The Great Elm Tree

Frances Keller Swinford

Rebecca Smith Lee

The Great Elm Tree

HERITAGE OF THE EPISCOPAL
DIOCESE OF LEXINGTON

By Frances Keller Swinford
& Rebecca Smith Lee

WITH AN EPILOGUE BY
THE RIGHT REVEREND
William R. Moody, D.D.

FAITH HOUSE PRESS
LEXINGTON, KY.
1969

The seal on the title page is a reproduction of the original seal of the Diocese of Lexington, designed by the Right Reverend Lewis William Burton, its first Bishop.

This book was set in Linotype Granjon and printed by Kingsport Press. Design by Jonathan Greene.

Contents

Illustrations

Meeting of the Transylvania House of Delegates,
1775. *George W. Ranck, Boonesborough (Louisville,
1901).*

Foreword

The Diocese of Lexington of the Episcopal Church includes the eastern half of the State of Kentucky, from Frankfort, the capitol, eastward to the Appalachians, and from the zigzagging Ohio River on the north down to the looping Cumberland on the Tennessee state line. It was organized in 1895 when the Diocese of Kentucky, established on the frontier in 1829 to include the whole Commonwealth, decided that its widely separated sections could make better progress if the Diocese were divided in half.

In the eastern portion that became the Diocese of Lexington were many of the oldest parishes in the state and a number of beautiful churches. Therefore, although the new Diocese yielded both its historic name and the formal episcopal establishment to the western division, it retained its traditional position as the seedbed of the Anglican Church in Kentucky.

As the first Bishop of Lexington and his seventeen clergymen faced the challenge of organizing a large and diverse area, they were heartened by a century of dedicated Churchmanship that had gone before them. This legacy, which enriched the Diocese in its beginning, is still one of its greatest treasures. The company of faithful Episcopalians who labored in this part of Kentucky in the earlier days left a goodly heritage to the Diocese of Lexington.

The noble phrases of the Prayer Book that were intoned beneath the leafy shade at Boonesborough before the founding of the nation have echoed down the years. The great elm tree has spread its branches over Kentucky.

Acknowledgments

In the preparation of this first general history of the early Episcopal Church in eastward Kentucky, the authors have had the help and encouragement of many persons, to all of whom they are sincerely grateful. Especial thanks are due to the following: The Right Reverend William R. Moody, Bishop of Lexington; the Right Reverend C. Gresham Marmion, Bishop of Kentucky; the Right Reverend H. V. Hallock, Bishop of Milwaukee; the Reverend Lockett Ford Ballard, Rector, Trinity Church, Newport, Rhode Island; Dr. V. Nelle Bellamy, Archivist, Church Historical Society; Dr. Jacqueline Bull, Archivist, University of Kentucky Library; Thomas Edward Camp, Librarian, Theological Library of the University of the South; the Reverend George J. Cleaveland, Registrar, Diocese of Virginia; Dr. J. Winston Coleman, Jr., Lexington; Mrs. Spalding Coleman, Louisville; the late Dr. Charles Ewell Craik and Mrs. Craik, Louisville; the Reverend George E. DeMille, Historian, Diocese of Albany; Dr. Gilbert H. Doane, former Director, Library, University of Wisconsin; the Very Reverend Robert W. Estill, former Dean of Christ Church Cathedral, Louisville, and presently Rector, St. Alban's Church, Washington, D.C.; the Reverend Canon Charles M. Gulbert, Secretary, Executive Council, Protestant Episcopal Church in the United States of America; Burton Milward, Lexington; Hendree Milward, Lexington; the Reverend Percy V. Norwood, Registrar and Historiographer, Diocese of Chicago; F. Garner Ranney, Archivist, Diocese of Maryland; the Venerable Charles F. Rehkopf, Archdeacon and Executive Secretary, Diocese of Missouri; the Venerable W. Leigh Ribble, Archdeacon and Executive Secretary, Diocese of Virginia; the Reverend Nelson Rightmyer, Historiographer, Diocese of Maryland; the Reverend Edward L. Sheppard, Historian, Diocese of Minnesota; Mrs. Frances Smith Shine, Historiographer, Diocese of Lexington; C. William Swinford, Lexington; Dr. Herbert D. Thomas, Registrar, General Theological Seminary; Professor Eugene Thompson, Greensboro, North Carolina; Earl R.

Thorne, Historiographer, Diocese of Kentucky; the Reverend J. Wesley Twelves, Registrar and Historiographer, Diocese of Pennsylvania.

We are indebted to the library staffs of the University of Kentucky, Transylvania College, the Lexington Public Library, the Episcopal Theological Seminary in Kentucky, the Kentucky State Historical Society, the Filson Club, the Cincinnati, Ohio, Public Library, the Church Historical Society, the University of the South, the University of North Carolina, Duke University, the University of Wisconsin, the Peabody Institute, the Maryland Historical Society; the rectors and lay historians of all the parishes included in this narrative, all of whom opened their records for our study and lent photographs and documents.

To Bruce Denbo, Director of the University of Kentucky Press, we are deeply indebted for counsel and practical guidance in the preparation of the text for publication. As an interested Churchman, he has encouraged us to believe that this documented account of the background of the Diocese of Lexington will be of interest and value not only to our own Communion but to all who are interested in the American past.

The Great Elm Tree

1 The Prayer Book Comes to Kentucky

The first public service of worship in Kentucky was conducted by an Anglican clergyman on May 28, 1775, at Boonesborough, beneath the spreading branches of a great elm tree.[1] The stately words of *The Book of Common Prayer,* traditionally heard within the walls of cathedrals across the Atlantic, did not seem out of place in this green wilderness. No brilliant trappings, no pomp and ceremony here; yet this setting was in its own way just as imposing.

The clergyman stood within the shade of the "Church Tree," as it was ever afterwards called, and on this first Sunday after Ascension Day asked God's blessing on those assembled. He prayed for England's "most gracious sovereign Lord King George" and "all the Royal family." The voices of the pioneers joining in the responses reverberated through the primeval forest. Some were Churchmen from the royal colonies of Virginia and North Carolina, some were dissenters, and many professed no religion at all. No matter, they welcomed this opportunity for orderly worship.

Two months earlier, Daniel Boone with a party of thirty men, acting for the Transylvania Company of North Carolina, had blazed a trail through Cumberland Gap to this point on the Kentucky River where it emerged from the steep hills, and had commenced building a fort.[2] Following Boone's party, Colonel Richard Henderson, leader of the Transylvania Company, with thirty more men, arrived at Boonesborough on April 20. Others came, and by May there were eighty men at the station. Although the fort was unfinished, Colonel Henderson proceeded without delay to organize a land office, appoint its officers, and summon a legislative assembly to meet there on May 23 for the purpose of establishing a proprietary government for the colony of Transylvania. Delegates from the four Kentucky settlements—Boonesborough, Harrodsburg, Boiling Springs, and St. Asaph's or Logan's Fort—assembled.[3]

One of the delegates from Harrodsburg was the Reverend John Lyth,[4] and it was he who conducted that first memorable service of worship in Kentucky.

The Church of England clergyman presumably came to Kentucky with the Transylvania Company,[5] but he may have been with some other party which crossed the mountains during the early spring of 1775. Certain it is that he spent some time in Harrodsburg during part of that year[6] and was prominent enough among the settlers there to be elected a delegate to the first legislative assembly west of the Allegheny and Cumberland Mountains. That he took an active part in the convention is attested by the "Journal of Proceedings of the House of Delegates of the Colony of Transylvania."[7] Immediately after the seating of the delegates and the appointment of the chairman and clerk, the meeting was opened with prayer by the clergyman. His name appears on several important committees, including the committee to draw up a compact between the proprietors and the people of the colony, and he introduced a number of bills in the convention, one of which was "to prevent profane swearing and Sabbath-breaking," and another dealing with the punishment of criminals. During its four-day session, the convention enacted nine laws and agreed upon a form of government. Colonel Henderson, according to his diary, had planned for religious services beneath the great elm, under which "one hundred persons might commodiously seat themselves." The tree, in Henderson's words "one of the many proofs of the existence from all

[1] Richard Henderson, "Journal of an Expedition to Cantuckey in 1775," in Draper MS 1 CC 83.

[2] Richard H. Collins, *History of Kentucky* (Covington, Ky., 1874), II, 520.

[3] *Ibid.*, II, 501.

[4] *Ibid.*, II, 501.

[5] Draper MS 17 CC 208. "Memorandum of information obtained from Capt. Nathaniel Hart of Woodford County, containing biographical data on persons mentioned in Ledger A of Richard Henderson and Company."

[6] Collins, *History of Kentucky*, II, 519. The Rev. John Lythe [*sic*], is one of 54 names in a list of persons who "were among those who resided or spent some time at Harrodsburg during some portion of the year 1775, after March 11th, which was the date of the first arrival and reoccupancy of the cabins built in 1774. . . ." The name is spelled "Lythe" by most Kentucky historians but Virginia records prove the correct spelling is "Lyth." See also Draper MS 4 CC 87. Statement of Mrs. Elizabeth Thomas that she knew Lyth at Boonesborough and Harrodsburg.

[7] Collins, *History of Kentucky*, II, 501–508.

eternity of its Divine Master," had served admirably as a council chamber for the convention, which adjourned on May 27. On the following day, Lyth conducted what history records as the first public service of worship in Kentucky.[8]

After divine service at Boonesborough most of the delegates returned to their settlements.[9] John Lyth, however, remained at Boonesborough as chaplain, continuing to conduct services on Sundays and ministering to the settlers.[10] There is no record of the length of time he remained there, but it was probably through the autumn of 1775. He then returned to Harrodsburg.[11]

During the meeting of the convention at Boonesborough but unbeknown to those assembled, stirring events were taking place elsewhere in the colonies. Back across the mountains the struggle of the American colonists against the British King had already begun. Two months before in St. John's Church, Richmond, Virginia, Patrick Henry had sounded the rallying cry for liberty or death. The "shot heard round the world" had already been fired at Lexington, Massachusetts, on April 19, but the news did not reach the Kentucky settlements until May 29,[12] the day after the worship service conducted by Lyth. It threw the settlements into a frenzy of excitement. The American colonies were at war with England, and Kentucky was a part of Fincastle County, Virginia.

Many a stout pioneer in that first congregation took up arms in defense of his country, and Kentucky's first ordained clergyman was no exception. Leaving Harrodsburg sometime in the late spring or early summer of 1776, he returned to Virginia and cast his lot with the colonies against England.

John Lyth's choice of America as his home had its origins in his character and early life. He was born in the early 1730's in Newton

---

[8] Undoubtedly John Lyth held religious services at Harrodsburg for some of the inhabitants of the station prior to the public service at Boonesborough. See Collins, *History of Kentucky,* II, 617; Maria Daviess, *History of Mercer and Boyle Counties* (Harrodsburg, 1924), I, 152.

[9] Henderson's Diary, May 28, 1775.

[10] Henderson's Diary, June 4, 1775.

[11] Draper MS 4 CC 84. Statement of Mrs. Elizabeth Thomas, which indicates the time she was at Boonesborough and when she went to Harrodsburg, establishing Lyth's stay in Harrodsburg until at least spring, 1776.

[12] Henderson's Diary, May 29, 1775. Letter with account of "battle at Boston."

Pickering, Yorkshire, England, where his middle class forebears had resided since at least the early sixteenth century.[13] He was admitted as sizar at Clare College, Cambridge in 1751, matriculating the next year. He received his B.A. degree in 1756,[14] and was ordained to the priesthood sometime prior to 1763, the year he was licensed for Virginia and received the King's Bounty.[15]

Lyth had arrived in Virginia by 1764 and very likely applied to the Governor or to the vestry of some parish for admittance as rector. There were at this time approximately 120 clergymen there, about 92 holding parishes and the remainder teaching at William and Mary College or in endowed parish schools, or else awaiting opportunities to be called to parishes.[16] Lyth may have been in this latter group or he may have served in a parish, the records of which were destroyed. In 1767 he left Virginia and went briefly to South Carolina, presumably to be rector of a parish there, but returned to Virginia that same year.[17] It is certain that he eventually settled in the southwestern part of the state, in Botetourt County. He owned five hundred acres of land in two tracts on the North Fork of the Holston River, in what is now Washington County.[18] Whether he lived on one of his plantations or resided near Fincastle, the county seat of Botetourt, is not known. At any rate here in the Valley of Virginia, Lyth lived the life of a gentleman bachelor. If he did not have a parish of his own, it may be presumed that he filled in from time to time in one or more of the parishes in the area. He numbered among his friends, in addition to the Anglican clergy in the Valley, many prominent families, including the Prestons, Breckin-

---

[13] John Venn, *Alumni Cantabrigienses, A Biographical List of All Known Students, Graduates and Holders of Office at the University of Cambridge from the Earliest Times to 1890* (Cambridge, 1924), III, 122.

[14] *Ibid.*

[15] George MacLaren Bryden, "The Clergy of the Established Church in Virginia and the Revolution," in *The Virginia Magazine of History and Biography*, XLI, No. 3, 237-238 (July, 1933). The King's Bounty was an appropriation of twenty pounds sterling from the public funds made to every clergyman licensed by the Bishop of London to the colonies.

[16] *Ibid.*, XLI, No. 1, 11-23 (January, 1933).

[17] Frederick Dalcho, *An Historical Account of the Protestant Episcopal Church in South Carolina from the First Settlement of the Province to the War of the Revolution* (Charleston, 1820), p. 434.

[18] Botetourt County, Virginia, Circuit Court, Will Book A, p. 139.

ridges, and Russells,[19] all staunch Presbyterians. He was particularly fond of Colonel William Preston, who was a Justice of the first County Court of Botetourt, escheator, coroner, and colonel of militia, and of his sister, Letitia, the wife of Colonel Robert Breckinridge, and of their daughter, Betty.

Perhaps it was the same adventurous bent that had brought John Lyth to the new world which caused him in 1775 to leave friends and comforts in Fincastle and set out across the mountains to the wilderness of Kentucky. Doubtless he was influenced by friends in the Valley who had already been there or were planning to go in the near future. His land holdings on the Holston were in the very center of the area through which the settlers had to pass on their way to Kentucky. They may have tempted him with stories of the abundance of fertile land to be acquired on easy terms or they may have convinced him of the need for a clergyman in the wilderness. Perhaps Lyth planned to settle permanently in Kentucky, but if this were the case his course was altered by the dissolution of the Transylvania Company in 1776 together with the Revolutionary War, causing him to return to Virginia.

Lyth's adventures in Kentucky during 1775/76 have already been recounted. In 1776 and 1777 he served with the Virginia militia in the campaign against the Cherokee Indians.[20] In a letter to his friend, Colonel Preston, written in April, 1777, Lyth stated that he had been engaged as chaplain to Colonel Russell's regiment and was already on his journey.[21] Before he left he ordered his affairs at

---

[19] *Ibid.* Lyth mentions these families in his will. Also see Deed Book 3, p. 56, John Lyth to Col. William Preston, April 3, 1777.

[20] Lyth appears on a number of lists as chaplain of Virginia militia in 1776/77. Virginia State Library Records, War, 23, 1777 Library Report (1912), p. 280, names him "Chaplain of Virginia Militia in expedition against the Cherokee Indians in 1776/77."

[21] Botetourt County Circuit Court, Deed Book 3, p. 56. The Colonel Russell to whom Lyth referred was Colonel William Russell, Colonel of militia of Fincastle County until December, 1776, when he was commissioned Colonel of the Thirteenth Regiment in the Continental Lines. All records show that the Reverend Alexander Balmaine, curate of Augusta Parish, was chaplain of the Thirteenth Virginia Regiment from February 20, 1777, until he became brigade chaplain, 1778–1780. It is highly probable that while Balmaine was chaplain of the Thirteenth Virginia Regiment in the Continental Line, Lyth acted as chaplain to Colonel Russell's regiment on a campaign against the Cherokees, Russell having returned to his home

home, wrote his will, and provided for the collection of certain promissory notes due him and the disposition of monies from the same in the event he did not return. He left his entire estate to Miss Betty Breckinridge, the young daughter of his friends, the Robert Breckinridges, and niece of Colonel Preston.[22] Tradition claims that John Lyth was killed by the Indians,[23] but contemporary records prove otherwise. After serving as chaplain with Russell's regiment in the campaign against the Cherokees, Lyth became, on October 1, surgeon of the Thirteenth Virginia Regiment,[24] still commanded by his friend, Colonel Russell.

In the winter of 1777/78, Colonel Russell's regiment was with Brigadier General Peter Muhlenberg's Brigade at Valley Forge, and undoubtedly it was at that place that John Lyth died on January 13, 1778,[25] probably succumbing to the rigors of that terrible winter. It seems likely that he was buried there. This American by choice, who had carried the Gospel across the mountains less than three years before, lies somewhere near Valley Forge, and his memory lives on in the hearts of succeeding generations of Kentucky Churchmen.

Although the Kentucky settlements were only about a year old when the Declaration of Independence was signed on July 4, 1776, Kentucky was to play an important role in the Revolutionary War. While the colonists were fighting the British on the eastern seaboard, the western frontier was having its troubles with the Indians, who were encouraged by the enemy to attack the settlements. While George Rogers Clark was capturing much of the northwestern territory, Daniel Boone and fellow settlers were holding the forts back home.

---

from the regular Continental Army to assist in defense of the frontier settlements on the Clinch and Holston Rivers.

[22] Botetourt County Circuit Court, Will Book A, p. 139; Deed Book 3, p. 56.

[23] See James T. Morehead, *An Address in Commemoration of the First Settlement of Kentucky, Delivered at Boonesborough, May 25, 1840* (Frankfort, 1840), p. 72. Morehead calls Lyth, "the peaceful minister of the Church of England whose sacred vocation could not exempt him from the death of the tomahawk."

[24] Francis B. Heitman, *Historical Register of Officers of the Continental Army during the War of the Revolution, April, 1775, to December, 1783* (Washington, D.C., 1914), p. 362.

[25] *Ibid.*

Throughout the new nation, the Revolution left a great prejudice against anything which hinted of English influence, and England's Church unfortunately came under this opprobrium. Those who opposed the Church ignored the fact that the founders of the new republic were chiefly Churchmen; that of the signers of the Declaration of Independence, thirty-four of the fifty-five were Anglicans; that the first session of the Continental Congress in Philadelphia was opened by the rector of Christ Church in that city, who, clad in vestments, read the prayers; that in the convention to prepare the Constitution of the United States, two-thirds of the commissioners were Churchmen; that the Constitution of the Protestant Episcopal Church in the United States of America was ratified in the very same room in which the Constitution of the United States had been adopted in 1787 and was modeled after the national Constitution. So strong was the antipathy toward the Church of England at the close of the war, however, that its dissolution seemed inevitable.

Six years were required to iron out the ecclesiastical differences among the churches in the several states. At the end of this time, however, the churches had united themselves into a national body and had obtained from England and Scotland the episcopacy necessary for its existence. The organization of the Protestant Episcopal Church was completed in 1789, and by the end of the eighteenth century it was beginning to recover from the shock of separation from the Mother Church of England.

Only then was the infant Church able to turn its attention to the vast and sparsely settled regions beyond the Appalachian mountains and to send missionaries for the propagation of the Anglican faith.

2 James Moore & Other Early Clergymen

Many of the controversies between the Anglican Church and denominations which had arisen before and during the American Revolution, especially in Virginia, were brought to the western country and were continued in Kentucky even after it became a state.

As a religious community, Kentucky was split among various sects, hotly contending amongst themselves on doctrinal issues. Presbyterians and Baptists made up the larger part of the population. Both were well supplied with preachers, the Presbyterians educated men, the Baptists usually unschooled, deeming learning unnecessary in expounding the Scriptures.[1] By the end of the 1780's the Presbyterians, Baptists, and Methodists were firmly established, with churches fully organized,[2] and during the next quarter of a century Unitarians, Shakers, New Lights, Socinians, Campbellites, and others organized religious societies in Kentucky. As early as 1785 there was a large colony of Roman Catholics near Bardstown, and the first priest arrived two years later.[3]

The Episcopal Church, preoccupied as it was with organizational and other problems, had thus far made no great effort to establish missions in the western country as had other Christian bodies. There were, however, scattered Episcopalians throughout Kentucky. Some of these had been absorbed into existing denominations, but others adhered to the faith of their fathers. Unable to exercise their faith in an organized manner, they continued to read their Prayer Books and hold family services in their homes.

It was to be another ten years before any eastern diocese made any effective effort to send missionaries into Kentucky. However, as early as 1789, an attempt was made, not by the Church in Virginia as would probably have been the case except for its struggles there, but by the Church in Maryland. At the Convention of the Diocese of Maryland in June of that year, greetings were sent "to all and every the professors of the Protestant Episcopal Church inhabiting

Kentucky Government," commending to them the Reverend William Duke, who was emigrating to Kentucky, and attesting to his regular canonicals and excellent character.[4] Duke set out for Kentucky and crossed the mountains beyond Harper's Ferry but was compelled by sickness to return to Maryland,[5] where he spent an active and useful life.

There were a few Episcopal clergymen residing in Kentucky prior to 1800, but these had ceased to pursue their calling and had entered other professions. The Reverend Benjamin Sebastian,[6] a Virginia clergyman, had settled in Bardstown in 1788 and had become a politician and Judge of the Kentucky Court of Appeals. Although he did not preach, he occasionally officiated at baptisms and marriages for friends. He died in Bardstown in 1832 at the age of ninety-three. The Reverend Edward Gantt, Jr.[7] was sent to Ken-

[1] Humphrey Marshall, *A History of Kentucky* (Frankfort, 1824), I, 440–465.

[2] See Collins, *History of Kentucky*, I, 416–490. The first Baptist minister to come to Kentucky was William Hickman in 1776. Four years later a great number of that faith moved from Virginia, and the first church was organized in Garrard County with the Reverend Lewis Craig as founder. The Presbyterians followed, with the Reverend David Rice of Hanover County, Virginia, arriving in 1783 and organizing three churches at Danville, Cane Run, and the forks of the Dix River. By 1802 there were enough Presbyterians in Kentucky to justify the organization of a synod at Lexington. The Methodist Church sent its first regular itinerant preachers, James Haw and Benjamin Ogden, in 1796, although they had been preceded by a few local preachers, among them Francis Clark, pre-eminent as the founder of Methodism in Kentucky.

[3] *Ibid.* The first Roman Catholic priest in Kentucky was the Reverend Mr. Whelan, 1787–1790. The second was the Reverend Stephen Theodore Badin, who labored for more than thirty years in the state.

[4] Maryland Diocesan Archives, Peabody Institute Library.

[5] *Ibid.* Diary of William Duke.

[6] See Bryden, "Clergy" in *Virginia Magazine*, XLI, No. 4, p. 299 (October, 1933). Benjamin Sebastian: licensed for Virginia Sept., 1766; received King's Bounty, Oct., 1767; Rector, Frederick Parish, 1767; Rector, St. Stephen's Parish, Northumberland County, 1767–1777; removed to Maryland; Rector, Christ Church, Calvert, 1782; Rector, William and Mary Parish, St. Mary's, 1785.

See also J. Winston Coleman, *Famous Kentucky Duels, the Story of the Code of Honor in the Bluegrass State* (Frankfort, 1953), p. 4. Sebastian is remembered as one of the famous Spanish conspirators in 1795, who was exposed for receiving a pension of $2,000 from the Spanish Government for services to that country. He had been drawn into the affair by James Wilkinson, who had arranged with the Spanish Governor Miro to deliver Kentucky over to Spain in return for trade privileges down the Mississippi River to New Orleans.

[7] Bishop Claggett to the Reverend William Duke, April 5, 1803, Maryland Diocesan Archives. Claggett states that he sent Gantt, Jr., to Kentucky but that he failed to establish churches there.

tucky in 1798 by Bishop John Thomas Claggett of Maryland, but failing health caused his departure. He is often confused with his father, the Reverend Edward Gantt, Sr., M.D.,[8] who became a resident of Louisville about 1807 and practiced medicine there for many years. The Reverend James Chambers,[9] a Virginia clergyman, was an early settler of Bardstown. He attained prominence as a physician and surgeon there around 1800 and married the daughter of Judge Sebastian. His posthumous fame is based, however, on his untimely death in a duel with Judge John Rowan of the Kentucky Court of Appeals.[10] The Reverend James Elliott,[11] another Virginia clergyman, settled in Franklin County in 1800, but he was not heard of again until nearly a score of years later, at which time he was residing in Lexington. Not one of these clergymen took the initiative in organizing a parish, doubtless regarding the prospects of the Protestant Episcopal Church in Kentucky as hopeless.

There was, during the early 1790's, at least one group of prominent citizens, designated as the "Episcopal Society," who met together and held services on the farm of Captain David Shely, near Lexington.[12] It was not until 1796, however, that this same group became the nucleus of the first organized Episcopal Church in Kentucky with a clergyman to minister to them. The clergyman was the Reverend James Moore.

This young man had come to Kentucky in 1791, fresh from his

[8] See Ethan Allen, D.D., *Clergy in Maryland of the Protestant Episcopal Church since the Independence of 1783* (Baltimore, 1860). Edward Gantt, Sr.: native of Prince Georges County, Md.; received holy orders in England, 1770; served as rector of several parishes in Md., removing to Georgetown, District of Columbia, where he was chaplain to the Congress of the U.S. Died in Louisville in 1837 at age of ninety-five.

[9] See Bishop William Meade, *Old Churches, Ministers and Families of Virginia* (Philadelphia, 1861), II, 323. The Rev. James Chambers was in charge of a parish in Staunton, Virginia, 1788.

[10] See Coleman, *Famous Kentucky Duels*, pp. 1-14. Also see Lewis Franklin Johnson, *Famous Kentucky Tragedies and Trials* (Cleveland, 1916), pp. 7-15.

[11] See Meade, *Old Churches*, II, 154. "The Reverend James Elliott was the last settled minister (of Cople Parish) up to the year 1800, when he removed to Kentucky."

[12] The Rt. Rev. Lewis William Burton, *Catechism on the Diocese of Lexington* (Lexington, Ky., 1911). Burton states that the first church was a log church, four miles out of the city of Lexington, erected on a farm of Captain Sheely. [sic.] The name is spelled "Sheely," "Sheley," "Shely." The latter is probably correct according to his signature on an answer filed in Fayette County Circuit Court, March 7, 1804. Later historians make no mention of a "log church" on the David Shely farm. The Episcopal Society probably met in a small log building there.

studies at Washington College[13] in his home county of Rockbridge in Virginia. Aware of the strong colony of Presbyterians in the Bluegrass Valley, James Moore came with the express purpose of settling there and becoming a Presbyterian minister. With him came his bride, née Margaret Todd, daughter of the Reverend John Todd of Louisa County, Virginia.[14] The Reverend Mr. Todd and his nephew, Colonel John Todd of Kentucky, had been instrumental in procuring through the Virginia General Assembly in 1780 the land grant of 8,000 acres of Kentucky County as an endowment for an educational institution which would become Transylvania University.[15]

The Todd family was well known in Kentucky. Colonel John Todd had in 1774 received a tract of land just outside Lexington for his services in the French and Indian War. Referred to as "Mansfield,"[16] it was the first place in Kentucky to receive a name. Colonel Todd was killed at the Battle of Blue Licks in 1782. His two brothers, Levi and Robert, were prominent citizens of Lexington and among the first settlers in Kentucky. Levi, the first clerk of the Fayette County Court, lived at "Ellerslie," an elegant estate, situated just beyond "Ashland," the home of Henry Clay. Robert was considered one of the ablest jurists in the state and was the first senator from Fayette County to the legislature after Kentucky was admitted to the Union. His wife was Nancy Todd, his cousin, who was the sister of Margaret Todd Moore.[17]

Most certainly the James Moores were warmly received by their many relatives upon their arrival in Lexington. They built a house on a lot purchased from Mrs. Moore's brother-in-law, Robert Todd, on the southwest side of Main Street and running back to Water Street,[18] living there until 1798, when they built a charming house

[13] Now Washington and Lee University, Lexington, Virginia.
[14] Malcolm H. Harris, *History of Louisa County, Virginia* (Dietz Press, 1936), p. 265. "Marriage Bonds in State Archives Dept., P. B. Porter, Clerk, 1767–1800: James Moore and Margaret Todd, September 6, 1790."
[15] Doctor Robert Peter, *The History of the Medical Department of Transylvania University* (Filson Club Publications No. 20, 1905), p. 3.
[16] Samuel M. Wilson, *The First Land Court of Kentucky 1779–1780* (Lexington, Kentucky, 1923), p. 70.
[17] Draper MS 27 CC 13–15. Newspaper clipping on the Todd family.
[18] Fayette County, Kentucky, District Court Book A, p. 110, August 13, 1796. Also see Deed Book B, p. 206, May 12, 1826, for an indenture describing the lot.

in the Georgian manner about three miles from Lexington on the Georgetown Pike.[19] They named their house "Vaucluse" after the adopted home town of Petrarch near Avignon in southern France.[20] Here on a sizable estate, tended by more than a dozen slaves,[21] they would raise six children and spend the rest of their lives.[22] An interesting feature of the house was the square, high-ceilinged parlor, built under the supervision of Moore and especially for the exercise of "the parson's passion," which was the flute.[23] The walls were of special material and the whole constructed to give the best acoustics possible at the time.

James Moore had been in Lexington for a very short time when he accepted in 1792 the offer of the Board of Trustees of Transylvania Seminary of the position of grammar master in the new school. At almost the same time he applied to the Transylvania Presbytery to become a candidate for the ministry and was accepted.[24] He entered on his candidacy and spent the next year in study and preparation for his trial examination before the Presbytery. Much to his disappointment, the Presbytery was forbidden by the Virginia Synod to proceed with his examination until proper testimonials could be received from Lexington, Virginia. He was thereby suspended as a candidate until "these obstacles be removed," the Presbytery pointing out that the action was not the result of "any fault we find with the natural abilities, literary acquisitions, or moral or religious character of the candidate."[25] Some months later

[19] Fayette County, Deed Book N, p. 224, July 1, 1815.

[20] Newcomb, *Architecture,* p. 49. "Among the older Georgian houses of Lexington is 'Vaucluse,' built in 1798 by the Rev. James Moore." Also see Elizabeth M. Simpson, *Bluegrass Houses and Their Traditions* (Lexington, 1932), pp. 28–34 for description of the house, later called "Eothan." The house, now known as "Malvern Hill" is the home of Mr. and Mrs. Sterling D. Coke.

[21] Fayette County Court, November, 1814. Inventory of the personal property of the Rev. James Moore, deceased, establishing the number of slaves he owned as sixteen.

[22] Fayette County Court Book O, p. 524, May 9, 1816. Refers to Margaret Moore, relict, and James E. Davis and Margaret T. Davis, his wife; John T. Moore, on part of Joseph Adam Moore, Jane Walker Moore, Nancy Todd Moore, and Elizabeth McCalla Moore, heirs of the Rev. James Moore, deceased. Inventory filed Nov. 18, 1814.

[23] James Lane Allen, *Flute and Violin and Other Kentucky Tales and Romances* (New York & London, 1899).

[24] Records of the Transylvania Presbytery, Book 1, 1792, pp. 63–69.

[25] *Ibid.,* April, 1793.

he was reinstated as a candidate and prepared and preached a number of sermons before the Presbytery. Finally, two years having elapsed, he delivered his final sermon together with a proper discourse, both of which were sustained. He had passed through all the different phases of preparation for Presbyterian ordination successfully. However, certain members of the Presbytery had not been present at the meeting when the sermons were sustained, and they requested that he repeat the two sermons at a later meeting. This he refused to do, considering himself rigorously treated, whereupon the Presbytery resolved that he be dismissed as a ministerial candidate.[26]

After his rejection by the Presbytery in 1794, Moore persisted in the course he had set for himself to become a minister of the Gospel, albeit within another body of believers. He was acquainted with the small group called the "Episcopal Society" which was meeting at the log church on Russell's Road[27] and soon made contact with its members. He was favorably impressed, as were they. After ascertaining that their religious tenets differed not appreciably from his own, he returned to his native state and was subsequently ordained an Episcopal priest by Bishop Madison in 1794. He hurried back to his frontier Episcopalians, to begin a ministry which would span a score of years and endear him to posterity. Obviously a man of great energy and determination, he "beat the canebreaks and scoured the buffalo trails"[28] for additional numbers and assiduously set about to knit them together into a faithful ecclesia. He began in 1796 to hold services in a dilapidated little frame house on the corner of Market and Middle Streets,[29] the present site of Christ Church, and was officially named minister, to hold services "once in every two weeks." So long had these Kentucky Episcopalians hungered for an ordained clergyman that they flocked to the little church to hear the Scriptures expounded and to receive the sacraments, so long neglected.

Since the day of his ordination, James Moore had devoted his whole time to his ministry, but now in the spring of 1796 he felt that his church was sufficiently organized to allow him to devote

---

[26] *Ibid.,* 1794, p. 135.
[27] Now Russell Cave Pike.
[28] Allen, *Flute and Violin,* p. 4.
[29] Middle Street is now Church Street.

some of his time and labor to his other profession, higher education. He thereupon accepted an offer as president of Kentucky Academy near Pisgah, and a little later, as director of Transylvania Seminary. When these two rival institutions consolidated in 1799 to become Transylvania University, James Moore became its president and professor of Logic, Metaphysics, Moral Philosophy and Belles-Lettres. He spent the next five years organizing and building up the first university west of the Alleghenies, laying the foundation for years of academic excellence.

Involved as he was in both administrative and teaching duties, Moore soon found it increasingly difficult to devote what he considered the proper amount of time to his church. He was fortunately blessed with a number of highly influential and dedicated laymen, such as his brother-in-law, Robert Todd; William Morton, or "Lord" Morton as he was usually called; David Shely, on whose farm Episcopal services had first been held; and Dr. Walter Warfield, prominent Lexington physician. These men had indeed held constant to the faith, even before they had a minister, and were ever ready to give of their time and their substance in its behalf. They had come to love the gentle parson who had taken their small group as a nucleus and built a sizable congregation around it, and who had been their minister and their friend for the past five years. Proud they were that he was now president of Transylvania University, but they felt, with him, that the responsibilities of this office were consuming the major portion of his time and energies.

About the time that Moore took upon himself the full duties of the presidency of the university, he and his congregation began to show concern that there was not another officiating Episcopal clergyman in all the vast region of Kentucky. They thereupon wrote to a number of the eastern bishops, informing them of their plight and begging aid in the form of missionaries. The Diocese of Maryland heeded the call. Bishop Claggett had long shown an interest in missionary enterprises beyond the Appalachian Mountains, but thus far his efforts to this end had failed. A decade earlier he had sent William Duke as missionary to Kentucky, but Duke had never reached his destination. A few years later the Reverend Edward Gantt, Jr., had been commissioned to found churches in Kentucky, but he too had failed. Upon receipt of the letter from Lexington, the

Maryland bishop commissioned the Reverend Samuel Keene, Jr., as missionary to Kentucky and at last met with some success.[30]

Samuel Keene arrived in Lexington in the summer of 1799 and immediately made himself known to James Moore and the members of the Lexington Episcopal Church, who greeted him with joy and hope.[31] He spent nine months in the region of Lexington and, according to Claggett, "effected great things," organizing several small congregations in the state and by his preaching and good conduct raising the character of the Church and converting "some of the most influential Presbyterian characters" to the Church's faith and practice.[32] He was particularly interested in Georgetown, Winchester, Paris, and other towns readily accessible from Lexington.[33] While in Kentucky, Keene made the acquaintance of a Methodist preacher, the Reverend Williams Kavanaugh, who resided in Clark County between Lexington and Winchester. He was greatly impressed with the character and preaching ability of the young itinerant and encouraged him to take Episcopal orders.[34] Keene returned to Maryland in the spring of 1800, and in April Moore wrote to him, "Were I acquainted with the Bishop I would write to him, informing him of the apparent success of your labors amongst us, and requesting him to send you back, or engage for us some other as zealous and as well calculated to give general satisfaction, for I can assure you that your visit to our country has, I believe, been of real service to the cause of Christianity here. The worst observation I have been able to gather with respect to you is that all parties speak well of you." The Lexington rector also informed Keene that Williams Kavanaugh had set out for Maryland, bearing testimonials from a number of the "most respectable citizens of Kentucky." "My own personal acquaintance with him," stated Moore, "is very imperfect—I have heard him preach once and was well pleased, and am credibly informed that his labors in that way are generally

[30] Bishop Claggett to the Reverend William Duke, April 5, 1803, Maryland Diocesan Archives.

[31] James Moore to the Rev. Samuel Keene, April 1, 1800, Maryland Diocesan Archives. Letter was written shortly after Keene's visit to Kentucky.

[32] Claggett to the Rev. William Duke, April 5, 1803, Maryland Diocesan Archives. Letter tells of Keene's 1799 visit to Kentucky.

[33] Joseph Jackson to Bishop Kemp, Nov. 24—Dec. 29, 1817.

[34] Claggett to the Rev. William Duke, April 5, 1803. The Bishop mentions Keene's acquaintance with Kavanaugh three years earlier.

acceptable. The provision, which in certain cases dispenses with an examination on the learned languages, will, I think, be very properly extended to him. He will expect your friendship in the business and I hope is deserving of it."[35]

After Williams Kavanaugh had been encouraged by Keene to seek Episcopal ordination, he made himself known to members of the Lexington Church. Dr. Walter Warfield was especially impressed with the Methodist minister, and he proposed that if Kavanaugh would take orders in the Episcopal Church the Lexington Episcopalians would employ him as their minister.[36]

As a Methodist circuit rider, Kavanaugh had been required to travel over a vast extent of territory, and the prolonged separations from his family had caused him to consider another profession. Like James Moore, his other love was teaching, and he had already started a school in Clark County. The call to the cloth was strong, however, and to Warfield's proposal Kavanaugh replied, "If I can do so without a violation of principle and preach the doctrines I believe to be true and Scriptural, I may accept your offer." He set about to examine the "Thirty-nine Articles" and to acquaint himself with the usages and customs of the Episcopal Church and soon concluded, as had Moore before him, that there would be no violation of principle in taking the proposed step.[37]

The Lexington Episcopal Church immediately drew up and signed an address to Bishop Claggett, requesting him to confirm Kavanaugh and after proper examination to ordain him and send him to Lexington as minister.[38] Kavanaugh went to Maryland, taking with him a number of testimonials from prominent citizens of Lexington, Winchester, Richmond, and other Kentucky towns, all attesting to his "unimpeachable moral character and excellent preaching ability."[39] One testimonial from Lexington, signed by Robert Todd, H. Coleman, John and Thomas Barnes among others, stated that Kavanaugh's "usefulness would be great" and that "he

---

[35] James Moore to Samuel Keene, Jr., April 1, 1800, Maryland Diocesan Archives.
[36] A. H. Redford, D.D., *Life and Times of H. H. Kavanaugh, D.D., One of the Bishops of the Methodist Episcopal Church, South* (Nashville, 1884), pp. 41–47.
[37] *Ibid.*
[38] *Ibid.*
[39] Maryland Diocesan Archives.

would have the support of three congregations."[40] Levi Todd wrote that he had known Kavanaugh for two years as he had lived near him and had heard him "urge publicly divine truths." "His conduct and profession are consistent, his talents are such as will make him useful," he stated.[41]

The Standing Committee of the Church in Maryland, after an examination of "the very honorable testimonials" of Kavanaugh's moral and religious character, recommended upon request of Bishop Claggett that he ordain Kavanaugh provided that he was convinced of the "soundness of his faith, of his determination to adhere to the doctrine and discipline of the Protestant Episcopal Church, and of his possessing a sufficient knowledge of theology, ecclesiastical history, and human learning for the work to be committed to him."[42] Bishop Claggett soon formed a great regard for Kavanaugh, who easily passed his examination. He was ordained deacon and priest in Baltimore on June 20, 1800.[43] Claggett later stated that the Church in Kentucky had by this act in some measure placed itself under his episcopal jurisdiction.[44] He continued to show concern and interest in Kentucky for some years afterward.

Back to Lexington came Kavanaugh to officiate as assistant to James Moore. In the spring of 1801 he corresponded with Bishop Claggett, keeping him informed as to the progress of the Church in Kentucky. In one letter he asked the Bishop to send "two able and faithful ministers," stating that he and Moore and some of the lay members of the Lexington Church "thought there would be no difficulty in making up five or six hundred dollars for each as a salary per year merely to be employed in ministering in the different churches." He further stated that if the gentlemen sent by Claggett were willing to take charge of an academy in the state "the emolument of each would amount in toto to ten or twelve hundred

[40] By "three congregations" the writers were referring to the several small congregations organized by Samuel Keene in 1799 and were anticipating the establishment of missions, probably in Winchester and Georgetown.
[41] Maryland Diocesan Archives. Testimonial of Levi Todd, March 15, 1800.
[42] The Standing Committee of Maryland to Bishop Claggett, June 6, 1800, Maryland Diocesan Archives.
[43] Redford, *Life and Times of H. H. Kavanaugh*, p. 46.
[44] Claggett to William Duke, April 5, 1803, Maryland Diocesan Archives.

dollars a year."[45] Claggett wrote his friend, William Duke, to whom he had given the first commission to Kentucky fourteen years before, asking him to consider Kavanaugh's proposition and go to Kentucky as minister and teacher.[46] Duke, now a professor at St. John's College, Annapolis, was in feeble health and declined the commission.

The Reverend Williams Kavanaugh remained in the neighborhood of Lexington, assisting James Moore and preaching to other small congregations at least through the spring of 1803 or for a period of nearly three years. Sometime in 1803 he left Lexington and settled in Louisville, where he began holding services in a small meeting house.[47] This was eight years before any other denomination of Christians can claim to have been there and twenty years before Christ Church, Louisville, was founded. Here and in a small mission in Shelby County, he continued for nearly three years until the itinerant urge, deeply rooted in his nature, once more compelled him to move on. He left Louisville early in 1806 to take charge of a church in Henderson, where he died that same year at the age of thirty-one.[48]

Meanwhile back in Lexington, the little frame building which had served as a church for seven years had been replaced in 1803 by a small brick church.[49] At first it was to have been built on Main Street on a lot owned by Robert Todd but it was later decided that it should be built on the site of the first and present house of worship on the corner of Market and Church Streets. William Morton and Walter Warfield accordingly purchased the lot from Mrs. Keziah Barton for the sum of eighty pounds and held the deed jointly.[50] The new lot was on high ground and secure from the danger of an overflow of Town Branch, which flowed through the center of the town. The previous lot had been quite close to this

---

[45] Claggett to the Rev. William Duke, April 5, 1803, Maryland Diocesan Archives. Reference made to an earlier letter from Kavanaugh.

[46] *Ibid.*

[47] Reuben Durrett, *The Centenary of Louisville* (Filson Club Publications No. 8, 1893).

[48] Zachariah Smith, *The History of Kentucky* (Louisville, 1901), pp. 414–415.

[49] Fayette County, Kentucky, Circuit Court Records, April 25, 1803, Fisher vs. Warfield.

[50] Fayette County District Court, Deed Book D, p. 131, August 12, 1802.

stream. The change of location was the cause of a lawsuit in Fayette Circuit Court in 1803 between the builder, Maddox Fisher, and several members of the American Episcopal Church, as it was now called.[51] Walter Warfield, David Shely, Robert Todd, William Morton, James Bullock, and the Reverend James Moore were named defendants. The plaintiff, Fisher, claimed in April, 1803, that the change of site was costly to him because of the distance from his brickyard to the Market Street lot and that he had been promised reimbursement for his losses. He further claimed that, the building having been completed, a balance of 229 pounds was due him. The defendants claimed that Fisher knew of the change of site and had raised no objection until the building was completed. In June, 1804, the court adjudged that unless the defendants or some of them paid the amount due before October next the church and lot would be sold at public auction to the highest bidder. Apparently Fisher was satisfied, for the auction never took place.

A proper church edifice in which to worship doubtless played a significant part in James Moore's decision to resign as president of Transylvania in 1804 in order to devote his full time to his ministry. He thereupon set about with steady enterprise to establish his church on a sounder basis, and during the next four years it enjoyed a substantial growth and increased in importance in the community. The parson became known far and wide and was deeply respected for his good sense and devoted piety. His dark good looks and courtly manners added greatly to his pulpit appeal. People came from a large part of the surrounding country and on Sunday many vehicles from the neighborhood drove up to the little church.[52]

All the while Moore grew in the esteem of his congregation. On a marble plaque just within the entrance of Christ Church today, he is described as "learned, liberal, amiable and pious," and most certainly he was all of these, but even more to his credit, he was beloved by all who knew him. One of his students at Transylvania described him as "one among the best men who ever lived,"[53] and

[51] Fayette County Circuit Court, April 25, 1803, Fisher vs. Warfield.
[52] George W. Ranck, *History of Lexington* (Cincinnati, 1872), p. 198.
[53] Robert McAfee, "Personal Papers," in *The Register of the Kentucky Historical Society,* XXV, No. 74, p. 134 (May, 1927).

James Lane Allen in a summation of his character depicted him as "humanly speaking, almost a perfect man."[54]

On August 25, 1808, at a meeting held at the church, the preliminary steps were taken toward the organization of the parish. Of a larger number present, twenty-six men, prominent in church and community, agreed to subscribe to pews, to pay for their erection and to rent them annually "at prices fixed by a committee appointed for that purpose to be applied to paying the salary of the minister." In this day of no plate offerings and pledged income, the sale of pews was a primary means of fund raising. The subscribers were: Henry King and Andrew McCalla, Matthew Elder, William Essex, David Shely and Robert Holmes, Thomas Hart, William Macbean and P. T. Robert, John Bradford, William Morton, Robert Todd, Charles Wilkins, Alex Parker, Walter Warfield, Henry Kelly, James Moore, John Postlethwait, Henry Clay, Rose and Shryock, John Wyatt, Thomas Church by G. A. Weaber, Henry Purviance, John Jordan.[55] It is noteworthy that in many cases, then and later, pewholders were not necessarily communicants of the Episcopal Church. For example, it would be forty more years before Henry Clay was baptized and subsequently became a communicant.

What had heretofore been simply a society of Episcopalians was at last on its way to becoming the first parish in Kentucky. Less than a year later, on the first Sunday in July, right after divine service, the parish was formally organized and the first vestry chosen. Appointed to that body were seven men: John Wyatt, John Johnson, William Macbean, John Jordan, William Morton, David Shely, and Walter Warfield. Mr. Moore was to officiate every fortnight at a salary of $200.00 per annum.[56] Enthusiasm ran high, and at a meeting the next day it was "resolved that a scheme of a lottery be attempted to raise $750.00 for the use of the Church."[57] The drawing took place at William Satterwhite's tavern at 3:00 o'clock on Saturday, September 16, 1809, and the money collected was used for finishing the church and for the organ.

---

[54] Allen, *Flute and Violin*, p. 8.
[55] Christ Church Records, Lexington, Kentucky.
[56] *Ibid.*, Minutes of the Vestry, 1808.
[57] *Ibid.*, Minutes of the Vestry, July 3, 1809.

For the next three years, church services were held every two weeks and Mr. Moore continued to preach, to administer the sacraments, to marry and to bury, but his health was beginning to fail. Never a robust man, he had found himself more and more incapacitated and confined to his bed. Once again, in 1812, the church suffered from the lack of a full-time minister, and there was discontent among some of the pewholders.[58]

There was in the congregation a clergyman, the Reverend James Elliott, one of the earlier nonofficiating clergymen in Kentucky, who formerly resided in Franklin County and was then making his home in Lexington, though not officiating as a minister. With the authorization of Moore, the parish requested Elliott to perform divine service until the rector was again able to officiate or until a suitable person could be procured.[59] He readily agreed to serve for a period of six months,[60] and carried on his duties as *locum tenens* throughout the spring and summer of 1813.

By midsummer it had become obvious that James Moore would never again be able to resume his pastoral duties; he remained rector in name only. Therefore, in July the vestry appointed John D. Clifford, son-in-law of "Lord" Morton and one of the church's most active laymen, a Philadelphian by birth, to correspond with the Reverend Jackson Kemper, assistant rector of Christ Church, Philadelphia, one of the oldest and most prominent churches in America, to ask his advice on securing a permanent rector for the Lexington church. Clifford was likewise commissioned to request recommendations from Bishops William White of Pennsylvania and John Henry Hobart of New York.[61]

The first phase in the life of the Lexington Episcopal Church as a loosely organized society of Episcopalians had come to a close. Nearly twenty years had lapsed since its beginnings, but the parish had never been fully organized nor had services been regularly held each Sunday. A new era, as an organized parish under a full-time rector was about to begin.

[58] *Ibid.*, Minutes of the Pewholders and Vestry, 1812.
[59] *Ibid.*, Minutes of the Vestry, March 27, 1813.
[60] *Ibid.*, Minutes of the Vestry, May 3, 1813.
[61] *Ibid.*, Minutes of the Vestry, 1813.

3 John Ward, Organizer of the Lexington Parish

When the Reverend Jackson Kemper received Clifford's letter, he conferred with his Diocesan, Bishop White, who was also rector of Christ Church, Philadelphia, and with Bishop Hobart, whom of all men he probably most admired. Both bishops had received like requests from Lexington.

Highly regarded by all three was a Connecticut clergyman in his mid-thirties, who had served for the past ten years in parishes in New Jersey and Rhode Island, and was presently in charge of a mission in Germantown, Pennsylvania, which Kemper had obtained for him only a few months earlier. Kemper was at this time acting head of the Society for the Advancement of Christianity in Pennsylvania and was also much interested in the Church's missionary endeavors to the west.[1] He, White and Hobart agreed that the Reverend John Ward was a likely candidate for the Lexington Church, and they thereupon recommended him for the position. It was to prove a most happy choice.

John Ward was born in Connecticut on September 12, 1779[2] and spent his youth and young manhood in the environs of Litchfield.[3] He was a candidate for Holy Orders in 1803 when he received an invitation from Trinity Church, Newport, Rhode Island, for a conference "upon the subject of settling him as assistant minister and school master."[4] He served as lay reader at Trinity for several months in the early part of 1804 and, after his ordination to the diaconate by Bishop Jarvis on December 1, 1805, returned there as assistant minister and schoolmaster "to ten poor children, whom he was to instruct in grammar and mathematics gratis."[5] He was ordained to the priesthood on October 11, 1807, at the age of twenty-eight. His ministry at Newport was during the rectorate of the dynamic Reverend Theodore Dehon, and it is likely that the impressionable young assistant acquired much of his skill at organization and formulated much of his Churchmanship from that able and dedicated prelate, who later became Bishop of South Carolina.[6]

During these years at Trinity he became associated with Bishop White and with Hobart, then assistant minister of Trinity Church, New York. He also numbered among his clerical friends William Smith, rector of St. Paul's, Norwalk, Connecticut; Alexander Viets Griswold, rector of St. Michael's, Bristol, Rhode Island; Richard Channing Moore, rector of St. Andrew's, Staten Island; and Philander Chase, missionary in New York and rector of Christ Church, Poughkeepsie.

When Theodore Dehon resigned as rector of Trinity Church in 1809, Ward remained there as rector for about one year.[7] In 1811, he accepted a fill-in position in St. Michael's Church, Trenton, New Jersey, but by the fall of the following year was still uncertain as to whether to accept the permanent rectorship.[8] At this time, he began a correspondence with Kemper, then a deacon and already assistant rector of Christ Church, Philadelphia. Although Kemper was ten years Ward's junior, a close personal relationship developed between them, and Ward sought the advice and counsel of his friend on matters both trivial and important at this time and for many years afterward.[9]

---

[1] The eastern clergy were already interested in this field, although it would be seven years before the Domestic and Foreign Missionary Society was organized in 1820.

[2] Archives of the General Convention, Episcopal Church Center, New York.

[3] Trinity Church, Newport, Rhode Island, Minutes of the Vestry, April 1, 1805 and November 4, 1805.

[4] *Ibid.,* November 2, 1805.

[5] *Ibid.,* November 3, 1805.

[6] William Wilson Manross, *A History of the American Episcopal Church* (New York & Milwaukee, 1935), pp. 234–235. Theodore Dehon was rector of Trinity Church, Newport, R.I. until 1809. It was one of the few flourishing parishes in what was to become, in 1811, the Eastern Diocese (made up of Massachusetts, of which Maine was a part, Rhode Island, New Hampshire, and Vermont) with Alexander Viets Griswold as Bishop. Dehon accepted a call to St. Michael's Church, Charleston, South Carolina, in 1809, and was Bishop of South Carolina from 1812 until his death in 1817. He was noted for his skill at organization, for his interest in the poor and oppressed, and his work among orphans and in poorhouses.

[7] Trinity Church, Newport, Minutes of the Vestry, letter to Ward from Sam Whitehorne, senior warden.

[8] Wisconsin State Historical Society, Papers of the Rt. Rev. Jackson Kemper; John Ward to Jackson Kemper, July 28, 1812; Ward to Kemper, October 22, 1812.

[9] *Ibid.,* Correspondence between Ward and Kemper, 1812–1822. Kemper was assistant rector of Christ Church, Philadelphia until his consecration as Bishop of Missouri and Indiana in 1835.

During the winter of 1812 and early months of 1813, Ward was lonely and in rather poor health, and he wrote his friend, Kemper, that he was considering the latter's suggestion that he move to Germantown, Pennsylvania, "provided his services would be acceptable to the bishop, clergy and people."[10] "Indeed I am averse," he wrote, "to setting myself for sale in the pulpit, as a jockey does his horse at the tavern or stable," pointing out that the situation in Germantown would have to be satisfactory for him to consider it.[11] Above all he was concerned with Bishop White's approval. "I am so much of a primitive churchman as to wish nothing to be done without the consent of the Bishop," he stated. "I should consider it the greatest misfortune of my life to be separated either in will, in affection, or deed from him I have solemnly sworn to reverence and obey."[12] Six days later the Society for the Advancement of Christianity in Pennsylvania commissioned Ward to go to Germantown as a missionary. He immediately wrote Kemper, outlining the pastoral and financial arrangements and begging his friend's "priestly counsel on the matter of removal."[13] He remained at the Germantown mission for less than six months[14] or until early fall when, acting upon the recommendation of Kemper and the Bishops of Pennsylvania and New York, he set out for Kentucky to meet with the vestry of the Lexington church.

On November 5, 1813, the Lexington Episcopal Church officially invited the Rev. John Ward to be its rector, and he accepted the post for a period of three years, beginning service without delay.[15]

Three days later the following item appeared in the *Kentucky Gazette:* "In consequence of the Rev. Mr. Ward having taken upon himself the duties of the Episcopal Church in Lexington, notice is hereby given that divine service will be performed in future on Sundays, to commence at 11:00 o'clock in the morning and at 3:00 o'clock in the afternoon."[16] John Ward was off to a running start.

[10] *Ibid.,* Ward to Kemper, March 3, 1813. (Catalogue No. 3G50).
[11] *Ibid.,* Ward to Kemper, March 6, 1813 (3G53).
[12] *Ibid.*
[13] *Ibid.,* Ward to Kemper, March 12, 1813 (3G55).
[14] Pennsylvania Diocesan Archives, Philadelphia. The Germantown mission is now St. Luke's Parish.
[15] Christ Church, Lexington, Minutes of the Vestry, November 5, 1813.
[16] *Kentucky Gazette,* November 8, 1813, p. 3.

His detailed letters to Jackson Kemper during the following years are a contemporary history of his new parish.[17]

On November 8 he wrote Kemper a glowing letter, full of anticipation, in which he expressed his pleasure at his reception in Lexington. "Yesterday I commenced my ministerial functions by preaching to a crowded and attentive congregation and have the satisfaction to believe that my services were gratifying," he wrote. "There are several Episcopalians here of a genuine stamp, whom you may be sure were elevated at beholding my canonicals and listening to our liturgy."[18] He mentioned that the Reverend James Elliott had turned farmer and was residing about twelve miles from Lexington, and he looked forward to a visit on the morrow with the Rev. James Moore, "who," he said, "is unhappily subject to a too common infirmity."[19] He stated that plans for enlarging the church building and establishing the society upon a permanent basis were under consideration, and asked Kemper to exert his influence with friends to procure a bell. "I could with confidence then apply for friends to erect a cupola and we should be complete except in a preacher," he stated.[20] The self-effacement of this statement was characteristic of John Ward.

He continued in his newsy letter to describe the "excellent and handsomely furnished house," belonging to John D. Clifford, where he was to be furnished with bachelor quarters as well as with a study in one of the four garden houses. In describing Lexington, he wrote, "It is a pleasant place, situated in the midst of land, more beautiful and fertile than any I have ever before seen. . . . I think I should be perfectly contented were it not for my distant removal from all my former friends and acquaintances and for the necessity of continuing a queer bachelor, concerning which state I have many unfavorable notions."[21]

Writing early in January, 1814, he stated, "For the first time on

[17] Kemper Papers, Wisconsin Historical Society, Letters from Ward to Kemper, 1813–1822.

[18] *Ibid.,* November 8, 1813 (3G116).

[19] The Reverend James Moore had not been in robust health for some years and had been confined to his home for the past year. He very likely suffered from consumption.

[20] Ward to Kemper, November 8, 1813 (3G116).

[21] *Ibid.*

the Sunday succeeding Christmas, I administered the Holy Communion to between twenty and thirty devout professors, a greater number than ever received at once in this church. The minds of many appear to be awakened so that we may soon expect an additional number of communicants. On every account, as far as the people in my charge are concerned, I am most happily situated. Divine services are well attended and devoutly performed by the congregation as far as I can judge."[22]

In the spring and summer of that year his letters reveal the continuing progress of the church and attest to the growing popularity and improving health of the new rector. In March, he wrote, "You cannot boast a more regular Episcopal Church east of the mountains than is ours." Already, however, he was informing Kemper of the need of additional Episcopal ministers in Kentucky. "As for myself," he said, "I can do nothing towards building up other churches. It is as much as I can do to take care of my own. I am confident it will be greatly to the benefit of the future Church in this quarter to have this well established. It will be like a parent possessing the strong influence of good example."[23] In general this was to be Ward's stand during his rectorate in Lexington. He devoted his full ministry to his parish and did not attempt to establish other churches. His congregation loved him and knew him intimately, but the missionary push in Kentucky and the establishment of a diocese under a bishop was to await another man.

A letter to Kemper, dated April 11, 1814, showed Ward to be happy, healthy, and popular in his new home. "I am writing sermons, delivering them, reading and building castles in the air," he wrote. "I have as complete a room for study as ever was entered by thinking beings." Again he stressed the great need for additional ministers in Kentucky, describing in some detail the type of person needed. "Everything here," he wrote, "will depend upon the popularity of ministers who must be extremely attentive to their whole deportment and be endued with fairness and keep themselves separate from the world. Indiscretions which in other parts would

[22] *Ibid.*, Ward to Kemper, January 5, 1814 (3G122).
[23] *Ibid.*, Ward to Kemper, March 15, 1814 (4G68).

hardly be noticed would here be considered criminal in a clergy-man. The settlers here are chiefly from Virginia, who have unfortu-nately been accustomed to clergymen of a peculiar cast and infre-quently are inclined to think all clergymen alike. These prejudices we must remove before we can do much good. A preacher of the Gospel, who is contented to seclude himself from the busy world and keep a bridle on his tongue when he is in company, will find little difficulty in gaining the good opinion of all, even of the sons of unbelief. He may be affable and at the same time dignified in his whole deportment." Ward informed Kemper of the progress of his church building which was "raised" to the foundations and told him that the twenty communicants were presently holding services in a room at Transylvania University. His gratification over the improving Churchmanship of his flock was apparent throughout the letter. "I recently baptized nine children," he stated, "and doubt not but I shall in due time prevail upon all the heads of families to offer up their offspring to the Lord as their duty obliges them. . . . If I can bring people to a position of soberness to the Gospel by making an impression upon their reason, I shall be better satisfied than I should when they do come forward through some violent excite-ment or passion. . . . I sincerely rejoice that my steps were directed here. The harvest is plenteous and what I can I will by God's help perform." He showed great interest in the upcoming General Con-vention in Philadelphia, stating that it should be "a delicious season if the Evangelicals[24] have not become numerous and are not conten-tious, which I very much fear." He ended with the hope that "should my life be spared, to dedicate our church in some way that will answer to prevent it from being employed to any other purpose than that of public worship," and asked Kemper to suggest how this might be done. "I am a bishop," he stated, meaning simply that he, being the only officiating clergyman in the state, had all the

[24] Ward's use of "Evangelicals" refers to a party in the Episcopal Church. The term was used extensively at this time and for many years afterward to describe the Low Church party. At this period Ward meant by an "Evangelical" one who minimized the order in faith and order, who stressed enthusiastic preaching and revivals, who urged rubrical relaxation and did not adhere strictly to the liturgy of the Book of Common Prayer, who considered the sacraments, memorials rather than means of grace, and who viewed the Episcopacy as expedient rather than essential.

authority. "As such," he queried Kemper, "would it be improper for me when we first meet in our new church to preach a sermon upon the occasion and endeavor to impress upon the minds of my people the duty and importance of considering that holiness becomes God's house?"[25] In Lexington, in the early days before the organization of the diocese and election of a bishop, the unconsecrated church building was often used by Transylvania University for its annual commencement exercises and at least once for a Fourth of July celebration. As indicated in his letter to Kemper, this concerned John Ward, but the practice was to continue until after the church was properly consecrated some years later.

Ward's letter to Kemper paints a fairly clear picture of his Churchmanship. It shows him to be concerned with order and decorum in worship, dedicated to the strict use of the liturgy of the Book of Common Prayer and opposed to rubrical relaxation, attributing a high place to the episcopacy and to the efficacy of the sacraments as means of grace. In his principles may be seen the influence of his years in Connecticut, indisputably the cradle of "High Churchism" in America, and his association with Jackson Kemper and John Henry Hobart. John Ward was most certainly the first Episcopalian of this type in Kentucky, a Churchman of the Hobartian stamp—an "Evangelical High Churchman."[26]

By late spring, or after John Ward had been in Lexington about five months, he became particularly concerned that his congregation should become an integral part of the Protestant Episcopal Church in the United States and enjoy all the privileges of its sister churches. On April 29 the parish agreed to the Constitution of the Protestant Episcopal Church in the United States of America and elected John D. Clifford a delegate to the General Convention in Philadelphia in May. Clifford, bound by ties of birth, friendship,

[25] Ward to Kemper, April 11, 1814 (3G143).

[26] The term "Evangelical High Churchman" may at this time in the Church's history appear obscure. It will be more fully explained and defined in a later chapter when the Church, riven by party strife, delineated more sharply the different types of Churchmanship. It is not to be confused, however, with "Evangelicalism" or Low Churchmanship. It is the type of High Churchmanship which, although stressing Catholic and Apostolic order, does not rule out zeal and evangelical preaching. At this period it was known also as "Connecticut Churchmanship" or Hobartian Churchmanship, for John Henry Hobart of New York was its chief exponent.

and extensive property holdings to the City of Brotherly Love, left Lexington in April to attend the Convention and also to solicit donations there for the Lexington church. With him he carried a letter of commendation from his rector to Jackson Kemper, begging the Philadelphia clergyman's help in procuring bell and organ for the still unfinished Lexington church.[27]

John D. Clifford arrived in Philadelphia and on May 17 presented himself at the General Convention held in St. James' Church, with a certificate, signed by the clerk of the vestry of the Protestant Episcopal Church at Lexington in the State of Kentucky, attesting his appointment as a representative to the Convention. To his disappointment, however, he was not admitted as a member of the House of Clerical and Lay Deputies but was given only an honorary seat in the Convention. It was resolved that "Whereupon the Protestant Episcopal Church in the State of Kentucky not being organized, not having in convention acceded to the Constitution of the Protestant Episcopal Church in the United States of America, Mr. Clifford cannot be admitted as a member of this House, but that he be allowed the privilege of an honorary seat."[28] John Ward had instructed Clifford to obtain the Convention's advice in regard to the regular steps necessary for organization as an official part of the Protestant Episcopal Church in the United States, and the resolution spoke clearly on the matter. It stated, in effect, that with no diocese, no bishop, and no state convention, the church in Kentucky was unable to be represented at the General Convention. It would be fifteen more years before the important work of organizing the Diocese of Kentucky was effected. John Ward had the vision but he lacked the means.

Back in Lexington, the rector contented himself with organizing the parish on a sounder basis. The new church was abuilding, membership was increasing, and Ward found his congregation amenable to his ideas and future plans. The size of the vestry was increased from seven to the traditional twelve, and the names of

[27] Ward to Kemper, April 16, 1814.

[28] William Stevens Perry, *A Half-Century of Legislation of the American Episcopal Church* (New Hampshire, 1844), Vol. I (1785–1821), p. 405. The book is a collection of the General Conventions of the Protestant Episcopal Church in the United States of America. Clifford's credentials were presented on May 17, 1814.

Thomas Bodley, John Bradford, William West, James Prentiss, and Robert Wickliffe[29] were added to the list of prominent Lexingtonians who had already served as vestrymen. Bernard Gaines was elected senior warden and John D. Clifford, junior warden. Ever ready to serve his church and assist his rector, Clifford served as either junior or senior warden during Ward's entire rectorate.[30]

By early summer, although still cheerful, Ward's letters to Kemper began to reflect a note of loneliness and sorrow that he had no fellow priest with whom to confide. "Were it not for my pious and intelligent friend, John D. Clifford," he wrote, "I should not be able to content myself." He still had high hopes for the church's prospects after the completion of the building. "We shall then be able to conduct our affairs in a rubrical, canonical, I hope evangelical manner. It is my intention to observe all the feasts and festivals of our Church and to establish a custom which will be calculated to build up my people in our holy faith," he said. He noted that when he came among them, his people were lax in their religious life, but that now they were bringing their children to Holy Baptism and regularly attending Holy Communion. "They were in general unacquainted with our liturgy. I am particular, as I am bound, not to omit any part. I believe my congregation derive more sincere pleasure from the service and consequently are more devout," he stated. He expressed gratification that his sermons had improved, but lamented that he had no talent at extemporizing for it would save him much labor. He showed concern that his people were not induced to read, stating, "How few will sit down at home in a composed and serious frame either to inspect the oracles of God or peruse the writings of pious men. Most men are ready enough to hear the Word preached and, while it sounds in their ears, are affected by it, but when they go away the seed has not fallen on good ground." He asked Kemper what he thought about the establishment of a missionary society, similar to the one Kemper headed in the East, "I am persuaded," he wrote, "that until we become more evangelical in our practice our Church will not be placed

[29] Christ Church, Lexington, Kentucky, Minutes of the Vestry, April 29, 1814.
[30] Ibid., 1813 to 1820.

upon the high eminence whence she will give light to those who are in darkness."[31]

John Ward had been rector of the Lexington Church for a little over six months when his predecessor, James Moore, pioneering parson who had brought to life in Kentucky two institutions, died on June 22, 1814, at the age of forty-nine.[32] He had, until nearly the end, followed his other profession once again, operating a school in his home, called Vaucluse Academy, in which he taught English, Latin, Greek, and the sciences to commuting and boarding students.[33] His church and the entire community mourned the loss of the educator-preacher whose name would be preserved for posterity by the pen of James Lane Allen.[34]

By the time John Ward had completed his first year in Lexington, a new and larger brick church, stuccoed to imitate stone and built to accommodate 800 persons, had replaced the now inadequate small brick building.[35] The building, though not completely finished, was at least comfortably habitable.

In spite of several mercantile failures in the town, which caused embarrassment to many citizens including Episcopalians, the sale of pews in the new church was encouraging. Of the eighty-two offered for sale at the church on December 26, fifty-one of the best sold for better than anticipated, and prospects for the sale of the remaining number were good.[36] The vestry rated the pews according to their situation in the church building, with the privilege of choice to be sold to the highest bidder. Those on the ground floor were rated from $50.00 to $100.00 each. The vestry hoped to raise $8,000 in this manner to cover part of the contract cost of the building and also a

[31] Ward to Kemper, June 11, 1814, Kemper Papers (4G4).
[32] Marble plaque just within the entrance of Christ Church, Lexington.
[33] *Kentucky Gazette,* January 3, 1814, p. 4.
[34] James Lane Allen, *The Choir Invisible* (New York, 1897), p. 180. Allen has the Reverend James Moore say, "The most that we can do is to begin a strain that will swell the general volume and last on after we have perished."
[35] Christ Church, Lexington, Minutes of the Vestry, November 25, 1813. "The subscribers propose to the vestry that they will pull down the present building and erect a larger church on the plan now presented." Ward's letters to Kemper reveal that the church was built before the completion of his first year as rector, although not completely finished.
[36] Ward to Kemper, February 3, 1815 (4G64).

further sum of \$2,000 for additional expenses and to remunerate the builders, Shryock and Gaugh, who through an unexpected increase of price of building materials stood to lose by their contract.[37]

Ward wrote to Kemper early in February, 1815, expressing his pleasure at the sale of pews. "I was much encouraged and flattered," he stated, "at having from sixty to seventy respectable families secured to my church." "But every rose has a thorn," he added. "We had held divine service but a few Sundays before it was discovered that the contractors had put on a roof entirely insufficient. Everybody was alarmed, all friends of the church grieved, few would venture to enter the doors, two Sundays we had no services. In the meantime we had the roof secured and engaged a new one to be put on in the spring as the only alternative. Our bell has arrived and our organ will soon be set up." "I assure you," he continued, "that we appear very much like a church and I flatter myself that time has not diminished my influence in this place."[38]

The month before the sale of the pews in the new church, with his customary regard for order and systematic organization, the rector had pointed out the propriety of having the church lot officially conveyed to the trustees of the church. When, in 1804, William Morton and Dr. Warfield had purchased the lot on which the church now stood from Mrs. Barton, they stated that they "were willing and ready to deed same to the trustees or otherwise for the benefit of the Society of the Episcopal Church,"[39] but this had never been done. Now, ten years later, the lot was the property of the trustees of the Lexington church.[40]

Through the spring and summer of his second year in Lexington, Ward wrote Kemper of his encouragement over the state of the church, of his happiness among his people, and of the advantages arising from his situation. "My being here," he stated, "keeps my

[37] *Kentucky Reporter,* Lexington, December 17, 1814. "Notice—Pews in the new Episcopal Church will be offered for sale at the church on Monday the 26th day of December at 10:00 A.M." An explanation of the sale followed.
[38] Ward to Kemper, February 3, 1815 (4G64).
[39] Fayette County, Kentucky, Circuit Court Records, William Morton's Answer to Maddox Fisher, March 1, 1804.
[40] Fayette County District Court, Deed Book M, p. 269, Indenture, March 18, 1815.

people from having itching ears. I am in no danger from any of those popular preachers who can talk from head to foot. . . . I go on in my own way, setting forth plain truths in a plain manner and I am certainly willing to depend for success upon the great Head of the Church."[41]

In answer to a letter from Kemper, delivered by Clifford upon his return from a trip to Philadelphia, Ward wrote in August, "My congregation is numerous and commendably attentive both to me and to the services of the sanctuary. I believe externally few churches can be found more orthodox, and I hope there is also a considerable portion of seriousness and piety among us." As in almost every letter since his arrival here, he lamented the lack of additional clergy, stating, "Had we clergymen to seek those gone astray, most respectable congregations might be collected." His beginning interest in other towns in Kentucky is first apparent in this letter. "I am shortly to spend a Sunday in a neighboring town, Paris," he wrote, "where there are many Episcopalians who appear confident that they can form a society fully adequate to the support of a minister. Though I probably cannot visit them but once, I hope it will be of spiritual use, to baptize their children of which they are desirous. I flatter myself that could I succeed in stirring them up and uniting them in one body, I might succeed in getting them a clergyman from the East."[42]

As Ward's intended tenure of three years flew by, the rector became "more and more revered for his piety and pastoral care" and more and more beloved by his congregation.[43] In August, 1816, he wrote Kemper, "When I left Philadelphia it was my determination to return after the expiration of my engagement. I see not, however, that I can get away. Not long since I mentioned my intention to them of giving up my charge at the time agreed upon but a unanimous solicitation on the part of my flock not to leave them, together with their profession of regard and attachment have in-

---

[41] Ward to Kemper, April 3, 1815 (4G71).

[42] Ward to Kemper, August 22, 1815 (4G93).

[43] Christ Church, Lexington, Minutes of the Vestry, June 30, 1816. Letter asking Ward not to leave Christ Church was made a part of the vestry minutes.

duced me to say that I will continue with them until some person can be found to fill my station to their satisfaction."[44] Indeed, the prospect of losing their beloved rector had filled the Lexington congregation with "melancholy and depression," and the vestry had presented him with a letter, imploring him in eloquent language not to forsake them "so early in their voyage." "We believe," the letter stated, "the well-being of our church, not only to be important as respects ourselves but as respects the future establishment of the Protestant Episcopal worship in the western states."[45]

Although heeding the appeal of his parishioners, Ward expressed in his letters to Kemper his desire to live where he could enjoy a portion of clerical society and stated that he would probably accept a situation where this could be so, provided a suitable man could be found for Lexington.[46]

Apparently Kemper at last began to take seriously his friend's appeal for additional clergymen in Kentucky, possibly with an eye to replacing him in Lexington, thus allowing him to return to the East. For, in a letter to Kemper dated October 11, 1816, Ward wrote, "I rejoice that you have concluded to employ your just and extensive influence in sending Mr. Douglas[47] as a missionary into these parts." He stated that he would offer Douglas every assistance and believed he could contribute much to the missionary's success. Ward further stated that he was having frequent attacks of fever, that his church had been closed for the past three Sundays, and that a missionary here would be of inestimable value. He informed his friend that a "Bible society was about to be formed here upon the most Catholic plan." I will have more influence," he said, "in this institution than is generally allowed Episcopalians in associations of this kind. It has been my determination not to be instrumental in digging the grave of Episcopacy. I believe now is the time for me to do good to our Communion, while the general interests of Christianity are advanced. Only one of a large number of people asked to subscribe has refused, and he is a professed deist. I expect to bring

[44] Ward to Kemper, August 7, 1816 (5G55).
[45] Christ Church, Lexington, Minutes of the Vestry, June 30, 1816.
[46] Ward to Kemper, August 7, 1816 (5G55).
[47] Jacob Morgan Douglas to Jackson Kemper, October 4, 1816, Kemper Papers (5G6).

forward numbers who have heretofore been inamicable to Bible societies."[48] This letter must have gladdened the heart of Jackson Kemper who, probably more than any other Churchman of his day furthered missionary societies and aided in the distribution of Bibles and Prayer Books throughout the country.

On the second week in December, 1816, the Rev. Jacob Morgan Douglas,[49] appointed by the Missionary Society of Pennsylvania, arrived in Lexington after a long and arduous journey by horseback from Pittsburgh, begun the first of November. The young deacon[50] came as a missionary to the western country and planned to visit several towns in Ohio and Kentucky, later going on to Tennessee, with Nashville as his final destination, before starting home for Pittsburgh.[51] The Lexington church had long awaited a missionary, and had eagerly looked forward to his visit among them. John Clifford, with characteristic hospitality, offered him his home and he received there the most cordial treatment. But the Rev. Jacob Douglas was to prove a disappointment in every way.

Upon his arrival he had stated, in answer to a request by Ward that he remain in Lexington while the rector visited New England, that he could on no account stay because his missionary duties, both to the west and south of Kentucky were too "sacredly important." He soon became enamored with the town, however, and began telling members of the congregation that he should be pleased to stay, without mentioning this to Ward. The result was that the rector dared not take his long-anticipated trip east for fear that Douglas's view, preaching methods, and personality would prove detrimental to the Lexington church. In a letter to a Philadelphia merchant and friend, John D. Clifford wrote, "Our church would

[48] Ward to Kemper, October 11, 1816 (5G8).
[49] Perry, *Half-Century of Legislation*, I, 472–473. At the General Convention of 1817, in the "Report of the House of Clerical and Lay Deputies," the Diocese of Pennsylvania stated, "During the last year a new Society was formed in this Diocese for the express purpose of sending missionaries into the western states. Under its direction a young clergyman has visited with success many parts of Ohio, Kentucky, and Tennessee." This was Jacob Morgan Douglas.
[50] *Ibid.*, p. 473. Douglas appears among twelve candidates for Holy Orders in Pennsylvania. He is one of those who had received deacon's orders since the last General Convention.
[51] Jacob Douglas to Jackson Kemper, October 25, 1816, Kemper Papers.

be destroyed by what Mr. Douglas calls his close preaching, but what we call a system of pretended inspired Calvinism, the sectarian doctrine of regeneration and grace, with a full admixture of endless perdition."[52]

Douglas made several trips to Georgetown, Paris, Frankfort, and Cincinnati, but he made Lexington his base of operation. He soon became extremely unpopular with the more orthodox members of the Lexington congregation but impressed those who still held "sectarian doctrines." He also greatly enraptured the Presbyterians and Baptists, with whom, according to Clifford, the Episcopalians were not on the best of terms. He preached for these denominations "in order to injure Mr. Ward, with whose large and respectable congregation they are not overly pleased."[53]

Douglas corresponded regularly with Kemper during his stay in Kentucky[54] but did not mention a breach with Ward. He did note, however, that Ward had some differences with his own brethren, "who have been so spoilt by the licentiousness of the old Maryland and Virginia clergymen that I have to apply the wormwood and the gall. As for understanding the articles, the rubrics, or the liturgy, this is out of the question."[55] Small wonder that John Ward, who prided himself on making real Churchmen of his Lexington Episcopalians, was incensed at Douglas's arrogance and pomposity.

Douglas left Lexington for Nashville in mid-February, 1817, but returned on his way to Pittsburgh.[56] It is doubtful that he remained long this time, for it is probable that Kemper, by now fully aware of the missionary's unpopularity, urged him to return to the East.

John Ward and the Lexington congregation, although disappointed with the character and missionary efforts of Jacob Douglas, did not abandon hope of obtaining an efficient missionary. A former associate of Ward from the Diocese of New Jersey, the Reverend

---

[52] John D. Clifford to Mr. Charles N. Bancker, January 23, 1817 (5G30), Kemper Papers. A confidential letter, which was to be shown to no one but Kemper. Bancker evidently forwarded it to Kemper, and it appeared among his correspondence.

[53] *Ibid.*

[54] Douglas to Kemper, December 13, 1816 (5G29); January 8, 1817 (5G77); January 22, 1817 (5G29).

[55] Douglas to Kemper, January 8, 1817 (5G77).

[56] Douglas to Kemper, February 27, 1817 (5G32).

John Churchill Rudd,[57] visited Lexington shortly after Douglas's departure for the East, either at the invitation of Ward or on commission of the Episcopal Missionary Society. He met with the approval of the Kentucky Episcopalians and was invited and expected to return to join Ward in his charge and also to endeavor to "raise up congregations in adjoining towns, such as Frankfort, Georgetown, Versailles, Paris and Winchester." A number of laymen in Lexington had already subscribed annually, for three years, as high as fifty dollars each for his support.[58]

While the Lexington church awaited the return of the Reverend Mr. Rudd, there came among them another of the young missionary visitors commissioned by the eastern bishops to make missionary contacts in the West. Like most of those before him, he too was from the Diocese of Maryland. The dedication and contributions of these Episcopal missionaries have been greatly overlooked and underestimated by Kentucky writers. Although they did not have the power to found churches, as did denominational preachers, they accomplished much toward sewing the seed and gathering together scattered Episcopalians in the West. A notable example of the best of this type of traveling missionary was the Reverend Joseph Jackson of Maryland.[59] He arrived in Kentucky in the late fall of 1817, with a commission from Bishop James Kemp, who had succeeded Claggett as Bishop of Maryland, to visit Kentucky, Ohio, Indiana, and Missouri with an eye to gathering together Episcopalians for the eventual establishment of churches. He planned to travel through these states for a period of six months, returning to Maryland in time for the diocesan convention in May.

Joseph Jackson endeared himself to fellow Churchmen and mem-

[57] Perry, *Half Century of Legislation.* Journals of the General Convention, 1808 through 1823 show Rudd to be rector of St. John's Church, Elizabethtown, New Jersey.

[58] Maryland Diocesan Archives. The Reverend Joseph Jackson to Bishop Kemp, November 24—December 29, 1817. Jackson wrote at length about Lexington, remarking, "Mr. Rudd is invited and expected to return. . . ."

[59] Perry, *Half Century of Legislation.* The General Convention Journal of 1795 lists Jackson as rector of Queen Anne's Parish, Prince Georges County, Maryland; 1799 through 1808 Journals show him as rector of St. Peter's Church, Talbot, Maryland. He later appears as rector of St. Thomas' Church, Baltimore. From time to time he is listed as on missionary duty in Kentucky and elsewhere.

bers of other denominations wherever he went. He was a zealous, devoted Churchman, kind and tolerant to all, who went about the country, sewing the seed in town and village alike. In almost every place he visited he was asked to remain as permanent minister or to return in the future. In many towns, subscriptions were offered for his support. He became strongly attached to many of his new acquaintances and personally interested in their welfare. In his letters to Bishop Kemp, he begged him to send other missionaries to the western country, and stated that he, himself, might return.[60]

There were many Marylanders in the state, and to these he soon introduced himself in each town he visited. Writing from Georgetown in December, 1817, he stated that he had been staying with members of the Keene family, relatives of the Rev. Samuel Keene, Maryland missionary who had visited Kentucky in 1799. "I am sorry to tell you," he stated, "that there is no regular Episcopal ministration here."[61] The next day, he wrote from Woodford County that he was visiting the Reverend James Elliott, formerly of Virginia and once the rector of his old parish in St. Mary's, Maryland.[62] After Elliott had retired as interim minister of the Lexington church in 1813, he had moved to Woodford County. Jackson wrote, "He is now become wealthy by marriage and, having a delicacy of constitution, does not officiate except occassionally. My hope is that he will be encouraged to further efforts by the growing prospects of cooperation and success." From Versailles the missionary set out for Frankfort, but was held up by an approaching winter storm. The next week he was on his way to Danville, and stopped in Lexington for four or five days. "I am exceedingly delighted with the progress of improvements there," he wrote. "The last evening I spent there I had the high gratification to hear a considerable part of Handel's *Messiah*, performed by a society of persons belonging to the church, several of whom were, previous to Mr. Ward's settling in Lexington, profane and heeless of religion in all respects."

In mid-December, he set out on horseback on the two hundred mile trip from Lexington to Nashville, Tennessee, where he stayed with a Col. Dallam, once of Maryland, who, with his wife, had

---

[60] Maryland Diocesan Archives, Joseph Jackson to Bishop Kemp, November, 1817.
[61] *Ibid.*, Jackson to Kemp, December 1, 1817.
[62] *Ibid.*, Jackson to Kemp, December 2, 1817.

become a Methodist "merely for the want of Episcopal ministration." On the way, he had stopped in Russellville, Kentucky, about fifty miles north of Nashville, and found there several families from Maryland. He preached there on Christmas Day and again on December 28, and promised to return. Of Russellville he wrote, "The Methodists appear generally friendly and I rejoice to see it as ominous of future good. When they look at my Prayer Book, it seems to be with a measure of regret." He wrote that he planned to proceed about eighty miles farther towards the Ohio River in a northwesterly direction to the town of Henderson, where there were several Episcopalians from Maryland and Virginia, and then to Huntsville, in the Mississippi territory, before returning home.[63] He evidently was persuaded to stay in the neighborhood of Russellville and Nashville for some months, for in April, 1818, he wrote of his regard for the people in the area and his hope that a minister might be obtained who could officiate in both places. "Their attention to the word of life has been eager. There are many characters of intelligence and refinement, who have no satisfaction in the rude vociferations which are too commonly substituted for preaching in different parts of this country. Our service has been approved by many and they have taken no offense at my written sermons, a thing never heard of before at Russelville."[64] He continued, "In one thing I have departed entirely from the mode pursued by the New England clergy who have visited Ohio. Whatever might be proper there, I have judged it to be entirely inexpedient to attempt any regular organization of the scattered, and at present lukewarm, professors of our persuasion. Good could not result from attempting to combine so heterogeneous a mass, and much evil, shame, and injury in all probability might. When a minister can be obtained, or a zeal something like that of rational and intelligent religion begins to appear in at least a few, it will be time enough." He stated that he had been asked to remain among them permanently but "could give no possible encouragement to it, from the situation of my aged parent. . . . However, I know not but I must yet return to them." Jackson was to return two years later.

Meanwhile John Ward continued as rector of the Lexington

[63] *Ibid.,* Jackson to Kemp, December 29, 1817.
[64] *Ibid.,* Jackson to Kemp, April, 1818.

church until September, 1819, three months before the end of his second three-year tenure. Then, instead of returning to his native East as he had long anticipated, he changed his plans and headed for Missouri and the growing town of St. Louis. Just why this frail and gentle man of forty-one years decided to sojourn once more among strangers instead of going home at last is a matter of conjecture. The most likely possibility is that he went at the request of several friends and acquaintances there. One of the town's most prominent citizens, Thomas Riddick, a devout Episcopalian, had married Eliza Carr of Lexington. Riddick had corresponded with Ward, who was the nearest clergyman to St. Louis, about the lack of Church ministration and the destitute spiritual condition of Churchmen there.[65] Doubtless he aroused Ward's interest enough to cause him to make the venture. Several other prominent St. Louis families had known Ward in Lexington,[66] and perhaps they too encouraged him to make the change. There is, moreover, a distinct possibility that Jackson Kemper, once more advising his friend, precipitated the move. It is interesting to note that sixteen years later, in 1835, Kemper, himself, would set out for Missouri as Missionary Bishop of the Northwest and that he would assume the rectorship of the parish founded by his protégé, John Ward.

John Ward arrived in St. Louis, a town of 4000 inhabitants, in the latter part of September, 1819. Almost immediately he made plans to preach in the Baptist Meeting House on October sixth,[67] but, becoming ill, had to postpone the meeting. On October 24, in a one-story frame building, which was occasionally used for holding court and as a dancing room, was held the first public service of worship by an Episcopal clergyman west of the Mississippi.[68] Dur-

[65] The Reverend Charles F. Rehkopf, "The Beginnings of the Episcopal Church in Missouri—1819-1844," in *Historical Magazine of the Protestant Episcopal Church,* XXIV, No. 1, pp. 39-65 (March, 1955).

[66] Missouri Historical Society, Letters of Maria Von Phul. Miss Von Phul had lived in Philadelphia, Lexington, and St. Louis. Her brother, Henry Von Phul of St. Louis had married Rosalie Saugraine, a native of Lexington. Ward's name appears a number of times in Miss Von Phul's correspondence.

[67] *Missouri Gazette and Public Advertiser,* October 6, 1819, as quoted in Rehkopf, *op. cit.,* "Saint Louis—The Rev. John Ward, an Episcopal clergyman from Lexington, Kentucky, will preach in the Baptist Meeting House on next Sabbath. Divine service to begin at 11 o'clock."

[68] The Reverend Montgomery Schuyler, D.D., *Historical Discourse Delivered at*

ing the ensuing week the Articles of Association and the list of subscribers were drawn up and the church which would become Christ Church, St. Louis, was born on November 1, 1819. The first vestry meeting was held on January 10, 1820, and the Rev. John Ward was officially called as rector. Under his ministrations the congregation gradually increased and prospects were favorable.

True to his promise to his Lexington congregation that he would not forsake them unless another man had been found to fill the pulpit, John Ward had left his parish in September, 1819, in the capable hands of his nephew, a young deacon, the Rev. Benjamin Birge[69] until the arrival of the Rev. John Churchill Rudd, still expected as rector. Birge had come from Connecticut three years before to complete his theological studies under his uncle. This young man, just two months before assuming his duties at the Lexington Church, had been ordained to the diaconate by the Rt. Rev. Philander Chase of Ohio. When Mr. Ward failed to return, Benjamin Birge was asked to continue until a permanent clergyman could be procured.[70] An "amiable" and "intelligent" young man, he soon became loved and admired by the congregation, and his untimely death on March 29, 1820, at the age of twenty-three, "cast a gloom" over the whole parish.[71]

The vestry made several futile efforts towards securing a suitable rector, again urging the Reverend John Churchill Rudd, long-expected assistant to Ward, to come as permanent pastor of the Lexington church, but he finally declined the call.[72] They thereupon

---

the Semi-Centennial Celebration of Christ Church, St. Louis, on All Saints' Day, 1869 (St. Louis, 1870), pp. 11–14.

[69] Christ Church, Lexington, Minutes of the Vestry, 1819. Several historians erroneously state that it was the Reverend Lemuel Birge who followed Ward. Lemuel was a brother of Benjamin. He is listed in the Journals of the General Convention, 1820 through 1826, after Benjamin had died.

[70] Christ Church, Lexington, Minutes of the Vestry, 1820. "Mr. Birge officiated for Mr. Ward from the 9th of September, 1819, until the first of December following. . . . Mr. Birge still continued to officiate as pastor of the Church (by contract made with him) 'till the 29th day of March, 1820, the time of his death."

[71] Kentucky Reporter, Lexington, April 5, 1820, p. 3. "Died on the 29th, the Reverend Benjamin Birge of the Episcopal Church at the age of 23." A lengthy obituary followed.

[72] Christ Church, Lexington, Minutes of the Vestry, April 3, 1820, "Resolved that the Vestry be authorized to renew their efforts to induce the Rev. Mr. Rudd to remove hither and officiate as pastor of this church. . . ."

once again communicated with several bishops in the eastern states, soliciting their aid in the matter. In a letter, dated June 1, 1820, to Bishop Kemp of Maryland, the vestry committee, composed of William Worsley, W. G. Hunt, Walter Warfield, William Morton and James E. Davis, stated that until the departure of John Ward the condition of the Lexington church was flourishing and "we were anticipating the rapid approach of the time, when new congregations being gathered and additional ministers obtained for them, we should be enabled to establish a new diocese, and to enjoy the benefit of a bishop in this Commonwealth. Our hopes, however, have been disappointed, and we now find ourselves in a situation extremely deplorable."[73] The letter further noted the smallness of the church's pecuniary means, stating that a salary of not more than $1000 per annum could be raised, but that additional emolument could come from the establishment of an academy. "Should we be so fortunate," it stated, "as to procure a gentleman of some years' standing in the ministry, whose sermons are already numerous, and to whom long continued habit has rendered professional duties light, the additional cares of an academy would not probably be burdensome, nor likely to interfere in the slightest degree with his obligations and responsibilities to the Church." The committee outlined the inducements connected with a ministry in the "largest and most populous town in Kentucky in the only Episcopal church yet established in the state." "In this place," the letter continued, "should be fixed the Bishop of the Diocese having under his care the churches which in a short time might be reared in different parts of this state." It was pointed out that no efforts would be spared to render the situation of a clergyman among them in the highest degree satisfactory.[74]

The spring of 1820 was indeed a woeful period for Lexington Episcopalians. Not only had they lost young Mr. Birge, whom they had come to revere and who doubtless would have been called as permanent rector, after his ordination to the priesthood, if death had not intervened, but they were also bereft of the services of their

[73] Maryland Diocesan Archives; Vestry of Christ Church to Bishop James Kemp, June 1, 1820.
[74] *Ibid.*

senior warden. John D. Clifford had become ill on May 1 and died on May 8 in the forty-second year of his age.[75] This extraordinary man who, along with his father-in-law, William Morton, had guided the lay activities of the church for the past decade, was probably the most beloved and esteemed of Kentucky Episcopalians. On a marble tablet in Christ Church, near the one in memory of the Reverend James Moore, are found today the following words: "Sacred to the Memory of John D. Clifford, Esq., Who exhibited in his character a rare union of private benevolence and worth, public spirit, liberal hospitality, social virtue, sincerity, warmth and steadiness in attachments, strength and compass of intellect, knowledge and enterprise in business, scientific attainment, cultivated taste, Christian fortitude, and practical piety. He died on May 8th, 1820, aged 41 years."

In addition to these severe losses, the failure of the Reverend Mr. Rudd, with whom many were personally acquainted, to accept the call as rector had saddened them. The state of affairs appeared black indeed as they awaited word from the eastern bishops with whom they had communicated.

Not only in Lexington were Episcopalians ready for missionary endeavors, but many people in Louisville and western parts of the state were Church inclined. The response to this need came again from the Diocese of Maryland when the Reverend Joseph Jackson responded to the challenge and returned to Kentucky after an absence of two years.[76]

From the vicinity of Louisville, while at the home of "a Marylander and Eastern Shore man of the name of Ward, once of Somerset," he wrote, "Certain it is that an Episcopal clergyman ought to have been settled here some years ago. The heart aches to think of the want of Episcopal seminaries and Episcopal ministers."[77] And from Bardstown in October he wrote, "The Lutherans, availing themselves of the known predilection for Episcopalians, have added to their number by pretending a nearer affinity than others to our

[75] *Kentucky Reporter,* Lexington, May 10, 1820, p. 3.
[76] Maryland Diocesan Archives, Joseph Jackson to Bishop Kemp, August 9, 1820; Jackson to Kemp, September 28—October 5, 1820.
[77] *Ibid.,* Jackson to Kemp, August 9, 1820.

Church, indeed an identity as descendants from Luther. There is therefore the more need of an Episcopal establishment here, that the real difference and the full and honest truth may appear at once. The Romanists, who are strong and numerous here, having a new and great cathedral in Bardstown, will not, it is generally believed, be won or influenced by any but Episcopalians." He begged Kemp to use his influence in sending missionaries to the area and pointed out that it was most important that a missionary fund be established in Maryland, in order to finance the venture. "Such expectations are naturally entertained of a state so ancient and so favored as Maryland," he wrote, and continued, "It puts me to shame to think that I come from a state so wrapped up in herself and so regardless of others, Maryland, in truth mother of most of the Episcopalians here, and yet she thinks not of her own offspring." Jackson's chief concern seemed to be that other denominations, particularly Lutherans and Presbyterians, were outstripping the Episcopalians in missionary enterprise in Kentucky. "There are places in both Kentucky and Indiana," he wrote, "where Episcopalians are eagerly desired, and the missionaries whom I would recommend, are those who might be useful hereafter, as settled ministers in these countries. . . . My wish is for a minister of the very first grade to officiate at Louisville —none other would answer. His eloquence especially must be winning, commanding, and irresistible." Jackson also called attention to the great need for a bishop in Kentucky. "Without a bishop," he wrote, "I see no prospect for a permanent Episcopal establishment in this state, nor indeed in any."[78]

Joseph Jackson's words were prophetic, for until the Episcopal Church in Kentucky organized itself into a diocese, further progress was impossible. The day was not far off when this would be accomplished, however, and the man who would effect it was the next rector of the Lexington church.

[78] *Ibid.*, Jackson to Kemp, October 5, 1820.

4 Chapman's "Sermons" & the Diocese of Kentucky

People on the older American frontier liked theological debates, and great crowds flocked to hear denominational preachers argue about predestination and salvation by grace. Early Episcopal clergymen such as James Moore and John Ward stayed aloof from this open controversy, partly because they were outnumbered but chiefly because they disapproved of the "enthusiasm" and vehemence of the participants. By 1820, however, the time had come when Episcopalians must enter the arena of religious debate in order to gain a foothold in the West. An able advocate of Anglican doctrine appeared when George Thomas Chapman was chosen as rector of the Episcopal parish in Lexington that year. With his coming the Episcopal Church took its place in Kentucky as one of the major denominations, in influence if not in numbers.

George Chapman was a scholar by temperament and training. Born in Pilton, Devonshire, England, in 1786, he was the son of Thomas and Charlotte Carnzue Chapman. His father, a well-to-do silk manufacturer, emigrated to New Jersey when George was a boy and soon settled at Greenfield, in western Massachusetts, where he reared his large family in a cultured and religious atmosphere. He was well read in theology and eventually became one of the leading members of St. James' Episcopal Church in Greenfield. George was sent to Dartmouth College, an excellent small institution in the area, from which he graduated in the Class of 1804.

Having an inclination for the ministry, he began his theological studies under the Reverend Henry Kollock of Princeton, New Jersey, a Presbyterian minister of considerable repute at the time. After about a year young Chapman gave up these studies, presumably because of his dissatisfaction with Presbyterian doctrines. An important result of his sojourn in Princeton under Kollock, however, was that he became acquainted with one of the most dynamic clergymen in the Episcopal Church, the Reverend John Henry

Hobart, then the assistant rector of Trinity Church in New York City, and already a leader in the High Church party. Hobart and Kollock had become friends during their college days at Princeton. After leaving Princeton Chapman read law in his home town and in 1808 began to practice successfully in Bucksport, Maine. In 1811 he married pretty Alice Buck, daughter of a prominent family.[1]

In 1815 he, in his own phrase, "resumed divinity studies privately" with the intention of seeking ordination as a priest in the Protestant Episcopal Church. His choice of a bishop under whom to seek his training—there was as yet no Episcopal theological seminary—was very probably determined by the needs of his growing family. He must have desired to move to New York City and study there under the Right Reverend Hobart, now Bishop of New York. Instead, he applied to his own diocesan, Bishop Alexander Viets Griswold, of the Eastern Diocese, which included all of New England except Connecticut, and in 1816 was made deacon. Griswold was a simple-hearted, humble man of burning evangelical zeal. He needed missionaries for the rocky back-country of his Diocese, and he promptly put Chapman in charge of a succession of rural missions both before and after his ordination to the priesthood in 1818 at St. Michael's in Bristol, Rhode Island, the Bishop's own parochial charge. Chapman wholeheartedly shared the missionary zeal of Griswold. During his lifetime of service to the Church he would minister to a score of parishes and missions, seven of which he helped to organize. But his thorough research into Scriptural and historical sources had led him to a doctrinal position closer to Hobart's moderate High Churchmanship than to Griswold's Evangelical views.

In May, 1819, Chapman's father died, leaving a comfortable estate to his family. Some eight or ten months later George gave up his three little mission parishes in Massachusetts and made a journey to the Ohio Valley. One of his sisters, the wife of Dr. Azariah Brigham, was living in Ohio, and George may have been visiting

[1] For biographical data on George Thomas Chapman see: George T. Chapman, ed., *Sketches of the Alumni of Dartmouth College* (Cambridge: 1867), pp. 116–117; Edward F. Battaille, *Grace Church in Newark: The First Hundred Years, 1837–1937* (Newark: 1937), pp. 18–19 *et passim;* also John McVicker, *The Early Life and Professional Years of Bishop Hobart* (Oxford: 1879), pp. 165–166; 316–317.

her when in the spring of 1820 he went over into Kentucky as far as Lexington. There is no evidence that he was invited to come by the Episcopalians there, but the register of the church shows that he conducted the funeral of the small son of one of the parishioners on June 12. The next day the vestry invited the visiting clergyman from the East "to preach for a few weeks until a permanent pastor could be obtained." Within a fortnight the members were so pleased with his sermons that the vestry invited Mr. Chapman to become rector of the Episcopal parish in Lexington at a salary of one thousand dollars a year.[2]

Even a traveler lately come from the settled Atlantic seaboard might well have been favorably impressed by the recently completed church building with its bell and organ and its list of substantial pewholders. This call to Lexington offered Chapman, now in his mid-thirties, a "settlement," in the phrase of the time, that was more commensurate with his abilities as a scholar and preacher than any he had heretofore obtained. On the first day of July he composed an eloquent letter of acceptance and forthwith leased a comfortable residence near the homes of some of his new parishioners in which to establish his wife and young daughters when he fetched them out to the "Athens of the West."[3]

The new rector set great store by records. Upon his arrival he carefully listed the forty-six "communicants" of the parish whom he had found upon his taking over his duties on July 1, 1820, and he made a record, too, of parishioners who counted themselves Episcopalians by baptism only or by preference. He started an "Annexed List" of the new members added by himself in all these categories. On the new list, for example, he inscribed the names of Mrs. Lucretia Hart Clay, wife of the Honorable Henry Clay, who was as yet unconfirmed, and that of Mrs. Mary Austin Holley, wife of President Horace Holley of Transylvania University, who had been confirmed in her girlhood by her Connecticut bishop. The irregular status of many of his most faithful parishioners suggested at once to

[2] Vestry Minutes of Christ Church, Lexington, Kentucky, for June 13 and June 17, 1820.

[3] Fifth Census of the U.S. (1830), KENTUCKY, Microcopies of Records of the National Archives, Vol. 3, Sheet No. 263.

Chapman's orderly mind the great need for the services of a bishop in this new country.

The parish prospered. The vestry, composed of many of the same dependable men who had served under the Reverend Mr. Ward, met somewhat more regularly under the new rector. The treasurer's books were audited. The sexton was required to scrub the floors and forbidden to toll the bell, even for funerals, without express permission. He was also instructed to put a stop to all noise during services. Chapman was a dedicated preacher, and without minimizing the importance of the Prayer Book offices, he delivered sermons that were intended to convince and convert his hearers. From the day of his arrival, the pews were filled morning and evening with parishioners and townspeople come to hear the quiet parson, who looked remarkably like an old-fashioned English barrister, outargue the "ranters" with his sharp logic. On each occasion Mr. Chapman removed his surplice and, clad in black silk gown and black silk gloves, mounted the pulpit and peered benignly through his small, thick-lensed spectacles at the congregation. They settled down to listen while he expounded pure Anglican doctrine from the Holy Scriptures and from the writings of the Church Fathers. He spoke with authority although without arrogance, and always in the most correct accent.

He was on friendly terms with his parishioners and with the townspeople, in a quiet sort of way. Most important, perhaps, was his real friendship with John Ward, which developed upon the latter's return to Lexington in the spring of 1821 for what was intended to be a short visit. Ward's plans changed suddenly when in May he married Miss Sarah Clifford, sister of his friend and benefactor, John D. Clifford, now deceased.[4] His new responsibilities required him to live in Lexington and so to give up his church in St. Louis. In Lexington there was no opening for him as a minister and so he became a schoolteacher, like James Moore and many another scholar of the cloth. He opened a select academy for young ladies on the southeast corner of Market and Second Streets which was at-

---

[4] *Lexington Reporter,* May 21, 1821, p. 3, col. 4. See also the will of Sarah Clifford (mother of John D. and Sarah), appointing her daughter Sarah as executrix, Will Book E, p. 297, Fayette County, Ky., probated October, 1820.

tended by the daughters of the town's first families for nearly forty years.[5] In the meantime he assisted Chapman as a fellow clergyman and friend, as a vestryman and sometimes warden, and as a benefactor to the parish, a role he continued to fill with all of Chapman's successors.

Chapman's scholarly attainments were recognized in 1824 when Transylvania University conferred upon him the honorary degree of Doctor of Divinity, and again when he was appointed its professor of history and antiquities. He enjoyed the friendship of President Holley, a distinguished liberal clergyman from New England, and remained on the university faculty until Holley's resignation in 1827. Chapman also seems to have maintained cordial relations with Transylvania's brilliant and eccentric scientist, Professor Constantine Rafinesque, who was often enough a guest in the Chapman home to execute charming portrait sketches of Mrs. Chapman and one of the daughters.[6]

Like Ward and the other clergymen of the town Chapman participated in civic and patriotic celebrations. He attended many of the festivities of General Lafayette's two-day visit to Lexington in May, 1825, joining in the procession with the Transylvania faculty and in the reception given for the General by President and Mrs. Holley. He must have gone to the reception, too, at the Dunham Academy since he was a "Visitor" of the institution. Next morning at the Masonic breakfast the Reverend Ward welcomed the General in what the local press called "a speech of great pertinency and excellence." The following year another memorable patriotic ceremony, held at Chapman's own church, was the mourning service for three statesmen who had recently died, Jefferson, Adams, and Shelby. It concluded with prayers by the rector.[7]

Chapman's significant achievement in Kentucky, however, was accomplished in his role as a priest of the Church. He was the first

---

[5] Fayette County, Ky., Court Records, Deed Book 10, p. 446: John Ward *et al.* to John B. Snead, Trustee. The building is known today as the Ridgeley House. John Ward died in 1860.

[6] The original sketches are preserved in the Rafinesque Papers, Transylvania College Library.

[7] Edgar Erskine Hume, *La Fayette in Kentucky* (Frankfort, Ky.: 1937), p. 96; also Ranck, *History of Lexington,* pp. 313-314.

Episcopal clergyman west of the mountains to defend Anglican doctrines and worship in direct confrontation to the powerful Presbyterian, Baptist, and Methodist preachers who were attracting the frontier people to their denominations. Somewhat earlier, in central Ohio, the scattered Episcopalians had organized a diocese under the indefatigable missionary, Philander Chase, but Bishop Chase was a rugged frontier builder, not a theological scholar. Chapman, a different kind of missionary, aimed to convert "good minds, divested of prejudice on the one side and disposed to investigate on the other, to read, think, and judge for themselves." He found an encouraging number of such minds in Lexington.

Chapman's preaching attracted so many listeners that about five years after his coming a "highly valued friend" suggested to him that he deliver a series of sermons about the Church to answer its critics. The suggestion was an inspired one. Chapman had spent much of his adult life in serious study of ecclesiastical doctrine, polity, and history. His firm convictions were supported by ripe scholarship. Fortunately he recognized his friend's suggestion as a God-given opportunity to proclaim the validity of Episcopal faith and order to inquiring hearers. During the years 1826–1827 he composed and delivered at intervals a series of twenty sermons setting forth the beliefs, organization, and worship of the Episcopal Church.

Believing that he was addressing people who had genuine interest in his subject, he presented his evidence in considerable detail, quoting from the Scriptures and the Church Fathers. He then argued logically from established premises to prove his conclusions. Among his major subjects were the validity of apostolic succession and the three orders of the ministry, especially the episcopacy; the soundness of the patristic writings as interpretation of the Scripture and as guide to the life of the Church; the value of formal and common prayer; and the true meaning of "baptismal regeneration," of infant baptism, of confirmation, and, above all, of the sacrament of the Lord's Supper. Countless other principles and practices were explained and defended. By the time he reached the end of the series he could declare: "On the whole, brethren, no one possessed

The Reverend
James Moore,
Rector of Christ
Church, Lexington
(1796–1813).
*Courtesy of Tran-
sylvania College.*

Marble tablet just
within the entrance
of Christ Church,
Lexington.

In Memory of
the Rev.ᵈ JAMES MOORE,
*First President of Transylvania
University & first Minister
of this Church.
He was learned, liberal,
amiable & pious.*
He departed this life June 22.ᵈ 18
aged 40 years.

The Reverend
John Ward,
Rector of Christ
Church, Lexing-
ton (1813–
1818). *Archives
of the parish.*

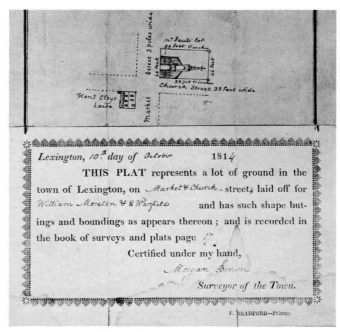

Original Plat of Christ Church site.
Archives of the parish.

The Reverend
George T.
Chapman, Rec-
tor of Christ
Church (1820–
1830). *Archives
of the parish.*

ABOVE: Dr. John Esten
Cooke (1783–1853). *Orig-
inal portrait is in possession of Robert B. Hamil-
ton, Claremont, Califor-
nia.*

RIGHT: Title page of Dr.
Cooke's *Essay. From a
copy owned by Frances
Keller Swinford.*

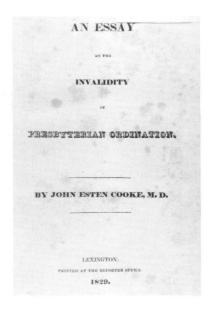

AN ESSAY

ON THE

INVALIDITY

OF

PRESBYTERIAN ORDINATION.

BY JOHN ESTEN COOKE, M. D.

LEXINGTON:
PRINTED AT THE REPORTER OFFICE.
1829.

The Right Reverend Benjamin Bosworth Smith, first Bishop of Kentucky, consecrated in 1833. *Portrait is in possession of Mrs. Ewing L. Hardy, Anchorage, Kentucky.*

Bishop Smith was also Presiding Bishop of the Protestant Episcopal Church in the United States of America (1868–1884). *Archives of the parish.*

Lithograph of the Episcopal Theological Seminary in Kentucky used by Bishop B. B. Smith on official stationary in 1837. *Archives of the Diocese of Lexington.*

Chapel, Old Episcopal Burying Ground, East Third Street, Lexington. *Archives of Christ Church, Lexington.*

The Reverend Henry Cas-
wall. *Archives of Christ
Church, Lexington.*

The Reverend Edward Win-
throp. *Archives of Christ
Church, Lexington.*

The Reverend Benjamin Orr
Peers. *Courtesy Transylvania
College.*

The Reverend Thomas W.
Coit. *Courtesy Transylvania
College.*

PROMINENT EDUCATORS OF THE EPISCOPAL THEOLOGICAL
SEMINARY IN KENTUCKY DURING THE 1830's

Trinity Church, Danville, rebuilt in 1860 on the site of the original church. *Courtesy of Mrs. R. S. Dulin.*

St. Peter's Church, Paris, "rebuilt and greatly enlarged" in 1870 on site of original church begun in 1832. *Archives of the parish.*

The Church of the Ascension, Frankfort. The present church is
essentially the edifice erected in 1850. *Archives of the parish.*

of reason to discriminate, and the opportunity to judge, can for a moment question the pre-eminence of our beloved Zion."

His friends at once urged him to publish the discourses, and he willingly did so, although he was advised that leaders of other denominations were preparing to reply strongly. The twenty sermons, along with a number of others on various topics, appeared in 1828 under the title of *Sermons upon the Ministry, Worship, and Doctrines of the Protestant Episcopal Church*. It was a substantial volume of 399 pages, bound in boards. The publishers were Messrs. Thomas Smith and James W. Palmer, members of the vestry.[8] It was dedicated to Bishop Hobart as a tribute of "esteem," "applause" and "admiration." Had there been any doubt as to the author's allegiance to Hobartian High Churchmanship, this dedication would have proved the point. The book was generally circulated in Kentucky and also among Church people throughout the country. After its republication in the East four years later in a condensed form (leaving out the miscellaneous sermons), it became known on both sides of the Atlantic as a standard exposition of the Anglican position, especially in regard to apostolic succession. Chapman lived to see it go into an eighth edition. A more immediate satisfaction came to him in the part played by his *Sermons* in the conversion of Dr. John Esten Cooke, an eminent physician residing in Lexington at the time. Dr. Cooke had come to Lexington in 1827 to occupy the chair of the Theory and Practice of Medicine in the Medical Department of Transylvania University. Most of the first forty-four years of his life had been spent in the Valley of Virginia, where he had begun the study of medicine under his father and, then, after graduating M.D. at the University of Pennsylvania, had practiced in Winchester, Virginia. Already a well-known writer in his own profession when he arrived in Kentucky, he soon afterward published his widely accepted *Treatise on Pathology and Therapeutics,* the earliest American systematic textbook of medicine.[9]

[8] G. T. Chapman, D.D., *Sermons upon the Ministry, Worship, and Doctrines of the Protestant Episcopal Church* (Lexington, Ky.: 1828).

[9] Edward F. Preble, "John Esten Cooke" in *Dictionary of American Biography* (New York: 1930).

Ere long the doctor turned his active and analytical mind to another and different field of research. Although his mother, daughter of the Acting Governor of Bermuda in the late 1700's, was reared an Anglican, Dr. Cooke had for eighteen years been an active member of the Methodist Society, a flourishing sect in the Valley. He and his wife (born Lucy Beale) and their ten children were affiliated with that denomination in Lexington, but his interest in theology caused him to subscribe to Dr. Chapman's *Sermons* as an addition to his fine library. In a rare leisure moment, curiosity led him to examine the argument that was to control his future religious position. It planted a doubt in his mind as to the ministerial authority of those to whose jurisdiction he had hitherto submitted. He ransacked libraries in order to read every available book on the subject, allowing himself only four hours for sleep and an hour daily for lecturing to his medical class. The rest of the twenty-four he devoted to the absorbing problem. At the end of six weeks his conviction as to the apostolicity and catholicity of the Episcopal Church was complete, and he immediately attached himself and his family to that body. The reasons for that conviction were set forth in his volume titled *Essay on the Invalidity of Presbyterian Ordination.* The book was widely read, and was credited with leading many clergymen as well as laymen into the Episcopal Church.[10]

Dr. Cooke soon began to take an active part in the affairs of Christ Church, as the parish in Lexington began to be called at that time, perhaps at Dr. Chapman's suggestion. In the spring of 1829 Cooke was elected to the vestry, adding his fresh enthusiasm to a group that proved to be among the most forward-looking and courageous vestries in the parish's history. One of the newly elected members was young Deacon Benjamin Orr Peers, a professor at Transylvania and head of the Eclectic Institute, his own progressive school for boys, located in Lexington. Son of the well-known Major Valentine Peers of Maysville, he had graduated from Transylvania and gone east to study for the Presbyterian ministry. Instead, he had been ordained deacon by Bishop Meade of Virginia, and had then turned to teaching as his chosen field. Already he was recognized as

---

[10] Published in Lexington in 1829.

one of the Commonwealth's influential educators.[11] The laymen on the 1829 vestry were mostly men who had served many times before: William Morton, B. W. Dudley, M.D., Joseph Logan, Thomas Smith, John Brand, and James Harper. There were also new faces. Besides Dr. Cooke there were E. Warfield, E. Yeiser, E. Warner, and A. Dumesnil, representatives of loyal parish families. In addition, the vestry could count on the support and wise advice of the Reverend John Ward.

It was a parish vestry eager to begin the task of spreading the Church's teachings throughout the Commonwealth. It is not recorded who first suggested that a diocese be organized in Kentucky. However, since George Chapman, ever a modest man, later wrote that he "effected the admission of that State [Kentucky] as a diocese in the Protestant Episcopal Church in the United States of America in 1829," it seems proper to recognize him as the organizer. The honor has never been disputed.

There were requirements to be met before the diocese could be formed. The rules of the General Convention called for three parishes and at least that number of clergy, but besides the Lexington church there was only Christ Church in Louisville, established in 1822. Obviously the first step was to form at least one more parish. Chapman, with his legal background, and his experienced vestry did not propose to organize prematurely as the Ohio churchmen had done a dozen years earlier.[12] With all this in mind the vestry at a meeting on May 19, 1829, requested its rector to visit Danville, Louisville, and Cincinnati "on business of the church" with "expenses paid."

George Chapman lost no time getting started. Late in May the sturdy, bespectacled parson set out on horseback with a "pedlar's pack" full of Prayer Books and copies of his *Sermons* to journey forty miles southward through the springtime countryside, crossing the Kentucky River where it cut a channel between high cliffs of limestone strata, to the small, important town of Danville. Its 849

[11] Grant C. Knight, "Benjamin Orr Peers," in *Dictionary of American Biography.* B. O. Peers was married on October 2, 1827, to Mary Ann Bell, of Lexington, by the Rev. G. T. Chapman (Register, Christ Church, Lexington, Ky.).

[12] Richard G. Salomon, *Philander Chase in Ohio* (New York: The National Council, n.d.), p. 8.

citizens, many of them from the Valley of Virginia, were uncommonly well educated for the period and the community was a stronghold of Presbyterians. His sermons would in all likelihood be the first Anglican doctrine ever preached there.

When Chapman rode into town along the main street and dismounted the bystanders asked what he was selling. "Some books on the subject of religion," was his reply. "A new religion?" they asked. He replied that it was new to this place but was really very old, and then offered to let them examine his books. They did so and each bought one for further study. The news of his arrival spread quickly, and crowds came out to hear him.[13]

Dr. Chapman was present on June 2 when a committee of citizens met for the purpose of establishing a Protestant Episcopal Church in the town. Its six members were James Birney, chairman, John Yeiser, secretary, Dr. Ephraim McDowell, John Finley, Frederick Yeiser, and Thomas Barbee. Twenty-nine other names were added later to the resolution pledging support to the new society. Some of the signers, like James Birney, the Yeisers, and Judge Edward Worthington, were "original Anglicans"; some, like the famous surgeon, Dr. McDowell, were coming over from the Presbyterians; still others were up to now members of no church. A short time after Chapman's visit an "adjourned meeting" was held which chose Trinity as the name of the new church and elected delegates to the organizing convention of a new diocese about which he had told them.

In later years the founder of the Danville church summed up his labors briefly: "Having in a few days collected these persons together, my object in visiting them was fully explained, and the result was the organization of a church, and the appointment of delegates to the proposed state Convention at Lexington in July."[14] Chapman understates the importance of his visit to Danville; actually it was the first effective domestic mission in Kentucky.

[13] For Chapman's founding of Trinity Church in Danville see Fackler, *Early Days in Danville,* pp. 91ff.; Minutes of Trinity Church, Danville, Ky., for June 2 and June 20, 1829; and "Reminiscences of a Remote and Recent Past in Danville," signed "G.C.," in *Kentucky Advocate,* Danville, Ky., January 7 and 23, February 6, 1905. "G.C." is undoubtedly the pen name of George Cowan, prominent early layman of Trinity Church.

[14] *The Spirit of Missions,* XIII, No. 4 (April, 1848), p. 97.

Leaving behind him several copies of his books for the edification of the new group and also a promise to come back to them at intervals until they could obtain the services of a clergyman, Dr. Chapman saddled up for the much longer ride to Louisville, more than eighty miles through the rolling hills down to the Falls of the Ohio. He apparently had no companion on the journey.

Louisville in 1829 was a thriving river town of about ten thousand inhabitants which because of its strategic location was surpassing Lexington as a center of trade and transportation. In earlier days there had been several Episcopal clergymen who conducted services there intermittently, notably the Reverend Williams Kavanaugh, who officiated regularly at a meeting house in the community between 1803 and 1806.[15] In the spring of 1822 a group of nine dedicated laymen, prominent among them Peter Ormsby and Richard Barnes, had organized a permanent congregation called Christ Church. One hundred and ninety-two subscribers pledged over six thousand dollars for the building of its house of worship, which was completed within two years. The career of the first rector, the Reverend Henry Shaw, was unsuccessful and brief, but the spirit of the parish remained firm. When word came to its leaders of the proposal to organize a diocese in Kentucky, they planned a friendly reception for Dr. Chapman. On June 7 the parishioners assembled to hear his exposition of the plan. According to his report, they "cordially concurred" and appointed delegates for the forthcoming meeting.

Having secured sufficient support in Danville and Louisville to insure the legality of the new diocese, Chapman returned directly to Lexington without continuing his journey on to Cincinnati as originally outlined. Instead he wrote to the Reverend Samuel Johnston of that city, extending an invitation to attend the organizing convention. The interests of Episcopalians in Kentucky were naturally bound up with those of the churches in southern Ohio, a fact which Chapman recognized. Another important preparation for the meeting involved correspondence with the Right Reverend John Stark

---

[15] Stoddard Johnston, editor, *The Memorial History of Louisville* (Chicago: 1896), Vol. II, Chap. VII, "The Episcopal Church" by the Rt. Rev. Thomas U. Dudley, pp. 136–137. Also James Craik, *Historical Sketches of Christ Church, Louisville, Diocese of Kentucky* (Louisville: 1862).

Ravenscroft, Bishop of North Carolina, requesting that he visit Kentucky at an early date to survey the prospects and especially to administer the rite of confirmation to many devout believers who had never had the opportunity to be received into the full fellowship of the Church. Since Ravenscroft's jurisdiction included also the state of Tennessee, it was natural to hope that he would be able to come to Kentucky. Chapman's invitation may have been influenced by the fact that the Bishop of North Carolina was also a follower of Hobartian High Churchmanship.

In the history of every organization certain scenes are illuminated by the light of their later importance. For all Episcopalians in Kentucky the gathering on Wednesday, July 8, 1829, in Christ Church, Lexington is such a scene. An excellent and commodious building for the time, its whitewashed walls gleamed in the summer sunshine, and its pews proved more than ample for the delegates and the numerous interested visitors. Its bell and organ welcomed the occasion, and the addresses were delivered from a handsome pulpit erected some three years earlier at a cost of more than five hundred dollars.

The official delegation was not large, only twenty-one in all, consisting of four clergymen and seventeen lay representatives. Their names should be remembered. The clergy were: Dr. Chapman, the only officiating parish priest in Kentucky at that time, and the Reverend Messrs. Ward and Peers. Also present was the Reverend Samuel Johnston, rector of Christ Church, Cincinnati, who was admitted an honorary member of the convention. The lay representatives from Christ Church, Louisville were Richard Barnes, John Bustard, and John F. Smith. From Trinity Church, Danville came Daniel Barbee, Henry J. Cowan, Ephraim McDowell, Edward Worthington, and Frederick Yeiser. The delegates from Christ Church, Lexington included Richard Ashton, John Esten Cooke, Anthony Dumesnil, Josiah Dunham, Charlton Hunt, John W. Hunt, William Morton, and Thomas Smith. The elevated mood of the gathering on this memorable occasion can be judged from the circumstance that to this opening session came elderly John Bradford, eminent newspaper editor and member of the group that in 1808 had formally organized the parish on this very spot. The convention invited him to take his seat as an honorary member, and he did so, perhaps feeling himself a representative of that earlier generation. All those who prayed and deliberated in Christ Church on that summer day must have realized that they were carrying on the work of those who had founded both the nation and the American Church within the memory of many of those present.

The meeting proceeded about its business with dispatch and in proper order.[16] The opening session started at "eight o'clock AM" with a prayer by Mr. Ward, and "an appropriate sermon" by Dr. Chapman, delivered of course, from the vantage point of his own pulpit. The convention then proceeded to organize, electing Chapman as president and Peers as secretary. The president appointed committees, headed by Judge Worthington and Dr. Cooke respectively, to report at the afternoon session with rules and a constitution; and, thanks to efficient previous preparations, it was so done. The constitution was adopted, and a committee was named to report a set of canons at the next convention. Other business was transacted with equal harmony, including the authorization of the Missionary Society of the Protestant Episcopal Church of Kentucky for the "support of the Missionaries . . . in destitute parts of this Diocese." The Reverend Johnston had preached a sermon on the need for missionary endeavors that encouraged such a step. Judge Worthington moved that an invitation be extended to Bishop Ravenscroft of North Carolina to include Kentucky in his current western visitation, whereupon Dr. Chapman read a letter from the Bishop stating that he proposed to come to Kentucky during the latter part of the present month. On motion of Dr. Cooke the convention authorized the use of lay readers by congregations "destitute of clerical services." This action was a recognition of the Church's difficulty in conducting formal services on the frontier.[17] The two days of the organizing convention closed in a spirit of

---

[16] *Journal of the Proceedings of the First Convention of the Protestant Episcopal Church in the Diocess (sic) of Kentucky, held in Christ Church, Lexington, July 8th and 9th* (Lexington, printed by Thomas Smith, 1829). Hereinafter it is referred to as the *Journal of the Diocese of Kentucky.*

[17] Delegates to the General Convention scheduled to meet in August in Philadelphia were elected: of the clergy, Chapman, Ward, and Peers; and of the laity, Dr. Cooke, Dr. Dudley, Joseph Logan of Lexington, and J. S. Snead of Louisville.

confidence with "Divine Service" by the Rev. Benjamin O. Peers. The new Diocese had accepted its responsibility to go out into all parts of the Commonwealth on its apostolic mission.

The Bishop of North Carolina kept his word and, after finishing his visitations to missions in Tennessee, made the hard four day journey by stagecoach from Nashville to Lexington. He was in poor health, and he must have been very weary when he at last reached the Chapman residence at about eight o'clock on Saturday evening, July 25. His host mercifully spared him from receiving any visitors that hot summer evening. The Episcopalians of the town and surrounding area were planning a full schedule of activities during his stay.

Until his coming no bishop of the Episcopal Church had set foot in the state and to many Kentuckians, even the habitual occupants of the pews in Christ Church, the doctrine of apostolic succession and episcopal authority seemed remote and somewhat alien. Fortunately Bishop Ravenscroft was a powerful preacher and a colorful personality. Son of a Virginia planter and born to a life of affluence, John Stark Ravenscroft was nearly forty when he was suddenly "convicted of sin" one day while riding alone across his wide acres. By reading diligently in the Scriptures he convinced himself of the divine authority embodied through apostolic succession in the Episcopal Church. He was ordained priest at forty-five and became a forceful, undiplomatic man of God. To his own surprise he was soon elected Bishop of the large and difficult Diocese of North Carolina that reached all the way to the Mississippi River. Lexingtonians had heard many colorful anecdotes about him—how when his clerical cravat started loosening during a particularly vehement sermon he had pulled it off and laid it aside without ever pausing; and how he had astonished a group of fellow travelers on a stagecoach by his astute knowledge of horseracing.[18] Not only Episcopalians but many townspeople were eager to hear and to meet him.

The congregation of Christ Church saw the Bishop for the first time the following day when he preached at the morning service. A large man, he seemed even bigger in his clerical robes, and his booming voice could easily be heard by the people who were stand-

[18] John N. Norton, *The Life of Bishop Ravenscroft* (New York: General Protestant Episcopal Sunday School Union and Church Book Society, 1868).

ing outside the doors. Above his lean, masculine face with its acquiline nose perched a small pair of spectacles in readiness when it came time for the Order of Confirmation. He must have been gratified when he looked down at the seventy-one persons whom Dr. Chapman was presenting to him to receive the Laying on of Hands. There were old people who had waited half a lifetime for this hour, and young people who would remember it vividly until the close of the century.[19] That day the Bishop preached twice more to a crowded church and at a second service on the 28th he confirmed another class numbering twenty. In the long lines that waited reverently to receive the Bishop's blessing were Chapman's two daughters, Dr. Cooke and his wife, Mrs. Clay and her daughter, Ann Clay Erwin, Benjamin O. Peers' wife, and scores of others. Among the confirmands from out of town were Dr. McDowell and Dr. Daniel Yeiser from Danville, Mrs. Eliza Marshall from Paris, and Mrs. Mary Paxton from Mason County.

In addition to holding public services during his three days in Lexington, Bishop Ravenscroft received many visitors who wished to meet him informally. Dr. Chapman's account of these days is detailed and lively.

On Monday and Tuesday my house was thronged with those desirous of testifying their admiration for this truly excellent and evangelical Bishop. On these occasions I took good care, by leading questions, to have him discourse on the great doctrines of the Cross, and this he did fully and freely to large numbers of delighted hearers. These interviews were altogether of a spiritual cast. The Bishop was the only speaker, and as it was with Paul at Athens, so it was with him. "His spirit was stirred within him" to declare the whole counsel of God with such fervor that all found it good for their souls to be there. The language I do not profess to remember, but the effect was electric and searching—"a solemn stillness reigned about."[20]

The visit of the Right Reverend John Stark Ravenscroft to Lexington clarified for his many hearers the doctrines of the Episcopal Church that Dr. Chapman and Dr. Cooke had set forth in their

---

[19] "The Old Register" of Christ Church, Lexington, Kentucky, Confirmations, July 26, July 28, 1829. Also Elizabeth King Smith and Mary LeGrand Didlake, *Christ Church, 1796–1946* (Lexington, Kentucky: privately printed, 1946), pp. 13–14.
[20] Norton, *op. cit.*, pp. 134–135.

learned books. Here was a bishop in the flesh who spoke with authority and yet was a practical man with a simple faith. His coming bestowed a certain distinction upon the Church in this region which, for all its intermittent lapses through the years, it has never lost.

Episcopalians in Kentucky now entered into a period of indigenous missionary activity. Dr. Chapman visited the new Danville parish once each month, assisting the Reverend Silas C. Freeman, a young deacon who ministered there for a few months.[21] It is of record that one day in September he baptized three small Yeisers and a child in the Birney family in Danville and went out into the county next day to perform the same rite for four young Worthingtons.[22] By an odd coincidence, one of his visits fell upon the same day as the arrival of a "Romish priest," and their appointments to preach were at the same place—the county courthouse—and the same hour. "The result," as the town remembered for half a century, "was a hard-fought contest over Protestant principles, but so conducted by Dr. C. that the Priest became his warm & ardent friend, while both widely differed & maintained their separate convictions."[23]

In August, 1829, Dr. Cooke represented the new Diocese as delegate to the General Convention in Philadelphia and made the acquaintance of the leaders of the national Church. He must have had contacts with the secretary and the advisers of the Domestic and Foreign Missionary Society, organized in 1820, which had shown interest in Kentucky. The Convention evinced its interest in domestic missions by authorizing Bishop Thomas Church Brownell of Connecticut to make an inspection tour of the southern and western states.

On Friday, December 3, Bishop Brownell, accompanied by the Reverend William Richmond of New York City, arrived in Lexington. The high point of the official visitation was his consecration of Christ Church, the first such office among Episcopalians in the state.

---

[21] *Journal of the Diocese of Kentucky* for 1859, p. 80.

[22] "Old Register" of Christ Church, Lexington, Kentucky, September 12, 13, 1829.

[23] George Cowan to James Craik, January 15, 1869 (James Craik Papers, by permission of the Reverend Charles Ewell Craik, Jr.).

Five clergymen assisted him and, as a local newspaper reported the occasion, at the communion service afterward there were "fellow Christians of other denominations." That evening three persons were confirmed and various contributions made to missions, including a handsome gift of book royalties from Dr. Cooke, a plate collection of forty dollars, and a hundred Prayer Books from the Domestic and Foreign Missionary Society. During Bishop Brownell's visit, arrangements were made for Mr. Peers to officiate at intervals in nearby Versailles and for Mr. Ward to preach in the vicinity of Lexington when invited. A new clergyman from Ohio was on his way to take charge of the parish at Danville.[24]

The visiting bishop and his companion, accompanied by Dr. Chapman, then proceeded to Louisville, where they were welcomed by the new rector, the Reverend David C. Page, who had arrived just in time to participate in the consecration of his church and to present thirty-one persons for confirmation. He was an eloquent preacher and well known to the congregation as the son-in-law of one of its prominent members. His coming was a good omen for Christ Church, Louisville.

The new year of 1830 opened auspiciously for the Diocese and especially for the Lexington parish. Its vestrymen were devout and responsible men. Its rector, during his years among them, had organized the new Diocese, published a volume of internationally recognized sermons, and served as both a professor and a trustee of Transylvania University. Nevertheless, in the spring the Reverend Mr. Chapman resigned as rector of Christ Church, Lexington, because he and his parishioners could not come to terms about the payment of his salary. The disagreement had been going on for several years, ever since he had given up his professorship at Transylvania. He had written the vestry from time to time about sums long past due. It had replied with promises and in turn chided him about neglecting parochial visiting and about his appropriation of the plate offerings. Finally, on April 23, 1830, he addressed a rather long letter to the vestry, stating his case with dignity and firmness.

[24] *Kentucky Reporter,* Lexington, December 9, 1829. Also "Extract from Bishop Brownell's Private Notebook—Itinerary (MSS), *Journal of the Diocese of Kentucky* for 1860, Appendix IX, pp. 70–72.

. . . When I took charge of the parish it was with the fullest determination to retain it to my dying day provided that my manner of life and labour proved acceptable. Most solemnly do I declare that it never entered into my mind that a congregation so generally blessed by a kind providence with worldly prosperity would have failed to comply with their engagements with respect to the salary tendered to my acceptance. Such, however, has been the result. It has in no one instance been punctually paid, and now after repeated and fruitless efforts to obtain a settlement of the arrearages due me has changed my original determination.

The letter closed by Chapman's tendering his resignation as of July 1 unless the total amount due him was paid. If not, he proposed to return to the eastern states.[25]

The vestry tried again to raise the money to pay the arrearages but met with no response among the parishioners. Wounded perhaps by Chapman's frank statement of their financial shortcomings, the pewholders unanimously accepted his resignation at a meeting on May 8. The vestry members, more aware of the justice of his demands, borrowed money to settle his account in full. They also rather curtly requested that he turn over all books and papers of the parish and that he purchase "with any parish funds in his hands" a book in which the records of the church were to be inscribed. He did so and spent a good many long days transcribing from his private notes all the baptisms, funerals, confirmations, and marriages during his ten-year ministry into a large and handsome leather-bound volume, which to this day remains among the most precious possessions of the parish.[26]

Dr. Chapman continued to fulfil his duties until July 1. In May he attended the second annual convention of the Diocese at Danville, serving as its presiding officer, with Benjamin O. Peers as secretary. The other clergy present were Mr. Page from Louisville and the newly arrived rector of Trinity, Danville, the Reverend Gideon McMillan from the Diocese of Ohio. Only three lay delegates were there: Dr. Cooke from Lexington, Dr. McDowell of Danville, and

[25] For Chapman's leaving see Vestry Minutes, Christ Church, Lexington, Kentucky, December 28, 1829 through June 30, 1830.

[26] "The Old Register" of Christ Church, Lexington, Kentucky contains the records from Chapman's coming in 1820 to the time of his departure and for about 30 years longer. Some of the later records are less meticulously kept than his.

Mr. J. Smith from Louisville. Judging from the scanty remaining records of this meeting, the principal business consisted of reports of correspondence with the Domestic and Foreign Missionary Society through its secretaries, the Reverend Messrs. B. B. Smith and F. L. Hawks, of Philadelphia. The convention officially invited the Right Reverend William Meade, Assistant Bishop of Virginia, to visit its parishes.[27] Brief as was this 1830 meeting, it preserved the continuity of the organization.

By midsummer Dr. Chapman, with his wife and two daughters, departed from Lexington, leaving behind them many friends in the community and throughout the Diocese. They went back to Massachusetts, probably at first to his brother's home in Williamstown. Chapman had reason to hope for advancement in the East on the basis of his now famous *Sermons,* but as it turned out, his prospects were little better than when he left. The two High Church leaders whom he knew best—Bishop Hobart of New York and Bishop Ravenscroft of North Carolina—both died during this year of 1830, and their associates knew little about Chapman. He again accepted posts under kindly Bishop Griswold in provincial parishes at Pittsfield, Massachusetts, Burlington, Vermont, and Portland, Maine. Meanwhile he got out a new edition of the *Sermons* (1834) and published another volume of discourses, *Sermons to Presbyterians of All Sects* in 1836.

During the 1830's Chapman was attracted to the early phases of the Oxford Movement in his native England. He was in sympathy with its emphasis on apostolic succession and the sacramental life, its reliance on the early Christian practices, and its desire for one catholic church. During the years 1837-41 he attained prominence as the first rector of a new High Church parish, Grace Church, in Newark, New Jersey. It is clear, however, that Chapman did not follow the Oxford Tractarians in their ceremonialism or in the doctrines that led some of them into the Roman Catholic faith. He

---

[27] No copy of the *Journal* of the 1830 Convention of the Diocese of Kentucky is known to exist, even in the otherwise complete file of the present Diocese of Kentucky. The above facts are taken from Appendix XI, "Synopsis of Thirty-one Annual Conventions," *Journal of the Diocese of Kentucky* for 1859. For the beginning of the collection of the *Journals* of past years, see *Journal of the Diocese of Kentucky* for 1871, pp. 28-39.

remained, for the rest of his long and useful life, essentially the same moderate Hobartian that he had been when he proclaimed that doctrine so vigorously from the pulpit of Christ Church, Lexington. He died in 1872 at the age of eighty-six, busily engaged in collecting and editing the biographical sketches of the alumni of his alma mater.

It is interesting to speculate about the development of the Diocese of Kentucky if George Chapman had stayed on for another decade or longer. His orderly, legal approach to administrative problems would have been valuable, and his scholarship would have lent distinction to the Diocese. His High Church leanings would not doubt have had considerable influence. He evinced no interest, however, in the sparsely settled, outlying regions of Kentucky and the limitations of a frontier diocese might have proved uncongenial to a scholar.

A further comment regarding Chapman's relationship with the Diocese of Kentucky seems pertinent. The man himself and the Diocese both suffered a genuine loss when he left it for financial reasons. This situation, however, exemplifies a problem that confronted the entire Church as well as the Lexington parish. The parishes of that period, especially in smaller communities, had no systematic fiscal policy. Their sources of income were precarious— special contributions and gifts, plate offerings, pew rents, and occasional lotteries. Sometimes it was a matter of dispute as to who should handle and distribute the money. Most serious of all, the clergyman's salary as agreed upon by the congregation was usually so small that neither he nor the people really expected that he would be able to support his family on it even if it was paid promptly and in full, which was not always the case. A new organ sometimes got priority over the minister's stipend. Clergymen without independent means often taught school in addition to their parochial duties, and in that case a related problem arose as to how much of his time the minister owed to his flock. Such financial difficulties were common in all denominations, but, considering the high requirements of the Episcopal Church as to the education and training of its candidates for the priesthood, its clergy were conspicuously underpaid. One of the problems sure to plague the new Diocese of Kentucky was money.

5 Benjamin Bosworth Smith, First Bishop of Kentucky

After its second annual convention in 1830 the new Diocese progressed in a quiet, orderly manner. The Reverend D. C. Page began a successful ministry of about seven years at Christ Church, Louisville with the full support of the devoted laity that had borne the full responsibility until his coming. Ere long the parish had both a bell and a proper organ. In Danville Gideon McMillan and his "small but interesting congregation," as he described his charge, began in July, 1830, to build Trinity Church, the third Episcopal edifice in Kentucky. By the end of the year, probably upon the recommendation of Bishop Brownell, the Domestic and Foreign Missionary Society assigned two young deacons then attached to the Diocese of Maryland to new stations in Kentucky—George F. Giddinge to Hopkinsville, Russellville, and parts adjacent, and Robert Ash to Shelbyville and Middletown.[1]

Christ Church, Lexington after Dr. Chapman's departure, relied upon the ever faithful Reverend Mr. Ward and upon transient clergy such as Deacon Giddinge to conduct its services. Meanwhile the vestry set about calling a new rector, asking advice of prominent eastern bishops and of the General Mission Board in Philadelphia. On August 8, 1830, it voted to extend an invitation to the Reverend Benjamin Bosworth Smith, editor of the *Episcopal Recorder,* an Evangelical organ, and priest in charge of Grace Mission Church in Philadelphia. He was known chiefly to the Lexington vestry through his duties as corresponding secretary of the Domestic and Foreign Missionary Society, but it is more than likely that he and Dr. Cooke had become acquainted at the recent General Convention. Dr. Cooke wrote to him on behalf of the vestry, but at a meeting on September 13th had to report that he had received a reply of "non-acceptance." Undeterred, the vestry instructed him to "re-invite" Mr. Smith "under a statement of the peculiar condition of the church in this place and in the western country at large," with a request that if he did not come would he please look for a suitable substitute. Rather promptly, all things considered, Dr. Cooke was able to report to the vestry on October 8 that he had received a letter of acceptance from Mr. Smith, whereupon it was voted to advance two hundred dollars to assist the new rector in moving to Kentucky as soon as possible. The salary was to be one thousand dollars per annum.

Since, more than any other individual, Benjamin Bosworth Smith was to shape the destiny of the Episcopal Church in Kentucky for the next half century, it is important to try to understand why this studious and conscientious clergyman gave up congenial editorial and administrative tasks amid the agreeable surroundings of an eastern city to move with his young family to a faraway border state he had never seen. With little prominence or preparation for leadership, he was suddenly, at thirty-six, faced with a choice between a quiet career, well adapted to his natural talents, and a challenging missionary task. He first elected to follow his modest inclinations and then, impelled by a sense of divine call and, perhaps, by a surge of unaccustomed ambition, he decided to take an active part in the Church's western expansion. The personality traits he brought to his new mission were part of his New England heritage: dedication and commitment, fortitude and stubbornness, and an extraordinary mixture of humility and pride.

He was born in 1794 in the prosperous seaport town of Bristol, Rhode Island, where his estimable Congregationalist forebears had settled nearly a century earlier to become the town's clerks and stone-cutters and, some of them, soldiers in the Revolution. By Benjamin's time the town had lost most of its puritanical rigidness and was living "in a theological temperate zone" of tolerance that verged upon indifference to religion.[2] The wealth of the community

[1] Domestic and Foreign Missionary Society Secretary's Papers, 1830–1831 (Church Historical Society Archives), Executive Committee Minutes for August 11, 1830, signed by B. B. Smith, re Giddinge; September 30, 1830, re Ash.
[2] M. A. De Wolf Howe, *Bristol, Rhode Island. A Town Biography* (Cambridge, Mass.: 1930). Written by a great-nephew of B. B. Smith, it contains an extended account of Bishop Griswold but only slight mention of B. B. Smith. The best accounts of B. B. Smith are the Rt. Rev. Alfred Lee, Bishop of Delaware, "Life and Ministry of Benjamin Bosworth Smith, First Bishop of Kentucky," *Journal of the Diocese of Kentucky* for 1884, Appendix A; and the several articles by the

derived in large part from the extensive slave trade of the port. The arrival in 1804 of the Reverend Alexander Viets Griswold to be rector of St. Michael's Episcopal Church and a little later to become Bishop of the Eastern Diocese brought about a change for the better in the religious climate of Bristol. He was a plain man who had been a farmer in his younger days, and it seemed natural to him to black his clerical guests' boots for them. Persons of all denominations were included in his wide tolerance, and, most importantly, he was a mighty preacher who "set the town afire" with his message of salvation.

The sixteenth of eighteen children, young Smith grew up in modest circumstances, especially after the death of his father when the boy was only five. His mother, born a Bosworth, sent him to dame school and saw to it that he knew Milton and Shakespeare and Gibbon and "some scraps of Greek and Latin." He would probably have become a clerk like his Grandfather Smith had he not been converted to the Episcopal faith during the Great Revival of 1812 by Bishop Griswold and prepared for college in the bishop's school. He was nearly nineteen when he entered Brown University in nearby Providence as a sophomore. He became a candidate for Holy Orders and soon organized a Sunday school at St. John's Church there, the first in the city. He was graduated in 1816, made deacon in 1817, and ordained June 25, 1818, on which day he married his cousin, Elizabeth Bosworth. They lived for a year at Marblehead, Massachusetts, where he had a small parish. He was a methodical young man of somewhat nervous temperament, who arose at five each morning to pursue his studies and to write letters, sometimes as many as twenty a day. He never touched tobacco or alcoholic stimulants of any sort, an abstinence he continued to the end of his life.[3] His great example then and ever after was Alexan-

Rev. Robert Insko: *Kentucky Bishop* (Frankfort, Ky.: Ky. Historical Society, 1952); "Benjamin Bosworth Smith (1794–1884), Early New England Clergyman," *Rhode Island History*, Vol. 18 (1959), pp. 65–82; "The Trial of a Kentucky Bishop," *Filson Club History Quarterly*, Vol. 35 (1961), pp. 141–158; "A Pioneer Educator on Horseback, Kentucky's Third Superintendent of Instruction," *Filson Club History Quarterly*, Vol. 32 (1955), pp. 284–295; "Benjamin Bosworth Smith," *History Magazine of the Protestant Episcopal Church*, XXII (1953), pp. 143–228.

[3] Obituary notice in *Standard of the Cross*, June 5, 1884.

der Viets Griswold, and their warm personal ties were strengthened when about 1818 Griswold took as his second wife the widow of Smith's brother. Like his friends and fellow ordinands under Bishop Griswold, Smith was Evangelical in his Churchmanship, which meant at that period chiefly that he was committed to the cause of missions and Gospel preaching, that he favored simplicity in the services, and that he was tolerant of other Protestant denominations.[4]

To help out one of these fellow ordinands during an illness B. B. Smith accepted a call in 1820 to a little mission church in Accomack County, Virginia, on the rural Northern Neck. In 1822 he took charge of two slightly larger missions in Charles Town near the Potomac. The four years the young Yankee priest spent in Virginia were very influential in shaping his later career. He proved himself to be a good missionary among the plain people of rural parishes, an asset he possessed to the end of his days. He came under the jurisdiction of the dynamic Bishop of Virginia, Richard Channing Moore, a New Yorker, who was reviving the moribund postcolonial Church in that state. He had just founded the Virginia Theological Seminary at Alexandria, the second in the American Church, to train young men for his oversize Diocese. The young New England priest had even more contact with another Virginia clergyman, the Reverend William Meade, a strong Evangelical and the leading figure in the "Clerical Association" west of the Blue Ridge where Smith served from 1821 to 1823.[5] One particular phase of his work in Virginia made a deep impression upon him. Although he had been reared in a town made rich by the slave trade, his own family had opposed the institution, and when he went south he already had an interest in the condition and salvation of the colored race. At this time he made a beginning in his lifelong ministry to them.

In 1823 he returned to New England to accept the rectorship of the well established church at Middlebury, Vermont, a move moti-

[4] See Insko Collection, Bishop B. B. Smith Papers, Sermons (Church Historical Society): pp. 66-117, Marblehead, October 14, 1817; pp. 66-118, Marblehead, October 5, 1817.

[5] See Lawrence L. Brown, "Richard Channing Moore and the Revival of the Southern Church," *Historical Magazine of the Protestant Episcopal Church*, XXXV (1966), pp. 39-40.

vated in part by the needs of his young wife and their growing family. He took advantage here of an opportunity to pursue his scholarly ambitions, and he plunged into a study of sacred languages, history, and theology that won for him an M. A. degree from Middlebury College. He joined with the Vermont Episcopalians who wanted to be detached from the Eastern Diocese and founded a journal, the *Episcopal Register,* to promote a movement toward organizing the Diocese of Vermont.

His talents were recognized in 1830 when he received a call to become editor of the *Episcopal Recorder,* the largest and most influential periodical in the Church, and to take charge of Grace Mission in order to supplement his salary. He accepted and soon after his arrival became also one of the secretaries of the Domestic and Foreign Missionary Society. His new and favorable situation put him at the center of the administrative affairs of the American Church and kept him in touch with its outreach toward the western frontier, which was beginning to quicken. He was understandably reluctant to consider the call that came from Kentucky, and friends in Philadelphia offered to increase his annual salary at Grace Mission to fifteen hundred dollars in order to keep him. The money seems to have mattered less than other aspects of his connections in Philadelphia. He wrote a friend that he was "loathe to let go of the Recorder and the Missionary Society." His fellow Evangelicals, whose great desire was to further domestic missions, urged him to accept.[6]

What Dr. Cooke wrote to the Reverend Mr. Smith in the "re-invitation" is a matter of conjecture. He may well have mentioned the obvious need for bishops in the west since that was much on Cooke's mind. Even if the chance of a bishopric was suggested to Smith that was a dubious reason for his coming. The only missionary bishop up to that time, the Right Reverend Philander Chase of Ohio, was having great difficulty in keeping his struggling parishes united. Smith himself never gave a direct reason for his acceptance

[6] B. B. Smith to Alonzo Potter, August 10, 1830, quoted in Insko, "Benjamin Bosworth Smith (1794–1884): Early New England Clergyman," *Rhode Island History,* Vol. 18 (1958), p. 76. Also Bishop Smith's Address, *Journal of the Diocese of Kentucky* for 1863, p. 14.

of the call to Lexington. His friend and first biographer, Bishop Alfred Lee of Delaware, wrote that "it must have been in consequence of his belief in a Divine call which he dared not refuse. . . ."[7]

In October the new rector of Christ Church, Lexington brought his wife and four small children, aged six to eleven, out from Philadelphia by stage and steamboat, and along with them came Deacon Robert Ash, sent out by the Domestic and Foreign Missionary Society to labor in the Kentucky field. It was a pleasant family journey, as small Lizzie Smith remembered it, enlivened by "tale and song" and by "wonder at the passing scene."[8] Smith was a devoted family man, with a way of charming all children, including his own. Being clever with his hands, he would whittle small figures or other trifles with his pocketknife. Among the trunks and boxes of books he brought with him to Kentucky was a chest of fine carpenter's tools with which as a pastime he made furniture, carvings, and miniature architectural models. There was a homely strain of Yankee craftsman in the man, along with his studious leanings, and he was always concerned about proper buildings and equipment with which to carry on his work. Within a year after his settling in Lexington he saw to it that his new parish had a service of communion plate and a rectory close by the church on Market Street.[9]

With the coming to the Diocese of Smith, Ash, and Giddinge, there were now five clergy at their posts, making available for their people the Church's offices and organizing Sunday schools and missionary societies for spreading the Gospel in their regions. In March, 1831, another mission was started in the "grassroots" fashion of the early days. Deacon Amos Cleaver, a former Baptist preacher from England, set up a "female school" in Paris, a town of twelve hundred inhabitants in a rich agricultural county north of Lexing-

[7] Lee, *op. cit.,* p. 68.
[8] *Journal of the Diocese of Kentucky* for 1852, p. 17; also Insko, "Benjamin Bosworth Smith (1794–1884): Early New England Clergyman," *Rhode Island History,* Vol. 18, pp. 65–82.
[9] Vestry Minutes of Christ Church, Lexington, Kentucky, May 27, 1831 and ff. Also Fayette County, Kentucky, Deed Book No. 7, p. 190: William Richardson to B. W. Dudley and James Harper, June 10, 1831, for 66 feet on Market Street.

ton.[10] There were a few Episcopalians there, and services had been held there as early as 1815 by the Reverend John Ward and 1820 by a Reverend William Wall, and during the 1820's by Dr. Chapman. Mr. Cleaver began as soon as he arrived to conduct morning prayer every Sunday in his schoolroom for the two Church families of the town and to preach frequently to large gatherings in the countryside. He decided that Paris was a desirable place for an Episcopal Church and singlehandedly set about securing contributions for a proper building. This seemed to him, "next to the conversion of souls, the most important thing to be accomplished."[11] A man of simple faith and great patience, Amos Cleaver set about establishing his parish.

In mid-May the Right Reverend William Meade, Assistant Bishop of Virginia, visited Kentucky to perform the "episcopal offices" which the "infant diocese" had requested of him at its last convention.[12] He had recently been elected as assistant to the aging Bishop Moore of Virginia, under whom he and B. B. Smith had served together a decade earlier. Since both men were Evangelical in their views, this visitation was a cordial reunion. Smith joined Bishop Meade at Maysville on May 19 as he left the steamboat to begin his overland tour of the Diocese. They preached in the vicinity, sometimes thrice daily, in the Presbyterian and Methodist churches and on one occasion to the colored people. When they reached Paris a similar program was carried out at the Baptist and Presbyterian churches and in Mr. Cleaver's schoolroom. In Lexington they were joined for several days by Robert Ash and Gideon McMillan for an even more extended preaching mission, this time in Christ Church, with excursions to Mr. Ward's schoolroom and on "one evening to the colored people in a meeting-house where Mr. Smith is accustomed to officiate for them."

Bishop Meade was active and vigorous, and became very much

---

[10] Advertisement in *Western Citizen*, Paris, Kentucky, April 2 and 9, 1831.

[11] *Journal of the Diocese of Kentucky* for 1831, pp. 12–13. There is a tradition that before settling in Paris Amos Cleaver consulted with B. B. Smith regarding the merits of Paris, Versailles, and other locations.

[12] "Report of the Right Reverend William Meade, D. D., of his Ministrations during a visit through the Diocese of Kentucky, made in the months of May and June, 1831, by request of the Convention of the aforesaid Diocese," *ibid.*, pp. 19–22.

concerned with the problems of the new Diocese as he visited parishes and missions as far west as Hopkinsville. In Danville he confirmed twenty-five persons and consecrated the Reverend McMillan's new building "to the service of Almighty God by the name of Trinity Church." In Louisville he confirmed twenty-one persons and ordained to the priesthood the three deacons who were serving in the Diocese: Robert Ash, George Giddinge, and Amos Cleaver. There he presided over the opening sessions of the Annual Convention of the Diocese on Monday, June 13, 1831. Besides the Bishop of Virginia, there were two other honored guests—the Reverend Samuel Johnston, of Cincinnati, who had been present at the organizing meeting of the Diocese of Kentucky and the Reverend B. P. Aydelott, also of Cincinnati. The Ohio clergy were genuinely interested in the Church's progress south of the river, and they must have approved of the reports made to this third convention.

All six of the active clergy of the Diocese were present: three rectors of parishes, two missionaries of the Domestic and Foreign Missionary Society, and the schoolmaster-preacher from Paris. Absent were Messrs. Ward and Peers, who could be counted upon for clerical services from time to time. The rectors reported a total of 178 communicants listed in their registers, plus as many more regular attendants at their services. The missionaries hopefully counted a hundred or more "prospects." Contributions from within the Diocese for its own missions were generous, especially from the parishes in Lexington and Louisville. Bishop Meade was favorably impressed by the response of the larger churches and later wrote in his report: "To these, and these alone, hath much been given, and from these will much be required." At the close of the clergy reports, Bishop Meade departed in order to continue his journey to the western part of the state.

The convention proceeded to approve various amendments to its 1829 constitution in order to make it conform with the procedures of the national Church. It adopted canons for more specific regulation of the Diocese, including one for the discipline of clergymen for certain misdoings, and a rather general Canon V requiring that any "presentment" against the bishop could be made only by order of the convention of the Diocese. Prominent in the drafting of these revisions were Dr. Cooke, lay delegate from Christ Church, Lexington and Judge Edward Worthington, of Trinity, Danville.

The next order of business was of even more interest to all present. A motion by Judge Worthington that "it is expedient for this Convention to elect a Bishop for this diocese" was accorded "full and mature deliberation" and then was carried by a vote of eleven to six. The minutes show that the Danville delegates voted unanimously for the motion, and that the delegations from both Louisville and Lexington were divided. One reason for the Danville delegates' support of this movement to elect Smith as bishop was undoubtedly his attitude toward slavery, which matched their own "gradual emancipation" views. After silent prayer the clergy balloted, electing the Reverend Benjamin Bosworth Smith, and the choice was approved by a majority of the lay delegates.[13] This convention was B. B. Smith's first visit as far west as Louisville, and the election was a gratifying vote of confidence. The members of the 1831 convention returned to their parishes thinking that only the formality of approval by the other dioceses and the ceremony of consecration remained before the Diocese of Kentucky would have a bishop. Fifteen months elapsed, however, before that end was achieved. During the course of the summer more than half of the other dioceses questioned the validity of the election, chiefly because of an insufficient number of clergy participating. In October, the Reverend Mr. Smith addressed a letter to the Standing Committee of the Diocese of Kentucky, requesting that the Kentucky Convention nullify his election as bishop and "proceed as if nothing had been done."[14] He apparently felt no ill will about the matter, nor is there evidence of any personal feeling in the action of the dioceses. The electing of a bishop by a missionary diocese was somewhat of a novelty. The election in Ohio in 1817 had been hastily done, and this one was being more closely scrutinized.

The work of the churches in Kentucky enjoyed a modest success during the ensuing year although without receiving any additions to the clergy. Christ Church, Louisville began its long career of extra-parochial good works with the activities of a Female Benefici-

[13] *Journal of the Diocese of Kentucky* for 1831, pp. 16–17.
[14] *Journal of the Diocese of Kentucky* for 1832, p. 12.

ary Society and an effort to establish a mission in the city. In Paris Amos Cleaver brought the number of parishioners up to twenty-five and journeyed to the cities of the northeastern seaboard, where he raised $560.00 for a church building. Upon his return, as he stated in his annual report, he "set about digging the foundation of the Church and building a wall round the church-yard, which were completed by April [1832], and at which, for economy's sake, I worked as the beloved Paul did, with my hands." Gideon McMillan's flock at Danville, having completed their church, worked at distributing Prayer Books and tracts while their rector devoted fully a third of his time to officiating at three stations in the countryside. In the western part of the state, George Giddinge settled down in Hopkinsville, having brought out Mrs. Giddinge from Maine with the aid of a gift of one hundred dollars from the ladies of Christ Church, Lexington. In Henderson a group of laymen organized St. Paul's Parish. At Shelbyville, Robert Ash endeavored with moderate success to gather the scattered Church families of the area into his Zion Mission.

B. B. Smith resumed his parochial duties after the convention as if nothing untoward had happened in his failure to be ratified as bishop. He organized missionary societies both for the ladies and for the men. He regularly gathered colored people in the vicinity for religious services. He promoted the lagging Sunday school and delivered lectures on religion to the medical and law students of Transylvania. His name appears in the minutes of the Union Philosophical Society, a student organization at the university. He certainly joined in the "vast throng" of people who attended the ceremonies at the laying of the first stone sill of the new Lexington and Ohio Railroad on October 21. The parade formed on the university campus and swung down toward Water Street to the clangor of all the church bells. The citizens of Lexington welcomed the railroad as an answer to the rise of the river cities with their steamboats, and the celebration was long and elaborate. There is no record of any toasts proposed by the Reverend Mr. Smith at the banquet and he may well have seemed to the town to be serious and somewhat puritanical. Very probably his abstemious habits and absorption in his labors made him something of an outsider in the more relaxed ways of Lexington society. He and his gentle, unassuming wife lived quietly with their children, apparently undisturbed by the fact that they had less money than most of their parishioners. She had only a modest patrimony to supplement his sometimes irregular salary.[15]

Meanwhile he made plans for the growth of the Diocese as if he were already its head. His concern centered upon its urgent need for more clergy. The American Church had as yet established only three theological seminaries: in New York City (1817), in Alexandria, Virginia (1820), and in Gambier, Ohio (1824). These fledgling institutions could barely supply the needs of their own areas and had few young men left for the western missions. When Smith arrived in Kentucky he found only one candidate for Holy Orders, Aldert Smedes, son of a prominent Lexington family, who was a student at General Theological Seminary in New York.[16] Smith's solution for the problem in Kentucky was to emulate Bishop Moore in Virginia and Bishop Chase in Ohio by "encouraging young men to seek a theological education within our own borders."

During the year that B. B. Smith waited for a valid election as the Diocesan of Kentucky—and apparently there was no question in any quarter that he would be so named when the Diocese had a sufficient number of qualified delegates for an election—he made a modest start on his plan for training young clergymen for Kentucky. As he himself recalled the matter some thirty years later, he placed his own library "in a public room like a lawyer's office" where a few young men began to study under his direction.[17] In his own parish he undertook to raise an education fund for aiding young men who had "the ministry of the Protestant Episcopal Church in view" and obtained one hundred dollars in cash plus three hundred more in pledges. When a few students came, nearly all from the eastern states, a residence was leased to accommodate them. Pending the time when the Diocese would take over the project, the rector and wardens of Christ Church, Lexington, were named as trustees of the

---

[15] Samuel B. Smith to B. B. Smith, June 20, 1854: a receipt for $600.00, which was his share of his mother's estate, with a like share going to each of his three sisters (Insko Collection, Bishop Smith Papers, Church Historical Society).

[16] *Journal of the Diocese of Kentucky* for 1852, p. 17.

[17] *Journal of the Diocese of Kentucky* for 1863, pp. 19–20.

fund. The first young men who became candidates for Holy Orders were Thomas H. Quinan, of Louisville; Daniel H. Deacon, graduate of Middlebury College; and Luther Halsey Van Doren, a young schoolmaster lately come to Lexington from Brooklyn, New York, to found an academy in conjunction with his father and brothers, who were distinguished Presbyterian ministers.[18]

The fourth annual convention of the Diocese met on June 11-12, 1832, in Hopkinsville, county seat of Christian County, one of the best agricultural sections of western Kentucky. Many Virginians had been among the early settlers who sought out this good land, and the town had strong Presbyterian and Methodist congregations. The loyal Episcopalians who made up the Reverend Giddinge's little Grace Church parish had as yet obtained "no stated place of worship" and so it is not certain just where this gathering, the farthest west diocesan meeting in the American Church up to that time, was called to order. Much important business was transacted by the little group of seventeen delegates. Four new parishes were admitted into union with the Diocese: Grace Church, Hopkinsville; St. Paul's Church, Henderson; St. Peter's Church, Paris; and Zion Church, Shelbyville. Thus the Diocese of Kentucky met the technical requirements for electing a bishop, and the delegates unanimously chose Benjamin Bosworth Smith. With equal unanimity they adopted the constitution which had been proposed at the 1831 meeting. Dr. Cooke, who had been on the committee for the constitution at the 1831 convention, was also present here and voted his approval. It is worth noting, in the light of later events, that this version of the constitution, as printed in the *Journal* for 1832, had one slight alteration from the 1831 version appended to the *Journal* for that convention. Article III (1831) permitted every clergyman of the Church canonically residing in the state, not having taken letters dismissory, to have a seat and a vote in convention. Article III as officially adopted in 1832 read "every officiating clergyman of this church." No explanation of this change is on record. It apparently attracted no attention in the *Journal* for 1832, which was prepared by the secretary of the convention, Gideon McMillan.

---

[18] *Journal of the Diocese of Kentucky* for 1832, pp. 6-7. Quinan became a lay reader instead; Van Doren withdrew and became a well-known Presbyterian minister; Deacon was ordained to the Episcopal priesthood in 1833.

To the newly elected bishop's great satisfaction, the convention in Hopkinsville approved his education fund, leaving the control of it with Christ Church, Lexington, and also admitted the three candidates for Holy Orders. Thus B. B. Smith was able to put into operation his major plan for his new charge even before his consecration. That ceremony was set for October during the General Convention in New York, and the vestry of Christ Church authorized its rector to arrange for a supply during his absence. B. B. Smith engaged twenty-two year old Henry Caswall, a deacon serving the mission at Portsmouth, Ohio, who had just graduated from Bishop Chase's new Kenyon College at Gambier. He was the son of an English clergyman, great-nephew of the Bishop of Salisbury, and married to Mrs. Chase's niece, Mary Batcheller, of an old New England family. He arrived in Lexington in time to baptize the Smiths' new baby, Ann, on July 29, 1832, probably just before the rector set off on his journey east. The young Caswalls made their home with one of the parish's prominent families and quickly became a part of the town's society.[19]

Before the General Convention the Bishop-elect visited his family in Bristol, Rhode Island, and renewed his contacts with former colleagues in the Eastern Diocese. Apparently feeling sure of his influence in Lexington, he went so far as to write to a friend who was teaching at Dartmouth to suggest that he become a candidate for the presidency of Transylvania, which had been without a head for the past year. It does not seem surprising that Smith wanted to see a Churchman of his own persuasion in this important post, but unluckily the letter turned up later in the hands of those who accused him of interfering in the university's affairs.[20]

As he noted with humility in his journal for October 31, 1832, he was one of four bishops consecrated that day in St. Paul's Church, New York City, by the Presiding Bishop, the Right Reverend William White, in the presence of the General Convention. Of the new diocesans, two were to preside over territories west of the mountains—Benjamin Bosworth Smith of Kentucky and Charles

---

[19] Vestry Minutes, Christ Church, Lexington, July 7, 1832; also Robert C. Caswall, "Memoir of the Reverend Henry Caswall," Caswall Papers, Diocese of Lexington Archives, University of Kentucky Library.

[20] B. B. Smith to Benjamin Hale, October 6, 1832.

Pettit McIlvaine of Ohio. This was a propitious sign of the Church's resolve to keep pace with the growth of the nation, and Smith was keenly aware of his strategic location. Years later he described himself at the time of his consecration as "the remotest sentinel of the Church—toward the South-West."[21]

The earliest portrait of the new Bishop of Kentucky in his ecclesiastical robes was probably painted at that time by H. Inman, the artist who executed a similar one of Bishop McIlvaine.[22] It shows a slender man with a proud, serious countenance and an air of reserve who, although he was in his thirty-ninth year, looks somewhat younger. He was just entering the vigorous prime of life, and he returned to his Diocese in November dedicated to the extension of God's kingdom within it according to the "great principles" of the Church, as he maintained them to be. According to his own statement these principles included:

. . . the Gospel preached in its purity and earnestness as nearly as possible after the example of the most zealous and successful ministers of the Church of England since the infusion of new life and power into her pulpit toward the close of the last century, and the noiseless carrying out of the Church system, in a strict adherence to all her rules and established observances. . . . And all this, with as complete forgetfulness as possible of the existence of other organisms; or at any rate, studiously avoiding to regard or treat them as hostile organisms; but, at the same time, with a full consciousness and acknowledgement, in every suitable way, and on every proper occasion, that we are very near and ought to be very dear, and they to us, to a great body of most excellent Christian people, far outweighing us in numbers, and fully equalling us, and in many instances, it is to be feared, not a little excelling us, in all the virtues and good fruits of the highest forms of Christian life. Conservative, but unaggressive, primitive Episcopacy . . .[23]

In this policy he was avowedly following in the footsteps of his beloved preceptor, Alexander Viets Griswold, and aligning himself

[21] *Journal of the Diocese of Kentucky* for 1855, p. 31.

[22] Photograph of the McIlvaine portrait in Papers of the Right Reverend Charles Pettit McIlvaine (27), Church Historical Society.

[23] *Journal of the Diocese of Kentucky* for 1852, pp. 14–15. In this Twentieth Anniversary Bishop's Address, B. B. Smith states the above to have been his aim during his whole administration.

with the Evangelical party in the national Church, which at the time of his consecration included the other missionary bishops, Chase and McIlvaine, also Meade of Virginia, and priests like Stephen H. Tyng, his fellow student under Griswold. It should be noted that Smith's position is "conservative but unaggressive" in his attitude toward other denominations. His natural bent was toward consensus and compromise, but when forced to a decision he could be counted on to agree with the Evangelicals. The first Bishop of Kentucky was a dedicated man who was wholly convinced of his vocation. Although somewhat diffident and unsophisticated in his personal life, he felt that as bishop he could speak and act with authority on the beliefs and policies of his Diocese. This type of leadership seldom appeared on the frontier, and, as B. B. Smith was to learn, it ran into opposition for being sometimes too indecisive and sometimes too arrogant.

Before his return to Kentucky in the late autumn the new Bishop received the degree of Doctor of Divinity from Geneva College (now Hobart College). He was ready to push forward his plans, but a hint of the tragic events which were to delay him for a year or more awaited him in the news that a promising new clergyman, the Reverend Nahum G. Osgood of Virginia, who had arrived during the past summer to serve the church at Henderson, had died in October of cholera.[24] The prevalence of the disease seemed, however, to diminish by the end of the year. B. B. Smith declared a Day of Thanksgiving throughout the Diocese on December 9 and began at once to exercise his episcopal authority. He ordained to the diaconate two candidates from other dioceses: Erastus Burr from Tennessee on the festival of the Epiphany, and Dexter Potter from Ohio on April 28, 1833. These ordinations were favors done for faraway bishops, a usual custom on the frontier. He visited all his churches and missions, preaching frequently and confirming many. By carriage or by horseback, his travels were rough and dangerous, enough to have daunted a less hardy man. His concern began in the settled areas near Lexington and Louisville, but his missionary view already reached northward to the Ohio and westward to the fara-

[24] For most events of the winter-spring of 1832–33, see *Journal of the Diocese of Kentucky* for 1833.

way Tennessee River, which had been until fairly recently the farthest limit of the Commonwealth.

Meanwhile, his group of young men desirous of entering the ministry of the Episcopal Church continued to grow. To the original three were added eleven more, some from distant states and a few recruited from other denominations.[25] The plan for their education was the most important item of business scheduled to come before the diocesan convention set to meet in June, 1833, in Lexington.

Only a handful of faithful delegates gathered at Christ Church, Lexington on the morning of June 13, and they scattered quickly when they discovered that they were in the center of the pestilential horrors that were sweeping the town. The convention minutes tersely record that "In consequence of the prevalence of cholera in Lexington at the time, the Convention adjourned to meet in Lexington on the third Thursday in October." It would have been relevant to add that on the previous day the Bishop had read the burial service beside the open graves of ten of his parishoners and that before that day was over he would do so three more times. Dr. Cooke, although he was a lay delegate, did not report that morning because he could not be spared for a single hour from his heroic efforts to save the victims.

The "cholera summer" of 1833 proved to be Benjamin Bosworth Smith's finest hour. There must have been several other clergymen who performed their sad duties, but he was conspicuous for his courage and endurance. No part of the community suffered more heavily than Christ Church. His parish lost nearly one third of its members, and it became necessary to use the new burying ground on the north edge of town (now East Third Street) known as the Episcopal Cemetery. His young daughter Elizabeth remembered long afterward the way her father met the crisis.

[25] They were Thomas H. Quinan (W); Luther Van Doren (W); Daniel H. Deacon (O); Edward Ashley (*June 18, 1833); James H. Brown (*June 19, 1833); William Douglass (*June 22, 1833); B. B. Sayre (W); A. A. Willis (O); Edmund Davis (O); Horatio E. Boyd (*March 11, 1834); M. L. Forbes (O); James B. Britton (O); William B. Cooke (W); these names are from the lists in *Journal of the Diocese of Kentucky* of 1833, pp. 8, 9-10. Also the name of Henry Page (W), listed in Communicant List, Old Register of Christ Church, Lexington, as of November, 1831.

(W)—Withdrew; (O)—Ordained; (*) Died while students

With the Roman Catholic priest, General Leslie Combs, and one or two physicians, he bore the brunt of the storm, and day after day he went forth, leaving anxious wife and little children, to nurse the sick, shroud and carry out the dead and bury them in hastily prepared graves. I well remember that a young theological student, who was buried at the same time with our mother, was carried to the grave in a common cart . . .[26]

Before the end of June the Bishop's personal sorrow would have broken a less dedicated Christian. On successive days he buried two of his most promising young theological students, and on the 22nd his wife died in his arms after giving her blessing to her children. At first prostrated by grief, he rallied and the next day he followed her corpse and that of yet another student to read the burial lines beside their hastily scooped out graves.[27]

By midsummer the dreadful epidemic had subsided. The last of the long list of funerals inscribed in the Register of Christ Church, Lexington, was that of the widow of the Reverend James Moore on July 9. With Christian fortitude, Bishop Smith comforted his four motherless little children and maintained a home for them. He ministered to his stricken people and even found time to visit the bereaved parish at Danville when they lost their beloved rector to the "mysterious disease." Providentially, a successor was immediately found in a local schoolmaster, the Reverend John Adams from the Diocese of Maryland; but the untimely death of Gideon McMillan deprived not only Trinity Church but the whole Diocese of an able clergyman whose influence might have offset or prevented a good many misunderstandings that arose later.

In October, when it was once more considered safe for people to congregate, the diocesan convention was summoned to reconvene in Lexington. It was the first for Bishop Smith since his consecration

[26] Quoted in Bishop Lee's "Life and Ministry of Benjamin Bosworth Smith, First Bishop of Kentucky," *Journal of the Diocese of Kentucky* of 1884, pp. 63–64. James Lane Allen's well-known fictional account of B. B. Smith during the cholera epidemic in his short story, "Old King Solomon," follows this account on the whole. For the part played by clergy of other Protestant denominations see Robert Davidson, *History of the Presbyterian Church in the State of Kentucky* (New York: 1847), p. 334.

[27] William Douglass, the student who died the same day as Mrs. Smith, was a patient of Dr. Cooke. His death is described clinically in Robert and Johanna Peter, *History of the Medical Department of Transylvania* (Louisville: 1905), pp. 66–67. Another student, J. B. Britton, recovered under Dr. Cooke's treatment.

but he was now well established. The lean, durable New Englander had won widespread respect for his courage during the epidemic. He was an officer in the Lexington chapter of the American Colonization Society, an organization to promote the transportation of free Negroes to the west coast of Africa to establish their own state. The society had been organized in 1817 by Henry Clay and other prominent leaders, North and South, whose consciences were troubled by slavery. A number of people in central Kentucky had freed their slaves and sent them to Liberia.

The routine business of the convention was climaxed by the new Bishop's address, in which he stressed his belief that the education of the theological students was the "very foundation of all our hopes as a diocese." It was encouraging to report that in spite of the ravages of cholera epidemic the house that had been rented as a residence for the students had been "sufficiently furnished by the pious liberality of a few Ladies in Louisville and Lexington." Loans had been made to several of the candidates. He now asked that the Diocese take over the management of the educational fund, and the motion to do so passed without a dissenting vote. Bishop Smith was now in a position to begin the development of his large ecclesiastical domain.

6 The Episcopal Theological Seminary in Kentucky

The Diocese of Kentucky was organized at a time when there was a growing interest throughout the Commonwealth in education at all age levels and for all social classes of its white population.[1] Inevitably the leaders of the Episcopal Church shared in this concern, since all of its clergy had some measure of formal training and its laity came for the most part from the better educated classes. Of the eight clergymen listed as resident in the Diocese in 1833, five were also practicing pedagogues. The Church itself, however, lacked the resources to establish an institution of higher learning to match the Presbyterians' Centre College (1819) at Danville, the Roman Catholics' St. Joseph's College (1819) at Bardstown, or the Baptists' Georgetown College (1829). Perhaps for this reason many Episcopalians favored a state-supported program at all levels. The Reverend B. O. Peers, then acting president of Transylvania University, called a General Education Convention in November, 1833, to discuss such a plan. Among those present were the Honorable Henry Clay, whose family connections were Episcopalian, Bishop Smith, and two of his parishioners, Robert Wickliffe and Charlton Hunt, both prominent citizens of Lexington.

Meanwhile the Episcopal Church in Kentucky focused its efforts on an attempt to solve its major problem—the lack of clergy to serve its parishes and expand its missionary reach. The secretaries in the office of the Domestic and Foreign Missionary Society in the East had never been able to recruit enough volunteers for the frontier. Bishop Chase needed more men in Ohio, and, as we have seen, B. B. Smith recognized the problem even before he was elected Bishop and promptly took steps to cope with it. As a result of these efforts, the Episcopal Theological Seminary in Kentucky was established, fourth oldest of seminaries in the American Church. The most complete and trustworthy account of its inception is that related by Bishop Smith as part of his testimony in his own defense during his ecclesiastical trial in 1837.[2] He testified that he began the project by hiring "a single room on a central street of the City, for my books, as a place of public resort for pious young men." Soon afterward he rented a small dwelling house for the use of the students, called the Theological Rooms, where five or six of them were "assembled." Shortly thereafter he raised money at a "public meeting" in Louis-ville to supplement what he had been able to raise in Lexington toward the purchase of buildings. In his testimony at the trial he did not mention the encouragement given to his plan by others, such as Dr. Cooke, but his earlier accounts make it clear that the Church people in the area were enthusiastic and generous. During the winter of 1833/34 he made a number of trips to Frankfort to secure a charter from the Legislature for the proposed theological seminary. Fortunately Attorney General Charles S. Morehead was a distinguished graduate of Transylvania and connected by marriage with the prominent Leavy family in Lexington. Smith had un-doubtedly met him the previous July when Morehead delivered an eloquent address on education for the Anniversary of the Van Doren Collegiate Institute for Young Ladies.[3] This excellent school was run by the Van Doren family, including Luther, one of the Bishop's candidates for Holy Orders. Smith's public endorsement of a Presbyterian school was in line with his belief that educational leaders of all churches and of the Commonwealth should work together. While in Frankfort he called upon several Episcopal fami-lies in the town and preached whenever a time and place could be arranged. He had already selected the little capital city as a good location for a mission church at some early date.

[1] Moses Edward Ligon, *A History of Public Education in Kentucky* (Bulletin of the Bureau of School Service, College of Education, University of Kentucky, XIV, No. 4, June, 1942), pp. 50–74.

[2] See papers regarding "Trial of Bishop B. B. Smith" in documents titled "Trials of Bishops," Archives of the General Convention, Episcopal Church Center, New York, New York. Information about the seminary appears in all the *Journals* of the Diocese from 1831 on; especially useful, for the charter of the seminary, are *Journals* for 1834 and 1843. Gossip about Smith's visits to Frankfort regarding the seminary is found in the Testimony of Mrs. Mary Hanna at the Smith Trial in *Papers of the Right Reverend John Henry Hobart*, Vol. 39, p. 14. The only history of the seminary is Robert W. Insko's valuable article, "The Kentucky Seminary," *Register of the Kentucky Historical Society*, Vol. 52 (1954), pp. 213–232.

[3] Charles S. Morehead, Esq., *An Address delivered on the Second Anniversary of Van Doren's Collegiate Institute for Young Ladies . . . on the last Thursday in July, 1833* (Lexington, Kentucky: Wm. M. Todd & Thomas T. Skillman, 1833).

The Kentucky Legislature acted on February 24, 1834, to grant to the Episcopal Theological Seminary in Kentucky a charter with, as B. B. Smith thought, "very liberal provisions." It was to be administered by the bishop of the Diocese as its rector, in conjunction with a board of trustees, of which he was to be a voting member. The organizing trustees were named: the Reverend Messrs. D. C. Page, Amos Cleaver, and John A. Adams, plus two laymen, Dr. Cooke and A. K. Smedes, both communicants of Christ Church, Lexington. Trustees were to serve for one year, and their successors to be elected by the diocesan convention upon nomination by the bishop. In the absence of the bishop at the time of the annual meeting, a trustee could serve as chairman. The rector and trustees shared the power to appoint professors. The institution could not be removed from Fayette County nor branches of it be established elsewhere without amendment of this charter by the Legislature. The trustees were authorized to handle financial transactions.

Just what made Bishop Smith consider this charter to be "liberal" is hard to see, unless he felt that in granting the right to teach denominational theology the Legislature had been so. His own control over the institution centered in his exclusive right to nominate the trustees. The power of the board of trustees, of course. rested on its management of the finances. All sides were apparently satisfied with the charter, and Bishop Smith reported to the Convention in June, 1834, that subscriptions in Kentucky had increased to approximately $3,500.

At about the same time the charter was granted, the Bishop engaged a full-time professor of sacred literature for the seminary in the person of the young Englishman who had served so successfully as assistant rector of Christ Church, Lexington, during the summer of 1832. The Reverend Henry Caswall, still a deacon, had left his Ohio mission and was then serving a small Massachusetts church under the direction of Bishop Griswold. He accepted the invitation to join the faculty of Bishop Smith's seminary "with pleasure" and must have realized that for a second time the Bishop was singling him out for advancement. Bishop Smith was genuinely fond of Caswall and regarded him as a trustworthy protégé, and at this time Caswall respected and cheerfully deferred to his Diocesan.

As Caswall journeyed to Kentucky in the early spring to assume his new duties, he was commissioned to visit a number of cities on the eastern seaboard to solicit funds for the seminary. He preached in Bristol, Boston, New York City, Brooklyn, and Philadelphia with good results on the whole. One New York church gave $500 toward his own salary as the only full-time member of the faculty and promised future assistance. Well-wishers in Boston presented some rare volumes to the future seminary library that he brought along with him. Most of his own household goods consisted of his library of several hundred excellent books, many of which, no doubt, had been sent him by his kinsmen in England. It sheds light on the scholarly career of Henry Caswall at the seminary to recall that his younger brother, Edward, the future hymn writer, was already a student at Oxford University in England and a follower of the Tractarian or High Church movement.[4]

An important step in the establishment of the seminary was the purchase on April 12, 1834, from the Reverend Benjamin O. Peers of the property which he had occupied for his Eclectic School before becoming president of Transylvania. It consisted of two acres admirably located on Second Street near the college, together with a large brick residence erected in the early years of the century for Thomas January, a wealthy hemp rope manufacturer. There were also several substantial brick service buildings and a little chapel that was probably added for the Peers' school.[5] It seems likely that it was also during the era of the Eclectic School that all the buildings were painted a dark blue, like the Presbyterian Church in Maysville which Peers attended as a boy.[6] The purchase price was $9,000, and Peers generously remitted $1,000 to be applied to the purchase of books for the seminary's library.

---

[4] For Caswall's career in Kentucky see Henry Caswall, *America, and the American Church* (London: Rivington, 1839), Chapter XIII "Lexington," and William K. Hubbell, "Henry Caswall and the Backwoods Church," *Historical Magazine of the Protestant Episcopal Church*, XXIX (1960), pp. 219–239. Previously cited is the brief Memoir of Henry Caswall by his son, Robert Clarke Caswall, who served as a priest in the diocese, 1900–1904. His brother, Edward, became an Anglican curate and followed John Henry Newman into the Church of Rome. Many of his hymns are included in the Episcopal Hymnal of today.

[5] Fayette County, Kentucky, Deed Book 10, p. 96.

[6] Alice Taylor Gill, *Glimpses of Kentucky and Early Maysville* (Maysville, privately printed, n.d.), p. 8.

Three or four acres adjoining the property thus purchased were sold by Peers to Josiah Dunham, a communicant of Christ Church and until recently head of a local school for girls, with a general understanding that he would at his death will the tract to the seminary. Colonel Dunham, a six-foot-four New Englander, graduate of Dartmouth, and between-the-wars soldier, was named intendant of the seminary to supervise the buildings and grounds, and to board the students.[7]

The seminary property was in good order on June 7, 1834, when the Reverend Henry Caswall arrived with his New England wife and their small daughter to assume his duties as resident professor in charge of seven students then enrolled. He found it "a very pretty place," as he soon afterward wrote his father, a clergyman in Wiltshire, England, giving him a full description and a "plan of the buildings and a rough sketch of the view . . . even to the cages of mockingbirds in the portico."[8] From the drawing and description we can reconstruct the well-kept lawn, dotted with acacia and poplar trees, and the main house, consisting of a two-storied central mass with a low porch across the front and one-story wings on each side and at the back. It contained a spacious room suitable for the library, a dining room to seat fifty if need be, and residential apartments for the resident professor and the intendant and their families.[9] In the rest of the main house and the adjoining buildings there was room to lodge thirty students.

Bishop Smith was not present to welcome the Caswalls. Not until about the first of July did he get back from a long tour of his own diocese and visits to three adjoining states, a journey of 1,350 miles, during which he preached forty-seven times. He had set out in mid-April, going first to Danville to give encouragement to its "new

[7] George T. Chapman, *Sketches of the Alumni of Dartmouth College,* pp. 50–51. For several years after his coming to Lexington in about 1821, Colonel Dunham's school for young ladies rivaled that of the Reverend John Ward; see account of Lafayette's visit to Lexington in *Kentucky Reporter,* May 23, 1825.

[8] Henry Caswall to R. E. Caswall, June 28, 1834 (Caswall Papers, Diocese of Lexington Archives, University of Kentucky Library).

[9] The seminary building, known today usually as either the Thomas January house or the Tobias Gibson house, stands at 437 West Second Street. See Clay Lancaster, *Ante-Bellum Houses of the Blue Grass* (Lexington, Kentucky, 1961), pp. 86–87; also, Norma Eckdahl, "January House To Open," *Herald-Leader,* Lexington, Kentucky, July 24, 1966, p. 15.

and laborious rector," John Adams, and to preach a few times in Harrodsburg. Thence he went south to Franklin, Tennessee, to visit with the Right Reverend James Harvey Otey, the newly elected first Bishop of the Diocese of Tennessee, and to attend a convocation of its clergy at nearby Nashville. His main purpose here was to explain his plans for a theological seminary in Kentucky, in the hope that Tennessee and other neighboring states would join in supporting it. His reception in Tennessee led him to hope that the new dioceses of the South and West would unite to build a strong institution, an excellent idea, as history would prove at a later date.[10]

The Bishop's route brought him back up into Kentucky again to Russellville where he met with a new priest, the Reverend William McCallen, newly arrived from Ireland the previous January and already serving as a missionary without salary. Grace Church at Hopkinsville had recently purchased a "most eligible lot" for a building, thereby making the Bishop's heart glad. In the Lord's vineyard no labor was ever more pleasant to Benjamin Bosworth Smith than seeing his people secure "a commodious place for the celebration of the various offices of religion." Heading steadily westward, he pushed on to the small communities of Princeton, Smithland, and "Paduca," where, as he reported later to the convention, "as yet we have few friends."

It was on this journey that B. B. Smith attained for the first time in his career, the dream of himself as a missionary bishop. At Paducah he took passage on a steamboat to St. Louis to spend a few days with the rector and 180 parishioners of Christ Church there. The city had never before been visited by a Protestant bishop, and it was a notable day when, on May 25, 1834, he "consecrated the church, administered confirmation to twenty-six persons, and the Lord's Supper to a large company of communicants," in addition to preaching morning and evening. It is to be hoped that he and some of his hearers remembered on that occasion that the church had been started by the Reverend John Ward of his own parish.

[10] Bishop Otey called as an assistant one of the Kentucky Seminary's "first fruits," M. L. Forbes, ordained deacon by Bishop Smith on the day of its first commencement, November 9, 1834 (*Journal of the Diocese of Kentucky* for 1835, pp. 4–5). The beginnings of the University of the South at Sewanee (1857) in Otey's last years may well have owed something to Smith's original suggestion.

For all his fruitful week in St. Louis, that city was not the prime reason for Bishop Smith's trip up the Mississippi. His objective was the village of Rushville, situated about a hundred miles north in the rich, sparsely settled Illinois prairie, to pay a visit to the family of his good friend, the late Judge Edward Worthington of Trinity Church, Danville. The Worthingtons, who had probably moved to Illinois because of their dislike of the institution of slavery, had gathered a few followers of the Church, including at least one colored person. Among this flock with no shepherd, the Bishop baptized, confirmed, and preached for five days. Another week was spent in Jacksonville, a larger Illinois town, where on June 9 he laid the cornerstone of the first Episcopal parish church in the state. His missionary work on this trip undoubtedly encouraged the handful of Episcopalians—six clergy and less than two hundred members— who organized the Diocese of Illinois the following year.[11]

The Bishop was a week late for the annual Diocesan Convention scheduled to meet on June 12 at St. Paul's Church in Henderson, located about a hundred and twenty-five miles down the Ohio River from Louisville. It was a prosperous town laid out on a gracious plan by the early settlers, many of whom resided on nearby plantations. There were a number of Episcopal families there, even in the early days of the Reverend Williams Kavanaugh, and St. Paul's Parish was organized in 1832. It suffered a set-back with the loss of its newly arrived rector during the cholera epidemic, but was now recovering under the successful ministry of the Reverend Daniel H. Deacon, one of B. B. Smith's original group of candidates for Holy Orders and the first young priest to be wholly trained and ordained by the Bishop for service in Kentucky.[12]

[11] For B. B. Smith's western journey see "Bishop's Address," *Journal of the Diocese of Kentucky* for 1834, pp. 8–11. Also Richard G. Saloman, *Philander Chase in Ohio* (New York: National Council, n.d.) for a brief account of the Church in Ohio and Illinois in the 1830's.

[12] Daniel H. Deacon, native of New Jersey and graduate of Middlebury College in Vermont, was a theological student in Lexington during the 1833 cholera scourge, was made deacon at Christ Church, Louisville, November 30, 1834. He was loyal to B. B. Smith during the trial years. He served St. Paul's, Henderson, from November, 1833, for most of the rest of his active ministry except for a few years in the Diocese of Mississippi (1842–1848) and died near Henderson in 1883 (*Journal of the Diocese of Kentucky* for 1883, opposite p. 110). He was a prominent citizen of Henderson for nearly fifty years, and was a brother-in-law of Governor Lazarus Powell.

The delegates who did come on the twelfth and the Henderson hosts waited with good grace until the Bishop and numerous other belated members arrived to open the convention on June 19. The reason for their tardiness was both understandable and pardonable. The date had been erroneously given as the nineteenth in *Sword's Almanac*.[13] As might have been expected, one of the few persons to arrive on the correct date was Dr. Cooke, lay delegate from Christ Church, Lexington and secretary of the convention. During the week of delay the doctor very certainly enjoyed warm hospitality and intelligent conversation in local homes, including that of Dr. Levi Jones, M. D., one of the delegates from St. Paul's at the 1832 Convention, who was now on the verge of emigrating to Texas, and of William Rankin, with whom the naturalist-painter Audubon and his family had lived during much of their stay in Henderson some years earlier.[14]

The convention heard encouraging reports from the parishes. Christ Church, Louisville, with 107 communicants, was now the largest parish in the Diocese, and it was fostering a small mission in the city. The rectors of the churches in Danville and Hopkinsville were holding services in nearby areas. Christ Church, Lexington, had raised nearly $3,000 above pew rents, two-thirds of it for the theological seminary. It was the Bishop's address, however, which measured the widening outlook of the Diocese. On his journey he had caught the vision of the Church's opportunity "to plant her foundations deep and firm, beside the foundations of civil society, where empire states are now beginning"—not only in Kentucky but on into the heart of the nation. In the founding of the seminary he had reason to hope that a way had been found to seize this great opportunity.

Support of the Bishop's program was unanimous. The convention elected the Standing Committee for the coming year, and the Bishop, exercising his right to nominate the trustees of the seminary, named the same five men. The clergy were all non-residents

[13] *Journal of the Diocese of Kentucky* for 1834, pp. 3–4. Other events of the convention are taken from the *Journal, passim.*

[14] See "Levi Jones," *Handbook of Texas* (Austin: Texas State Historical Society, 1952), I, p. 925. Also Edmund L. Starling, *History of Henderson County, Kentucky* (Henderson, Ky., 1887), pp. 463–471.

of Lexington: Page of Louisville, Cleaver of Paris, and Adams of Danville. The laymen, Dr. Cooke and Abraham K. Smedes, were members of Christ Church, Lexington. The organization and support of the seminary were given priority in the plans for the coming year.

When Bishop Smith got back to Lexington he found Mr. Caswall conducting classes at the seminary for the "seven or eight students" that had been reported at convention. Although the students were not named in the report they apparently were: Edmund Davis, a native of England; M. L. Forbes, a former Presbyterian preacher; J. B. Britton, of Louisville; A. A. Willis, from Delaware; Luther Van Doren, formerly of Brooklyn; and B. B. Sayre and William Beale Cooke (son of Dr. Cooke) of Lexington. Besides Henry Caswall as professor of sacred literature, the original faculty consisted of the Bishop, who taught doctrinal theology and pastoral duties, and Dr. Cooke, who gave his services as lecturer on Church polity and history. A three-year course was planned, consisting of a junior year devoted to Mr. Caswall's classes in sacred literature and the Bishop's tutelage in sermon-writing; and a senior year divided between lectures by the Bishop and Dr. Cooke in their fields plus an introduction to Hebrew and Greek and more sermon-writing. The graduate year was to be devoted to practical pastoral theology under the rector of some parish. Study hours were long—eight hours daily, with no visitors. All students were expected to attend daily Morning and Evening Prayer in the chapel and to practice early morning personal devotions.

This general plan must have been set up during the summer of 1834 after the Bishop and Dr. Cooke got back from Convention. At the same time, the three professors collaborated in establishing an extraordinarily fine library of theological and historical books for the new seminary. A nucleus was purchased or donated, but in addition the three men made their own personal collections available to the students, thus raising the total number of volumes to more than three thousand by the end of the first year. The library room was kept open constantly, and books were circulated among the students systematically, not more than four at a time. It is easy to see why. In the first catalogue issued by the seminary, three pages are devoted to a selected list of the titles in this admirable collection. Texts, Versions, and Commentaries for study of the Scriptures; Lexicons, Concordances, and Grammars; Sacred Literature and Criticism and Ecclesiastical History; the Fathers, Doctrinal Theology, Classical History—the titles are grouped in the catalogue under the headings of the professors' lectures, just as the books themselves must have been arranged on the library shelves.[15]

Soon a busy schedule was in operation throughout the seminary. Mr. Caswall, disturbed that his scholars were so poorly prepared in the classics, undertook to teach them to read "the more striking portions of the Greek and Latin fathers" and had them take their Septuagints to chapel to follow the lessons as they were read. The students who stayed with the course made satisfying progress. For some of them there was also the problem that they did not have the seventy-five dollars to pay Colonel Dunham for the year's board, and so they worked long hours in the garden to pay for it. Lodging was free.

Caswall's duties and responsibilities were heavy. In addition to teaching, tutoring, conducting chapel services, and serving as resident professor at the seminary, he was designated as assistant rector of Christ Church and immediately upon his arrival was put in charge of the Sunday school. For this service, as well as substituting for the Bishop during any absences, he was promised a modest stipend of $300.[16] He and his wife were already well known in the

[15] *Charter, Regulations, Course of Study, Etc., of the Theological Seminary of the Protestant Episcopal Church in the State of Kentucky* (Lexington, Kentucky: J. Clarke & Co., 1834), pp. 8–10. The library, augmented by gifts and purchases, was removed to Shelby College about 1842, and to Louisville about 1870. There it was kept in a warehouse, in rented rooms, and in the Kentucky Church Home, remaining in the possession of the Diocese of Kentucky when the Diocese of Lexington was organized in 1895. In 1921 what remained of the library was presented by the Diocese of Kentucky to the University of the South, which acknowledged the receipt of "some 1,500 volumes, being the Library of the Diocese of Kentucky" (Proceedings of the Board of Trustees, University of the South, 1921, p. 16). The books are now lodged in the library of the School of Theology, University of the South, whose librarian, Mr. Thomas Edward Camp, graciously furnished the present writers with Xerox copies of the title pages of such volumes in the collection as contain the original bookplate of the Episcopal Theological Seminary in Kentucky. The above data about the library are taken from the Diocesan *Journals,* and other scattered information is available. There is need for a study of this famous library, one of the best theological collections of its period.

[16] Vestry Minutes, Christ Church, Lexington, Kentucky, May 31, 1834.

parish and the town. The silver spoons they purchased shortly from Asa Blanchard, the silversmith, were no doubt needed for Mary Chase Caswall's modest teaparties.[17]

B. B. Smith was clearly depending upon Henry Caswall to run the academic affairs of the seminary. It was Dr. Cooke, however, who did more than anyone else besides the Bishop himself to establish it. He served on the first Board of Trustees, and was its only active member; the three clergymen lived outside Lexington, and Abraham K. Smedes died within the year.[18] Cooke served on the faculty gratuitously and made his library available to students. In September, 1834, he made a trip East, especially to Philadelphia, where he was well-acquainted, during which time he solicited funds for the seminary. As a warden of Christ Church, Lexington, he joined in the parish's generous financial support of the seminary. His zeal for the institution increased with the coming of Caswall. The doctor approved of the Englishman's scholarly background and of his Churchmanship.

The seminary progressed well enough to hold its first commencement exercises on November 9, 1834, in Christ Church, Lexington, for two graduates, Edmund Davis and M. L. Forbes, both of whom were that day ordered deacons. The Bishop's address for the commencement was a long exposition, titled "The Dignity of the Sacred Sciences," which he included in the seminary catalogue printed at this time. The catalogue consisted of nineteen pages setting forth the charter, course of study, faculty, library facilities, and other information for prospective students.[19] It was also designed for promotional purposes and was issued in time for the Bishop to distribute it widely during his forthcoming trip to the eastern states to secure students and financial support for the institution.

The Bishop's vestry gave its permission and blessing for his ab-

---

[17] Mrs. Caswall's Blanchard spoons are in the possession of the present historiographer of the Diocese of Lexington, Mrs. Frances Smith Shine, a gift from Mary Chase Batcheller, Caswall's granddaughter.

[18] A. K. Smedes died August 2, 1835 (*Journal of the Diocese of Kentucky* for 1860, p. 73).

[19] *Charter, Regulations, Course of Study, Etc., of the Theological Seminary of the Protestant Episcopal Church in the State of Kentucky* (Lexington, Kentucky: J. Clarke & Co., 1834).

sence, and he departed by steamboat from Louisville on December 1, his last official act being the induction into the priesthood of his favorite theological student, Daniel H. Deacon, at Christ Church, Louisville on November 30. Since he planned to be in the East until General Convention the following autumn, he took his children with him for a prolonged visit with their relatives in Rhode Island. Kindly ladies in the Louisville and Lexington churches made proper clothes for the children's journey. The rectory in Lexington was kept for the family's return.[20]

Bishop Smith was confident that he was making progress with his frontier diocese. A few years earlier, Philander Chase had felt compelled to go to England to obtain funds for his Ohio seminary, but Smith was sure he would get the help he needed from the generous, mission-minded churches in his own country.

Events moved on apace in Kentucky after his departure. About the end of the year 1834, Transylvania University called a new president to take the place of B. O. Peers, who had resigned some months earlier, and again it chose an Episcopal clergyman, Dr. Thomas W. Coit of Boston, known for his scholarly edition of the Bible.[21] Dr. Coit showed much interest in the seminary and within a few months was added to the faculty as professor of ethics and evidences of Christianity, but without remuneration. He was a High Churchman and he joined with Dr. Cooke and Henry Caswall in stressing the sacramental and "ritualistic" character of the seminary's daily services.

At this point in the growth of the Church in Kentucky, the modern reader must note what constituted the "ritualism" that was current in the seminary. Caswall's biographer defines the term so accurately that a quotation will serve as a guideline for the moderate High Churchmanship that appeared in Kentucky during the nineteenth century.

[20] See Vestry Minutes, Christ Church, Lexington, November 29, 1834; Papers of Rt. Rev. Jackson Kemper, Wisconsin Historical Society, Diary No. 3, June 8, 1836 (re: clothes given to B. B. Smith's children); Deed of Benjamin B. Smith and Harriet L. Smith to Catherine Harper, March 24, 1836, Fayette County, Kentucky, Deed Book No. 12, p. 350.
[21] "Thomas Winthrop Coit," in *Dictionary of American Biography*, IV, 278.

[Caswall's] own "ritualism" . . . is mild by today's standards: use of the sign of the cross in baptism; wearing of surplice, gown, and bands; observation of the feasts and fasts of the Church, including saints' days; bowing at the name of Jesus Christ. He expresses disapproval of omitting the word "regenerate" in the baptismal service; of the substitution of non-denominational Sunday School material for the Catechism; of the shortened marriage service (including dispensing with the ring!); and of irresponsible shortening of appointed Sunday services.[22]

Caswall was a tolerant and broadminded man, whose inclination was to see good in the more Protestant Evangelicals such as Bishop Smith and his wife's uncle, Philander Chase, and also in the more Catholic High Churchmen of the Oxford movement. Caswall was tolerant, too, in his concern for the salvation and education of the colored people, and here, of course, he found himself in accord with Smith. He encouraged the theological students to conduct a Sunday school for all who would attend, including about twenty-five slaves from the numerous Negro quarters near this prosperous residential section. To his disappointment, however, the mayor requested him to desist from such a "dangerous proceeding," and Caswall did so.[23] He also agreed with the Evangelicals in their enthusiasm for foreign missions, and during the year he served as rector of Christ Church, Lexington, the weekly collections for the Episcopal mission in Athens added up to more than six hundred dollars, plus the donations of the Ladies' Sewing Society.

Henry Caswall's busy days were occupied with teaching and his pastoral duties. Dr. Cooke, meanwhile, sought wider fields in which to expand the influence of the Church in the West. On January 10, 1835, appeared the first issue of the *Church Advocate,* a bi-weekly journal edited and supported by him. On its very first page, he stated his object.

Friends of the Church in Kentucky have for some years earnestly desired to establish a paper for the purpose of informing the public in regard to her doctrines and institutions . . . since incorrect views are

[22] Hubbell, *op. cit.,* p. 235.
[23] Henry Caswall, *America and the American Church* (London: 1851), p. 209.

prevalent. We shall be reasonable and adhere to Apostolic truth, but there will be opposition. We address the good diverse sects—the mischievous and the nonreligious. Let us discuss doctrine freely with all. We want *one* Church—this is the object of the *Advocate*.[24]

The *Church Advocate* was a better magazine than Cooke's rather belligerent announcement promised. It contained forceful theological articles and arguments by the doctor, many excellent biographical sketches and an occasional poem by Caswall, and considerable Church news from foreign, national, and diocesan sources. The first issue is typical. Caswall contributed the first installment of "The Lay Reader—An Authentic Narrative," praising the good works of a Connecticut Churchman who emigrated to Ohio. Dr. Cooke began a series titled "Dialogue between a Young Man and a Clergyman," setting forth the logical steps by which the youth is converted "by reason." The highlight of the issue, and certainly the most widely noticed item, was by Dr. Cooke under the heading, "The Theological Seminary Vindicated." It was a direct reply to various statements about the seminary which Cooke considered untrue and invidious, remarks made by certain Presbyterians regarding the dismissal from Holy Orders of Luther Van Doren at his own request on November 12, 1834.[25] The statements had appeared in the *Western Luminary,* the most influential Presbyterian journal in the West. Some of the remarks were contributed by the Reverend Dr. Robert Davidson, minister of the Second Presbyterian Church in Lexington and the brother-in-law of Luther Van Doren.[26] Among other charges against the seminary, he had accused the institution of teaching "High Church doctrines" such as that nonapostolic Protestants were "outside God's grace." Cooke angrily denied the charge and declared the Presbyterians were much "narrower" than Episco-

---

[24] *The Church Advocate,* Lexington, Kentucky, January 10, 1834. Microfilm, University of Kentucky Library.
[25] *Journal of the Diocese of Kentucky* for 1835, p. 4.
[26] Dr. Davidson was president of Transylvania University in 1840–1842 and author of *History of the Presbyterian Church in the State of Kentucky* (New York, Pittsburg, and Lexington: 1847). Luther Van Doren came from two families, the Van Dorens and the Halseys, noted for eminent Presbyterian clergymen. He, with his father and brothers, ran an excellent school for girls in Lexington during the 1830's.

palians in that they excluded from God's salvation all those outside the "visible church."

In the issue for February 2, 1835, Davidson was allowed a rebuttal, to which Dr. Cooke added a reply. There, apparently, this particular controversy ended, but the open clash of these two worthy opponents marked the emergence of the Episcopal Church into the arena of violent religious controversy, where the other Protestant denominations in Kentucky had been attacking each other for a generation. Such acrimonious arguments and doctrinal debates were not included in Bishop Smith's plan of "conservative, but unaggressive Episcopacy" for his Diocese, and it is doubtful that he would have participated in this quarrel in the pages of the *Advocate* if he had been in Kentucky at the time. There seems to have been no contribution by Bishop Smith to the *Advocate* prior to the publication of the annual address he sent to the 1835 Diocesan Convention in June, although he claimed upon his return that he had forwarded two or three reviews. The *Advocate,* during the rest of the year, included more and more of Caswall's well-written articles and occasional pieces by the Reverend George Giddinge and other persons in the Diocese. It was a good Church paper, and from it a reader would get the impression of a seminary and a diocese much stronger than they really were. Actually, when the Bishop went East to get men and money for the Church in Kentucky, he had only six parishes with officiating rectors and as many small missions, and the seminary, for all its excellent faculty and library, had as yet less than a dozen students. The bright prospects for the future rested upon a group of unusually dedicated leaders and upon the generosity of the churches in the eastern cities.

Bishop Smith had remarkable success in securing contributions for his Diocese, chiefly in and near New York City. The Right Reverend Benjamin T. Onderdonk, Bishop of New York, evidently sanctioned his widespread solicitations and was on friendly terms with him. In particular Smith was made welcome by his longtime friend, the Reverend William Jackson. Jackson, a native of England who had been ordained in Maryland, was rector of St. Stephen's Church in New York City. He and Smith had both served as young priests in Eastern Virginia under the guidance of Bishop Meade, and Jackson was likewise an Evangelical in theology and manner of preaching, although not given to controversy. Other clergy in the city with High Church leanings thought less kindly of the Kentucky Bishop's projects, but they did not oppose him openly. In this Smith was fortunate, for Bishop Hobart had openly objected to Bishop Chase's raising of funds for the Ohio seminary.[27] Party lines on the basis of Churchmanship were not so tightly drawn at this time in the American Church as they would be a decade later. By the end of May, 1835, Bishop Smith's address, sent to the Diocesan Convention, could report that funds had been contributed "sufficient to relieve the Trustees from all anxiety as to meeting the payments upon the [seminary] buildings, which may now be considered the property of the Church."[28] He told of other gifts, too, including books and money for the library and the promise of a press from a well-wisher in Boston. The Church of the Ascension in New York not only pledged $1,500 toward a seminary professor's salary but made a gift of a $1,000 to be lent to "feeble parishes" to aid them in building places of worship. The high esteem in which B. B. Smith was held in the national Church and particularly in New York is shown by his being selected to deliver the address at the commencement exercises of the General Theological Seminary in St. John's Chapel on June 26. He spoke on "The Character of a Good Minister."[29] He stayed on in the East awaiting the General Convention scheduled to meet in Philadelphia on August 19.

In contrast to the Bishop's achievements, the 1835 Annual Convention of his own Diocese at Paris in early June was a very diminished gathering. The Reverend Mr. Cleaver's church, on which he had been laboring for more than three years, was still not ready for use, but that mattered little for a group of only seven delegates. From the ranks of the clergy, D. C. Page of Christ Church, Louis-

[27] See *The Reverend William Jackson, Late Rector of St. Paul's Church, Louisville, Kentucky. With a Brief Sketch of His Life and Character* (New York: Stanford & Sworde, 1846), which contains Bishop Smith's funeral sermon for the Rev. William Jackson. Also George W. Doane to William R. Whittingham, April 13, 1835 (Maryland Diocesan Archives in Maryland Historical Society), advising Whittingham not to accept a call to the Episcopal Theological Seminary in Kentucky.
[28] *Journal of the Diocese of Kentucky* for 1835, p. 4.
[29] W. Robert Insko, "The Kentucky Seminary," *Register of the Kentucky Historical Society*, Vol. 52, p. 218.

ville, and young Daniel Deacon of St. Paul's, Henderson, made the trip to be present; and Amos Cleaver, of course, and Henry Caswall, representing Christ Church, Lexington. Lay delegates were Dr. Cooke, the perennial secretary of the convention, James Arnold of Paris, and Frederick Yeiser of Danville. The cheerful tidings in the Bishop's Address were included in the minutes. The Standing Committee and seminary trustees were re-elected, and, after much balloting, eight delegates to the forthcoming General Convention were chosen, of whom only Dr. Cooke was at all likely to attend.[30] The parochial report from Louisville was excellent. With 111 communicants, it was now the largest parish in the Diocese, and the Sunday school was flourishing "under the immediate direction of the Reverend B. O. Peers." The other parish reports were brief and indicated little progress. Indeed Mr. Caswall spoke of small congregations and a dwindling Sunday school at Christ Church, Lexington. As a last piece of business the delegates ordered the printing of five hundred copies of the *Journal* for this seventh convention of the Diocese. It would be interesting to know what became of this eight-page pamphlet, which is now so rare a collector's item.

When information about the Kentucky seminary was spread about the Anglican Communion a few new students from widely scattered places enrolled. They came from North Carolina, Virginia, New England, New York, Pennsylvania, and Ireland, and three from within the Diocese.[31] The printing press promised to

---

[30] *Journal of the Diocese of Kentucky* for 1835.

[31] The list of students must be compiled from the *Journals,* the *Catalogue* of the seminary for 1837, and the Communicant List of Christ Church, Lexington. Insko in his "The Kentucky Seminary," previously cited, gives the enrollment for 1835 as follows: *Seniors*—J. B. Britton (Philadelphia), William B. Cooke (Lexington), J. H. Drummond (North Carolina); *Juniors*—R. Randolph (Virginia), R. A. Ferguson (New York), James Young (Pennsylvania), William Newton (Pennsylvania). He also gives a list of the students in April, 1836, as follows: *Graduates*—John H. Drummond (North Carolina), Edward Winthrop (Connecticut); *Seniors*—Charles Higginson (Ireland), James S. Green (Ireland), M. F. Maury (Kentucky); *Juniors*—John O. Bradford (Pennsylvania), James Young (Pennsylvania), N. N. Cowgill (Pennsylvania), Francis B. Nash (Connecticut), Willard Presby (New Hampshire), Charles Bronson (Connecticut), and William F. Halsey (New York). The name of the Reverend W. H. Purviance, A.B. (New York) is in the 1837 *Catalogue* as a graduate in the Class of 1835. The 1837 *Catalogue* lists the following in its Middle Class: C. B. Smith (Rhode Island), J. M. Putney, A.B. (New Hampshire), Edward Berkley (Maryland), and J. B. Noblitt (Delaware). The names of J. O. Youngblood

Bishop Smith in Boston was duly received and set up at the seminary, with the intention that the students would run it. It was christened the Griswold Press in honor of the great Bishop, who now resided in Boston and who very certainly approved the generous gift. The ladies of a Philadelphia church gave funds to provide "a great magic lantern representing Scriptural subjects for the Sunday school and the Negroes," who were instructed by the students, and somewhere else money was provided for the purchase of an "organ with three stops" for the chapel.[32]

The ranks of the Episcopal clergy in Kentucky were augmented in mid-July, 1835 by two newcomers, who arrived in Lexington quite unofficially and with considerable fanfare. They were brothers, the Reverend Hamble James Leacock, of St. Nevis, and the Reverend William Thomas Leacock, of Jamaica, both priests in the West Indian Church of the Anglican Communion. Descended from an established English family of plantation owners, they had served for a number of years on various islands, but after an earlier visit by William to Kentucky they had decided to settle in the area and rented a large residence. Along with their immediate families they brought with them various near relations and a number of their former Negro slaves, whom they had already freed before leaving the Islands.[33]

Henry Caswall welcomed these Britishers heartily and, according to his own later recollections, invited Hamble Leacock to preach at Christ Church the first Sunday after his arrival. He had been rather superficially educated in the West Indian schools and, indeed, had never been confirmed, but he was a "fervid" preacher who spoke dramatically and with "expressive action." He won a following among the parishioners and caught the attention of Dr. Cooke, who set about completing Leacock's theological education. The doctor

and John C. Boorom appear in the Communicants List of Christ Church, Lexington. The enrollment at its peak would seem to have been about eighteen.

[32] Henry Caswall to Olivia (his sister), March 23, 1835, Caswall Papers, Archives of Diocese of Lexington, University of Kentucky Library.

[33] See Henry Caswall, *The Martyr of the Pongas: being a Memoir of the Rev. Hamble James Leacock, Leader of the West Indian Mission to Western Africa* (London: Rivington's, 1857). Hamble J. Leacock was confirmed in Christ Church, Lexington by Bishop Smith on December 6, 1835 (Old Register of Christ Church, Lexington).

did strengthen his orthodoxy by convincing him that apostolic succession alone validated the Church's claim to authority. Leacock also read with deep interest a copy of St. Thomas à Kempis, given him by Caswall, and treasured it through the years.

William Leacock, who had a degree from Queen's College, Oxford, was made professor of languages in the seminary during the winter. He also advertised a plan for opening a "school for boys and young gentlemen on Church Street" but apparently gave up the idea when he moved out of town to a farm he bought in an adjoining county near Midway.[34] He seems to have retained his connection with the seminary for at least a year and added distinction to a faculty that was already prestigious for so new an institution. The General Convention of 1835, the first attended by Smith since his consecration, was a milestone in the forward progress of the American Church. The convention enacted a canon authorizing the election of missionary bishops to serve in parts of the United States or in foreign lands where the Church was not yet organized. In addition, it re-organized the Domestic and Foreign Missionary Society and put it under the direction of the Board of Missions, consisting of all the bishops plus thirty members elected by each General Convention and a small group of early contributors to the work. Thus the Church as a body could direct and support its missionary program. For convenience of administration, the domestic and foreign mission fields were separated, and on motion of B. B. Smith the Committee for Foreign Missions was located in New York. Perhaps upon his recommendation, Dr. Cooke was made a member of the Board of Missions.

The convention chose two missionary bishops, one of whom, the Reverend Jackson Kemper, accepted election to serve in the states of Indiana and Missouri. He had been graduated from Columbia, trained for the priesthood by Bishop Hobart, and schooled in church diplomacy by twenty years spent as assistant to Presiding Bishop White in Philadelphia. A vigorous man of forty-six with an outgoing, generous personality, Kemper busied himself even before his consecration on September 25, 1835, raising three thousand

[34] *Journal of the Diocese of Kentucky* for 1836, List of Clergy; *ibid.*, for 1860, p. 73; *Lexington Intelligencer,* March 1, 1836.

dollars in Philadelphia and New York for his new mission work, and early in November set out for the West, with St. Louis as his distant goal. He was well acquainted with the affairs of the Church in Kentucky, having worked with the missionary society in Philadelphia along with B. B. Smith. The two were on friendly terms. He had long known John Ward, and had had ample opportunity to know George Chapman. Quite certainly Kemper had the widest acquaintance of any man in the American Church at that time, and his presence in the western country was to prove significant for the Diocese of Kentucky.[35]

The enthusiasm for missions at the time of the General Convention helped B. B. Smith as well as Kemper to secure contributions. On September 17 the Bishop made "public acknowledgements" of the receipt of "$11,220 in the Diocese of New York for Kentucky." He also received $1,233 for the seminary from churches and individuals in Philadelphia.[36] With this handsome sum in cash or pledges he could go back to his Diocese to implement some of the ambitious plans of its leaders.

He remained in New York for a month after the Convention, extending his absence from home to almost a year. He had good reason for lingering. At St. Thomas' Church on Wednesday evening, September 23, 1835, he married Mrs. Harriet Staples Douglass, relict of the Reverend Sutherland Douglass and daughter of Judge Seth P. Staples, of New York City, one of the organizers of the Yale Law School. The ceremony was performed by the Right Reverend Benjamin T. Onderdonk, Bishop of New York.

The new Mrs. Smith, some ten years younger than the Bishop, was a childless widow, having lost an infant son born of her first

---

[35] E. Clowes Chorley, "Missionary March of the Episcopal Church," in *Historical Magazine of the Protestant Episcopal Church,* XVII (1948), pp. 4–5. Details of Kemper's numerous contacts with the Diocese of Kentucky are to be found in the Kemper Papers, Wisconsin Historical Society. The present writers are indebted to the Right Reverend Donald H. Hallock, Bishop of Milwaukee, for permission to make use of the Kemper Papers; and to the Reverend Gilbert H. Doane, D.D., formerly director of the library of the University of Wisconsin, for generously sharing with them his arrangement and abstracts of the documents.

[36] The only precise accounting rendered by Bishop Smith of his collections at this time appears in *Journal of the Diocese of Kentucky* for 1860, p. 73. The secretary of the Diocesan Convention in 1860 included this and other historical material in the *Journal* by order of the convention (*ibid.,* p. 25).

marriage. The Reverend Mr. Douglass (Yale, 1824) had been ordained to the priesthood by Bishop Hobart and had served at
Rochester, New York, until compelled to resign by illness that
proved fatal in 1831. Harriet Staples Smith was intelligent, well-
educated, and widely acquainted among the established families of
New York City and Connecticut. One of her friends was Mrs. Lydia
Sigourney, the poetess of Hartford.[37] Her family ties (including
those with her first husband's relatives), her social and literary
interests, and her contacts with prominent Church people became
an immediate asset for her new husband.

In mid-October Bishop and Mrs. Smith and his children made the
long trip to Kentucky, accompanied probably by William H. Purviance, a well-educated young Sunday school teacher at the Church of
the Ascension in New York, who had decided to become a candidate for Holy Orders under the Bishop. There was plenty of time for
the Bishop to tell them what to expect in Lexington. Because of the
growing importance of river traffic, it had lost its commercial
preeminence to Louisville and Cincinnati in recent years. Nevertheless it was an agreeable and cultured town of more than six thousand
inhabitants, one-fourth of whom were Negro slaves or, in a few
instances, "free men of color." Streets were lined with acacia
(locally called locust) trees, and the houses were substantial and
sometimes elegant. Banks, bookstores, silversmiths, carriagemakers
—all did a thriving business. The citizens supported a subscription
library, and also a lunatic asylum for one hundred patients, the first
west of the mountains. It was a community of many churches: two
Presbyterian, one Methodist, and several Baptist; and two African
congregations (Methodist and Baptist) who had erected their own
places of worship. The one Episcopal Church seated six hundred,
rather more than the number of its regular worshipers, but its size
was commensurate with its status and influence.[38]

---

[37] For Sutherland Douglass see Franklin Bowditch Dexter, *Biographical Sketches
of the Graduates of Yale College* (New York: 1903), supplement, pp. 918–922; and
for Harriet Staples Smith's activities see her letters in the Bishop Smith Papers
(Church Historical Society).

[38] This is virtually the description of Lexington in 1834–1837 that Henry Caswall
includes in his *America and the American Church* (London: Rivington, 1839),
Chapter XIII, "Lexington."

Bishop Smith had scant time to introduce his wife properly to Lexington society or even to the ladies of Christ Church and her neighbors on Market and Mill Streets. He was caught up at once in the brisk activity going on when he arrived. His first commitment was to a series of meetings held by the Episcopal clergy of the Ohio Valley at Christ Church, Louisville, beginning on Sunday, October 25. It was the first such gathering in the region, with both Bishop Smith and Bishop Charles P. McIlvaine of Ohio present. McIlvaine did the lion's share of the preaching, but Smith also addressed the ladies of the Sewing Society on behalf of the seminary. Caswall read the prayers and preached once, and B. O. Peers presented a program for the Sunday school children one evening in an upstairs room to see the magic lantern illustrations of Bible stories.

This convocation undoubtedly met with Bishop Smith's approval, but it could hardly have been arranged by him in the short time since his return. It was the work of the very considerable number of Episcopalians in Louisville, many of whom had influential connections in the Church. Bowes Reid McIlvaine, brother of the Bishop of Ohio, was head of a commission house in the city and a prominent layman in Christ Church, as was Henry Augustus Griswold, son of Bishop Griswold. Henry had taught at Transylvania while B. O. Peers was there and had recently come to Louisville to enter the successful printing and bookselling business of John P. Morton, who was soon to become the husband of his sister Harriet. Over a long lifetime, Morton remained a benefactor of the Church. Such men as these gave strong support to the joint meetings, and after a fruitful three days the clergy traveled in a body up the river to Cincinnati to start another series of meetings at St. Paul's and Christ Church, with consecration services for the latter. Bishop Smith spent one day of this expedition looking over the missionary prospects at Covington and Newport, small towns on the Kentucky side opposite Cincinnati.[39] Because of the increasing steamboat traffic on the Ohio River these communities were sharing in the prosperity of the "Queen City" across the river. They were even then virtually suburbs of the larger city, but the river divided them, setting up not

[39] *Church Advocate*, November 14, 1835, "Interesting Intelligence from Cincinnati and Louisville," signed by H. C.

only a state but a sectional boundary. They awaited missionaries from the Diocese of Kentucky to meet the competition of the other churches, especially of the Roman Catholics. Bishop Smith was on the verge of persuading the newly constituted Board of Missions to provide support of three more missionaries in his Diocese, making six in all, but the new men were already assigned to necessary tasks. The missions on the upper Ohio would have to wait a while.

Back in Lexington, Smith found plenty of business awaiting him, old and new. There probably was some sort of formal exercise to mark the end of the seminary's academic year and the graduation of J. B. Britton, the earnest recruit from the Louisville parish, and William H. Purviance.[40] Both were ordained deacons (January 3, 1836), as was (November 29, 1835) Albert A. Willis, a talented, roving young man from the East who had studied at General Theological Seminary. For these recruits the Bishop meant to use the additional missionary stipends the national Board had allotted Kentucky. On Sunday, December 6 he confirmed M. F. Maury, a seminarian from a staunch Church family in Bath County, Kentucky, and also the Reverend Hamble Leacock, who had never had the opportunity in his youth to receive this episcopal laying on of hands.

The situation in his own parish was in some respects a happy one. The number of communicants was again about one hundred, overcoming the losses of the cholera epidemic, and contributions were generous, not only to the seminary but to missions at home and abroad. An annual Ladies Fair for furnishing the church edifice and the work of the Ladies Missionary Society and a Ladies Sewing Society showed the interest of the women. However, Henry Caswall, as a part-time, poorly paid assistant to the rector, had been unable to meet the parish's pastoral needs. He was not only a full-time resident professor at the seminary and its priest, but increasingly he was editing the *Church Advocate*. He gladly relinquished the post of assistant rector as soon as B. B. Smith returned. Everybody, including the Bishop, agreed that Christ Church, Lexington, needed an assistant if he continued to serve as rector. That

[40] *Catalogue* for 1837, p. 7. Purviance, listed as holding an A.B. degree, may have been graduated on the basis of examinations.

raised the question of the assistant's salary, and the people of Christ Church did not welcome taking on that responsibility in addition to supporting the Bishop of the Diocese. He could, of course, give up his parochial charge and its stipend in the hope that the Diocese would raise the money for his salary, but no effective action had been taken as yet to do so. The support of its episcopate was a serious problem all over the American Church, but particularly so in this instance.

From all outward appearances, however, the Episcopal Church in Kentucky was making good progress as the new year began. In addition to its material gains, there had arisen a genuine zeal for winning converts, especially among the able, sophisticated group concentrated at the seminary. Caswall described the movement in one of his books, written years later, as an effort to reach the many "unbaptized and unbelieving folks" in Kentucky and praised the contribution made by each of the group: Coit's proof of the inspiration of the Scriptures, Cooke's "professorial instructions" demonstrating the existence of the Deity, and Hamble Leacock's appeal to the "heart's conscience."[41] He might well have mentioned also his own faithful use of the services of the Prayer Book. It all had the effect of a small "Episcopal revival," more aggressive than Dr. Chapman's orderly sermons and far more certain to elicit rejoinders from the other denominations regarding points of doctrine and ceremony. Caswall flung out the challenge boldly in the "Christmas Address of the Carrier of the *Church Advocate* to its Patrons," a poem he wrote, after the fashion of the day, to be distributed to the subscribers.

> Old Thirty-five is nearly gone,
> Good Churchmen all, in Lexington!
> Soon Thirty-six will be our date,
> Good Patrons of the Advocate!
> We pray you, lend a little time,
> To listen to our humble rhyme,
> And get a little information,
> Without much trouble or vexation.

[41] Henry Caswall, *The Martyr of the Pongas,* p. 23.

"What is the Church?" all men inquire;
Some say, "A building with a spire,
Where gentlemen and ladies go
To lounge away an hour or so."
Some say, "The Church, the Kingdom come,
Is every sect in Christendom,
Quakers and Shakers and Socinians,
As many Churches as opinions."
Some say (to whom great praise is given)
"Tis all good folks in earth and heaven
But who they are we cannot tell,
The Church is quite invisible."

If such be then their doubtful state,
What says the "little Advocate"?
"The Church is all that mighty host,
In every land, in every coast,
Baptized and taught (through heavenly love)
By those commissioned from above
To spread the tidings of salvation
In every age and every nation."[42]

The poem, naturally, roused the anger of the Presbyterians and the Baptists and the other denominations outside the apostolic succession, but Caswall, who called it a "Hudibrastic effusion," no doubt meant for it to do so. Such doctrinal quarreling with other denominations, however, did not meet with the Bishop's approval. The poem, like many other activities during his long absence, was not in accord with his Churchmanship or his plans for the Diocese.

[42] Henry Caswall, *America and the American Church* (London: Rivington, 1839), pp. 232–233.

7 Dissension in the Diocese

Soon after Bishop Smith came back from New York in the autumn of 1835 dissension arose between him and some of the seminary faculty members. The dispute involved control of the *Church Advocate* and the seminary, then of Christ Church, Lexington, and eventually of the Diocese. For almost two years the struggle for power continued, despite intermittent truces, culminating in an ecclesiastical trial of Benjamin Bosworth Smith.

The "Bishop Smith Trial," as the whole affair has usually been called, aroused strong partisan feelings and proved to be the most disruptive episode in the history of the Church in Kentucky. The present writers have searched for contemporary records and documents in an attempt to reconstruct impartially what actually took place. This has not been an easy task. The records are widely scattered, some in special collections devoted to other subjects. Most of them are highly partisan, telling only one side of the case; the rest are so noncommittal as to reveal little of what took place. The official court records of the trial itself were retained by the senior judge, Bishop Charles P. McIlvaine of Ohio, who eventually deposited most of them with the Registrar of the General Convention. In this custody they have remained, virtually overlooked for over a century, until the various packets of papers were untied for the furtherance of this study. These neglected records contain valuable testimony on both sides, including the defense of B. B. Smith by his attorney. The most widely known contemporary account of the details of the trial was a broadside published very soon afterward, titled "Sentence of the Court in the Case of Bp. Smith," which set forth the charges and specifications against him in full, plus a brief summary of the court's decisions. This broadside, which omitted entirely the Bishop's refutation of the charges, has been chiefly responsible through the years for the unfavorable image of Benjamin Bosworth Smith in his own Diocese and in the Church at large.

Smith's personal defense is preserved in his private papers, which have been brought to light in recent years by his able biographer, the Reverend W. Robert Insko. Much information about the whole Kentucky controversy of 1835–37 is contained in the extensive papers of the Right Reverend Jackson Kemper, a missionary bishop in the western country at the time. Such contemporary documents as these, together with newspapers and periodicals of the time, provide the sequence of events and, more importantly, some understanding of the motives that prompted these Kentucky Episcopalians to quarrel so bitterly over a tangle of issues that ranged from such important matters as the proper extent of a bishop's authority to such trivia as the sinfulness of holding a Ladies' Fair to raise money for a parish.[1]

Disagreements between Smith and his faculty members began immediately upon his return from the East, although he had corresponded with them on the most amicable terms during his long absence. An early confrontation concerned the management of the *Church Advocate*. The Bishop disapproved of the Cooke-Davidson controversy which had appeared in its columns, and also complained that the editorial board had refused to publish two reviews by himself because they praised the work of Evangelical writers. Angered by these criticisms Dr. Cooke resigned from the editorship of the *Advocate*, withdrew his financial support, and turned the publication over to the Diocese. On November 23 Henry Caswall was named editor by the Standing Committee, with the promise of

[1] Basic contemporary sources for the trial include: *Proceedings of the Eighth Convention of the Protestant Episcopal Church in the Diocese of Kentucky . . . 1836* (Lexington, Ky.: 1836); *Proceedings of the Ninth Convention . . . 1837* (Lexington, Ky.: 1837); Minutes of the Vestry of Christ Church, Lexington, Kentucky; Papers regarding "Trial of Bishop Smith" in documents titled "Trials of Bishops" Archives of the General Convention, Episcopal Church Center, New York, N.Y.; Broadside titled *Sentence of the Court in the Case of the Diocese of Kentucky vs. the Rt. Rev. B. B. Smith, D.D.* (Archives of Diocese of Lexington, University of Kentucky Library); Papers of the Rt. Rev. B. B. Smith (Church Historical Society, Austin, Texas); Manuscripts of the Rt. Rev. John Henry Hobart, Vol. 39, pp. 1–16 (Church Historical Society); Papers of the Rt. Rev. Jackson Kemper (State Historical Society of Wisconsin). Attention should be called to W. Robert Insko, "The Trial of a Kentucky Bishop," *Filson Club History Quarterly*, Vol. 35 (1961), pp. 141–158, in which Mr. Insko summarizes the material about the trial in Bishop Smith's private papers lent to him by the family.

a small stipend. He edited the journal under a skimpy budget until the end of 1836, but its influence steadily declined.[2] From the beginning of the battle between Smith and Cooke, Henry Caswall was caught in the crossfire.

A much more serious disagreement arose concerning the contributions the Bishop had collected in the East for the seminary. Dr. Cooke, as treasurer of the Board of Trustees, asked for an exact accounting of the money, with a pronouncement that all such funds should be turned over to the trustees and spent by them for the purposes indicated by the donors. Smith viewed the demand as "prying into his accounts," and explained that he had expended almost all of his own year's salary traveling for the seminary and therefore had been compelled to make a "temporary use" of some of the contributions for his personal expenses and other of the institution's current needs. The amount "unaccounted for" ranged from four hundred to about eleven hundred dollars, depending upon whose later testimony one accepts.

Dr. Cooke was indeed a formidable opponent. In addition to his brilliant mind and sincere devotion to the Church, he had the advantage of holding most of the important offices in it which were open to a layman. He was a member of the national Board of Missions, of the Diocesan Standing Committee, and of the Board of Trustees of the Episcopal Theological Seminary, and was senior warden of Christ Church, Lexington. With so much of personal commitment, he felt a deep sense of responsibility for the welfare of the Church in Kentucky. As treasurer of the seminary, he contended that it should be managed on an exact business basis. The Bishop, never a precise man about records, took a different view of contributions to the seminary. Having collected most of the money personally, he looked upon it as a sort of missionary gift, to be administered by him for the good of the Diocese. He felt free to reallocate the contributions, if need be, in order to take care of urgent current expenses for which no other funds were available. For example, B. O. Peers had remitted one thousand dollars of the purchase price of the seminary property, with the stipulation that

---

[2] *Journal of the Diocese of Kentucky* for 1860, p. 73; Henry Caswall to A. Durant, December 28, 1835 (Caswall Papers, Archives of Diocese of Lexington).

the full nine thousand dollars price was to be raised and then one thousand spent for library books. Smith was able to raise only eight thousand dollars for the property, but upon receiving a special donation from some Philadelphia Presbyterians for the purchase of library books, he counted that as fulfilling the Peers' stipulation. Peers objected strenuously and from this time forward joined Dr. Cooke in opposition to Bishop Smith. It is doubtful that the Bishop ever set up any formal system of bookkeeping for the seminary, even with regard to the maintenance and boarding arrangements with Colonel Dunham. If he did so the records have not been found.

In fairness to Bishop Smith, it should be noted that such informal handling of the financial affairs of the Church was no new thing in the Diocese of Kentucky. At its organization, the body possessed no funds of any kind, and the convention minutes for the first three years scarcely mention money except to provide meticulously for the publication of the minutes. The delegates in 1833, 1834, and 1835 were content to have the Bishop report to them that he had collected "about a thousand dollars" or "sufficient" to complete payment on the seminary buildings. In 1835, volunteer contributions were solicited from all communicants for diocesan support, and the following year the convention elected a treasurer to safeguard the disbursements of diocesan funds. It is not surprising that, as one of the trustees of the seminary expressed it, the Bishop thought "that all the money that came into the Seminary could with propriety be thrown together, and that it might justifiably be applied to any known want of the Seminary."[3] In his handling of such money, the Bishop did indeed have both custom and expediency on his side, for there were no other funds available for student loans or current expenses. Nevertheless, the businesslike trustees, at their March meeting, forced him to transfer the funds in question to their control in order to meet the payments due on the property. They also collected from him part, or perhaps all, of the money he had used for personal expenses in the East.

Still another area of controversy at this time was the proposal to

[3] Deposition of B. R. McIlvaine, of Louisville, at the trial of B. B. Smith (MSS of Rt. Rev. John Henry Hobart, Vol. 39, p. 3).

call an assistant rector for Christ Church, Lexington. During the Bishop's absence Mr. Caswall had filled the post as best he could in view of his heavy responsibilities at the seminary, but he had resigned at once when Smith returned. It was felt by all that Smith could not single-handedly fill the three offices of bishop, rector of Christ Church, and head of the seminary. The vestry, desirous of having more pastoral care for the parish, agreed that Smith should select his assistant, with a general understanding that he would relinquish part of his own salary to him. Smith was, however, a man of modest means; in fact, the least affluent man who had ever been the rector of Christ Church for any length of time.[4] With a sizable family to maintain, he could ill afford to give up any considerable portion of his modest salary as rector. On this occasion and many others during his career in Kentucky, his relationship with his people would have been more amicable if he could have afforded to waive his remuneration in difficult times as frequently as some of his colleagues did.[5] At this time it was also unfortunate that he was capricious in exercising his prerogative of choosing an assistant. He first considered the possibility of calling the Reverend Mr. Aldert Smedes, member of a prominent family in the parish, who had trained at General Seminary in New York, and he imprudently allowed the young man's mother to think her son had been called. Smith then discussed the matter of a possible call with the Reverend Hamble Leacock, who likewise considered the talk an

---

[4] Nearly all the early Episcopal clergymen had some independent means. The Deed Books of Fayette County, Kentucky, show that James Moore and John Ward (and their wives) were large property owners; B. O. Peers and Henry Caswall owned more modest estates. George Chapman, Thomas W. Coit, the Leacock brothers, and Edward Winthrop came from families of substantial means. B. B. Smith, according to his own testimony at his trial, spent all his "hard earned patrimony" in the service of the Church. He owned no property in Fayette County other than an equity left him by a parishioner in the rectory on Market Street, which he sold for one thousand dollars (Catherine Harper to B. B. Smith, January 15, 1833, Fayette County, Kentucky, Deed Book No. 8, p. 379; and Benjamin B. Smith and Harriet Smith to Catherine Harper, March 24, 1836, Fayette County, Deed Book No. 12, p. 350).

[5] See Vestry Minutes of Christ Church, Lexington, September 14, 1830, for one of John Ward's many waivers; also the *Journals* of the Diocese *passim* for generosity by John Adams and M. F. Maury in Danville, John Nicholas Norton in Frankfort, and others. B. B. Smith later relinquished a few sums (*Journal of the Diocese of Kentucky* for 1843, p. 24).

offer. Neither man was formally called; their friends and relatives were incensed. Along in March Dr. Cooke, in his capacity of senior warden, and accompanied by Henry Caswall and Amos Cleaver, called upon the Bishop to remonstrate with him about the state of affairs. A violent quarrel ensued. Smith said the doctor asked him to resign as Bishop; Cooke denied it and accused the Bishop of falsifying himself about Smedes and other matters. The long battle had now begun, and nearly everybody of consequence in the Diocese and also in the town was eventually drawn into it on one side or the other. There was one exception—the gentle and magnanimous John Ward remained on good terms with all parties.

By Easter Monday, the customary date for the election of vestry members at Christ Church, both factions were trying to control the voting. The Bishop, according to his opponents, called a meeting of the theological students to obtain their votes since they were listed as communicants of Christ Church, and even dismissed them from their studies to attend the parish meeting.[6] At all events, the faction favorable to Smith elected its candidates, and for the first time since his joining the Anglican communion, Dr. Cooke was not a member of the vestry. His place as senior warden was filled by Colonel Josiah Dunham, a most loyal follower of the Bishop.

The election precipitated an open split in the parish. About thirty or forty members, headed by Dr. Cooke and George W. Anderson and consisting chiefly of their families and friends, organized a new church, to be called St. Paul's.[7] They held services in the chapel at Transylvania, which were conducted by Mr. Caswall, Mr. Hamble Leacock, and probably by Dr. Coit as well. The Bishop refused to give permission for the organization of St. Paul's and declared its members to be "schismatics" for proceeding without his approval. His opposition to the new parish was increased by the fact that its members preferred to follow High Church custom instead of the

[6] Deposition of James Young, a theological student, at the trial of B. B. Smith (MSS of Rt. Rev. John Henry Hobart, Vol. 39, p, 15), but testimony in the court records from Nash, Winthrop, and other students defends Smith from this charge.

[7] G. W. Anderson (Testimony at the Smith trial) claimed 20 communicants, but Bishop Smith, in the *Journal of the Diocese* for 1838, p. 9, reports the loss of only ten communicants to St. Paul's.

Evangelical practices he maintained at Christ Church. Their moderate kind of High Churchmanship had very little to do with ceremonialism but centered rather in following the Prayer Book services strictly and in recognizing the efficacy of the Holy Communion only when administered by ordained priests of the apostolic succession to confirmed believers. High Churchmanship was not a major issue in this Kentucky controversy, although it was one of the factors that drew Cooke, Caswall, and Coit together during the Bishop's absence and set them at odds with him upon his return.

Spring of 1836 found Dr. Cooke supported in his opposition to the Bishop by a small but influential group: Caswall, Coit, Cleaver, the Leacock brothers, B. O. Peers, and Robert Ash, the early missionary who was now teaching in Louisville. A glance at the list reveals that, with one exception, the anti-Smith men were not parish priests but educators. Only Amos Cleaver had charge of a church. Caswall, Coit, and Peers were still deacons. With some justification, the Bishop felt that these academic clergy of lesser rank had no authority to criticize and oppose him in the administration of the Diocese.

He recognized from the start that Dr. Cooke was the "leader of hostilities," but it was Henry Caswall's opposition that hurt and angered him most. He had looked upon the young Englishman as his protégé, having brought him out of obscurity first to be his parish assistant and then a full-time professor in the seminary. To Caswall had been allotted the only salary connected with the institution, a three-year stipend, contributed by the Church of the Ascension in New York City, that was paid directly to him. The two men had much in common, despite the difference in their ages and backgrounds. Both were bibliophiles and talented craftsmen. They originally held each other in high regard. Shortly after Caswall's arrival at the seminary, he wrote in a letter to his family that his Diocesan was "eminently holy in life and perfectly blameless and harmless in conduct."[8] Smith's affection for Caswall had grown through their years of association to such an extent that on one occasion during the strife he exclaimed to a lady parishioner, "Oh,

[8] Henry Caswall to Mrs. R. C. Caswall (his mother), July 31, 1834 (Caswall Papers, Archives of Diocese of Lexington).

Caswall! Caswall! My son! that you should have treated me so!"[9] His affection turned to anger, and he himself testified later that as early as March he meant to "get rid of Caswall along with the rest." In April he wrote to the treasurer of the Church of the Ascension in New York to send Caswall's salary in the future directly to him (the Bishop) for further disposition.[10] Thus Caswall's salary and tenure became another issue in the larger controversy.

In the midst of this bickering in Lexington, the affairs of the rest of the Diocese proceeded much as usual, registering losses and gains. A distinct loss was the resignation in April of the Reverend David C. Page as rector of Christ Church, Louisville. He had been persuaded by Bishop Otey, whose supervision included the state of Mississippi, to accept a call to Trinity Church in Natchez, where the former incumbent had become a Roman Catholic. Page's place was filled temporarily by young Deacon Britton. One gain for the Diocese was the missionary work of Deacon Purviance at Frankfort. Another was the admission of six new candidates for Holy Orders: John Drummond, James S. Green, Charles Higginson, M. F. Maury, Edward Winthrop, and James Young. Two candidates withdrew—William B. Cooke, the doctor's son, and B. B. Sayre— probably because of the controversy.

The last week in April, when the weather and his recent "low state of health" improved, the Bishop made a visitation to most of his parishes. He was accompanied by Edward Winthrop, the most mature and promising of the new candidates. In about six weeks they covered 650 miles, getting as far west as Henderson and Hopkinsville. B. B. Smith preached twenty-one times, wherever groups congregated to hear him. This visitation made him all the more certain, as he declared soon afterward in his address to the convention, that the greatest and first need of the Church in Kentucky was a supply of "living ministers." Next to this he named the urgent need for the "erection of small and cheap church edifices" that could be simply floored and "covered in" as soon as possible so that

[9] Deposition of Mrs. Eleanor M. Anderson at the trial of Bishop Smith (MSS of Rt. Rev. John Henry Hobart, Vol. 39, p. 13).

[10] M. F. Cary to B. B. Smith, April 29, 1836; also Henry Cary to B. B. Smith, July 21, 1836 (B. B. Smith Papers, Church Historical Society).

Episcopal missionaries need not officiate for months and years in schoolhouses or even less proper places while awaiting the erection of expensive buildings.[11] It was on these rugged journeys over his sparsely settled domain that Benjamin Bosworth Smith was at his best. He followed the winding roads and ferried the countless streams without fear or complaint. His Evangelical preaching, although on the sober side, suited the practical frontier people, and his simple manners fitted easily into their way of living, which was for the most part still plain. Whatever his shortcomings as an administrator, he was an effective missionary in the field.

During Bishop Smith's western visitation the Right Reverend Jackson Kemper arrived in Louisville for a fortnight's stay. During these early years of his missionary work, Kemper made this city the headquarters for his Indiana visitations. Here he claimed his usual comfortable room at the Galt House, which he considered "one of the most splendid taverns in the country." Here he answered the mail that awaited him and exchanged visits with his many friends in the community and area. He was always invited to preach and was cordially entertained in the homes of the parish families.[12] On this visit, without seeking to do so, he became inextricably involved in the troubles of the Diocese of Kentucky. First the "Bishop's Lady" wrote to him "most earnestly requesting him to attend the Convention." Then B. O. Peers, in whose educational theories he had already evinced an interest, asked him to assist in restoring peace. The Louisville people urged him to stay, and as time for the convention drew near, virtually everybody called upon him to confide all that had been going on. Among them were President Coit, whose clergyman brother Kemper knew back in Connecticut; Henry Caswall, whom Kemper trusted on sight; and George Giddinge, who spoke for most of the clergy of the Diocese in wanting peace irrespective of seminary rivalries. When Dr. Cooke came he seemed to Kemper to be a man of harsh countenance and abrupt manners.

[11] *Journal of the Diocese of Kentucky* for 1836, p. 23.
[12] Kemper's earlier diary for 1836 mentions visits with J. B. Britton, the Reverend and Mrs. D. C. Page, B. O. Davis (a longtime intimate of Kemper's), J. P. Smith, Dr. Maddox, Mr. and Mrs. Gwathmay, Mr. and Mrs. B. R. McIlvaine, and others of Christ Church, Louisville.

Kemper very properly called promptly when Mrs. Smith appeared at the Louisville Hotel, escorted by young seminarian Nash, to meet her husband upon his arrival from western Kentucky. When Bishop Smith came, only a few days before the opening of the convention, he too began a series of conferences with his long-time colleague in order to present his own side of the story. And it was indeed a tangle of contradictions and honest differences, of prejudices and trivialities, that Kemper jotted down each night in his confidential diary, along with bits of gossip and his own shrewd evaluations of the men and the issues. He decided to remain in Louisville for the convention, from a sense of duty and concern for the "peace and purity" of the Church in the West,[13] but it must be admitted that as a sort of father confessor to half the American clergy he likewise took a lively interest in the minor details and personal relationships revealed to him. Long before the day of psychoanalysis he noted in his diary the personality traits of the chief antagonists with great discernment and shrewdness.

All pre-convention efforts at reconciliation between Bishop Smith and Dr. Cooke failed, and the atmosphere was tense as the first session opened on Thursday, June 9, in Christ Church. In addition to the delegates, it was attended by several visiting clergy, theological students, and local visitors. The Bishop lost no time in making the opening move for control of the body. He handed to Dr. Cooke, the holdover secretary from the previous convention, a list of eligible clerical delegates for the rollcall. It was marked "Officiating Clergymen" and consisted of only nine names. They were the Bishop himself, Cleaver of Paris, Giddinge of Hopkinsville, Deacon of Henderson, Adams of Danville, and McCallen of Russellville, plus three deacons, Britton, Purviance, and Willis. Of this list two were absent; Adams was in Virginia and McCallen in Ireland. Omitted from the roll of eligibles and thus without seat or vote in the convention were eight other clergymen resident in the Diocese: Coit, Caswall, Peers, the Leacock brothers, Ward, Robert Ash, and Edmund Davis. Davis now maintained only an intermittent connection with the mission at Leesburg.

---

[13] Jackson Kemper to his daughter, Elizabeth Kemper (Adams), June 4, 1836 (Kemper Papers, Wisconsin Historical Society).

In answer to vigorous protests the Bishop defended his ruling as being in accordance with Article III of the constitution of the Diocese, which awarded seats to "officiating clergymen." He interpreted this to mean "regularly officiating in a parish"; and to support his interpretation he had obtained a written opinion from the Right Reverend H. U. Onderdonk, Assistant Bishop of Pennsylvania.[14] In reply Dr. Cooke asserted that he had himself written the article in question and that it meant "all clergy who officiated, even seldom." The Bishop ignored the protests and organized the convention with only the delegates he had declared eligible. He then proceeded with routine business. At this point Bishop Kemper, with assistance from some of the neutral clergy, tried to effect a compromise between the disputants and seemed to have achieved it. That evening he preached a ringing sermon on missions that must have struck home because through the years he continued to receive contributions from Kentucky for his faraway missions.

Early Saturday morning, having done what he could to make peace prevail among his Kentucky brethren, Bishop Kemper took the steamboat up the river to keep appointments in Philadelphia. In his diary for that day he wrote with judicial resignation: "I think the Bp having stated his own views sd have let the convention organize as they pleased." He then added a comment on the two men whom he had tried vainly to reconcile. "He and Dr. C., with perhaps equal zeal, are antipodes. And when by rather harsh, suspicious and severe judgement on the one hand and high claims of dignity and office on the other all friendship was withdrawn Dr. C. and his friends established a minority no human being could withstand. I don't see how Dr. C. & the Bp could ever dove-tail." Time proved his observations to be very astute.

Jackson Kemper's steamboat had scarcely backed out into midstream above the Falls when the truce between the opposing parties was ended and the contest began in earnest. Bishop Smith had been mistaken when he counted on his accredited clerical delegates to

[14] Bishop Onderdonk's opinion supporting this interpretation is omitted entirely from the convention minutes in the *Journal of the Diocese of Kentucky* for 1836, which was prepared by Dr. Cooke. It is mentioned in Bishop Kemper's private record of the convention (Diary No. 3, June 9, 1836).

support him in excluding the rest of the clergymen. The accredited delegates, led by George Giddinge, amended Article III to admit all missionaries and clergy canonically residing in the Diocese, and then voted to seat Coit, Ash, Peers, and, last of all, Caswall. It was not legal to put the amendment in force the same year it was voted, but that technicality was overlooked. It stood to reason, as Kemper had shrewdly thought, that any convention on the American frontier, whether political or ecclesiastical, would eventually exercise the right to determine its own membership.

Three new parishes had previously been received into union at this convention: St. Paul's, Louisville; St. Peter's, Trenton; and Christ Church, Leesburg. Now two more were added: St. Paul's, Lexington, of which Dr. Cooke was the lay delegate; and St. Mark's, Bourbon County, of which the lay delegate was George W. Anderson, a strong anti-Smith man. The membership on the newly elected Standing Committee and seminary board was altered to suit the anti-Smith party, and several canons amended to curtail the Bishop's power. Then at last the main issue under contention was raised in a resolution that the convention resolve itself into a committee of the whole to ascertain "whether the rumours now afloat concerning the character of our Bishop be of such nature as to warrant an impeachment."

As a consequence, the convention met for the next three days and a half from eight-thirty in the morning until very late in the evening at the home of the Reverend and Mrs. Peers to weigh the evidence. Bishop Smith declined to attend in order, so he said, to give the advantage to the others. Several delegates went home. There remained some fourteen or fifteen—eight clergymen and six or seven laymen. The minutes of the meetings are phrased in a parliamentary jargon that carefully indicates nothing at all about what was actually said. They do record that on the afternoon of the fourth day of such deliberations the committee rejected George W. Anderson's motion to bring the Bishop to "presentment," a term officially substituted for "impeachment." The vote was critically close. On the following day the convention accepted the report, thus dropping any immediate proceedings against Smith, by the same close vote. The minutes give no hint as to how the Bishop's friends

managed to block the "presentment," but it was generally understood afterward that the defense owed its success to Garnett Duncan, the lay delegate of St. Peter's Church, Paris. He was actually a
Presbyterian, but the laymen of St. Peter's sent him as their accredited delegate to try to prevent an open break between their
Bishop and his opponents, among whom was their own rector.
Garnett Duncan's knowledge of law and his diplomatic arguments
proved more effective than Bishop Kemper's appeals, and the reunited convention paid its respects to Duncan by naming him a
trustee of the Episcopal theological seminary.[15]

The vote to save Bishop Smith from "presentment" was his only
victory during the Convention of 1836, and that a dubious one. Dr.
Cooke and his adherents prevailed in all the other issues at stake.
They aired their grievances and took control of the meeting. They
amended the constitution at will and loaded the canons with restric-
tions on the episcopal prerogative. They elected their men to the
key offices, and in particular named Dr. Cooke as treasurer of the
Diocese. They did, to be sure, recommend that an effort be made to
provide a salary for the Bishop, but also urged that he resign as
rector of Christ Church, Lexington. When the convention finally
adjourned on June 18 the Cooke party felt, as they afterwards
testified, that there was now an "understanding" and that matters
were arranged so as to restore peace. B. O. Peers made a special
report of the meeting to the vestry of Christ Church, Lexington, in
which he spoke as if the past misunderstanding had been settled.

Bishop Smith seemed likewise at that time to be in a mood to
forget and forgive. Before leaving Louisville he wrote Kemper a
long, somewhat effusive letter thanking him for aid in "our late
difficulties," adding a fervent hope for the "thorough reconciliation
that is now promised." Back in Lexington, however, he found that
his adherents were proclaiming that he had won a triumph. One of
the local newspapers, edited by Colonel Dunham's nephew, Julius
Clarke, reported the meeting as having been favorable to the
Bishop, and the account was copied by the papers elsewhere. This
version of the matter pleased the considerable section of the public

[15] For one version of Duncan's part in the convention see B. B. Smith to Jackson
Kemper, June 20, 1836 (Kemper Papers, Wisconsin Historical Society).

who favored the Smith cause. Their reasons for doing so were varied. Many people remembered his courage and faithfulness during the cholera epidemic; others thought his high office deserved support; and a sizable element liked him for his enemies. Dr. Cooke was not widely popular in the town at this time.

The support of the Bishop by his Lexington following seems to have influenced his course of action to a considerable degree. He was sensitive to praise as well as criticism and, as Kemper described him about this time, he was "so dependent upon the support and kindness of all around him that he lived in a fictitious atmosphere."[16] Once again Kemper was right for Smith unwisely interpreted the decision of the convention and the approval of his friends to be a mandate to resume his former aggressive policies. His pride and vanity were involved, too. Harriet Staples Smith was disappointed with her life in Kentucky, and she may well have encouraged his renewal of opposition to the Cooke faction. She was expecting the birth of her first child in the early fall.

By way of partial reconciliation, Bishop Smith cooperated with the vestry of Christ Church in attempts during the summer and fall to obtain an assistant rector, even agreeing to relinquish part of his salary. The post was offered in turn to Professor French of Bristol College and to Mr. Adie, of Leesburg, Virginia, but both declined.[17] Then, disregarding the peaceful "understanding," Smith proceeded to get rid of George W. Anderson as junior warden of the parish, on the ground that he had given up his pew there and was now properly a member of the new St. Mark's Mission, which he had represented at the recent convention.[18] Proceeding still further in disciplining his subordinates, Smith continued to withhold Caswall's salary, and at a meeting of the trustees in Louisville on July 21 requested his resignation from the seminary faculty on the grounds that his usefulness was at an end. Caswall, who up to this time had been respectful in his opposition to the Bishop, flatly refused to resign. He demanded an investigation of the charges against him

[16] Kemper's Diary, June 11, 1836 (Kemper Papers, Wisconsin Historical Society).
[17] Vestry Minutes of Christ Church, Lexington, Kentucky, August 9 and 14, October 14, 1836.
[18] Ibid., July 11, 1836.

and a chance to defend himself. Within a fortnight he purchased a house and twenty acres on the Tate's Creek Pike two miles south of town and moved his family out of the seminary building.[19] He took with him his fine library, and thus the students lost the privilege of using his books as they had already lost those of Dr. Cooke. Caswall continued for the time being to teach his seminary classes and to edit the *Church Advocate*. At the trustees meeting on November 2 he was cleared of the charges against him and awarded the right to the salary that had been withheld. The full amount due him was not paid for several years.

Henry Caswall now turned country gentleman, exchanging social courtesies with his new neighbors, including the Clay family. Meanwhile he advertised in the local press his willingness to "receive a limited number of *Young Ladies as boarding scholars*" with extra charge for French, music, and drawing.[20] About the time of his removal to the the country, Caswall completed and published his first important literary work. It was a twenty-four page pamphlet titled *The History of the American Episcopal Church* that appeared under the imprint of J. (Julius) Clarke & Co., publishers of many of the academic and professional writings in the community. It was a pioneer work in the field, both accurate and readable, and was so well received that Caswall published a much fuller edition within a few years.[21]

Bishop Smith was not sorry to see the Caswalls move out of the seminary building. He had thought of living there upon his return from New York, and now that he had sold the small equity he owned in the Christ Church rectory to repay the seminary funds for his expense money on the eastern trip he promptly moved into the professor's quarters there. Very probably his daughter, Harriet Chester, whom he himself baptized on September 28, was born at the seminary. For his growing family it was a commodious and comfortable residence, and also it permitted him and his wife to

[19] Fayette County, Kentucky, Deed Book No. 12, p. 530. Also references to this home in Caswall Papers (Archives of Diocese of Lexington).

[20] *Intelligencer*, Lexington, Ky., January 4, March 16, 1837.

[21] Henry Caswall, *The History of the American Episcopal Church* (Lexington, Ky.: 1836). See also his *America and the American Church* (London: 1839, 368 pp.). The *Catalogue* of the British Museum lists 22 publications by Henry Caswall.

advertise the opening of a boarding school for about fifteen young ladies.[22] The school began during the following winter and continued as long as the Smiths lived in Lexington.

Another advantage for the Bishop in living at the seminary was the opportunity it afforded him and Mrs. Smith to know the students personally and to have them as guests in their home. The men that year were, on the whole, the best the seminary had enrolled. The third commencement was held on October 26, 1836, for six graduates: J. H. Drummond; J. S. Greene, A.B.; Charles Higginson, A.B.; M. F. Maury; and Edward Winthrop, A.M. The Bishop's address for the occasion was an unexciting sermon titled "Piety."[23] Higginson was a well-educated Irishman. Maury was a Kentuckian from Bath County whose forebears had been Episcopal ministers in Virginia. Winthrop was from a distinguished Connecticut family and a graduate of Yale.

Christ Church, on the other hand, was not benefited by its rector's removal to the seminary before an assistant had been secured. The new St. Paul's flourished with thirty-three communicants and a total congregation of about eighty, counting children. The Reverend Hamble Leacock served as temporary minister and then rector with such success that sometimes a hundred and fifty persons attended the divine services he conducted in the Transylvania chapel. Despite the High Church beliefs of Dr. Cooke and some others in the parish, the Reverend Hamble had no leanings one way or the other and, in particular, cared little for "liturgical minutiae" such as candlesticks and even architectural styles. What he did care about was earnest preaching and pastoral visiting, and as a consequence he attracted a few of the Christ Church people who felt with some justification that they saw very little of their own rector. The St. Paul's congregation evinced no desire to build their own church.

For a time a sort of stalemate was reached in the diocesan controversy, possibly because the chief participants became involved in other matters. We have already taken note of Caswall's other ventures. Peers was in poor health and gave up all "public service,"

---

[22] B. B. Smith, "Glimpses Backwards Over Two Hard Years of Life," MS in Bishop Smith Papers (Church Historical Society).
[23] *Catalogue of The Episcopal Theological Seminary in Kentucky* for 1837.

including church duties, in order to arrange for the publication of
his book on American education stressing the need for a national
system of schools and colleges.[24] Both Coit and Cooke were concerned with the movement among some of the professors in the
Medical Department at Transylvania to move that part of the
university to Louisville. The Transylvania medical school was one
of the outstanding ones in the nation, having graduated about nine
hundred medical doctors since its founding in 1799. The discon-
tented professors, led by Dr. Charles Caldwell, a brilliant, arrogant
theorist, and Dr. John Esten Cooke, argued among other things that
Lexington was not a large enough metropolis to permit the "pro-
curement of a sufficient supply of material for anatomical instruction," that is to say, of cadavers for dissection. The plan to move was
aided by the offer of a bonus to the proposed Louisville Medical
Institute made by generous businessmen of Louisville such as B. R.
McIlvaine.[25] Sweeping changes were made in the Transylvania
medical faculty as a result of this proposed move.

It seems likely that the changes in the Transylvania medical staff
suggested to Bishop Smith that he reorganize the faculty of the
theological seminary in spite of the conciliatory promises exchanged
by both factions at the close of the diocesan convention in 1836.
Changes occurred among the trustees of the seminary; A. K.
Smedes died and B. R. McIlvaine resigned, leaving only B. O. Peers.
Smith appointed two new trustees from his own party and at a
called meeting on December 27, 1836, the board dismissed the entire
seminary faculty, including the Bishop. Peers protested violently.
The next day the trustees met again and reinstated Smith. Surprisingly they also reappointed Caswall to his professorship, but Peers

---

[24] Benjamin Orr Peers, *American Education; or Strictures on the Nature, Necessity, and Practicability of a System of National Education* (New York: 1838). With
an Introduction by Francis L. Hawkes, D.D.

[25] See Robert Peter and Johanna Peter, *The History of the Medical Department of
Transylvania University* (Louisville: 1905), pp. 61–63 *et passim* for a fair, dispassion-
ate account of the medical school controversy by the famous Dr. Peter, one of the
participants. For a very biased version see the *Intelligencer*, Lexington, Kentucky,
for 1837, which attacks Caldwell, Cooke, and the *Louisville Journal* (George D.
Prentice, editor) in almost every issue. The mistaken idea that the Episcopal
seminary was a part of Transylvania appears in Peter, *op. cit.*, p. 161, and Alvin
Fayette Lewis, *History of Higher Education in Kentucky* (Washington, D.C.: 1899),
p. 70.

was not placated and the diocesan quarrel flared again. Peers immediately laid twelve "charges" against Smith before the board. Smith declared them to be "cruel and unfounded" and the board dismissed them. Peers then demanded that he himself be put on trial before the proper authorities to prove that he had not falsified in the "charges" and further offered a proposal that three other bishops be invited to meet in Lexington at an early date to settle the differences in the Diocese of Kentucky. The board took no action on these requests, and the Bishop proceeded with his plans to rebuild his seminary faculty by using his best graduates. Caswall declined reappointment but stayed on with his classes for a month.

Over in Louisville the Right Reverend Jackson Kemper had been occupying his favorite room at the Galt House since the middle of December while waiting out a month of extremely bad weather. The leading Episcopalians of the town hastened to welcome him and to give him their versions of what had happened since the previous June. He listened to all their repetitious stories, being chiefly impressed by responsible laymen such as Garnett Duncan and B. R. McIlvaine. They, together with the clergy of the small churches and missions, urged that harmony be restored in the Diocese by whatever means necessary. Some wanted Bishop Smith to resign, as Bishop Chase had done recently in Ohio under somewhat similar conditions. Kemper, always a man for reconciliation, favored this plan and wrote on January 13 to B. B. Smith hinting "pretty broadly at resignation." Smith, in some of the frequent letters he was dispatching to his colleague, firmly rejected the idea. At this point Kemper confided to his diary: "I have done my duty, and now I must be silent."[26] But if he expected to be rid of the troubles of the Diocese of Kentucky so easily he was mistaken.

B. O. Peers now took the lead by proposing that three bishops be invited to mediate the disagreement, and consequently an invitation was extended to Bishops McIlvaine, Kemper, and Otey to serve. McIlvaine first consented to come and then declined, on the ground that the attempt at mediation was premature. Otey accepted, and on February 15 he arrived in Louisville, where he and Kemper agreed

[26] Kemper's Diary during January, 1837 (Kemper Papers, Wisconsin Historical Society).

to do what they could. They were fully aware that, having no precedent and no canonical authority, they could only advise and hope to reconcile the parties. On their own responsibility they undertook to help these troubled frontier Episcopalians and wrote to them from Louisville with a "proposal" for peace. Each side was to state its grievances, confess its faults, and forgive the other side, and then accept the counsel of the mediators. Such a sane and Christian solution deserved to be accepted, but each party petulantly demanded what the visiting bishops must do. Smith wanted them to limit their duties to determining the truth of the charges the convention had made against him and rule as to whether a trial was in order. The Cooke-Peers contingent, fearful lest a reconciliation should rescue Smith from the formal trial they had wanted so long, arrogantly questioned whether any action by the bishops, even a mediation, would be legal.

Exercising great forbearance and patience, Bishops Kemper and Otey journeyed over to Lexington on or about February 22, only to find that all hope of reconciliation was gone. Since they were on the ground, they consented, somewhat reluctantly, to hear "the matter of disagreement" between B. B. Smith and B. O. Peers, not to determine guilt but to advise whether or not Peers should have a trial. And so, for a long week, a semiprivate hearing was held at the seminary, during which B. B. Smith withdrew most of his accusations against Peers but Peers defended himself by repeating and embellishing the charges against Smith which had been made at the 1836 convention. Various clergy and laymen were called to testify, and the community buzzed with curiosity and rumors. Otey and Kemper insisted they had not come to adjudge anyone guilty or not guilty, only to bring about a reconciliation; but they did give an opinion that no trial was indicated for Peers. They also persuaded the opposing parties to sign an agreement, dated March 5, 1834, designed to restore a measure of order in the Diocese. First, it was agreed that Bishop Smith would not object if the next convention moved a presentment against him; second, that the canons of the Diocese of Pennsylvania should govern in the trial by consent of the convention; third, that Henry Caswall was to be restored to his professorship in the seminary upon the resignation of the new incumbent, Edward Winthrop; and finally, "that the signers to these articles of agreement will use their efforts to allay the agitations and excitement and work together in their respective spheres as God shall enable them for the promotion of peace, piety, and godliness amongst men." The document was signed on March 6 by ten persons, five from each party. Dr. Cooke's signature was not on it.

The visiting dignitaries called at the seminary that evening to say goodbye before leaving early next morning, and found Smith deeply depressed at the rumors brought in by Colonel Dunham and other friends that the town thought his enemies had defeated him in the hearing. His visitors reassured him, and Bishop Otey harshly rebuked Dunham for "gabbling" such frivolities and making matters worse. Otey was weary of the long hearings and had formed a low opinion of Smith in the course of them. He wanted no more of the Kentucky controversy. Kemper, characteristically, was more tolerant and still a little hopeful of compromise. While in Lexington he had called on Mrs. Smith and also driven out to Caswall's country place to see his wife and two small daughters. He had renewed acquaintance with John and Sarah Clifford Ward from Philadelphia days, and called at Ashland, only to find the Clays away from home. No experience ever failed to provide Jackson Kemper with a chance to make friends.[27]

The visit of Bishops Otey and Kemper to Lexington actually did nothing to end the conflict in the Diocese. Caswall declined reelection to the seminary faculty. The Cooke-Peers faction ignored the agreement, which Dr. Cooke had not signed and Caswall had signed with exceptions. They planned consistently and relentlessly to bring the Bishop Smith to trial and to force him out of the Diocese. He, for his part, acquiesced in the agreement but continued to exercise his episcopal prerogatives, at times in a highhanded manner. Thus a handful of angry leaders moved on a collision course toward the confrontation at the 1837 convention.

This sort of strife naturally attracted attention among the general

[27] Vol. 17 of the Kemper Papers (Wisconsin Historical Society) is the chief source for the visit of Bishops Kemper and Otey to Lexington in February-March, 1837, containing correspondence, private and official, and minutes of the hearing.

public. A group of influential citizens of Lexington, already agitated by the departure of several of the medical faculty to Louisville, were indignant at the opposition to the Bishop that seemed at this point to be centering in that city. On March 11, a few days after Bishops Otey and Kemper had departed, a number of these citizens gathered to express their appreciation of B. B. Smith's "private virtues and public worth" and, as they wrote him formally, to demonstrate "their esteem, affection, and respect in a manner which should be suitable for the present and enduring for the future." For that purpose they formally passed resolutions to tender to him a service of silver plate. The subscription paper was signed by thirty-three gentlemen who agreed with this favorable view of the Bishop and who pledged the sum of $412 for the testimonial. The list included not only several of his supporters in Christ Church but many who were not Episcopalians. The service of plate they procured and had engraved consisted of "a superb pitcher, six goblets, and a splendid server . . . on each piece [of which] is an inscription of the object for which it is made, and on the pitcher is the following, beautifully engraved: 'A Testimonial of Esteem, Friendship, and Confidence, Presented to the Rt. Rev. Benjamin Bosworth Smith, Bishop of Kentucky, by a number of his fellow-citizens of Lexington, March, 1837. I WAS SICK AND YE VISITED ME.' "[28]

However mixed may have been the motives of the citizens who presented the handsome testimonial, the gift proved that there were many who remembered Smith's devotion during the cholera epidemic and who approved his forward-looking plans for the Church in Kentucky. This recognition did much to offset the embarrassment of the charges against him and the unfavorable publicity. With the stubborn ability to endure hardship that was his greatest asset, he proceeded to issue a new *Catalogue of the Episcopal Theological Seminary in Kentucky* for the year 1837, containing a revised set of rules and regulations raising the academic requirements and the announcement of a new faculty. It was composed of himself, Daniel H. Deacon, Edward Winthrop, and Albert T. Bledsoe, the Assistant Rector of Christ Church, Lexington, who was

---

[28] *Intelligencer,* Lexington, Ky., May 23, May 26, 1837.

newly arrived from Ohio.[29] As things worked out, neither Deacon nor Bledsoe did any teaching, but Edward Winthrop became a worthy successor to Henry Caswall. Holder of a Master of Arts degree from Yale, Class of 1831, Winthrop was the best-trained teacher in the seminary up to that time. Life at the institution went on as usual, and for the most part the students were loyal to the Bishop.

The opposition, however, was mobilizing in anticipation of the 1837 convention to be held in Danville, beginning on May 11. The Cooke-Peers group planned their strategy with care in order to make sure that Smith would not escape impeachment a second time. They knew that a number of the clergy in the western part of the state were remaining aloof from the quarrel and so would not be present: Deacon of Henderson, Giddinge of Hopkinsville, Willis at Smithland, and McCallen of Russellville. John Ward was likewise refraining from taking any active part in it. The anti-Smith faction, therefore, felt that they had only to make sure that their delegates, clerical and lay, were present to dominate the convention.

At the opening session the Bishop tried again to deny a vote to clergy who did not officiate in a parish regularly, and again he failed to do so. With great lack of judgment he tried to exclude the Reverend John Adams, who, in spite of poor health and teaching duties, had until a short time previous rendered considerable service gratuitously to the Danville parish. Adams was seated by the convention but significantly the Bishop lost the Danville votes he customarily counted on. At this same session each faction sought the admission of new parishes favorable to its views. The Bishop's side gained Calvary Church, Smithland while his opponents added Ascension, Frankfort. Admission was denied to two parishes being organized by theological students loyal to the Bishop. The convention was organized with a decisive majority of fifteen to five against B. B. Smith. Committees were elected to investigate the Bishop and the diocesan funds, using much the same procedures as in 1836. On the second day the Bishop protested in a formal speech that the

[29] *Charter, Regulations, and Course of Study . . . of the Theological Seminary of the Protestant Episcopal Church in the State of Kentucky* (Lexington, Kentucky: 1837).

convention was clearly prejudiced against him and demanded a trial by his peers instead of another secret investigation. He asked specifically for a trial according to the agreement signed by representatives of both sides during the visit of Bishops Kemper and Otey in Lexington.

Since the Danville parish declined to be host to an impeachment the convention adjourned to reconvene on May 15 at Christ Church, Lexington. The delegates who gathered on that date were even more anti-Smith than those at Danville. Ward and William Hearne, lay delegate from Leesburg, both moderate men, had dropped out, and J. B. Britton, temporarily serving at Christ Church, Louisville, was now the first rector at Indianapolis while his successor in Louisville, the Reverend William Jackson, had not yet arrived.[30] Both would have favored Smith. As a result, the vote from Louisville was controlled by Dr. Cooke and two lay delegates, both of them his medical colleagues. William Leacock appeared at the adjourned session with the clerical credentials from Ascension, Frankfort. The opponents of the Bishop were in complete control of the convention. Dr. Coit was named head of the committee to draw up the "Charges and Specifications" against him; and by a vote of 16 to 3 the convention ordered that he be presented for trial. The votes against the motion were cast by Josiah Dunham, Edward Winthrop, and Charles Higginson. The seminary remained loyal to him. The opposition proposed to include the charges and specifications in the *Journal* containing the minutes of this 1837 convention, thus giving them wide circulation before the trial.[31] Probably with this in mind the delegates voted to authorize the printing of one thousand copes of the *Journal* for this session, double the number usually ordered from the printer.

The case against the Bishop was set up after the manner of a

[30] The Reverend Mr. Jackson arrived in Louisville on the third Sunday in July, 1837 (James Craik, *Historical Sketches of Christ Church, Louisville*, Chapter 4). J. B. Britton followed Bishop Kemper to Indiana. See Eli Lilly, *The History of the Little Church on the Circle: Christ Church Parish, Indianapolis, 1837–1955* (Indianapolis: 1957), Chapter III "Mr. Britton and His Dilemma," pp. 41–74.

[31] Bishop Kemper wrote in his notes on the trial that the charges and specifications should not have been published before the trial (Kemper Papers, Wisconsin Historical Society). However, he and the other judges permitted them to be used during the trial.

military court martial. The charges, six in number, were supported by specifications, 134 in all, many being repetitions. The specifications told essentially the same story that Cooke had related to the 1836 convention and that Peers had recounted to Bishops Otey and Kemper. Virtually everything B. B. Smith had done for the past three and a half years was exposed in detail: the Smedes affair, control of the *Church Advocate,* the disposition of the money collected in the East for the seminary, Caswall's dismissal and salary, the Ladies' Fair, and letters he had written and statements made, usually to erstwhile friends. All this was made the basis for the charges, which were: first, originating and keeping up the disturbed state of the Diocese; second, mental reservation, equivocation, insincerity, duplicity, and making statements partial, contradictory, and untrue; third, defaming and persecuting the clergy and official laymen of the Diocese; fourth, illegal and arbitrary conduct in office, and improper use of influence; fifth, arrogating unreasonable privileges, and making unbecoming demands on the grounds of the episcopal office; and sixth, conducting the monied and other business operations of the Diocese in a loose and improper manner, and disregarding obligation in money matters.[32] The charges hardly corresponded to the offenses which the General Convention Canon 37 named as indicating trial for ministers: crime, gross immorality, disorderly conduct, drunkenness, profane swearing, and specific violations of the canons. But for the trial of a bishop there was no precedent, and Smith's opponents proposed to make their own rules.

As judges for the trial the convention selected Bishops McIlvaine, Kemper, and Otey, all of whom were promptly notified by Amos Cleaver, president pro tem of the convention after the vote against the Bishop. Cleaver also presided at the "Adjourned Convention" held on August 11 to decide upon the mode of trial, a privilege given each diocese under the Sixth Article of the constitution of the General Convention. Disregarding the agreement signed by some of the opponents to abide by the canons of the Diocese of Pennsyl-

[32] *Journal of the Diocese of Kentucky* for 1837, pp. 46–68; also *The Sentence of the Court in the Case of the Convention of the Diocese of Kentucky vs. the Rt. Rev. B. B. Smith* (broadside).

vania, The Adjourned Convention passed five new canons on the
subject, the most drastic being Canon 18, which required the judges
"to declare the accused to be guilty, or not guilty, of each charge
and specification."[33] Christ Church, Lexington was chosen for the
place of the trial, and the visiting bishops were urged to set a date
early in September.

Bishop Otey declined to serve, giving as his official reason the
state of his health, his many engagements, and the fact that he had
heard the evidence before. His real reason was that while in Lexington in March he had "formed conclusions" adverse to B. B. Smith
which "imperiously forbade" his serving as judge. He had also corresponded rather confidentially afterward with Dr. Coit.[34] An invitation was then extended to the Right Reverend Samuel A. McCoskrey, recently elected Bishop of Michigan, who accepted. The
change of judges had several advantages. Bishop McCoskrey, who
had formerly been a lawyer, brought a fresh point of view to the
situation. He was a moderate in matters of doctrine and so provided
a good balance between the High Churchmanship of Kemper and
Otey and the Evangelical position of McIlvaine and Smith. There is
no evidence that the opinion of the court was influenced by the
Churchmanship of the accused or that his accusers in the Diocese
made an issue of the matter. Only twice in the lengthy specifications
is the subject discussed (I,8 and II,15), and in both cases Dr. Cooke
protests against being accused of High Church partisanship. This
Kentucky trial was less concerned with doctrines and ceremonialism than with ecclesiastical polity and fiscal responsibility and personal antagonisms. It greatly resembled the frequent political im-
peachments in the Commonwealth of that era.

Both parties worked diligently through the summer, gathering
evidence and aligning witnesses. The prosecution was largely
turned over to Dr. Coit and B. O. Peers, who arranged for most of
the depositions and consultations. They seem to have engaged no

[33] Amos Cleaver to Jackson Kemper, May 25, 1837, and August 7, 1837 (Kemper
Papers, Wisconsin Historical Society).
[34] James H. Otey to Jackson Kemper, August 15, 1837 (Kemper Papers, Wisconsin
Historical Society).

professional counsel. Smith, on the other hand, secured as chief counsel the Honorable Charles Morehead, newly elected member of the Kentucky legislature, and as his assistant counsel, Robert Wickliffe, Lexington attorney and political pundit. Smith also sought counsel from the Honorable Henry Clay on various aspects of the difficulty. On the advice of Clay and Wickliffe he refrained from answering the charges and specifications when they were improperly published in advance of the date of the trial. The Bishop did much of the work of securing witnesses, especially character witnesses, for his case, and he liked to think of himself at times as conducting his own defense.

It must have been more on his own responsibility than on the advice of his eminent legal counsel that the Bishop continued hostilities with his opponents while awaiting trial. For example, when Mr. Bledsoe, the new assistant at Christ Church, obtained the consent of the vestry to exchange pulpits from time to time with the Reverend Hamble Leacock in order to renew friendly relations with the people of St. Paul's, Smith, as rector, refused his consent. As a result Bledsoe and most of the vestry resigned. New vestrymen favorable to Smith were elected, and for the sake of the long-suffering parishioners, John Ward offered to serve as assistant for the time being without remuneration. Still another less conspicuous skirmish served to widen the breach between the opposing parties. When Henry Caswall decided in early July, 1837, to accept the rectorship of the parish at Madison, Indiana, in Bishop Kemper's jurisdiction, he asked for the usual letter of dismissal from the Diocese of Kentucky. Bishop Smith's formal letter contained a statement that he might at some future time investigate Caswall's "course of opposition" to his former diocesan.[35] Kemper, who entertained a high regard for Caswall's "piety, learning, and simplicity," had already ordained him to the priesthood in Madison on July 2, and so B. B. Smith's unforgiving threat did his former protégé no harm. However, the departure of Caswall and Bledsoe and the Leacocks hurt the prestige and strength of the Church in Lexington.

[35] B. B. Smith to Jackson Kemper, July 6, 1837 (Kemper Papers, Wisconsin Historical Society).

Elsewhere in the Diocese the parishes were progressing normally. At the suggestion of Bishop Smith, Christ Church, Louisville called as its rector the Reverend William Jackson of St. Stephen's Church in New York City. Jackson, one of the most popular preachers in the metropolis, was induced to come west on account of his health. His parish, now the largest in the Diocese, welcomed him whole-heartedly, and, according to his first parochial report, he found it in a "perfect state of harmony and general prosperity," with a well-supported Orphan Society and flourishing Sunday schools for both white and colored. The new rector was a peace-loving man and wholly devoid of personal ambition. He took no part in the conflict he found upon his arrival, and his church was soon crowded at every service with people of all faiths or none, who came to hear his sincere and eloquent Evangelical sermons. He was the most distin-guished Episcopal clergyman who had settled in Kentucky, and his presence in Louisville at this particular time did much to maintain the prestige of the Church in that area. In the smaller parishes and missions, too, modest progress was being made. The lay people at Henderson and Paris were building their churches, and in May, 1837, the enterprising congregation at Smithland laid the corner-stone for their own edifice. The Reverend Giddinge at Hopkinsville and Deacon Higginson, a seminary student, did missionary preach-ing beyond the bounds of their particular parishes.

The trial of Bishop Smith, decreed for September by the diocesan convention of 1837, loomed up ahead like a darkening storm. Both sides busied themselves through the summer, collecting evidence to prosecute or refute the charges that had been so unwisely published abroad over the Diocese and nation. Most of the prosecuting com-mittee (Dr. Cooke, B. O. Peers, George W. Anderson, and Dr. J. T. Maddox) lived in Louisville, and so it was Peers who persuaded witnesses in that city to come to his residence for depositions, while President Coit gathered similar evidence from Lexington citizens and a few seminary students. Points in the specifications were meticulously documented: how the Bishop had contradicted him-self about the propriety of church fairs, how he refused on occasion to shake hands with Caswall, and so on. One lady, belonging to a very influential family, remembered that back in 1834 he had talked in her hearing about naming the seminary for Mr. Robert Wickliffe in hopes of getting a donation.[36]

Bishop Smith likewise worked diligently, preparing his side of the case. Witnesses were found to testify for him, including fellow clergymen, past colleagues, and parishioners, mostly as character witnesses.[37] Because the opposition had based its charges on a series of actions by Smith, many of which admittedly had taken place, the defense must necessarily rely upon showing those actions to have been justified by the circumstances. The defense was astutely planned to (1) offer the character and record of B. B. Smith as the answer to the charges of dishonesty, mendacity, and irascibility, (2) declare the diocesan convention illegal in its canons specially enacted for this trial and because of broken agreements regarding the trial, and (3) permit the prosecution to become repetitious and trivial in meticulously proving its six charges and one hundred and thirty-four specifications. In later years the Bishop liked to recall that he "conducted his own defense," but clearly it was planned and directed by his three eminent legal advisers.[38]

All the while, B. B. Smith was conducting the seminary with the assistance of Edward Winthrop. He also supplemented his income by conducting a school for boys on the premises in conjunction with an earnest senior student from Connecticut, Francis B. Nash.[39]

[36] In the MSS of the Rt. Rev. John Henry Hobart, Vol. 39, pp. 1-16 (Church Historical Society) is preserved a little collection of depositions: R. Ash, B. R. McIlvaine, Dr. J. P. Maddox, J. P. Smith, H. A. Griswold, William F. Pettit, William B. Cooke, Dr. Joseph Martin, Mrs. Eleanor Anderson, Mrs. Mary A. Holley, James Young, and Mrs. Mary S. Hanna. Mostly anti-Smith and chiefly from Louisville, they seem to belong to Peers' work on the prosecution. No explanation has yet appeared as to how they got in the Hobart MSS. Caswall and other anti-Smith witnesses are included in the "Papers of Bishop Smith Trial" (Archives of General Convention).

[37] Witnesses for B. B. Smith included General Leslie Combs, the Reverend John Ward, the Reverend William Jackson, Dr. John Eberle (of the Transylvania Medical Department and a former parishioner in Philadelphia), John Brand, Josiah Dunham, Julius Clarke, Dr. Pinkard, Francis B. Nash, Edward Winthrop, Wilhelm Iucho (organist at Christ Church and relative of the Van Doren family), Dr. James Blythe (former member of the Transylvania faculty and eminent Presbyterian) and others ("Papers of Bishop Smith Trial" in Archives of General Convention).

[38] Evidence of B. B. Smith's turning to Henry Clay for advice in this difficulty is found in B. B. Smith to Henry Clay, August 16, 1836; and Henry Clay to B. B. Smith, August 17, 1836 ("Trial of Bishop Smith Papers" in Archives of General Convention).

[39] Advertisement in *Kentuckian-Citizen*, Paris, Kentucky, June 9, 1837.

Bishops McIlvaine and Kemper arrived and were lodged at one of the hotels in time for the trial to begin at eleven o'clock on the morning of September 25, although Bishop McCoskrey's stage did not get in until late that same evening. As the senior member of the court, Bishop McIlvaine presided. Two clerks were appointed: J. L. Hickman, who apparently did the clerical work, and Edwin Bryant, editor of the local *Intelligencer* and a strong Smith partisan, who served without remuneration. Apparently the judges were trying to be impartial, and Bryant's position enabled him to report the trial at first hand. Visitors were admitted, and at times the church was crowded with ladies as well as gentlemen. Bishop Kemper, who always kept an eye on the passing scene, wrote his daughter back in Philadelphia that he found "fashion and splendid dress as much in Lexington as in the Atlantic States."[40]

At the opening session, Robert Wickliffe asked that the court consider only such offenses as were specified as pertaining to the trials of clergy in Canon 37 of the General Convention but his motion was overruled. Thereupon the prosecution began calling its witnesses to prove the charges and specifications that had been previously published and distributed. Witnesses were examined and cross-examined; depositions and exhibits were collected by the clerks; brief minutes were set down in paperback account books. Once again Smith's opponents described the numerous wrong things he had said and done for the past three or four years, with emphasis on an indiscreet letter he had written to B. O. Peers on April 5, 1836. By now this was a familiar story to everybody present, except possibly Bishop McCoskrey. The prosecution took a little more than two weeks to present its case, attempting to prove each detail of each specification. This mode of trial was, in effect, the method of a military court martial, in which each allegation is adjudged "guilty" or "not guilty" whether or not the alleged action was in itself wrong. In this way the prosecutors might accumulate enough verdicts of "guilty" on provable facts to get a judgment on the charges that dealt with such grave matters as moral turpitude and fitness for office. The bishops acting as judges, having no

[40] Jackson Kemper to Elizabeth Kemper, September 28, 1837 (Kemper Papers, Wisconsin Historical Society).

precedent for such a trial in the American Episcopal Church, felt bound to proceed according to instructions of the Kentucky convention's revised canons. Consequently, they patiently permitted the prosecution to drag the case through all of the 134 specifications.

On October 9 the defense began to present its case. Local interest increased, perhaps because of the certainty that new views would be brought out in this shopworn quarrel. Christ Church was so crowded with Smith's adherents that Kemper scribbled a note to his daughter during the session with the comment that "9/10's of the people are in favor of him." The character witnesses for Bishop Smith were an impressive group. John Ward testified that he had always found Smith to be charitable toward his opponents. Dr. John Eberle, one of the new professors in the Transylvania Medical Department, told of having been a member of Smith's parish in Philadelphia. Smith was, he said, "a man of sincere piety, moral uprightness, and gentleness of heart." Another old friend came to defend the accused when the Reverend William Jackson, now settled at Christ Church in Louisville, took the stand. And there must have been a ripple of amusement when Wilhelm Iucho, the German music teacher who had been an organist at St. George's in New York, testified that B. B. Smith was so forgiving of his enemies that he, Wilhelm, had often said publicly that "if Bishop Hobart had been treated thus he would have excommunicated every soul of them!"

Other witnesses followed to justify and explain the circumstances of the various wrongdoings imputed to Smith, but the highlights of the week during which the defense was heard were the speeches of the Bishop and his legal counsel. Attorney General Morehead made an oratorical plea that the character of his "Right Reverend Client" ought to be answer enough to the charges. Robert Wickliffe's sound address attacked the legality of the way the court had been set up for the trial, and the propriety of the charges under Canon 37 of the General Convention. He also refuted some of the evidence of the prosecution. Smith, too, delivered a long defense, speaking from carefully prepared notes, after the manner of a sermon.[41] Reiterating

[41] Insko in his "The Trial of a Kentucky Bishop" (*Filson Club History Quarterly,* Vol. 33, 1961, pp. 141-158) summarizes Smith's arguments from the notes in his

the claims of the trial's illegality made by his counsel, he went farther to avow that his opponents had taken his trivial words and deeds out of their context to defame him. He challenged the judges themselves to reflect what would be the result if all their own "accidental or imprudent betrayals of confidence" were brought out in "one startling catalogue." He rested his case finally on his "general character" during the nearly twenty years he had served as a priest in six dioceses.

At the conclusion of the public trial the weary judges faced the necessity of rendering a verdict upon each of the 134 specifications according to the formula prescribed by the Kentucky canon: "guilty" or "not guilty." This mode of proceeding was distasteful to them, as Kemper recorded later in his private notes on the trial together with his hope that "this case will not be adopted as the precedent."[42] The Bishops recognized the difference between declaring the facts recounted to be true *per se* and declaring that the actions thus established involved moral guilt. For that reason they qualified many of their decisions regarding the specifications and said "Guilty without criminality" or "Guilty of inconsistency—reconcilable however with honesty" or "Guilty of the words charged without blame." Many of these same decisions rebuked Smith as having been "imprudent," "unwise," "mistaken," "unduly severe," or "arrogant."

With the specifications disposed of, the Bishops proceeded to render verdicts on the six main charges, which dealt directly with moral turpitude or, at least, with defects of character. Did the actions recounted over and over in the specifications justify their declaring B. B. Smith to be guilty of mendacity, deceit, cruelty, arrogance, and financial irresponsibility? The Bishops thought not, and rendered a verdict of "not guilty" on all six charges, although they interpolated a series of admonitions and rebukes in the written sentence and a hope that both sides would "scrupulously avoid whatever may tend in any way to renew the controversy."

own writing preserved in the papers of Mrs. Charles A. Christian, of East Orange, N. J., his grand-daughter-in-law. The speeches by Morehead and Wickliffe are preserved in the "Papers of Trial of Bishop Smith" in the Archives of the General Convention.

[42] Kemper Papers (Wisconsin Historical Society), Vol. 18, No. 19.

Christ Church was crowded with excited parishioners and interested townspeople on Wednesday morning, October 18, at eleven, for the closing session of the trial. The verdicts seem to have been kept secret until that time and both sides were hopeful. The organist and choir were in their places. The visiting Bishops, in full regalia, occupied the chancel. B. B. Smith, "habited in his rochet" (bishop's surplice), was seated facing them in the left aisle of the church, with John Ward and William Jackson on either side of him. Smith's robes were draped on a chair in front of him.

Bishop McIlvaine read the "Sentence of the Court, in the Case of the Convention of the Diocese of Kentucky vs. the Rt. Rev. B. B. Smith, D.D.," and when it became apparent that the verdicts were "not guilty" on all the charges against him the audience began to clap. McIlvaine raised his hand for silence and continued with his solemn concluding remarks. Declaring the method of the trial to have been in some respects inequitable and the spirit of both parties uncharitable, the court urged them to seek to make peace. The sentence concluded with this statement:

In conclusion, the Court consider that in the publication of so much of this sentence as contains an opinion of guilt and expressions of censure of the Court, the accused has received the merited admonition and penalty, and are now, therefore, prepared to reinvest him with his robes of office, and receive the Rt. Rev. Benjamin Bosworth Smith as Bishop of the Diocese of Kentucky, within the rails of the altar and reinstate him in their affectionate regard.[43]

Choir and people joined in an appropriate hymn to the tune of "Old Hundred" while Benjamin Bosworth Smith was re-invested and welcomed within the sanctuary of his own church. Many in the congregation wept as the benediction was pronounced by Bishop McIlvaine and Smith's friends crowded forward to congratulate him and to express their appreciation to the judges for their services. Two days later the *Intelligencer* published a dramatic account of the session with the comment that Smith had been "fully and

---

[43] Broadside of the *Sentence of the Court* cited *supra*. See *Intelligencer*, Lexington, Kentucky, October 20, 1837, for details of the closing session.

honorably acquitted." The other local papers were less partisan, but the community seemed to feel that the Bishop had won.

The visiting Bishops left town immediately, having authorized the publication of the sentence as a broadside in lieu of any formal report to the Convention of the Diocese of Kentucky. The official records of the trial were committed to the keeping of the Presiding Judge, Bishop McIlvaine, who took them with him to his home in Ohio.[44] Despite the efforts of the judges to do their duty "without fear or partiality," there was no evidence that the trial had reconciled the opposing factions. As Kemper wrote soon afterward to a friend in Louisville, "you say true—there was no cause for triumph —there would be some for congratulation had we created peace. But this I fear is far from being the case!"[45]

The anti-Smith party was deeply disappointed in the result of the trial. Caswall complained to Bishop Kemper that not only the Lexington *Intelligencer* but the *Louisville Journal* and the *Churchman* had called it "altogether triumphant" for B. B. Smith.[46] Peers brooded over the failure of the judges to file the records of the trial with the Kentucky convention. This continuing animosity mattered less than might have been expected, however, because within a few months none of the Bishop's chief opponents remained in Lexington, and most of them had left the state. Caswall was residing in Indiana at the beginning of a distinguished career as priest and author, in both America and England. Peers won deserved recognition for his pioneer volume on education and was called to New York City to become director of the educational work of the Episcopal Church and editor of the *Journal of Christian Education.*[47] Bledsoe returned to Ohio, and Coit resigned the presidency of Transylvania in September, 1837, to accept a professorship at Trinity University in Connecticut. The Leacocks lingered a while in the Lexington area, but William soon became the long time rector of

[44] Charles P. McIlvaine to the Secretary of the Convention of the Diocese of Kentucky, October 6, 1840 (*Journal of the Diocese of Kentucky* for 1841, pp. 13–14).

[45] Jackson Kemper to B. O. Davis, January 3, 1838 (Kemper Papers, Wisconsin Historical Society).

[46] Henry Caswall to Jackson Kemper, November 4, 1837 (Kemper Papers, Wisconsin Historical Society).

[47] *Dictionary of American Biography*, Vol. XIV, p. 389. Also Collins, *History of Kentucky*, pp. 442–443.

Christ Church in New Orleans and Hamble went temporarily to a little parish in Franklin, Tennessee. He eventually became a world-famous missionary to the Pongas. Dr. Cooke continued for several years to hold a professorship in the Louisville Medical Institute and was an active member of Christ Church, Louisville, but it is not of record that he ever again participated in the affairs of the Diocese of Kentucky.

The most critical and damaging account of the trial was a scathing anaylsis of the *Sentence of the Court* which appeared in the December, 1837, issue of the influential *Western Messenger,* a Unitarian journal published in Louisville and widely circulated in New England. It was written by the editor, James Freeman Clarke, who based his devastating article entirely upon a reading of the broadside. As a result, he declared the "ambiguous verdicts" such as "Guilty without criminality" were condemnations of the Bishop which rendered his reinstatement "illogical, meaningless, and ridiculous." Most damaging of all was Clarke's pronouncement that the "whole bad business" was caused by the dangerous influence of the episcopal office upon Smith's character, a view agreeable to nonapostolic Christian denominations as well as to the Unitarians. Bishop Kemper had probably read Clarke's article when he wrote to Caswall on January 16, 1838: "The charges ought not to have been printed with the Journal. I regret the publishing of the Sentence—and should the whole trial be laid before the public in a volume I shall weep and tremble for the prosperity of the Church in the West."[48]

Prominent among those who were satisfied with the results of the trial was B. B. Smith himself. His attitude is revealed in a letter he drafted in reply to a protest he received regarding his acquittal:

Considering that the public mind of this whole community is more than satisfied; that all the malcontents are scattered abroad; and that they were completely foiled in their purpose to ruin me, I concurred with my friends in acquiescence to the Bishops' decision . . . and for the sake of

[48] Jackson Kemper to Henry Caswall, January 16, 1838 (Kemper Papers). Also "J. F. C.," "Sentence of the Court in the Case of Smith," *Western Messenger,* Vol. IV, No. IV (December, 1837), pp. 262-270. (Published in Louisville, Kentucky: Conducted by James Freeman Clarke, 1837).

peace we shall prefer that the matter be dropped. . . . But if you or anyone want further inquiry, if it be honorable, I'll meet it.[49]

Bishop Smith went beyond simple acquiescence in the verdict of his judges. He accepted it as a manifestation of God's will that he should continue his labors as Bishop of the Diocese of Kentucky. A few weeks after the trial, he received a letter from a fellow bishop advising him to resign his episcopal office. His reply, refusing stubbornly to abandon his lifework because a colleague deemed him a failure, is an extraordinary mixture of humility and pride. It reveals Smith's best qualities.

You think, and no doubt conscientiously, that fixed and unalterable traits of character in me are at fault. I think that the character of the opposition which I have had to contend with, and the circumstances in which I have been placed are mainly at fault. Which is right, which is wrong, can only be tested by time and experience. If, as I hope and believe, God has called me to this ministry, has not accounted me unworthy of it, has sustained me in it, and amongst many traits of character singularly unsuited to it, has nevertheless invested me with some which heretofore extensively have been estimated in a different manner, I cannot but trust Him that he will mould and fashion me, by His providence and Holy Spirit, that I may do some little good before I die . . .[50]

Public interest in the trial soon died out. The panic that swept the country in 1837 diverted the people's attention to financial and political issues. In such troublous times the Bishop emerged from the trial rather well. He was still in control of his diocese, seminary, and parish, although with diminished prestige and resources. He may even have been glad to be rid of the brilliant, ambitious group of men with whom he had surrounded himself in the seminary. Now he could count on the loyal, disinterested support of William

[49] Draft of a letter dated December 28, 1837 with no addressee (B. B. Smith Papers, Church Historical Society).

[50] B. B. Smith to "Rt. Rev. and dear Sir," November 2, 1837 (B. B. Smith Collection, Church Historical Society). This MS seems to be a first draft, and internal evidence indicates it was addressed to Bishop McIlvaine as it is in reply to a "letter from Cincinnati."

Jackson in the affairs of the Diocese and on the scholarly assistance of Edward Winthrop in the classroom.

Like most proud, shy persons Benjamin Bosworth Smith needed the approval and loyalty of those around him. This reassurance he had in full measure from his wife. She revered his office and defended his policies. While making a home for her stepchildren and her own infants she assisted her husband in conducting the school for young ladies on the premises. She was hospitable to the theological students, who found her intelligent and gracious. Along with the seminarians who gathered in her parlor was young Joel T. Hart, a self-taught sculptor whom the Bishop allowed to use the little gray brick building at the rear of the seminary for his studio. The Smiths probably watched Hart chisel the bust of Cassius M. Clay that launched the fledgling artist on his career. The Bishop, a woodcarver himself, took an early interest in Hart, and Mrs. Smith's kindness won his lasting regard.[51] With such friendships and activities Harriet Smith enriched her husband's life and enabled him to go on in his vocation almost as if the near tragedy of the trial had not occurred.

In order to carry on the work of the Diocese during these troubled times and after the departure of many of his talented opponents, the Bishop utilized the candidates who were enrolled in the seminary. He ordained twelve of them as deacons during 1836 and 1837, and eight of them accepted assignments in Kentucky. They were without exception worthy young men: J. B. Britton, trained at Columbian College, Washington, D.C.; Edward Winthrop, A.M., Yale; Charles Crowe, graduate of Dublin University; Charles Higginson, also educated in Ireland; Matthew Fontaine Maury, enrolled at Kenyon College before coming to the seminary; Francis B. Nash, student of history and government; Willard Presbury, Dartmouth graduate; and N. M. Cowgill, teacher from Pennsylvania. To this list should be added the name of Edward F. Berkley, ordained deacon in 1838.[52] This group of young clergymen shared

---

[51] J. Winston Coleman, *Joel T. Hart* (Lexington, Kentucky: 1962), p. 10.

[52] See "Ordinations in the Diocese of Kentucky, 1833–1927," a useful list abstracted from the *Journals* and other records (Archives of the Diocese of Kentucky, Christ Church Cathedral, Louisville). The other four ordinands were W. H. Purviance and

the uphill tasks of the Church in Kentucky at this critical period regardless of whether they remained for a long period or for a short time only. Without their assistance Bishop Smith could hardly have resumed his leadership of the Diocese.

Unhampered by High Church opposition, he participated within a month after his trial in an interdenominational meeting under the auspices of the American Sunday School Union that was held at the local Presbyterian church. The meeting featured an address by his friend and fellow student under Bishop Griswold, the Reverend Stephen Tyng, now a famous preacher residing in Philadelphia. Smith gave the opening prayer, and the benediction was pronounced by the same Reverend Mr. Davidson who had quarreled with Dr. Cooke in the columns of the *Church Advocate*.[53]

Encouraged by such friendly relationships in the community, Smith turned his attention to the problems of education in the whole Commonwealth, and in mid-December delivered a formal address before the Adelphi in Lexington titled "On Classical and Collegiate Education in Kentucky." The Adelphi was a recently chartered learned group that had its headquarters on the Transylvania campus. Among its members were the Bishop, Colonel Dunham, F. B. Nash, and Edward F. Berkeley.[54] The speech was well received, and within a short time it was published in a local newspaper and copied in other papers over the state. It was a well organized argument for state supported universities and scholarships for needy students as well as for better grammar schools. The proposed plan was not a novel one. Similar ideas had been discussed for more than a decade, conspicuously by Benjamin O. Peers; but the address reminded the public that Bishop Smith was interested in the whole field of education as well as theological training in his own denomination.

James Young, who were not sympathetic with Bishop Smith, and J. R. Drummond and J. S. Greene, who left the Diocese for personal reasons.

[53] *Intelligencer*, Lexington, Kentucky, November 3, 1837.

[54] Julius P. Bolivar Maccabe, *Directory of the City of Lexington for 1838–1839* (Lexington: 1838), p. 19; and Alumni File of Transylvania College Library for Adelphi Society. For B. B. Smith's speech see *Intelligencer*, Lexington, Ky., December 29, 1837; and *Commonwealth*, Frankfort, Ky., January 10, 1838. Similar ideas appear in "A Friend of Education," *Intelligencer*, January 10, 1837.

When the Bishop officiated that year at the Christmas Eve service in his own parish church, he had reason to be grateful to the faithful flock gathered there before him. The parish was not flourishing, having less than half as many communicants as when he had come to it seven years before. The reasons were many. Christ Church had never recovered from the ravages of the cholera epidemic; it had lost many parishioners to St. Paul's, which was still holding aloof; and it had suffered also from the limited attention it had received from its rector. In a way it had borne the brunt of the long controversy, but it was a sturdy parish, with roots deep enough to withstand a long drought. According to custom the pillars of the church were wreathed in cedar on this holy night, and all the candles were lighted. Professor Iucho played music such as he had been accustomed to render on the occasion at St. George's.[55] In the Bishop's family pew Harriet Smith sat with her brood of children and step-children, and perhaps one or two young lady boarders. She and the children loved Christmas Eve especially because it was the Bishop's favorite service in all the round of the Christian year.

At last the open struggle between Benjamin Bosworth Smith and his adversaries in his own Diocese was concluded. No individual connected with it had gained a victory or any real advantage, and the memory of it was a sorrow for generations. Providentially, some good did eventually come to the national Church because of it. Soon after the Smith trial the General Convention enacted canons regulating the discipline of bishops that prevented a repetition of the inappropriate judicial proceedings connected with the Kentucky presentment. After the trial the financial affairs of the Diocese of Kentucky began to be conducted in a more businesslike manner, and the controversy undoubtedly hastened the provision for a salary for the Bishop. Best result of all, this strife among the leaders brought about an "in-gathering" of loyalty and zeal at the parish level which carried on the Church's mission in the Commonwealth.

[55] Henry Armistice, *History of St. George's Church in the City of New York* (New York: 1911), Chapter IV "The Milnor Period."

8 Reconciliation & Recovery

As calm returned to the troubled Diocese of Kentucky during the winter and spring of 1838, there were unmistakable signs that it had lost much of its early position of leadership on the Episcopal Church's southern frontier. No further contributions came now from churches and individuals on the Atlantic seaboard to supplement the stipends from the Board of Missions. This setback was in part a result of Bishop Smith's loss of prestige in the Church at large after the trial, especially among his fellow Bishops. Even some of his Evangelical colleagues charged him with bad judgment, self-will, and other faults.[1] Another cause for the lessening of interest in Kentucky was the establishment of newer mission fields and dioceses such as Tennessee, Indiana, Illinois, and Missouri under the dynamic leadership of Bishops Otey and Kemper. As the Diocese of Kentucky entered into its second decade, it became apparent that the Church at large expected it to assume a larger share of responsibility for its own missions and even to contribute to the work in newer areas.

During the twelve months between the catastrophic convention of 1837 and the one in 1838, the Bishop was able to make very few visitations and confirmed only seven persons. Nevertheless, the parishes were steadfast and in some cases prosperous. The abiding loyalty of the lay members, especially where they had erected a church or even begun to build one, and the devoted labors of the parish clergy maintained the structure of the Episcopal way of life —the sacraments and the prayers, the baptisms and marriages and burials.

Christ Church, Louisville, under the eloquent preaching and benign ministrations of the Reverend William Jackson, numbered 145 communicants and a large congregation. Already it was aiding the establishment of the new St. Paul's mission in the city. At Henderson and Paris the church buildings were now complete, and the one at Smithland was nearly so. In most of the parishes and missions the

Sunday schools flourished, often in conjunction with other denominations, some having a larger attendance than the parishes themselves. Understandably, the parishes had done little to carry out the resolutions of the 1837 convention to raise funds to support the episcopate. Dr. Cooke, treasurer of the Diocese during the 1837–1838 term, had done little besides endeavor to raise money to pay for the expensive publication of the 1837 *Journal*. There are no records to show how B. B. Smith managed to stretch the slender funds at his disposal to pay Winthrop his salary as professor and to support the new deacons who were manning the posts over the Diocese.

Fortunately, the Bishop's young men were resourceful. During their years in the seminary they had sustained themselves in various ways. A few had personal funds, some had contributions from churches in the East, and others got jobs. E. F. Berkley worked for the American Bible Society. F. B. Nash tutored in the family of Robert S. Todd, a prominent citizen whose pretty young lady daughters thought him a dictatorial Yankee.[2] N. M. Cowgill taught school. The young theologians mingled in social circles with notable success; many of them married Kentucky girls.

The Annual Convention that gathered on May 10 at Christ Church, Louisville was small, quiet, and uneventful. The Bishop presided without opposition, chiefly because of the helpful support of the host rector. William Jackson was an able leader, but it was well known that he had no personal ambitions, and the convention showed its confidence in him by electing him to virtually all the influential posts in the Diocese. He became a member of the Standing Committee, a trustee of the seminary, delegate to the next General Convention, and chairman of the important committee appointed by the Bishop to revise the constitution and articles and canons of the Diocese. Bishop Smith desired especially to get rid of the various regulations that had been adopted directly in opposition to him.

Among those present at this peaceful convention were Henry

---

[1] See Francis T. Hawkes to Jackson Kemper, September 19, 1837; James H. Otey to Jackson Kemper, September 21, 1837; Charles P. McIlvaine to Jackson Kemper, April 23, 1838; and James H. Otey to Jackson Kemper, July 5, 1838, all in the Kemper Papers (Wisconsin Historical Society).

[2] William H. Townsend, *Lincoln and the Bluegrass* (Lexington: 1955), pp. 63–64.

Caswall, who was seated as an honorary member from Indiana, and B. O. Peers, delegate from St. Paul's, Louisville, where he was temporarily officiating. Caswall, of course, took no active part, but Peers had two items of business to put before the body. One was to present the treasurer's report on behalf of Dr. Cooke, who did not attend. The other was to offer a resolution that the convention demand a formal report of the recent trial from the bishops who served as judges and further demand that the official records of the court be returned to the archives of the Diocese of Kentucky. The convention ended, however, by sending a very mild request to Bishop McIlvaine to return the trial papers. The delegates wished no more altercation. It was time to overlook the past and unite the Diocese. Most especially they wanted to expand their mission field, and with this in mind they voted to hold the next convention in Smithland, a village more than two hundred miles down the river from Louisville at the confluence of the Ohio with the Cumberland, nearly the westernmost settlement in the Commonwealth.

This interest in the far reaches of the Diocese may well have originated with the Bishop himself. Immediately after the convention he set out "to the western part of the Diocese, upon a more leisurely and extended tour than any that had been attempted for years." It proved to be a journey during which, according to his own account, he "travelled nearly 1,000 miles, preached 46 times, consecrated two churches, confirmed 22 persons at five different places, and delivered 12 public addresses upon the subject of Education, chiefly on the importance and value of a system of Common Schools."[3] The reason for his considering such an expedition to be leisurely was doubtless that he traveled much of the time by steamboats on the Ohio and Mississippi rivers, skirting the northern and western boundaries of his episcopal domain. His extended journey in the spring of 1834 had been somewhat similar, extending on up the Mississippi above St. Louis. This time his travels were all within the state of Kentucky.

A short distance below Louisville he stopped off at Brandenburg in order to talk with a "few zealous Episcopalians there," and much

[3] *Journal of the Diocese of Kentucky* for 1839, p. 9.

farther on he paid a visit to Owensboro. He thought this thriving settlement "a fine little town for a mission if only there were enough missionaries." Thence he proceeded to Henderson, the next sizable town down the river. Here, on Sunday, May 20, he consecrated St. Paul's Church, a dignified little edifice served by the Reverend Daniel Deacon. It was notable among Kentucky mission churches because it had been built "without foreign aid" by the stout little parish, which included some of the town's most eminent citizens. Bishop Smith found the town and the parish significant because of the Episcopal families whose attachments to the Church went back to Virginia and the Carolinas, and because, too, he found traces of the influence of the Reverend Williams Kavanaugh, even though Kavanaugh's three sons had become Methodist ministers. From Henderson Smith drove fifteen miles to Morganfield, a smaller community where he undoubtedly preached one or two of his many sermons.

The next stop recorded by him was at the busy little river town of Smithland, some of whose leading citizens owned large cotton plantations in the Natchez area. He inspected Calvary Church's nearly completed building, and preached at both of its regular Sunday services, one for the whites and one for the colored people. The rector was A. A. Willis, a gifted misfit from the East, to whom B. B. Smith had assigned this outpost on the frontier. Ten miles farther down the Ohio River, at the mouth of the Tennessee, he visited the still newer community of "Paduca." The town was slowly recovering from the effects of a devastating fire, and the prospects for Deacon Nash's mission there were so discouraging that the Bishop consented for him to come back up the state to relieve ailing Amos Cleaver at Paris.

At Paducah the Bishop took a steamboat down to the village of Columbus at the southwest tip of the state, a strategic spot overlooking the winding Mississippi River and facing the Missouri shore beyond. There were only a few Episcopal families in the whole region, but he thought it a suitable location for a mission. When he started home he evidently took the boat back up as far as Smithland and then traveled by stage to Hopkinsville.

He was well acquainted with this prosperous community, where

George Giddinge's parishioners were now worshiping in a modest new church of their own and were about to purchase an organ. During his stay in this region he preached at Princeton and Eddyville, at Cadiz and Trenton (where three persons were confirmed), and at Elkton and Russellville. At Russellville the little congregation worshiped in a "small but neat little sacred edifice" that had been erected through the exertions of dedicated Irish-born William McCallen, who served gratuitously as rector.

This journey and many others made by Bishop Smith are enough to refute a traditional notion that Episcopal clergymen shunned the hardships and dangers of travel on the American frontier. This rugged small man, clad in the plainest clothes his office permitted, conducted Prayer Book services in borrowed meetinghouses or schoolrooms or wherever two or three gathered to hear him. During his long career he would officiate in many prestigious places but never more effectively than on these missionary journeys.

In the autumn of 1838 he attended the General Convention in Philadelphia. It was on the whole a harmonious meeting, marked by enthusiasm for Sunday schools and all forms of religious education, and by the provision for missionary bishops in sufficient number to supervise the entire nation. Apprehension had not yet arisen among the leaders of the American Church about the High Church tracts that were being published in England by John Henry Newman and his associates in the Oxford Movement.

In December, Bishop Smith went to Cincinnati to participate in the consecration of the Reverend Leonidas Polk as the first missionary bishop of the Southwest. It was the first consecration of an Episcopal bishop to take place west of the Alleghenies, and it seemed all the more appropriate for it to be in Cincinnati because Bishop McIlvaine during his years as chaplain at West Point had confirmed Cadet Polk.

On account of these various travels and other episcopal business, Bishop Smith was away from Lexington for half of the year and during his absence left Christ Church in the care of Professor Edward Winthrop. By now the new St. Paul's congregation was diminishing for want of leadership. The Reverend Hamble Leacock had gone to a church in Franklin, Tennessee, and a number of the principal laymen, including Dr. Cooke and his family, the Andersons, and Mrs. Nellie Hart, were now residing in Louisville and affiliated with Christ Church there. The St. Paul's flock had not undertaken to build a church, and had still never won recognition from the Bishop.[4] Most of the "old parish," except the Bishop and a few of his undeviating followers such as Colonel Dunham, were ready to welcome back the people of St. Paul's. In the autumn of 1838 the will of the majority prevailed and there was a reorganization of the vestry that replaced the irreconcilables with moderate, nonpartisan members such as William M. Brand, Edward McAllister, and D. Vertner. Seeing that his policy toward St. Paul's was being overruled, B. B. Smith tendered his resignation as rector of the parish, and it was accepted at a meeting on October 22. The separation, concluding eight years of service to Christ Church, was amicable on both sides.

In December Edward Winthrop asked that he be relieved of his position as assistant rector in order to devote himself to his seminary teaching and to his school for young ladies. His young wife having died, he had married a successful music teacher in the city who assisted with the school.[5] Sometime in 1840 Winthrop gave up his professorship in the seminary, which had so few students that the Bishop could carry on their instruction.[6] Winthrop continued to reside in Lexington, preaching frequently, especially to the colored people. In 1842 he served for a short time as an assistant at influential St. Paul's Church in Cincinnati before returning to the East. One of his notable contributions to the Church in Kentucky was his active participation in religious services for the inmates of the "Lunatic Asylum" in Lexington, one of the earliest institutions of its kind in the West.

[4] James Craik, *Historic Sketches of Christ Church, Louisville, Kentucky,* p. 84. In the *Journal of the Diocese of Kentucky* for 1838 St. Paul's, Lexington, is not listed, represented, or mentioned.

[5] Burial services for Marion Penny Winthrop, May 7, 1838, by the Reverend John Ward (Old Register, Christ Church, Lexington); also the Penny Family Letters, University of Kentucky Archives.

[6] The Bishop's Address (*Journal of the Diocese of Kentucky* for 1841) reports only two candidates ordained as deacons (R. S. Adams, who removed to Indiana; and J. M. Putney, who died before May, 1842); and only three new candidates received (J. A. Shepherd, J. Sweet, and William Harlow).

The vestry was now in a position to call a rector who could and would devote his full time to the parish. Christ Church had indeed suffered hardships during the previous five or six years. The ravages of the cholera, the prolonged controversy leading up to the trial that was conducted within its walls, the breaking away of the St. Paul's congregation—all these had diminished the parish both within and without. Throughout this period the Reverend John Ward had acted as a mediator, and was serving on the vestry in December, 1838, when the meeting was called at his home on the day after Christmas to select a new rector. Several clergymen from outside the Diocese were considered and rejected. It was agreed, in view of the grave necessity for calling the right man to reunite and restore the parish, to defer calling a permanent rector. The vestry resolved, instead, to engage temporarily the services of the Reverend Edward F. Berkley, who less than two weeks before had been ordained to the diaconate in Christ Church.[7] A native of Washington, D.C., he had come to the seminary as a student in 1835 and proved himself a diligent, useful young man. He was wholeheartedly loyal to Bishop Smith, who may well have suggested him to the vestry. Mr. Ward also knew and befriended Berkley, occasionally helping him out with a timely loan. Young Deacon Berkley preached his first sermon on January 2 and proved so satisfactory to his listeners that on April 1 they raised his salary from $900 to $1,000 per annum and decided to make him their rector as soon as he could be ordained to the priesthood. This was accomplished on Christmas Day of 1839, and thus he began a service of nearly twenty years in his first parish. The "Berkley Era" at Christ Church, Lexington will be recounted in a separate chapter, but it is interwoven with every phase of the antebellum Church in Kentucky.

At about this same time Trinity Church, Danville terminated a frustrating five years of part-time ministers by calling another of Bishop Smith's young seminary graduates, Matthew Fontaine Maury, member of the Kentucky branch of a Virginia family that produced distinguished Episcopal clergymen for several generations. Not since the death of the beloved Gideon McMillan had

[7] Minutes of Vestry of Christ Church, Lexington, Kentucky, December 26, 1838; Edward F. Berkley, Diary-Account Book, Christ Church, Lexington Archives.

Trinity had the full-time services of an active rector, and in M. F. Maury it found its leader for the next twenty years.

Now the missionary spirit began to reach out in a quiet, neighborly way to numerous other communities in the vicinity of Lexington. At Leesburg, a prosperous village in rich farming land to the north, a few well-to-do Episcopalians organized a parish, which was admitted to the Diocese at the 1836 convention. Chiefly through the efforts of William Hearne, a frame church building was erected, and in 1838 Deacon Charles Crowe, a seminary recruit from Ireland, was assigned to preach there every other Sunday. His duties were also to arouse interest in nearby Cynthiana and "to attend the Versailles station," where there were a few Episcopal families.

Expansion took yet another direction when the Bishop sent a newly ordained seminarian, Deacon N. N. Cowgill, as missionary to Maysville. This early settlement on the Ohio River, about fifty miles above Cincinnati, had become an important commercial town. Bishop Meade had preached there during his visitation in 1831, not only to the several Episcopal families in the community but to larger gatherings in the Methodist and Presbyterian churches. Cowgill was able to stay only a few months on this assignment, but made a start toward the parish that would be organized five or six years later, and did considerable preaching in the surrounding country. Such modest ventures were the most that Bishop Smith could undertake at the time with the limited resources at his disposal, but they kept alive the spirit of missions in Kentucky.

All these evidences of progress appeared in the reports that were read to the annual convention at Calvary Church, Smithland, in June, 1839. The meeting consisted actually of the Bishop and six delegates: The Reverend Willis and Dr. Sanders, of Smithland; the Reverend Giddinge and Major S. P. Gower, of Hopkinsville; the Reverend T. E. Paine, of Princeton; and Mr. George Tyler, of Trenton. The absence of representatives from the rest of the state was not because of any disapproval or dissension but because a journey to Smithland seemed too long and difficult for a two-day meeting. Nevertheless, several notable things were accomplished.

The Reverend William Jackson's committee to revise the constitution and canons sent in an excellent report, recommending the

restoration of the 1831 constitution, with only "a few slight amendments," and the adoption of the 1835 canons plus "certain additions
on a Missionary, Education, and Sunday school organization, without, however, touching on the subject of clerical trials, upon which
it was thought best not to legislate, pending the action of a Committee of the General Convention upon a uniform system of Ecclesiastical Jurisprudence."[8] The committee thus proposed to get rid of the
controversial regulations passed by the Cooke-Coit faction and to
stress the diocesan program for missionary and educational support.
Quite properly, this recommendation was laid upon the table for
consideration at the next convention, but there was no doubt that it
would be approved. Other important new business included a resolution seeking consideration for the establishment of a college in the
Diocese and another resolution asking consideration for the removal
of the seminary "to any point where said College shall be established." The seminary now had only two professors and four
students.[9] The Bishop had by no means given up his plan to educate
priests for his Diocese, but he was resolved to make a new start
elsewhere than in Lexington.

Throughout his career, Smith was essentially an educator, with
deep concern for providing opportunity for all willing students. He
was himself neither a learned scholar nor a gifted writer, but he was
well versed in educational theory and method. His first youthful
service to the Church was the founding of a Sunday school. He was
a teacher during most of his years in Kentucky, participating in
numerous educational meetings, oftentimes as a speaker. It was
appropriate, therefore, that late in 1839 he was appointed to the
office of Superintendent of Public Instruction in the Commonwealth of Kentucky. It was customary at the time to name clergymen from different denominations in turn to this post.

B. B. Smith's own account of his appointment is that Bishop
Hubbard Hinde Kavanaugh of the Methodist Church, holder of the
office during 1838 and 1839, wrote him of his own impending
resignation and suggested that Smith "might make interest to become his successor" if he so desired. Kavanaugh, son of the pioneer

[8] *Journal of the Diocese of Kentucky* for 1839, p. 17.
[9] *Directory of Lexington for 1838 & 1839,* p. 16.

Episcopal clergyman in Henderson, was well disposed toward the bishop of his father's Church. The "interest" that Smith employed was to ask Robert Wickliffe, of Christ Church, Lexington, his erstwhile parishioner and legal counsel, to communicate with his brother, Governor Charles Wickliffe, who then saw fit to appoint B. B. Smith. Charles Morehead, now in the legislature, may well have been helpful, also. It was a fortunate choice, both for Smith and the Commonwealth. The new Superintendent's travels over the state fitted admirably with his episcopal duties, and during his term he managed in the joint role of bishop and school superintendent and "friend of education" to visit seventy-six out of the then ninety-one counties in Kentucky. The salary of one thousand dollars a year relieved the financial stress he had suffered since relinquishing the rectorship of Christ Church.[10]

During his decade in the western country B. B. Smith had traveled much, by stage and steamboat, on the railroad cars that now ran between Lexington and Frankfort, and sometimes with his own horse and buggy. A new and more strenuous experience awaited him as he began his survey of the educational condition of the state with a six-week trip on horseback into the mountain country of East Kentucky. He had never made a journey on horseback before, and at the end of the first day on the raw-boned "fast walker" a friend had lent him, he thought he could not possibly go on. Along the way he had fallen in with a Methodist circuit-rider, and the two spent the night at a settler's cabin, where they were glad to be able to get corn dodger and sour milk for the evening snack and to share a pallet on the floor for the night. The Bishop had been advised to go well-armed on trips like this, but as a matter of principle he carried neither gun nor pistol. He was not molested or harmed on this trip or at any time afterward. His fearlessness served as his passport among the backwoods people, who respected courage in any man, especially in a parson.

[10] B. B. Smith, "Glimpses Backwards Over Two Hard Years of My Life, from 1839 to 1841, Whilst I Was Superintendent of Public Instruction in the Commonwealth of Kentucky," MS (B. B. Smith Papers, Insko Collection, Church Historical Society). Also Governor Wickliffe's Appointment of B. B. Smith as Superintendent of Public Instruction, dated February 1, 1840 (photograph, Archives of the Diocese of Lexington, University of Kentucky Library).

At county seats and country schoolhouses and lonely crossroads settlements he gathered the "first statistical information regarding the progress of the common schools in the new Commonwealth," which he incorporated in his valuable Report for 1841.[11] He drew up plans for a common school system, with districts under the direction of superintendents, and devised printed forms and instructions for maintaining records. In later life he called his term as superintendent "the hard years," but they undoubtedly constituted one of the most satisfying periods of his career. During this interlude he was able, while still pursuing his sacred calling, to bring a little closer the day when, as he hoped, "every Child in Kentucky would be within reasonable distance of a good Common School, under competent Teachers, furnished, both for boys and girls, with Instructors well educated & duly trained for their work in our own Normal Schools."

Meanwhile, Smith pushed forward his plan for establishing a "Literary Institution of an elevated character under the auspices of the Church in this Diocese." The convention of 1840 authorized an attempt to locate it at Richmond, but after a summer's work it was decided that the necessary subscription of ten thousand dollars could not be raised in Madison County, and this proposed location was abandoned. Then in November came overtures from the trustees of Shelby College, located in Shelbyville, a prosperous town halfway between Lexington and Louisville, offering to turn their institution over to the Episcopal Church. It consisted of "a fine College building and a handsome lot, which, together, may be estimated at $10,000.00."[12] With the offer were included also some sixty-five students, two professors, and two thousand dollars per annum, this "being the proceeds of a lottery conducted for the benefit of the college." The sole condition was that "it be continued at Shelbyville, and as a Literary Institution." The college had been

[11] Moses Edward Ligon, *A History of Public Education in Kentucky* (*Bulletin of Bureau of School Service,* College of Education, University of Kentucky, Vol. XIV, No. 4, June, 1942), p. 84.

[12] See *Journal of a Special Convention . . . in Shelbyville, December 29th and 30th, 1840,* bound with the *Journal of the Diocese of Kentucky* for 1841, especially the Bishop's Address, pp. 29–30.

founded four years earlier by public-spirited citizens of the community, who now felt the need of organized denominational support similar to that which undergirded most educational establishments of the time.

At a special diocesan convention held in Shelbyville on December 29 and 30, the offer of the trustees of Shelby College was now accepted without dissent, and a committee was appointed to seek the alteration of the charter of the Episcopal Theological Seminary to permit its removal "from Lexington to Shelbyville, or to any other point in the state they [the trustees] might deem expedient." It is noteworthy that the Reverend Edward Berkley was the only representative from Lexington at this meeting, and that the committees for carrying out the plan were composed mostly of clergy and laymen from the Louisville area, headed by the Reverend William Jackson. It was Jackson's support that enabled the bishop to carry out the plan to acquire Shelby College and to remove the seminary to that location. His cooperation virtually guaranteed the support of the several churches in the Louisville area. During the previous year he had transferred from Christ Church, Louisville to St. Paul's, Louisville, which had a newly completed and handsome building seating nine hundred persons. He took along with him most of his parishioners, and all without hard feelings. The diminished Christ Church called a young man from Indiana whom Bishop Kemper recommended, the Reverend T. C. Pitkin. St. Matthew's parish, located five miles east of the city, had erected "a neat little Church edifice" that was consecrated May 11, 1839, and had called the Reverend Charles H. Page, of Virginia, as its rector. This area was the strongest in the Diocese, both in numbers and in financial support.

The convention in May, 1841, at Danville was chiefly concerned with the acquisition of Shelby College and the naming of a long list of trustees from all over the Diocese. It was agreed to "dissolve" the seminary in Lexington and transfer theological training to the new college. The number of candidates for Holy Orders (who constituted the student body of the seminary) had dropped to about six, and their training was being carried on somewhat sporadically by the Bishop and others of the clergy officiating near Lexington.[13] The Board of Trustees, to which was delegated the task of closing down the institution, included: the Bishop, ex officio, the Reverend William Jackson, Henry Cowan, of Danville, the Reverend John Ward, William Iucho, and Alfred Warner, treasurer—the last three from Lexington.

In accord with the Bishop's wishes, the board authorized the transfer of the extensive seminary library to Shelbyville (at a cost of seventy-five dollars); the sale of the Griswold Press (which fetched the sum of seven hundred dollars); a formal request to Dr. Cooke to turn over any "monies, papers or records of the seminary now in his possession"; and immediate efforts to sell the entire seminary property. These business matters were attended to by Alfred Warner, but he could find no purchaser for the handsome property. The trustees then offered to let B. B. Smith continue to occupy it as his residence and school for one or two years at an annual rent of five hundred dollars. When he declined the offer, the place was rented to Tobias Gibson, Esquire, for the same sum. The trustees, certainly those who resided in Lexington, proceeded with very deliberate speed in selling the seminary property until the final steps were completed in amending the institution's charter to authorize the sale. The plan of renting the property for a time appealed to them also because it would provide a way to settle the debts of the seminary. Winthrop presented his bill for unpaid 1837 salary in the sum of $59.61, and Colonel Dunham's overdue account for boarding the students amounted to $683.64 plus accumulated interest. There must have been some disagreement between the Bishop and the treasurer during the year these matters were being settled, because Alfred Warner turned in his resignation along with his report and the records at the next annual convention. But the seminary did pay finally its debts, even if the last of the interest due to Colonel Dunham was not remitted to his widow until January 1, 1845.[14]

---

[13] The Bishop's Address in the *Journal of the Diocese of Kentucky* for 1841 reports two candidates for Holy Orders made deacons; also three candidates received.

[14] *Journal of the Diocese of Kentucky* for 1845, p. 19. See *Journal* for 1842, pp. 14–15, for the Report of "A. Warner, late Trustee of the Seminary, and late Secretary and Treasurer of the Board."

The reason Bishop Smith declined to rent the seminary property was that he had decided to leave Lexington. His resignation as rector of Christ Church had already severed most of the ties that held him here, and during his travels over the state as Superintendent of Public Instruction he had found that Louisville was a more influential and flourishing city. In the autumn of 1841 he removed his official residence to Louisville and settled his family at the east edge of town near the Bardstown Road, in an ample house which he named "Kalorama." Here he and Mrs. Smith promptly established a school for girls. It attracted an excellent clientele, with a dozen or more boarding pupils enrolled for the first session.[15] The Bishop's older daughters were now well-bred young ladies, ready to assist their stepmother with the teaching and the management of the school. They had been brought up to be studious. One of them recalled in later life that her parents' invariable reply to a child's query as to what to do was "Get a book and read it!"

Harriet Staples Smith was a capable and gracious mistress of the big household at "Kalorama" that included her own babies, her several stepchildren, the boarding pupils, and numerous guests. To at least one of the guests she seemed a great lady. Joel Hart, by this time a successful sculptor with commissions from all over the state, was a caller who left a treasured *carte de visite,* an original poem in her honor titled "A Mother's Love." The verses showed none of the genius that made his marble creations come to life, but the little note at the end was sincere enough to be treasured through the years: "Mrs. Smith will please accept these lines from the writer, in token of his esteem and admiration for her virtues and talents. J. T. Hart. Kalorama, April 9, 1843."[16] The Bishop continued to be interested in the young sculptor's work, visiting his studio when in Lexington and arranging at least one commission for him.[17]

Smith's term as Superintendent of Public Instruction ended in early 1842, when the appointment went to a Methodist clergyman.

[15] B. B. Smith to E. F. Berkley, February 2, 1842 (Berkley Papers, Filson Club).

[16] "A Mother's Love" by Joel T. Hart (Manuscript in Bishop Smith Papers, Church Historical Society).

[17] B. B. Smith to E. F. Berkley, March 12, 1844 (Berkley Papers, Filson Club) regarding a bust of the Reverend William Jackson.

The Bishop was now in fairly good financial condition. During the past two years he had received his salary from the state and the sum of $350 from the Diocese, plus the income from the school. He could now devote his primary attention to his "Literary Institution" at Shelbyville, only thirty miles from "Kalorama." His plans met with some opposition at the annual convention in May, 1842. The seminary property was still unsold, and the delegates from Christ Church, Lexington put through a resolution requiring any sale to be approved by the convention and forbidding the proceeds of such a sale to be invested in Shelby College. At that point the Reverend William Jackson effected a compromise permitting the income from the seminary property or its sale to be used for Shelby College, on the condition that the school offered theological training for candidates. The institution had no president, although it was hoped there would be one by the end of the year. It was being run by two deacons, the more efficient one being Joshua Sweet, Professor of Mathematics. The man who finally accepted the post in 1843 was a person of considerable distinction. Dr. Robert B. Drane, recently rector of a parish in Wilmington, North Carolina, had been ordained, as had B. B. Smith, by Bishop Griswold and doubtless was also an Evangelical Churchman.[18] Drane may well have been influenced to accept the position by the presence of William Jackson in the Diocese.

The trustees of the theological seminary, whose sole business now was to look after the Lexington property, found it a bad investment, and by authority of the 1844 convention sold it at auction on June 27 of that year to Messrs. Tobias Gibson and Henry Duncan for the aggregate sum of $11,500, to be paid over a period of six years with interest. The money was to be invested and only the income expended as ordered by the convention. The treasurer of the board of trustees at the time of the sale was D. M. Craig of Christ Church, Lexington, a careful businessman and a firm advocate of keeping

[18] MS notes by Eugene Thompson (Archives of Diocese of Lexington, University of Kentucky Library). Dr. Drane served as alternate delegate from the Diocese of North Carolina at the organizing convention of the Protestant Episcopal Church in the Confederate States of America [*Journals of the P.E.C. in the C.S.A.* facsimile (Austin, Texas: Church Historical Society, 1962), III, pp. 12, 204].

the seminary funds intact. He held the office until his death in 1868, and more than any other one person was responsible for the fact that this first "educational fund" of the Diocese of Kentucky remained almost intact until the end of the century.

With B. B. Smith's removal to Louisville and the sale of the seminary property, the first, or "Lexington," period of his episcopate ended. Only his close relationship with Edward Berkley and a continuing friendship with John Ward bound him now to the parish and city where he had lived for eleven years. His new projects were all located elsewhere. His supporters and advisers came mostly from the growing churches in Louisville, and within about two years the custom was established of regularly electing them to at least half the places on the important committees. The new "prime minister"—and B. B. Smith always needed a chief adviser to direct his policy—was the Reverend William Jackson, a fortunate choice.

Jackson was unquestionably the most eminent and widely known Episcopal clergyman to officiate in Kentucky up to this time. His popularity rested not only upon his personality but upon his tolerant and persuasive statement of the Evangelical position. The titles of some of his sermon outlines indicate his attitude toward the theological doctrines discussed in his day: "The Lord's Supper, A Token of the Covenant," "Baptismal Obligations (address to parents)," and "The Holy Catholic Church." His position was very close to that of B. B. Smith, but Smith lacked his friend's clarity of thought and speech. He lacked also the sense of humor that made Jackson reply to a suggestion that he stand for election as Bishop of Indiana that "rather than be called to the thankless and self-destroying duties of a western bishop, he would pray that he might first be taken to his Master's more immediate service in Heaven."[19]

William Jackson took much interest in the training of the Shelby College theological students, whom he called his sons, and when he fell mortally ill in February, 1844, two of the young men walked the thirty miles from Shelbyville to attend his last sickbed. Hundreds of

---

[19] [Mrs. Margaret A. Jackson], *Rev. William Jackson, Late Rector of St. Paul's Church, Louisville, Kentucky. With a Brief Sketch of His Life and Character* (New York: 1846), p. 28. Bishop Smith's Funeral Sermon, pp. 87-98.

people stood outside St. Paul's the day Bishop Smith preached the funeral sermon. The tolerant, peace-loving rector of St. Paul's had done much to build up the Episcopal Church in Louisville and to restore harmony in the Diocese. Few men have exerted a greater influence or contributed more to the Diocese than William Jackson.[20]

Within about three months after the death of Jackson and while Bishop Smith was still filling his pulpit at St. Paul's, the rector of Christ Church, Louisville, the Reverend Thomas Pitkin, accepted a call to Rochester, New York. The vestry deliberated a very short while and within a week called the Reverend James Craik, rector of St. John's Church in Charleston, Virginia (now West Virginia). This extraordinary promptness suggests that they were already well acquainted with the man, by reputation if not in person. Dr. Cooke may well have recommended him since the two families were acquainted back in Virginia.

Grandson and namesake of the Scottish born doctor who was Washington's personal physician, James Craik chose medicine as a career. In 1825 at the age of twenty he rode on horseback to Kentucky to pursue his studies at Transylvania University, and on the way he stopped at Maysville with a letter to Major Valentine Peers. In college he formed lasting friendships with fellow students— H. I. Bodley, Henry Clay, Jr., Alexander Bullitt, and Aldert Smedes. None of these were medical students, however, a fact which may have influenced him in changing to the study of law. Family tradition says that he did so on the advice of President Holley.[21] After leaving the university in about 1826 he established a successful law practice in Kanawha, Virginia, a busy river town, and in 1829 married Juliet Shrewsbury.

At this time in his life Craik had lost touch with the Church of his childhood and became an agnostic. Then a family connection who was a Roman Catholic introduced him in Cincinnati to the

[20] This opinion is quoted from the Right Reverend Thomas U. Dudley in J. Stoddard Johnston, *The Memorial History of Louisville* . . . (Chicago: [1896]), II, p. 143.
[21] *Catalogue of Transylvania University, 1826;* also "Autobiography of James Craik" (MS in the possession of the Reverend Charles Ewell Craik, Jr.); also Reverend Charles Ewell Craik, Jr., to Rebecca Smith Lee, October 18, 1966.

distinguished Bishop Spalding in the hope of converting him to that faith. The Bishop lent him various doctrinal books, presenting him with a copy of Eusebius' *History of the Early Church*. Reading Eusebius failed to convert him to Roman Catholicism, but it started him on years of serious study that led him to become a candidate for Holy Orders under Bishop Meade of Virginia, who ordained him deacon and then priest in 1839. He was a handsome man in the prime of life, with a lawyer's logical mind and a natural habit of command. The call to a larger church in a flourishing city came at an opportune time.

Characteristically, before giving an answer Craik took a steamboat down the river to look over the situation. He told the story of this visit many years later in a book of historical sketches about Christ Church.

Then as now the mailboat from Cincinnati arrived in the night, and the passengers were aroused at early dawn. Before sunrise Mr. Craik was traversing the streets of Louisville with curious interest. It was Friday morning, and the Church was open for early morning prayer. He entered the sacred Courts, and so the first house which gave him shelter in Louisville was the House of God, and nearly the first words which he uttered in this city were words of prayer and praise in communion with the people of God in the very place of his future labors.[22]

During the following days he met the Christ Church parishioners who had called him. He must have conferred with longtime vestryman Benjamin Outram Davis, who had been the frequent host of Bishop Kemper, and who was sometimes credited with having saved Christ Church by his benefactions when the majority of its people went over to St. Paul's. Almost certainly Craik soon met a new vestryman, Laurence Pike Maury from Bath County, postmaster of the city, who was treasurer of the Diocese, and very probably G. W. Anderson and G. Robinson—there were members of the Robinson family in all three Louisville parishes—were among his callers. There were many others. They all approved his Churchmanship, which rejected both the Tractarians and the "so-called

[22] James Craik, *Historical Sketches of Christ Church, Louisville, Diocese of Kentucky* (Louisville, Kentucky: 1862), p. 95.

Evangelicals" in favor of a true *via media* based on the Prayer Book. He in turn admired the Medical Institute, the banks and printing houses, and the many handsome churches and residences of the burgeoning community. He wrote his letter of acceptance on June 18 before he left town, designating the "first of August following" as the time he would return to assume his duties as rector.

Craik's arrival in the Diocese so soon after the passing of Jackson was a great boon to Bishop Smith. Like Jackson, Craik supplied the decisive leadership and judicious counsel that Smith needed and which, with the exception of his 1836-1837 controversy, he habitually welcomed from his colleagues throughout his long career. Craik and Smith were not warm personal friends, but each respected the other's office, and for more than a quarter of a century each worked in his own way for the advancement of the Diocese and the American Church. It is proof of the Bishop's Christian humility that he seems at no time to have been envious of Craik's superior talents and great influence.

9 Antebellum Expansion in the Bluegrass

At this point, it may be useful to define the region destined to become the Diocese of Lexington. It is generally recognized that a theoretical line divides the part of Kentucky which looks eastward from that which looks westward. For practical purposes we may start at a point on the Ohio River about halfway between Cincinnati and Louisville where the Kentucky River empties into it and follow a course due southward to the Tennessee state border. To the eastward of this line lies first a belt of fertile land, including a rich limestone plateau and the upper Ohio Valley, and on beyond are hills and knobs and then the ancient forest-clad mountains of Appalachia, forming a barrier across the horizon. West of the line, too, lie good farming lands that become less fertile as the terrain drops gradually to become wooded watersheds for four great inland rivers and innumerable lesser streams, all flowing eventually into the Mississippi and on to the Gulf. Of the eastward half of the Commonwealth the economic, educational, and cultural center has always been Lexington, set in the heart of the bluegrass area. In the westward half Louisville, at the strategic Falls of the Ohio, has from the beginning dominated commerce and politics and influenced cultural patterns all the way to Mills Point on the Mississippi. It would be misleading to speak of the two sections of the state as being opposed to each other, but travelers and historians have always been aware of their divergent points of view. The existence of the two sections is taken for granted by Kentuckians themselves.

It is very unlikely that Benjamin Bosworth Smith realized this basic dichotomy in the Diocese over which he presided. Although he lived in Kentucky for nearly forty years and continued as its bishop for another fourteen, he never was really at home among the high-spirited people who made up his charge, nor did he fully understand their mores and loyalties. He was so little a Lexingtonian that he was indifferent to the fact that closing the seminary and removing his official residence would inevitably wound the pride of the whole community and diminish the prestige of the Episcopal Church there for a generation. Shortly after his departure from Lexington he wrote complacently to Edward Berkley that he felt sure that Christ Church "would eventually flourish again"[1] and he maintained for the rest of his days only an aloof interest in the parish that had originally called him to the West.

When Bishop Smith took up his residence in Louisville in 1841, conditions seemed ideal for him to remain there the rest of his career. The school at "Kalorama" prospered as his daughters gained experience and reputation. With his own hands he built a quaint chalet-study on the grounds for his books and craftwork. Financial support from the Louisville churches increased his modest salary and underwrote his attempts to keep up the ill-starred college at Shelbyville. He preached and published locally a number of sermons setting forth his position as "a large-hearted, Catholic, evangelical Episcopalian."[2] For a quarter of a century Louisville Churchmen gave him loyal support. When, however, in 1866 he selected a location for the permanent home that the Diocese purchased for him, he chose to live in Frankfort, and even before his duties as Presiding Bishop necessitated his permanent residence in the east he spent much of his time there. He was always something of a stranger in his Diocese, a fact which sheds light upon his whole career.

There being no real *rapprochement* between the Bishop and his people, he had little intuitive knowledge of the traditional attitudes and loyalties of the different parishes in his domain. He moved the administrative center of the Diocese from Lexington to Louisville as a matter of expediency, to promote his personal and educational plans. There is no evidence that he gave any thought to the effects of shifting the leadership of the Diocese from one section to the other or that he weighed the differences between the growing urban outlook of Louisville and the agrarian society of the Lexington area. Nevertheless, the shift began to take place immediately,

---

[1] B. B. Smith to Edward Berkley, February 28, 1842 (Berkley Papers, Filson Club).
[2] B. B. Smith, *The Position of Episcopalians in Relation to Christians of Other Names* (Louisville: 1850), p. 14.

and from this time forward the parishes in eastward Kentucky were notably less involved in the formulation and support of diocesan projects. The change is apparent in the roster of officers and committees in the *Journals* from 1842 on. For the next fifteen years, Edward Berkley was the only clergyman in the Lexington area whose name appeared regularly on important committees. The laity of the area held no responsible posts, with the exception of D. M. Craig, who retained the treasurership of the seminary funds. There was no dearth of able men elsewhere for the diocesan offices. The Louisville clergy were often named, especially William Jackson and James Craik. The many active Louisville laymen were citizens who matched their services to the Diocese with labors for their own parishes. Except for the misfortunes that plagued Shelby College, Bishop Smith's years in Louisville saw much progress in the Diocese.

Inevitably the parishes in and near Lexington had borne the brunt of the unfavorable publicity resulting from the Smith trial, and their prestige was further diminished by the removal of the episcopal headquarters and the seminary from the city. Nevertheless these parishes set about patching up any differences among their own members and renovating their church buildings. They called new rectors, nearly all young men, and joined with the rest of the Diocese in working to enlarge the Church in Kentucky.

This concern that the Diocese should establish and support its own missions was not new; the organizing convention had authorized a diocesan missionary society for that purpose. In every annual address the Bishop begged for missionaries and for money to support them. In 1839 the annual convention in new Canon X set up the "Education and Missionary Society" of the Diocese. In 1847 the convention went much farther and made it the duty of every parish priest, especially in the larger parishes, to become an active missionary in the surrounding area without remuneration other than his traveling expenses. At that time, and until 1852, the Domestic and Foreign Missionary Society contributed toward the salaries of missionaries and some of the priests in charge of the small churches in the Diocese.[3] In 1857 the convention organized its domestic missions

[3] See *Journal of the Diocese of Kentucky* for 1851, pp. 22–23, for the financial statement from 1837 to 1852.

under the convocation plan, combining the work of the central portion of the Diocese under the direction of a general agent, the Reverend John West, a missionary from Massachusetts.[4]

In the bluegrass region and along the upper Ohio the results of these diocesan missions were good, resulting in steady, albeit modest, progress and enlargement. This kind of outreach from established parishes into nearby communities was admirably adapted to the homogeneous social pattern of the area. It was made possible, however, by a remarkable generation of parish priests in the area during that time. It was the period of Edward F. Berkley at Lexington, John Nicholas Norton at Frankfort, John W. Venable at Versailles and Georgetown, John Austen Merrick at Paris, G. G. Moore at Covington and Newport, Robert McMurdy at Washington, and others whose tenure was briefer. In this part of the Diocese the years from 1837 to the Civil War may well be called the Era of Rector-Missionaries; and its history is best set forth in the annals of their individual parishes. Because so much of the early story of Christ Church, Lexington has already been related it seems appropriate to begin with Trinity Church, Danville, second oldest of the parishes that would one day become the Diocese of Lexington.

ANTEBELLUM TRINITY CHURCH, DANVILLE

The organization of Trinity parish in Danville in 1829 at the instigation of Dr. George Chapman, rector of Christ Church, Lexington and its participation in the first decade of the Diocese have already been related. From the first it was a steadfast, responsible parish, whose influence exceeded its modest numbers, a maximum of some thirty-five communicants and about twice that number in the congregation. Its importance lay in the purposeful fellowship of its members. Some, like the Worthingtons and the Yeisers, had inherited the Anglican faith, while others, like Dr. Ephraim McDowell and Henry J. Cowan, had read themselves into the Episcopal Church in reaction against the dissenting denominations

---

[4] *Journal of the Diocese of Kentucky* for 1857, pp. 16–17, for the initial convocation plan; *Journal* for 1859, pp. 23–29, for report of West's work.

that flourished around them. They were mostly physicians, lawyers, bankers, merchants, and landowners, and after the manner of solid citizens they at once proposed to erect a substantial church building on Main Street. Under the leadership of the Reverend Gideon McMillan, the energetic missionary-in-charge from the Diocese of Ohio who became their first rector, they soon built it and paid for it. The largest contributor was James Birney, a wealthy Irish-born merchant who zealously maintained his loyalty to the Episcopal faith although his children married into the ruling Presbyterian families of the state.[5]

Trinity Church was ready for consecration by Bishop Meade during his visit in the spring of 1831. By that time the parish, increased to more than double its original number of communicants, supported regular services, a Sunday school, two Bible classes, and an active "Female Prayer Book and Tract Society." The rector spent a portion of his time on preaching expeditions to several nearby communities, including Harrodsburg and Lancaster. Gideon McMillan became a victim of the cholera epidemic of 1833 after exposing himself fearlessly in ministering to the entire community. His devoted parishioners buried him in the churchyard beside the east wall near the chancel.

With the death of McMillan Trinity Church lost some of the impetus of its auspicious founding, but it loyally supported the new rector, the Reverend John Alexander Adams, who, with his wife, had recently opened a female seminary in the town. A native of Washington, D.C., he had been ordained by Bishop Meade of Virginia and had served in several small parishes in Maryland. Never a strong man—he may have come west for his health—he always divided his limited strength between his school and his parish, sometime to the detriment of the latter. He did, however, keep alive the sacramental life of Trinity Church even when he was not its officiating clergyman, and he always had the esteem and respect of the congregation. He served as a trustee of the Episcopal

<hr>

[5] For James Birney and his famous son, James Gillespie Birney (1792–1857), see William Birney, *James G. Birney and His Times* (New York: 1890), Chapter II *et passim.*

Theological Seminary in Kentucky but seems to have taken very little part in its affairs.[6]

During the diocesan controversy of 1835–37 the Danville parish desired to remain aloof, and Frederick Yeiser, its lay delegate to the acrimonious convention of 1836, went home when the long investigation of the Bishop's conduct was begun. Because the convention of 1837 was scheduled to be held in Danville the Trinity Church vestry served notice in writing that it did not wish any arraignment of Bishop Smith to be conducted there.[7] Available evidence suggests that the parish and the community originally favored the Bishop in the contest. Unfortunately for his own cause B. B. Smith attempted as presiding officer to deny the Reverend Mr. Adams a seat in the convention on the grounds that he was not an "officiating clergyman in the Diocese of Kentucky." The meeting ruled in Adams' favor but the Trinity delegates were naturally displeased. Perhaps because of that both of them voted in favor of conducting a trial. Nevertheless, the parishioners remained on friendly terms with the Bishop and after the trial accepted one of his seminarians, Deacon Charles Higginson, as their temporary minister, with the stipulation that Mr. Adams hold communion services. The young deacon was diligent, and as hard times ended over the nation the ladies erected "a small, neat vestry-room," complete except for the plastering, which had to wait until the next spring.

Early in 1839 the parish called as its rector another young man from the seminary, the Reverend M. F. Maury, who had been ordained as priest the previous October in Christ Church, Lexington. When he entered upon his duties on February 7 he was rightly pleased to find the Sunday school in operation, with about twenty-five scholars and six teachers, and to be able to add four new communicants before time to report to the convention in June.

[6] Sources for Trinity Church, Danville, include: Fackler, *Early Days in Danville* and "G.C.," "Reminiscences of a Remote and Recent Past in Danville," *Kentucky Advocate*, January 7 and 23, February 6, 1905, both previously cited; and J. Rice Cowan, "The Hundred Years of Trinity Parish," *Danville Daily Messenger,* June 4 and June 5, 1929. Also the Minutes of the Vestry of Trinity Church, and the *Journal of the Diocese of Kentucky,* 1829ff., and a brief historical sketch of Trinity Church by Mrs. C. E. Newlin.
[7] B. B. Smith to Jackson Kemper, June 20, 1836 (Kemper Papers); and Minutes of the Vestry of Christ Church, Lexington, Kentucky, April 12, 1837.

Matthew Fontaine Maury, of Bath County, Kentucky, was descended from a well-known Virginia family, being the great-grandson of James Maury, who prepared Thomas Jefferson for college, and grandson of Matthew Fontaine, both Anglican clergymen of Albemarle County.[8] A cousin, who bore precisely the same name as his own, was already rising to prominence in the United States Navy, and it may have been for that reason that the Kentucky clergyman elected to be known as M. F. Maury, or sometimes as M. Fontaine Maury.

From the start M. F. Maury was quietly successful with his parish. Services were held regularly in the church and often in the surrounding countryside. Slowly but steadily the roster of communicants and of worshipers increased. He set up the first systematic record of births, deaths, marriages, and burials in Trinity Church. Within a little more than a year's time his happy parishioners installed a six-hundred dollar organ in the gallery opposite the chancel, the first in the Diocese outside of Lexington and Louisville. In the Bishop's annual address at the 1839 convention he thanked the people of Trinity Church for their hospitality during two visitations and with unwonted enthusiasm expressed his belief that "its zealous supporters are about to reap the temporal reward of all their toil and sacrifices."

The Danville Episcopalians were a building parish, always concerned with making the house of the Lord a proper place for worship. Soon after the organ was installed and paid for, they requested the Bishop to draw a "draught" of the cupola that was needed to complete the design of their church building. He did so competently and with great satisfaction, being, as one of the parishioners put it, "somewhat of an expert in that line and in making models, as guides in construction."[9] The money was contributed promptly, more than six hundred dollars, and the cupola was completed by the autumn of 1842, the bottom of it constructed of brick and the upper portion of frame. Not to be outdone in good works,

---

[8] *Journal of the Diocese of Kentucky* for 1857, p. 41. Two of M. F. Maury's sisters were married to his fellow seminarians: Sarah Anne to Edward F. Berkley, and Elizabeth A. to Francis B. Nash (Christ Church, Lexington Register of Marriages).

[9] "G.C." [George Cowan], "Reminiscences . . ."

the ladies raised funds to order a bell from Boston, and with a little cash left over they enclosed the front of the church with "a neat iron railing."

It is not surprising that B. B. Smith esteemed the Danville congregation. No phase of his ministry to his people brought him so close to them as his practical participation in the building and renovating of their churches. Beginning with his plans for the first small mission church at Frankfort, he took great interest in additions here in Danville and also in Paris, Lexington, Louisville, and parishes in the western part of the state. He made designs for chancel furniture and suggested workmen to carve baptismal fonts.[10] Later on he drew plans for excellent churches in Harrodsburg, Georgetown, Cynthiana, and Mt. Sterling, even carving a small-scale model for the Harrodsburg edifice.[11] Some of these products of his architectural taste and craftsmanship still remain, intact or incorporated into later structures, as monuments to Kentucky's first bishop.

The first decade of M. F. Maury's rectorship augmented the dignified position held by the Episcopalians among the several strong denominations in Danville. His Churchmanship conformed to the Virginia Evangelical school but without controversy. He and one or two lay delegates attended most of the conventions, but they seem to have taken no active part in the fortunes of Shelby College. Perhaps their pride in the local Presbyterian Centre College accounted for their lack of interest. About 1850 Maury's health became poor and he was compelled to spend several months in the warmer climate of Alabama. He tendered his resignation to the vestry in the spring of 1851 and received a letter that must have warmed his heart.

The Vestry of Trinity Church, Danville, would further report that the Parish is suffering materially from the want of a Pastor, and fully appreciating the past services of their beloved Rector, they would still indulge the hope, that it may comport with his plans and health, to continue among them, they having made no attempt to supply his place, as will appear from the following extract from the proceedings:

---

[10] B. B. Smith to Edward F. Berkley, October 28, 1848 (Berkley Letters, Filson Club).

[11] Neva A. Williams, *The History of St. Philip's Episcopal Church* (Harrodsburg, Kentucky, Historical Society, April, 1948), p. 5.

"On motion of the Secretary, it was *unanimously* Resolved, That the Vestry call the Rev. M. F. Maury again as Rector of this Parish; and in case he accepts the call, that the Vestry make arrangements with him so soon as he returns from the South, or so soon as his health is sufficiently restored again to take charge of the Parish."[12]

He agreed to this proposal and probably it was he who arranged for a substitute minister, the Reverend Thomas R. B. Trader, who took his place from June, 1852, to June, 1853. There is no record that Mr. Trader was formally transferred into the Diocese of Lexington, and M. F. Maury came home to his people in 1853 to spend the rest of his days among them, fulfilling his parochial duties to the limit of his precarious strength. For the most part his services were rendered gratuitously. Among the steadfast laymen who supported the work of the parish were Dr. Daniel Yeiser; three members of the Cowan family, H. J., George, and John; Alexander S. McGrorty; and George C. Shaeffer.

Because of his health Maury was unable to have any large share in the concerted movement of the parish rectors to establish missions in nearby communities. Nevertheless, he maintained contact through the years with the little group of Church people in and around Harrodsburg that had been hoping since the time of Gideon McMillan for a missionary to be sent to them. Harrodsburg and Danville being only about ten miles apart, it was natural that when the movement to organize a parish in Harrodsburg began to crystallize in 1857 the Trinity Church people shared their rector and lent their aid. The history of St. Philip's, Harrodsburg will be recounted in a later chapter, but its beginnings are closely related to the Episcopal group in Danville.

Toward the end of the Reverend Maury's ministry, on Ash Wednesday, February 22, 1860, Trinity Church was partially destroyed by a fire that all but wiped out the town. Scarcely anyone in the community escaped heavy losses. Yet early the following morning, even before estimating their personal misfortunes, the members of the vestry met in the churchyard and planned to rebuild at once on that same site. The Reverend Mr. Maury traveled widely over the south and east to seek aid for his parish and succeeded in

---

[12] *Journal of the Diocese of Kentucky* for 1851, p. 23.

obtaining generous contributions. An appeal in *The Churchman,* published in New York City, elicited the sum of $2,200.[13] On January 27, 1861, services were held for the first time in rebuilt Trinity Church. Plain and neat, without a font or an organ or a bell as yet, it stood once more in the heart of the town as a symbol of the stout parish about which Bishop Smith had written prophetically at the time of the cholera epidemic: ". . . in steadfast devotion to the best things it is behind none in the Diocese."[14]

ANTEBELLUM ST. PETER'S CHURCH, PARIS

In the slow but steady progress of the Episcopal Church in antebellum Kentucky, St. Peter's Church in Paris was an outstanding example of the small parish that continuingly reached out to found missions in its own area. One reason for this activity was the area itself. Bourbon County, of which Paris is the county seat, lies in the heart of the good "level land" that was settled early by large owners, so that by 1830 it was dotted with small towns and communities as well as many sizable country places. Paris, with a population of about 1,200, had a bank, a newspaper, private schools, and numerous churches—Methodist, Presbyterian, Baptist, and the new Disciples of Christ, all of which made it a center for people within a radius of thirty or forty miles, especially to the north and east. Amos Cleaver saw these advantages when he located his school here in 1831. Paris must have reminded him of the excellent provincial towns in his native England.

The remarkable Cleaver, a tall, black-bearded man of great physical energy, was another reason for the missionary zeal of the small group of Episcopalians he gathered in his mission. It has already been noted how he raised money on long preaching expeditions to the East, how he literally built some of the church, and how it was finally ready for consecration in 1838. What should also be emphasized is that he devoted at least half his clerical duties to preaching in the countryside and nearby towns. He was, meanwhile, support-

---

[13] J. Rice Cowan, "The Hundred Years of Trinity Parish," Danville, *Daily Messenger,* June 5, 1929. Also *Journal of the Diocese of Kentucky* for 1861, p. 41.
[14] *Journal of the Diocese of Kentucky* for 1833, p. 9.

ing his family by teaching. However modest the attendance might be in town, the "country stations" drew large congregations, and within five years two had become small missions, Christ Church, Leesburg and St. Mark's, Millersburg. Amos Cleaver was not only a teaching parson in the tradition of James Moore and John Ward; he seems to have been a good and convincing preacher, following modestly in the footsteps of the famous English clergyman, George Whitefield, and Bishop Ravenscroft. It is not surprising that he found ready hearers, for in Central Kentucky people liked powerful preaching.

The building of St. Peter's Church was a long process, in which the community shared. The lot on the courthouse square and adjacent to busy Duncan Tavern was donated by "a gentleman, formerly of the Episcopal Church." After the first funds were secured from donors in Paris and Lexington and the eastern cities there was a long spell of wintry weather when no building could be started and Cleaver could not ride out to his country stations. The townspeople must have watched with amazement as, in his own words, "I set about digging the foundation of the Church, and building a wall round the church-yard, which were completed by April, and at which, for economy's sake, I worked as the beloved Paul did, with my own hands."[15] He was assisted by his two sons and a hired Negro. When the cornerstone was laid in June, 1832, a large concourse of citizens witnessed the ceremony. When the completed edifice with its "classic porch" and "fine Corinthian columns"[16] was at last consecrated by Bishop Smith, St. Peter's took its place among the important churches of the town and county. Within a year an organ was "contracted for and sufficient money raised to pay for it when completed." Among the prominent laymen who represented St. Peter's at conventions during these early years were Jefferson Scott and James Arnold.

During the diocesan controversy of 1835–37, Amos Cleaver adhered to the position taken by the Cooke-Coit-Peers-Caswall party. He must have done so as a matter of principle, as he had no

---

[15] *Journal of the Diocese of Kentucky* for 1832, p. 9. The *Journals* from 1831 to 1857 furnish the information about Cleaver unless otherwise noted.
[16] "History of St. Peter's, Paris," *Diocesan News*, May, 1904.

personal stake in the quarrel and his parish apparently did not wish to become involved. It was generally understood that the vestry of St. Peter's sent Garnett Duncan, a Paris attorney, as their representative to the 1836 convention in the hope that he could effect a compromise. When the excellent compromise he brought about failed to prevent the final confrontation of the Bishop and his opponents the parishioners of St. Peter's had no further recorded share in the matter. In 1839 Cleaver was replaced as rector by a young seminary graduate from Massachusetts, the Reverend Francis Burdette Nash, who remained for about a year. Somewhat later another young clergyman, J. A. Shepherd, filled the place for a short time. Cleaver, residing in the town as a teacher, always filled in when needed for the services at St. Peter's. He moved to Louisville in the fall of 1843 to teach in a school for young ladies and to act as supply for Christ Church, Louisville and other parishes. In 1845 or early 1846 he removed to Mississippi, where he conducted a large Church school for girls in the environs of Jackson and acted as chaplain to the inmates of the penitentiary.[17]

With the departure of Amos Cleaver the early era of St. Peter's came to a close. He had left his imprint on the parish. Its commitment to nearby missions, its responsible financial policy of keeping out of debt, and its preference for rectors who were teachers or at least men of scholarly turn—these were characteristics developed during his years of devoted ministry. After he ceased to officiate actively the success of the nearby mission stations fluctuated. St. Mark's, Millersburg died out after the controversy of 1835–37, having been organized, apparently, for partisan reasons. Christ Church, Leesburg was for a brief time considered a promising mission and shared its rector with the mission at Cynthiana in an adjoining county.

In 1845 the Vestry of St. Peter's Church filled its vacant pulpit by calling the Reverend Green Grove Moore, one of the most extraordinary and energetic of the missionary priests in the early Kentucky Church. Having served as first rector of the new Episcopal church at Covington he was now engaged in literary projects and preach-

---

[17] Craik, *Historical Sketches of Christ Church, Louisville,* p. 99. Cleaver died of yellow fever in 1853.

ing missions. He preached several times at St. Peter's and impressed his hearers by his zeal and eloquence. In a letter dated January 23, 1845, calling him to become rector of the parish, the vestry offered him an initial salary of four hundred dollars from the pewholders, plus an allowance of two hundred from the General Missionary Society. Moore accepted on condition that he be allowed to complete his travels and studies and that his salary be paid quarterly.[18] In June, after the annual convention, he moved his wife and children to Paris and took active charge of the church.

The three years of his incumbency were profitable ones, and a modest gain in membership and contributions resulted. Chiefly, however, his labors bore fruit in new missions. In September, 1846, he held divine service in Maysville for a small, faithful group. He and the Reverend Mr. Berkley, of Lexington, were the chief organizers of the Church of the Nativity established there. In November of the same year Moore and Berkley together began holding regular monthly services for the small dedicated group at Cynthiana that soon organized the Church of the Advent. With the consent of the people of St. Peter's Moore served as rector for both the new missions, a generous contribution on their part. Throughout his ministry in Paris the Reverend G. G. Moore succeeded in involving the parish in the expansion of the Church northward to the Ohio River and in bringing its leading laymen back into the councils of the Diocese. In February, 1848, he returned to Covington as rector of Trinity Church.

The town of Paris and the surrounding countryside, meanwhile, were becoming more prosperous and cultured at this period. It is not surprising that St. Peter's parishioners were pleased with their next rector, Deacon Horace Hill Reid, a well educated young man from the Diocese of New York. He likewise was pleased and reported that he found his new charge excellent "both in a spiritual and temporal point of view." During his stay the chancel of the church was enlarged and improved, with the addition of "chaste and beautiful Font, the gift of a lady of the Parish." The improve-

[18] Vestry of St. Peter's Parish to G. G. Moore, January 23, 1845, and G. G. Moore to the vestry of St. Peter's Parish, February n.d., 1845 (Archives of the Diocese of Lexington, University of Kentucky Library).

ments were assuredly completed in time for Mr. Reid's ordination
to the priesthood on May 27, 1849, a ceremony most gratifying to
the people of St. Peter's. It was the first time they had seen their
rector ordained before their own altar. His congregations were large
as they were also at Cynthiana for his semi-monthly services there.
The ladies at Paris raised more than five hundred dollars with a
Fair, and the money was given for the purchase of a lot on which to
erect a rectory. It was a real disappointment when Mr. Reid departed to Connecticut at the end of a year.

The next rector called by the Paris church was the Reverend Tobias H. Michell, M.D., from the Diocese of Pennsylvania, who had
been practicing medicine for about a year in the nearby town of
Winchester. His five years at St. Peter's were a time of retrenchment,
partly in order to pay off debts previously incurred and also because
of a "migration" to the new West such as frequently occurred in
early American communities. There is no record of any missionary
activity by Dr. Michell but he was a diligent shepherd of his own
flock and a respected schoolmaster in the town. The new parishes at
Maysville and Cynthiana were being served by various clergy in the
area. Prominent laymen of St. Peter's at this time were Jefferson
Scott, Dr. Henry Hopson, Jacob Spears, and Robert Davis.

St. Peter's Church reached a high point during the incumbency
of its next rector, the Reverend John Austen Merrick, D.Ph., who
entered upon his duties on the Third Sunday in Advent, December
17, 1854. He came from the Diocese of Pennsylvania, already an
ordained priest and dedicated to the frequent celebration of the
Holy Eucharist and the observance of the chief Holy Days of the
Church.[19] The parish had never before had a rector who possessed
his qualifications or who devoted himself so completely to his
parochial duties. The response was immediate. Within six months
Merrick could report to the annual convention that his parish had
paid their assessment for the support of the episcopate, repaired the
organ, bought books and magazines for the Sunday school, as well
as other contributions. Most significant was the attendance at Holy
Communion and the "devout reverence" at all the frequent services.

[19] See John A. Merrick's detailed parochial reports in *Journal of the Diocese of
Kentucky*, 1855–1863.

The rural Gothic Church of the Ascension, Mt. Sterling, erected in 1878 on site of an earlier building. *Archives of the parish.*

All Saints' Church, Flemingsburg, begun in 1860, sold in 1888. The building is now used for commercial purposes. *Courtesy of the Bishop of Lexington.*

Old Mason County Court House, Washington, where services of the Church of the Epiphany were conducted (1848–1857). *Courtesy of J. Winston Coleman, Jr.*

The Church of the Nativity, Maysville, as built in 1850. *Archives of the parish.*

St. Paul's Church, Newport, erected in 1870 on the site of the first building of 1844. *Archives of the parish.*

Trinity Church, Covington, "completely renovated and greatly enlarged" in 1886, with brick bell tower and round baptistry tower added. *Archives of the parish.*

The Church of the Advent, Cynthiana,
as built in 1855. *Archives of the parish.*

St. John's Church, Versailles, as built in 1885
on site of the first church building of 1851.
Archives of the parish.

St. Philip's Church, Harrodsburg, as built in
1861. *Courtesy of the Reverend John S. Akers.*

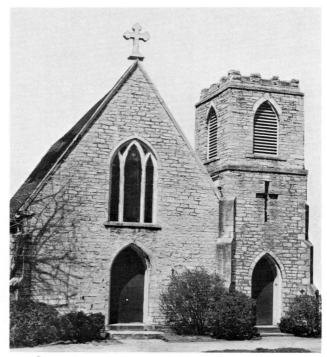

Holy Trinity Church, Georgetown, as built in
1869. *Courtesy of J. Winston Coleman, Jr.*

The Reverend Edward Fairfax Berkley, Rector of Christ Church, Lexington (1839–1858). *Archives of the Diocese of Lexington.*

Henry and Lucretia Hart Clay on their fiftieth wedding anniversary, April 11, 1849. *Courtesy of Mrs. H. Clay Brock.*

Christ Church, Lexington, completed in 1848 during the Berkley era, is the fourth building on the same site. *Archives of the parish.*

The missionary effort in the nearby area was now made in Mt. Sterling, an excellent town over in Montgomery County. "Uphill work," the new rector called it, but he must have been effective, as a parish was formed there about three years later. Meanwhile he preached also at Millersburg and Blue Licks, a community to the north at the site of the last battle fought during the American Revolution.

John Merrick's labors were prodigious. He was keenly aware of the needs of the national Church and the Diocese as well as those of his own parish, and he increasingly broadened the horizons of the parishioners of St. Peter's. Beginning at home, they got completely out of debt, and in 1857 by voluntary offerings rearranged "the choral and ecclesiological ordering of the Church (involving) an ample chancel arrangement, the removal of the organ from the loft-gallery to the choir, a proper communion Table, with its credence, an octagonal Font of stone, an Episcopal chair, with its sedilia, and a mural tablet to the memory of the martyr-founder of the parish, Amos Cleaver, who had died in 1853." All this was with the Bishop's approval, and it may be assumed that it was also with his consent that the seats in the church were "made free to all persons, at all times, without distinction or difference." The women organized a Parish-aid Association to visit the sick, poor, and ignorant. Especial attention was given to the Sunday school children, including the colored pupils, who by 1857 numbered 57 out of a total of 124 enrolled. "Colored servants" were baptized and confirmed in modest numbers.

The prosperous people of St. Peter's began to give to western missions. In 1857, for example, they sent $17.00 to Bishop Kemper's Nashota Mission in Wisconsin, and $30.00 to the Minnesota Missions "in part for the support of a Chippewa child named John Austen Merrick . . . he being the first baptized at Kesahgah Mission." Nor did the parish forget its domestic missionary commitments. In 1859 it gave $60.00 to the Mt. Sterling congregation for a melodeon, and $81.00 to Cynthiana for a surplice and other aid. By now its rector was preaching from time to time in Winchester and Carlisle, as well as Mt. Sterling and Millersburg.

The end of the antebellum period found St. Peter's, Paris, with 58

communicants and their families. Its achievements under John Austen Merrick were outstanding, even in an Era of Missionary-Rec-
tors.

ANTEBELLUM CHURCH OF THE ASCENSION, FRANKFORT

In 1829, when the Diocese of Kentucky was organized, Frankfort,
the capital of the Commonwealth, was a crowded community of
2000 inhabitants nestled on the banks of the Kentucky River beneath high limestone cliffs. Situated on the way west from Lexington to Louisville, it was geographically and culturally a part of the
bluegrass area. The neat little eighteenth century town encompassed
the Capitol grounds, where a beautiful building of "Kentucky marble" in classic style had just been completed during the year. A score
of handsome residences were located near the river. Hotels and inns
abounded, for Frankfort "lived on the Legislature" during the
winter, as the saying went.[20] In addition, it was a prosperous commercial and manufacturing center, with numerous factories and a
brisk steamboat trade with Louisville. By this date there were
churches of many denominations: Presbyterian, Baptist, Methodist,
Disciples, and Roman Catholic.

The desirability of establishing an Episcopal Church in Frankfort
was apparent to Bishop Smith at least as early as the winter of
1833–1834, when he spent considerable time there securing the
incorporation of the seminary by the legislature. He preached there,
as he had done with Bishop Meade in 1831, and visited with the few
Church families in the community, including that of John Harris
Hanna, a successful lawyer, banker, and millowner from Pennsylvania. The following year, during Smith's long stay in the east, he
so roused the ladies of the Church of the Ascension in New York by
his pleas for Kentucky missions that they donated one thousand
dollars for a "revolving fund" to aid in the erection of new church
buildings. While still in New York he seems to have decided to

[20] Richard Lightbourne McCready, *The Church of the Ascension, Frankfort,
Kentucky* (Privately printed, 1939), p. 6 and ff. See L. F. Johnson, *History of
Franklin County, Kentucky* (Frankfort, Ky.: 1912), especially Chapter XVI,
"Churches in Franklin County"; and Willard Rouse Jillson, *Literary Haunts and
Personalities of Old Frankfort* (Frankfort, Ky.: 1941).

allocate the loan first to Frankfort. He brought back with him young William Purviance, a teacher and a worker in the Ascension Sunday school, whom he accepted as a candidate for Holy Orders and located in Frankfort to start a mission. Purviance supported himself by teaching in an academy, along with B. B. Sayre, another candidate. In 1836 a group of eight communicants organized informally, and a lot on Washington Street was purchased for $600. A contract was immediately let for a small frame church, modeled on the Greek temple style of the Church of the Ascension in New York, for which the new mission was named. Unfortunately, the cost was more than twice the "revolving fund" plus local contributions. Purviance went back to New York in the midst of the controversy of 1836–1837, and the little congregation dissolved. The property was sold for debt, but it was bought in by John Hanna, who eventually deeded it to the parish. In 1837, after the trial was over, the determined group of Episcopalians welcomed another young minister, Willard Presbury (Presbry, Presby), a student at the seminary from Dartmouth College, whom the Bishop ordained as deacon in the little mission church on November 17, 1837. Presbury soon organized the vestry and started the parish records and attempted to straighten out the parish's financial affairs. His wardens were O. G. Cates and M. Barstow; the lay delegate to the convention was O. H. P. Anderson. Other families entered in the parish register are those of "Dr. Lloyd, Mr. Stealey, Mr. Hanna, Mr. Lemuel Stoughton, and Mr. Charles Morehead." These efforts inspired a subscription of five hundred dollars for the purchase of an organ, said to have been the first in Frankfort. The rector's salary, however, was so small that he continued to teach in order to support his family. He had married, soon after becoming rector, Margaret Penny, a well-bred young Englishwoman residing in Louisville, whose sister was Edward Winthrop's wife. There is a touch of pathos in successive entries in the Old Register of Christ Church, Lexington: the marriage of Edward Winthrop to Marion Penny on August 3, 1837; the marriage of Willard "Presby" to Margaret Penny on February 1, 1838; the death of Marion on May 7, 1838; and an entry for July 6, 1839: "Sarah, daughter of the Reverend Willard and Margaret Presby, died in Frankfort, buried in Lexington on the Reverend John Ward's lot." The Presburys departed from the Church of the Ascension in Frankfort on July 11 to Ohio, overwhelmed perhaps by their sorrow. He had rendered a real service to the new parish.[21]

For the next seven years the stouthearted people of Ascension persevered in their determination to free their church building from debt and to beautify it. By 1842 the debt was lifted, thanks to a thousand dollars from John Hanna and substantial aid from Louisville and Lexington. "The Church was carpeted throughout, whitewashed, partially painted and furnished with lamps, and two valuable air-tight stoves. A lady in Louisville presented a pair of elegant branch candlesticks for the pulpit."[22] That summer, shortly after the annual convention, the church was consecrated, bringing great credit to A. F. Dobb, the young clergyman who was ministering to the growing congregation at that time. Dobb left, however, after a short stay, as did three other young clergymen who succeeded him and the parish lost ground. At the annual convention of 1846 the lay delegate from Ascension, H. I. Bodley, read a discouraging parochial report from his parish, which had been without a rector for eight months. The new organ and the air-tight stoves and even the elegant branch candlesticks had not enabled the Church of the Ascension to seize the opportunities awaiting it in the capital city.

The efforts of the past decade were not in vain, however. In December the parish called another new rector, the Reverend John Nicholas Norton, a twenty-six year old native of the New York Lake Country, graduate of Hobart College and the General Seminary, and but lately ordained to the priesthood by Bishop DeLancey of the Diocese of Western New York. Descended from Virginia families who settled along the lakes after the Revolution, he was the son of the Reverend George H. Norton, an early, much-loved frontier missionary. He was also related to Judge George Nicholas, early

[21] Willard Presbury returned to Kentucky to serve at Elizabethtown and at Paducah; he went to Mississippi in 1860. See *Journal of the Diocese of Kentucky* for 1844, 1845, 1856, 1857, 1860.
[22] *Journal of the Diocese of Kentucky* for 1842, p. 18, Parochial Report of the Reverend A. F. Dobb, Rector of Church of the Ascension. He went to Ohio in July, 1842, and thence to Alabama. He served in the Confederate P.E.C. Back in Kentucky in 1868, he died at Lexington in 1869.

jurist and statesman in Kentucky. John Norton's boyhood in villages along the Erie Canal where his father's parishes were located was a factor in his choice of the priesthood and his lifelong missionary zeal.[23]

He was a student at the General Theological Seminary from 1843 to 1845 at the height of the excitement there over the publication of the Oxford Movement tracts. Like most of the students, he was stirred and influenced by the tracts. He must have been acquainted with Arthur Carey, the seminarian whose views made his ordination by Bishop Onderdonk of New York the center of the controversy between the High Church and Low Church factions. Norton's views were already influenced by the High Church tradition of the Diocese of Western New York as interpreted by Bishop DeLancey in his famous article, "What Is *Not* Puseyism" (1843).[24] This classic statement affirmed that long before the Oxford Movement the American High Churchman had believed in certain catholic truths: episcopacy, apostolic succession, the inward grace of the sacraments, both the "real" and the "spiritual" presence of Christ in the sacraments, baptismal regeneration, and the rest of his twenty-two points. DeLancy's affirmation was very like the substance of Chapman's *Sermons,* and it is interesting to note that Chapman's book was used in western New York at that time to defend the Anglican faith.[25] This catholic doctrine, set forth by Hobart and Chapman and DeLancy, was the faith of the slender, gaunt young Norton when he accepted the call to Frankfort, and to it he adhered for the rest of his life.

Just why John Nicholas Norton came to Kentucky is obscure. After his graduation from the seminary in New York City he

[23] For George H. Norton see Charles Welles Hayes, *The Diocese of Western New York: History and Recollections* (Rochester, N.Y.: 1904), pp. 31–33, 66. For John Nicholas Norton see *In Memoriam. Rev. John Nicholas Norton D.D. Late Associate Rector of Christ Church, Louisville* (Louisville, Ky.: 1891); Richard Lightburne McCready, *The Church of the Ascension, Frankfort, Kentucky* (Privately printed, 1939), pp. 19–37. Also John Nicholas Norton, *Allerton Parish,* a thinly disguised account of Allen's Hill, one of his father's parishes.

[24] Published in *Gospel Messenger* (1843) and recapitulated in Hayes, *op. cit.,* 166–167; also George E. DeMille, *The Catholic Movement in the American Episcopal Church,* p. 52. See also E. Clowes Chorley, "The Oxford Movement in the Seminary," *Historical Magazine of the Episcopal Church,* V (1936), pp. 177–201.

[25] Hayes, *op. cit.,* p. 45.

served at St. Luke's Church in Rochester as assistant to the Reverend Thomas C. Pitkin, formerly at Christ Church, Louisville. Norton also was related to the influential Nicholas family of Lexington and Louisville. He was primarily attracted to the West, however, as his father had been, by the call for priests on the Church's frontier. With no private means to supplement a precarious salary, he was clearly free from any selfish ambition when he accepted the call to minister to a small parish whose pulpit had been vacant for nearly a year.

In reality, the people of Ascension Church were ready for a dedicated leader, and the new rector wasted no time. His parochial report to the convention of 1847 shows remarkable achievement in a period of six months. He knew precisely the statistics of his parish: families, 20; adults, 51; children, 47. He had preached 39 times, lectured 24 times, and officiated 50 times at sessions of the legislature. The church had been open for services on Christmas Eve, Christmas, Ash Wednesday, and Good Friday, with four meetings during Passion Week. Among contributions listed were: $24.25 for domestic missions, $5.00 for Bishop Kemper's Nashota Mission in remote Wisconsin that had been founded by three High Churchmen whom he had known at the General Theological Seminary, and $13.00 for "Jew's Chapel in New York."

At this same diocesan convention, he made the proposal that the rules recently prepared by the House of Bishops "for the proper postures to be used in the communion office, with a view of effecting uniformity" be entered in the *Journal of the Diocese of Kentucky*. Thus early he identified himself as a High Churchman in his new Diocese.

The annual report for 1848 from the Church of the Ascension was even better. It listed sixty baptisms, a third of them colored children; twelve persons confirmed; Divine Service celebrated 126 times; 119 sermons preached; 59 lectures delivered on Fridays and Holy Days; Holy Communion 14 times; 30 legislatures; and a monthly appointment at the penitentiary. Contributions increased threefold, including a new bell for the church. Most significant of all was Norton's prompt response to the Resolution of 1847 regarding domestic missions. He had made two long trips to Maysville to preach to the little group of Episcopalians N. N. Cowgill had found some years earlier. Five times he had been to Georgetown, chief town in adjacent Scott County, where four loyal communicants attended services by a lay reader each Sunday. Even oftener he had preached in Versailles, another fine little county seat halfway between Frankfort and Lexington. Here he and Edward Berkley had so encouraged the six communicants and their families that a parish had been organized the previous June. Meanwhile, his own people were supporting two parish schools in which 60 poor children were "taught gratuitously, the ordinary English branches, and carefully trained up in the Church's ways."

Ascension's original little frame "greek temple" church was the scene of the 1949 Annual Convention of the Diocese. It is a famous meeting, in part because the Honorable Henry Clay was a lay delegate from Christ Church, Lexington. He had recently been baptized and confirmed. The distinguished statesman entered into the proceedings of the small assembly with the same interest that he was to manifest a few months later in the United States Senate on behalf of his great compromise, and he was elected a lay delegate to the forthcoming General Convention. Ascension's report was again one to be proud of, even in the presence of the distinguished Mr. Clay. All the projects previously reported were flourishing, especially the two parish schools, and a special Friday evening service for colored persons was being held during the winter months. Norton's concern for the colored people, especially children, of Frankfort was in accord with Bishop Smith's longstanding practices, as well as those of other parishes in the Diocese.

In midsummer of the next year the cornerstone was laid for a handsome new Church of the Ascension, entirely the gift of John H. Hanna, which was located near the original one. The Bishop once more exercised his talent for designing ecclesiastical architecture and furnished the plan, together with a wooden model for the new structure. This he did in accord with the wishes of the donor, who had made a special trip to Europe in order to study suitable styles for the building and its furnishings. Dr. Craik, with whom Norton had been warmly congenial ever since their coming into the Diocese at so nearly the same time, was named the preacher for the occasion. Even more elaborate was the consecration of the beautiful Gothic church on August 12, 1852.[26] It seemed ample for the nearly 150 communicants and other persons who flocked to the services "twice every Sunday, once on all Fridays, and on the greater Fasts and Feasts," but it was soon too small for the congregations that increased steadily throughout the years of Norton's rectorship. It was at one time the largest parish in the Diocese.

In 1851 the strain of Norton's tireless labors compelled him to call an assistant, Deacon John W. Venable, a scholarly artist who had become a candidate for Holy Orders after being one of the laymen who organized the parish at Covington a decade earlier. Venable soon took charge of the services at Versailles and shared the missionary preaching at Georgetown, Bridgeport, and the Kentucky Military Institute located near Frankfort. In 1855 Norton married Mary Louisa Sutton, daughter of a wealthy Lexington manufacturer. She joined in his concern for people in every walk in life. Their charities ranged from large endowments to the very coins in his pockets, which he emptied each day for the cripples or paupers or children whom he met.

In the midst of all his commitments to his parish and diocese, Norton found time to publish regularly in the Church journals and to write books widely circulated throughout the country. Sermons, some of the best of them written for children; a series of lives of Anglican bishops, including those of Alexander Griswold, John Stark Ravenscroft, Thomas J. Claggett, and other early leaders in the American Church; and several semi-autobiographical narratives. *Rockford Parish* (1856) is a thinly disguised account of his Frankfort experiences. He preached very informally, often extemporaneously, with anecdotes and examples from everyday life. His literary style is cultivated and agreeable.

So satisfactory was the condition of the Church of the Ascension in the spring of 1860 that the Reverend Mr. Norton and his wife made a journey to Europe for his first vacation in nearly fourteen years. Deacon Henry Martyn Frost, his assistant, diligently served the 223 communicants under the watchful eyes of a vestry that

---

[26] McCready, *op. cit.,* pp. 25–26.

included John Hanna, W. P. Loomis, Michael Barstow, George W. Doxon, William B. Holeman, and Colonel E. W. Morgan, Superintendent of the Kentucky Military Institute. The parish school was flourishing. The parish library numbered 409 volumes. The Orphans Home, established two years before, sheltered twelve little girls. The rector had earned a vacation.

By the time the Nortons returned to America, Abraham Lincoln had been elected to the presidency and war clouds were gathering over the nation. The Ascension parishioners and their rector would respond to the challenge of the troubled sixties by even better achievements in the community and the Diocese.

10 Antebellum Expansion Along the Upper Ohio

THE NEWPORT—COVINGTON AREA

The northernmost "Point" of Kentucky projects up into the state of Ohio exactly where on the Kentucky side the Licking River flows into "La Belle Riviere" that divides the two states. At this strategic location history was made in the pioneer days. Here, in the summer of 1780, George Rogers Clark's companies of "good Woodsmen armed with good rifles" gathered to launch their expedition against the Piqua Shawnees. At the close of the Revolution settlers located near the Point, first on the Kentucky shore below the mouth of the Licking at Kennedy's Ferry. Then a village was established over on the Ohio side that was first called Losantiville, but soon renamed Cincinnati. About 1790 a few cabins were erected on the Kentucky side, east of the Licking, where General James Taylor from Virginia had extensive holdings. In 1794 the part of Kentucky in the "bulge" behind the Point became Campbell County, and the next year the town of Newport was founded on Taylor land near the Point. The town of Covington was settled in 1815 on approximately the site of the old ferry.

Cincinnati, favored with a fine harbor for steamboats, soon became one of the important cities on the Ohio, ranking with Pittsburgh and Louisville. The towns across the river grew more slowly, but from the first were closely related to the economic and social life of the Ohio side. Newport acquired a church in 1806, a library in 1815, a bank in 1819, and another library in 1832, Covington began a little later but grew more rapidly, with a log schoolhouse as early as 1819, a banking institution in 1821, a newspaper in 1831, churches almost from its beginning, and a Baptist Theological Institute by 1834. June 1835 saw the beginnings of the Covington, Georgetown and Lexington Turnpike Company that would in time connect the Point towns with the communities in the central part of the state.[1]

In addition to being thriving commercial communities, the Kentucky towns were a pleasant residential area for many citizens whose business interests were located in Cincinnati. By the mid-twenties a steam ferry across the Ohio and a rope ferry over the Licking afforded convenient public transportation that linked the three towns and made them in effect a single widespread community. Visitors noted the beautiful residences on the wooded hills across the river, and some of them took passage on the steam ferry to explore the United States Arsenal grounds in Newport or stroll the streets of Covington, which were "so laid out as to appear a continuation of Cincinnati."

Newport and Covington people not only shopped in Cincinnati but often attended church there. After the founding in 1817 of Christ Church, Cincinnati, the first Episcopal parish in the city, the Churchmen on the Kentucky side looked to it for contact with their own communion. The name of General James Taylor of Newport, along with that of William Henry Harrison, appears on the list of vestrymen who gathered on Easter Monday, March 23, 1818, to welcome the parish's first rector, the Reverend Samuel Johnston. In 1828, after a successful decade at Christ Church, Samuel Johnston led more than half of its parishioners in a movement to leave it and found a second church called St. Paul's. This was accomplished, apparently, without discord, and the Kentuckians tended to follow the popular Mr. Johnston to St. Paul's.[2] He was invited by Dr. Chapman to attend the organizing convention of the Diocese of Kentucky in 1829, and so was present at that historic meeting in July at Christ Church, Lexington. It is recorded in the minutes that he "was admitted an honorary member of the Convention, and he took his seat accordingly." He thus became the first of the many Ohio clergymen who have shared the concerns of the Church in northern Kentucky.

_____

[1] Collins, *History of Kentucky,* Vol. II, articles on Campbell and Kenton counties. Also Helen Bradley Lindsey, "Early Days in Campbell County," *Kentucky Historical Society Register,* Vol. 36, pp. 35ff.; Harry W. Stevens, *Six Twenty; Margaretta Hunt; and the Baker-Hunt Foundation* (Covington, Ky.: 1942), *passim.,* and *Kenton County Centennial, 1940* (privately printed pamphlet).

[2] William Henry Venable, *A Centennial History of Christ Church, Cincinnati* (Cincinnati: 1918), *passim.*

TRINITY CHURCH, COVINGTON

The prime mover in gathering the Episcopalians of Covington for services in their own community was Dr. Thomas Bird, an energetic Englishman of about thirty, who was partner in the town's drugstore on Lower Market Corner. There must have been numerous meetings before January, 1842, at which time he wrote to Bishop Smith calling attention to the need for a missionary in the town. The Bishop's reply, dated February 25, expresses his long-standing interest in the Covington area, which he had visited frequently, and then makes suggestions for Bird's further endeavors. Sometime during the following May, just before the diocesan convention, the Bishop paid a visit to Covington in response to Dr. Bird's appeal. On May 7 he endorsed a lay reader's license which Bishop McIlvaine of Ohio had issued to G. G. Moore, thereby authorizing Moore to officiate in Kentucky also. The next day Bishop Smith conducted evening prayer services in Covington for a small group that included five communicants and other interested persons. The following Sunday Moore began holding regular morning and evening services, plus Thursday evening lectures, in a schoolroom on Madison Street. The group soon secured a more adequate room on the third floor of a building on the "Market Space."[3]

G. G. (Green Grove) Moore was a Methodist minister of fourteen years' standing, who came to Cincinnati about 1838 from Maine with his wife, Violette Woodward, a native of Middlebury, Vermont, and their young family. Invigorated by the new city's lively interest in culture, he edited and published a monthly magazine, titled *The Rose of the Valley; or a Flower of the West,* that lasted at least during the year 1839. He also read a course of

---

[3] The many sources for the early history of Trinity Church, Covington include: Parish Records; and parochial reports in *Journals of the Diocese of Kentucky* for 1843ff. Also *Annals of Trinity Episcopal Parish, Covington, Kentucky, from the Parish Registers* (Covington, Ky.: 1917); Harry W. Stevens, *op.cit.,* pp. 1–11 *et passim.;* R. Grattan Noland, "History of Trinity Church," MS in Archives of Diocese of Lexington, University of Kentucky Library. Also John W. Venable to Frederick P. Wolcott, March 29, 1892; Melville M. Moore to Frederick P. Wolcott, June 1, 1892 (Archives of Diocese of Lexington).

theology that induced him to apply to Bishop McIlvaine for a license as a lay reader on February 2, 1842.

The unorganized group of Episcopalians attended Lay Reader Moore's services faithfully for the six months before he was ordained deacon by Bishop McIlvaine at Chillicothe, Ohio, on November 13, 1842. Deacon Moore lost no time in meeting his new responsibilities. The organizing meeting of the parish of Trinity Church, Covington, was held on November 24, with fourteen persons in attendance. Elected to the vestry were: George W. Southgate, senior warden, Jackson Sparrow, junior warden, John K. McNickle, treasurer, John W. Venable, secretary, Charles A. Withers, J. L. Newby, J. W. Clayton, John W. Stevenson, and Dr. Thomas Bird. Others present were William J. Brockenbrough, James Clayton, D. Clayton, M. L. Littlefield, Ellen Sparrow, and Eliza Mildtead. John W. Stevenson was not present at the meeting, but his well-known loyalty to the Church made his election appropriate. Two days later the newly elected vestry formally called Deacon Moore to become their rector. Everybody in the new parish set about furnishing their third-story meeting room more fittingly and organizing a choir and a Sunday school.

No member of the organizing group was more serviceable than John Wesley Venable, a young Cincinnati artist and art teacher who was residing in Covington. A charming account of those early days was his contribution to the parish's Fiftieth Anniversary Celebration. He wrote: "It was my privilege to serve . . . in various ways . . . the male element being small . . . as vestryman, Sunday School teacher, member of the choir, and lay reader in the absence of the rector. Artists being proverbially poor I had nothing to give but my services." He subsequently became an Episcopal priest, the first of Trinity's many sons who have become candidates for Holy Orders.

The dedicated little parish felt keenly the need for a "convenient church edifice," all the more so when the ordination of its rector to the priesthood on November 5 had to be held in the Covington Baptist Church. A subscription of a thousand dollars was raised locally, and Moore made a trip east to raise money that netted little above his expenses. Nevertheless, the cornerstone for the first Trin-

ity "church edifice" was laid on June 24, 1843, and almost exactly a
year later services were held in it. That summer the ladies of the
parish gave a very successful concert and tea party to raise funds,
welcoming many guests who ferried over from Cincinnati for the
occasion. From the beginning the women of Trinity were active.
An example of their loyalty took place some years later when,
during a financial difficulty, they independently pledged four
hundred dollars "to be raised by their own efforts."

From mid-April, 1844, to the end of that year the Reverend Mr.
Moore's activities in northern Kentucky were expanded. At that
time the Episcopalians in Newport organized St. Paul's Church and
proposed that it "unite" with Trinity in sharing the services of its
rector. The proposal met with the approval of both parishes and of
Mr. Moore, whereupon he worked diligently with the Newport
people to get their parish started. He made a valuable contribution
to both parishes in their period of organization, but, being a man of
many interests, he resigned both posts in October for a new venture.

The Reverend Green Grove Moore was an unusual sort of clergyman. Intelligent, adventurous, and undoubtedly somewhat domi-
neering, he ministered to five parishes in Kentucky while exerting
considerable influence in other localities. To offset the persistent
idea that early Episcopal clergymen were less vigorous than the
circuit riders of other denominations, his report to the 1845 convention deserves to be recorded.

The subscriber reports that having resigned the Rectorship of the joint
parishes of Covington and Newport, which took effect on the first of
October, he has since been engaged in publishing the celebrated "Letters
of certain Jews to Voltaire." During the progress of this work, he has
delivered 11 sermons in Newport, 2 in Frankfort, 3 in Lexington, 4 in
Danville, 2 in Madison, Ia., 1 on Steam Boat ascending the Mississippi, 1
in St. Louis, 2 in Quincy, Ill., 2 in Portsmouth, Ohio, 1 in Christ Church,
Cincinnati, and 5 in St. Peter's Church, Paris. Having accepted a call to
this parish, he expects to enter upon his labors there immediately after the
present Convention rises.

The neat manuscripts of two of the sermons G. G. Moore used on
this journey have been preserved: "The Excellency of the Scrip-

tures" (12 times) and "Change of Heart" (6 times). Both were delivered at St. Peter's, and it may have been their evangelical earnestness that prompted the parish's call to him.[4]

Moore's rectorship of more than three years at Paris was marked by his missionary efforts in that area. Meanwhile, the new parishes at Covington and Newport had the services for about a year of the Reverend Edward Lounsbury, a young missionary from Ohio, and at other times had no rector. In February, 1848, as suddenly as he had departed, G. G. Moore returned to the rectorship of the two churches at the Point. He established his now sizable family in Covington in a large house opposite the church. There he opened a Young Ladies Seminary, meanwhile performing the duties connected with the two parishes. The school evidently did not prosper, and in addition Moore was not suited for the tedious task of paying Trinity's building debt. After a year he elected to go out to the western country he had visited a few years earlier, and accepted a missionary post with the hard-pressed little church at Smithland. Very soon after reaching there he died of a sudden illness and so never entered into this "new field of duty for which he seemed peculiarly fitted," as the Bishop said in a moving eulogy to him at the next diocesan convention.

The activities of Trinity parish during these early years were mostly bound up with the struggle to pay off the debt incurred in erecting its excellent brick church in 1844. According to parish tradition, Dr. Bird, who had first proposed the plan for the building, mortgaged his own home in 1848 to prevent the sale of the church by the sheriff. In spite of these financial burdens, the corporate life of the church was sound. It provided fellowship for its 24 communicants and their families, for 45 children in the Sunday school, and for "respectable congregations."

At this time the parishes in Covington and Newport discontinued the practice of sharing the services of one rector. After consulting the Bishop, the vestry of Trinity called the Reverend Mason Gallagher of the Diocese of New York. He was the second of three

---

[4] These two sermons are preserved in the Archives of the Diocese of Lexington, University of Kentucky Library. The present writers have not been able to authenticate the publication of Moore's edition of "Letters . . . to Voltaire."

priestly brothers from a prominent family in Geneva, New York, and was a graduate of Hobart College. His older brother, the Reverend John B. Gallagher, was at this time rector of St. Paul's, Louisville, having succeeded the beloved William Jackson.[5] As Trinity's first full-time rector, Mason Gallagher increased the church's stature in the community and the Diocese. He added dignity and ceremony to the services, and the church acquired a bell. In spite of a cholera epidemic in the area, he increased the number of communicants and decreased the size of the church debt. His distinguished brother having died in 1849, he resigned in 1851 to return to New York.

The new rector in December of that year was Deacon William Newton, a Shelby College theological student from Pennsylvania. He was loved by his parishioners and was ordained priest in their midst. Pledges were made to pay off the debt, and improvements were made in the church interior, where a marble font, a handsome set of lamps, new reading desks, and a new chancel were installed. The walls and pews were painted, all in a fashionable shade of blue.

After promising Mr. Newton went back to Pennsylvania the parish had several rectors who served even shorter terms. First came the Reverend William F. Bryant, of New Jersey, under whom the Sunday school passed the one hundred mark. In December, 1857, the Reverend Hodges from the Diocese of Maryland became the incumbent, and six months later was able to report that prospects were "flattering" and contributions to both domestic and foreign missions were generous. Trinity Church was indeed a "sunny spot in the Diocese," as Bishop Smith had called it in a recent convention address. The town of Covington was thriving, with nearly fifteen thousand inhabitants. The original parishioners, still loyal in their support, were now augmented by new members, many of them prominent in civic and business circles. Thus in 1857 Dr. Bird was still senior warden and Jackson Sparrow served as a lay delegate to the diocesan convention. John W. Stevenson, recently elected to the United States Congress, was still an active Churchman, both in Trinity and at the diocesan level. So likewise were M. M. Benton,

[5] Charles Wells Hayes, *The Diocese of Western New York* (Rochester, N.Y.: 1904), p. 168 footnote.

who had been Covington's first mayor, and John W. Baker, a successful Cincinnati merchant who moved his family residence to Covington in 1854 and shortly thereafter became a member and then a vestryman and warden of Trinity Church.

The last of Trinity's succession of ministers during the fifties was Dr. Thomas N. Ralston, a very able convert from the Methodist faith, who took up his duties in August, 1858, only a few weeks after his ordination to the diaconate by Bishop Smith. Within less than a year the number of communicants increased to 100 and the total congregation numbered 390. The vestry announced with pardonable pride to the parish: "The present is an interesting and important crisis in the history of our church. It has now become necessary to enlarge our accommodations. We have numerous applications for pews and sittings which we cannot accommodate." By the end of another year two lots adjacent to the church were purchased; the church building was enlarged; the total cost was paid off; and on March 1, 1860, Trinity Church was at long last consecrated.[6] Later that year, Dr. Ralston returned to the Methodist ministry, with no hard feelings between him and Trinity parish. His successor, Dr. Charles George Currie, who had been officiating in Cincinnati, came in September, 1860, to begin a memorable rectorship of eight years that spanned the difficult war period. An eloquent preacher and much loved pastor, he kept his parish united. In the account of the Church in Kentucky during the war, Dr. Currie and Trinity Church figure prominently.

ST. PAUL'S CHURCH, NEWPORT

Both Newport and Covington flourished during the decade of the forties, more than doubling their population. In 1840 the Legislature of the Commonwealth created the new county of Kenton, with Covington as its principal community, leaving Newport as the principal town of Campbell County. Rivalry between the towns

[6] *Journal of the Diocese of Kentucky* for 1860, p. 31: "No doubt attended the question of the consecration of Trinity Church, Covington, since the old portion of the Church had never been consecrated, in consequence of the pressure of a debt which had long crippled the growth of the parish . . ."

increased, so that each wished to have its own institutions. Within a year after the admission of Trinity Church, Covington, into the Diocese the Episcopalians in Newport began to organize a parish. Its beginnings were independent of the Covington group and different in procedure. The Church-minded people in Newport were counseled and ministered to in the beginning by the Reverend Nicholas Hamner Cobbs, rector of St. Paul's Church, Cincinnati, a newcomer from the Diocese of Virginia. He was a tall, spare man of saintly mien, a great preacher and a zealous missionary. He may well have suggested to the Newport people who attended his services that they form their own parish.

Dr. Cobbs was present at the home of Michael Jones in Newport on April 11, 1844, when a group gathered to make plans. Present were several of the town's most influential citizens, men who had helped to found the academy, the library, the bank, and the bridge company. With Samuel Winston and John W. Stevenson as chairman and secretary, respectively, a parish was organized and on Stevenson's suggestion was called St. Paul's Church. The name was perhaps a compliment to Dr. Cobbs, who agreed to serve as "acting rector" until a permanent one could be secured. A vestry was elected, consisting of Michael Jones, Samuel Winston, John W. Stevenson, Thomas Armstrong, and James Taylor, Jr., with the names of Colonel James Taylor and Captain N. C. McCrae being added several days later. Also included among the very early members were E. J. Harper, Mr. Clough, and M. T. C. Gould. The secretary was instructed to inquire of the Covington parish whether it would be willing to "unite" with the new parish in sharing the services of its minister, the Reverend G. G. Moore. The proposal was agreeable to all concerned, and Mr. Moore took up his additional duties in Newport on May 1st.[7]

---

[7] See the well-preserved records of St. Paul's Church, Newport; and parochial reports in *Journal of the Diocese of Kentucky* for 1844ff. Also "History of St. Paul's, Newport" (MS in Archives of Diocese of Lexington, University of Kentucky Library); B. H. Crews, *History of St. Paul's Parish, Newport, Kentucky* (mimeographed pamphlet, 1935); and Beryl L. Schwarberg, "St. Paul's Through the Years" (printed program of Centennial Celebration, Saint Paul's Episcopal Church . . . April 30, 1944).

Within a few weeks after the organization of the Newport parish, Dr. Cobbs was unanimously elected Bishop of Alabama and was consecrated in the office the following October. For that reason he was able to assist the group for only a very short time, but his influence on its early members was lasting. They considered him as their founder and inscribed in the first minute book their belief that "no parish ever had a safer, truer earthly guidance in the beginning." His love of the liturgy guided their efforts to convert their bare little meetinghouse into a setting for Prayer Book services.

Money was no problem in the organizing of St. Paul's. The vestry immediately raised five hundred dollars for the purchase of a small brick church on Court Square that had been built by the Methodists and then abandoned. The purchase was arranged even before the parish applied for admittance to the Diocese. That petition was presented by G. G. Moore to the convention in May, along with an invitation for the next meeting to be held at Newport. The invitation was accepted, even though a technicality delayed the admittance of the parish until the following year.

The renovation of the little brick church was a labor of love; the parishioners themselves did much of the work. One historian of the parish recalls that because there was no altar in the building "at each celebration of the Holy Communion Mrs. Barlow, one of the devoted members of the parish, provided a table and fair linen for each service." In September, 1844 Bishop Smith consecrated the "neat little house" with the assistance of Mr. Moore and "in the presence of a large and interested congregation." At that time the organ was located in the gallery over the front entrance of the church, and the choir also. The organist was Mrs. Sally Morgan, and the singers were Edward Morgan together with William Morgan and his wife. A "family choir" they were called.

Mr. Moore departed shortly after the consecration, and the two parishes called the Reverend Edward Lounsbury, a young missionary from the Diocese of Ohio, whose stay lasted about two years. Although he was successful in his endeavors with the parish in Covington he seemed never to become well acquainted with the close-knit group in Newport. In his parochial report for 1845 he made the strange statement that St. Paul's parish had no records and no full communicants. The secretary of the vestry, John W. Stevenson, was serving in the Legislature at the time, which may account for Lounsbury's not seeing the records. Nevertheless, the parish was intact and thriving when G. G. Moore returned for a few months in 1848–1849. He found ten communicants and a regular Sunday school, consisting of about fifty scholars.

In the early months of 1849 the Newport and Covington parishes decided to secure separate rectors, and St. Paul's called the Reverend Charles Henry Page, who came to them after a decade at the mission parish of St. Matthew's near Louisville. After ordination in his native state of Virginia he had come to Kentucky in 1838 to take charge of the mission and also a girls' school in the community. In addition, he ministered to the needy and unfortunate, including Negroes, inmates of the workhouse, and patients at the Marine Hospital. On coming to Newport he gave up teaching and devoted his whole time to pastoral and missionary duties. His first report, made in May, 1849, reveals his enthusiasm for the new parish and for the challenge of the untended area around it.

Having been in charge of this Parish not two months, the Minister has done little more than begin his duties. He has preached as yet but once upon the Sabbath, and held service of Friday afternoons. He has made one trip to Jamestown, a growing place two miles above, where a lot of ground is offered for the erection of a house of worship.

The congregation here is said to be better than it has ever been; the number of Episcopal families about 16. Sunday school teachers 8. Pupils from 65 to 70. Communicants 24.

Within a year, Page obtained the chaplaincy of the United States Army Barracks situated in Newport, thus supplementing his small stipend as a minister. The soldiers as well as his parishioners loved him for his Gospel preaching and his frequent administration of all the Church's offices. After he resigned his pastoral position in 1852 in order to assume full time duties at the barracks, he frequently officiated at St. Paul's. He also went out to various small communities in Campbell and Kenton Counties, usually as the first Anglican priest ever to appear in the locality. No Episcopal clergyman of his day, not even Dr. Norton, ministered more devotedly to the under-privileged than did Charles H. Page.

After Page's resignation St. Paul's had four ministers, each of them serving for approximately a year. At first glance, this record appears unfavorable, but such is not the case. At that time many newly ordained clergymen volunteered to serve short assignments in the undermanned frontier dioceses. Bishop Smith accepted many such recruits for his mission parishes, with the understanding that they might stay only a limited time. Just such a recruit was the Reverend J. Rice Taylor, an earnest young man from the Diocese of Ohio who was at St. Paul's in 1852–53. He probably came from Cincinnati, since the Ladies' Sewing Society of St. Paul's Church in that city presented the Newport parish with a "beautiful surplice" during his stay. He brought the list of communicants up from 36 to 44.

During 1854 the rectorship was held by the Reverend W. W. Dodge, one of the Bishop's most promising ordinands. He resigned after a short stay and Mr. Page filled in the vacancy until the vestry, on the advice of Bishop Smith, called the Reverend Frederick C. Boyd. Boyd was a man of considerable force and ability. He had recently left "Kilmarnock," his plantation near Natchez, to enter the Episcopal ministry, and he still retained his executive skill. He had just succeeded in arousing Grace Church, Paducah, in less than a year's stay. There was no need for him to arouse St. Paul's, but in the brief time between his arrival on July 1, 1855, and his leaving in March Boyd undoubtedly accelerated its progress. He added 34 names to the communicants list, bringing the total to 60. He per-suaded the parish to enlarge its crowded church building, and in the course of renovation a tower was erected. The first floor of the tower was made into a Sunday school library, presided over by Mr. Thompson. A new organ was purchased, and the children of the Sunday school donated a new baptismal font. In a spirit of senti-ment and frugality the first, hand-crafted font was preserved and would one day be given to a nearby mission. The work of renova-tion was well under way and a portion of the money collected to pay for it when a "Providential indication of duty" compelled Mr.

Boyd to return to Mississippi, where he continued his clerical vocation by holding services in his own house for the neighbors. He was still there when his name was listed in 1862 as a clergyman in the Confederate Episcopal Church.

St. Paul's last transient missionary at this time was a physician-turned-priest from Indiana, the Reverend Colley A. Foster, M.D., who filled the post in 1856. On him fell the sobering responsibility of paying off the debt incurred in the rebuilding and improvements. He, too, increased the membership, but he stated a little sharply in his only parochial report that eleven of the communicants included by his predecessor had informed him upon his arrival that they belonged to other parishes and had therefore been dropped from his own list. The doctor was evidently more of a realist than was Frederick Boyd.

The parish was in good condition in March, 1858, when the Reverend Peter H. Jeffries arrived to begin a memorable rectorship that lasted for eight years. He was a devoted pastor, absorbed in the fellowship of his parish. At year's end he announced that it was "progressing silently and permanently" and that the indebtedness was almost paid, thanks in part to a handsome gift from Edward Morgan toward the purchase of the organ. To the convention of 1860, he reported with pardonable pride that the parish was free of debt in spite of a tornado in May that had blown off the gable. "Peace and prosperity are in our midst," he wrote.

It is difficult to see how he could have felt so confident of his parish's future when the nation was already torn by internal conflict that caught him and his parishioners on a precarious borderline between sections. Jefferies seems to have been much less involved in public affairs during the war period than was Currie, rector of Trinity, but the position of the two parishes was the same—a moderate pro-Union stand combined with many personal ties connecting its members with the Confederacy. The proximity of the Newport Barracks, where Charles H. Page still served as chaplain, and the presence of Army people in the congregation at St. Paul's doubtless had some influence in determining its allegiance. The parish prospered, attaining a communicant strength of more than one hundred by the end of the conflict. At the end of Dr. Jeffries' rectorship—he was awarded a D.D. before he left in 1866—he might well have felt that he and his parish had managed to maintain internal peace and prosperity during the strife.

CHURCH OF THE NATIVITY, MAYSVILLE AND
CHURCH OF THE EPIPHANY, WASHINGTON

Many of Kentucky's early settlers came down the Ohio from Pittsburgh and tied up their flatboats at the mouth of Limestone Creek, generally thought to be the best landing place on the entire length of the Kentucky side. It was sheltered by surrounding hills, and just beyond them began the fertile limestone soil that at this point reached all the way to the river. Here began the winding road that followed the "good land" southward toward Lexington. First comers got valuable tracts near the landing, and in 1786 the town of Washington was located four miles back from the settlement at the river that was first called Limestone and then Maysville. When Mason County was organized, Washington was the county seat and became the first post office west of the Alleghenies, with service to five western states. In 1794 the county contracted with the Reverend Lewis Craig, who was also a stonemason, for the erection of a handsome two-story courthouse of native stone. Craig was a famous Baptist preacher who had brought his "Traveling Church" out from Virginia to Kentucky during the Revolution. The town of Washington contained substantial homes and excellent taverns, and by 1810 it boasted four newspapers, a book publisher, a library, and two churches. Its leading citizens were landowners and influential politicians.

A representative citizen of early Washington was Judge Adam Beatty, a Marylander who emigrated to Lexington, Kentucky, in his youth, read law, and became a friend of Henry Clay. In 1802 he located in Washington, where he became a circuit judge, a successful farmer, and a Whig leader. It is believed that he assisted Clay in composing the "substance of the Missouri Compromise." He remained a loyal churchman despite there being no Episcopal services within a day's journey of Washington.

The town of Maysville grew slowly at first, but by 1830 it began to rival Louisville as a commercial river port. By the end of the decade it had a market, a handsome city hall built in the Greek Revival style of architecture, a bank, a theatre, and a population of over 2,000. Washington was only a third as large, but it controlled the county politically.[8] The importance of these two towns was not overlooked by the Domestic and Foreign Missionary Society of the Episcopal Church. In 1830, when it sent the Reverend Amos G. Baldwin, a missionary from western New York, to look over the prospects in the Ohio Valley, he held services six times in Washington.[9] There is evidence that the Society in 1831 appointed the Reverend S. C. Freeman, who had been officiating at the new church in Danville, to act as missionary at Maysville and Washington with an annual stipend of $250, but there is no record that he ever served there.[10] The Church's interest, however, continued, and in May, 1831, Bishop Meade of Virginia preached several times at Maysville and Washington during his visitation to Kentucky, as did the Reverend B. B. Smith, then rector of Christ Church, Lexington, who accompanied the Bishop on the visitation. In his official report of the journey Meade said that "those who are best qualified to judge" told him that a "suitable minister" might well establish an Episcopal church there.

B. B. Smith was likewise impressed with the opportunities in Mason County, but he was unable to do anything about the matter during the first crowded years of his episcopate. Finally, in December, 1838, during a trip to Cincinnati to participate in the consecration of Bishop Polk, he went on to Maysville to look up the Episcopalians who had attended the services when he and Meade were there. According to a parish tradition, upon his arrival he encountered a friendly Methodist who offered to drive Smith

---

[8] See G. Glenn Clift, *The History of Maysville and Mason County* (Lexington, Ky.: 1936), *passim;* Collins, *History of Kentucky,* Vol. II, section on Mason County; Edna Hunter Best, *The Historic Past of Washington, Mason County, Kentucky* (Cynthiana, Ky.: 1944), pp. 37–39 *et passim.*

[9] Manross, *History of the American Episcopal Church,* p. 254.

[10] Chief source for history of Episcopal churches in Maysville and Washington is their parochial reports in *Journal of the Diocese of Kentucky* for 1839ff. Also a pamphlet titled *The History of the Church of the Nativity, Maysville, Kentucky: One Hundredth Anniversary, 1837–1937* (n.d.), probably by Alice Gill, parish historian.

ANTEBELLUM EXPANSION ALONG THE UPPER OHIO   203

around the region in his own carriage to seek out the twelve
members that were deemed needful to organize a parish in the
locality. After two days, the story goes, they returned, the Bishop
quite jubilant at having found "the apostolic number." Just who the
twelve were we are not told, but very certainly they included Mrs.
Mary Paxton, whose family owned the well-known Paxton Inn in
Washington, because she had been confirmed by Bishop Ravenscroft at Christ Church, Lexington in 1829. Nor could they have
failed to pay a call on Judge Adam Beatty, whom Bishop Smith had
confirmed in Lexington more recently. A Churchman of longer
standing in Washington was Dr. Basil Duke, prominent physician,
who had remained loyal to his Maryland upbringing.

The following April the Bishop assigned one of his seminarians,
Deacon N. Newlin Cowgill, as missionary in Maysville. Cowgill
soon gathered six communicants and their families into a little
society, baptized eight persons, and persuaded forty-five children to
attend Sunday school. He preached to congregations of from sixty
to one hundred in the crowded council chamber of the Maysville
Market House, and every other Sunday afternoon he held services
in the Presbyterian church in Washington. Cowgill, a hardworking
schoolteacher from Pennsylvania, won the confidence of his people,
who pledged the considerable sum of fifteen hundred dollars toward building an Episcopal church in Maysville. Unfortunately, the
funds allotted to the Bishop for missionary work in that area were
exhausted at the end of six months. Cowgill was transferred to
another mission, and his labors bore no real fruit for nearly a
decade. The Bishop kept in touch with the leading Episcopalians in
Mason County, as was shown when Judge Beatty was elected by the
diocesan convention of 1840 to serve as one of the first trustees of
Shelby College.

In the fall of 1846 the Reverend G. G. Moore, then the rector of
St. Peter's, Paris and the Reverend Edward F. Berkley, rector of
Christ Church, Lexington agreed to undertake the project of organizing a parish at Maysville, and on September 13 they began holding regular services there. They continued to do so on at least a
monthly basis throughout the winter and spring, with occasional
assistance from Dr. James Craik and the Reverend J. B. Gallagher,

both of Louisville, and the Reverend Maury from Danville. Moore, being nearest at hand, had charge of the Maysville group in the beginning.

The first recorded meeting was held on February 10, 1847, at which time the parish was organized as the Church of the Nativity and six vestrymen were elected. They were Judge Adam Beatty, Richard Henry Lee, Horace H. Hill, Colonel David Lindsey, George Dodson, and A. A. Wadsworth. At about this time a letter was addressed to Bishop Smith about securing a minister for the church, and subscriptions amounting to fifteen hundred dollars were obtained for erecting a church building. The subscriptions were apparently a confirmation of the ones made ten years earlier. It was nearly a year before the Bishop found a minister for them in the person of J. S. Chadbourne, newly ordained deacon. The enthusiastic young clergyman held services every Sunday in the courtroom of the new Mason County courthouse in Maysville. That very year (1848) progressive Maysville had wrested away the privilege of being county seat from aristocratic Washington and converted its beautiful city hall to the county's use.[11]

The new parish made progress. Vestrymen were added: James Wormald, E. C. Phister, and Peyton R. Key. At the diocesan convention on May 25, 1848, the Church of the Nativity was admitted into union. In July the vestry bought a fifty-foot lot on Third Street not far from the court house, and in November approved a plan for a "beautiful Gothic church edifice" drawn for them by Bishop Smith. The contract called for the stone and brick work to begin immediately. On October 8 the Bishop ordained Deacon Chadbourne to the priesthood in a service at the courthouse. At the same service the Bishop ordained to the diaconate Professor Robert McMurdy, who had just opened an excellent school for young girls in Washington, using the old courthouse for his classes.

McMurdy, who came to Kentucky from Louisiana, was a well-known educator, holder of an A. M. degree and schooled in philosophy. For his Female College, as he usually called it, he set up a

---

[11] See J. Winston Coleman, Jr., *Historic Kentucky* (Lexington, Ky.: 1967), p. 145 and p. 152 for photographs and brief histories of the two Mason County courthouses, both used for Episcopal services.

Boarding Department in a spacious residence directly opposite the courthouse. It combined two houses built earlier by Dr. Basil Duke and Judge John Coburn. In addition to conducting an excellent school that was patronized by the best families locally and attended by pupils from many other states, Deacon McMurdy took his priestly duties seriously. Daily exercises during the week for the McMurdy Female College began with morning prayer in the former courtroom, now the college chapel. On Sundays and other appropriate days Mr. McMurdy conducted public services in the chapel for Episcopalians and other residents of Washington who came to hear his learned sermons. A goodly portion of his congregations consisted during the school year of his comely, attentive students. He preached frequently at the Church of the Nativity and also in Cincinnati, taking advantage of the convenient packet boat service between Maysville and the Queen City.

In the latter part of 1848 the Episcopalians worshiping with Mr. McMurdy in the old courthouse chapel in Washington organized a parish known as the Church of the Epiphany. Prominent members were Adam Beatty, Peyton R. Key, and W. Lashbrook. Communicants were only six but the congregations were large for the size of the community. There was very certainly no hard feeling between this group and the Maysville parishioners. At the convention the following June in Frankfort the rector of the Church of the Nativity presented the petition for Epiphany's admission to the Diocese, which was favorably recommended by the Committee on the Admission of New Parishes, of which Dr. Craik and the Honorable Henry Clay were members. The recommendation must have given pleasure to Judge Beatty as well as to Deacon McMurdy. McMurdy was ordained to the priesthood in August at Dr. Craik's church in Louisville.

Already popular as an educator, McMurdy was very soon esteemed also as a clergyman. Within five or six years he increased the number of communicants to twenty-five, almost entirely by confirmation. Divine services numbered about 150 a year and in addition he preached in various other states. Epiphany had no financial problems because the rector headed a prosperous academy, and the parish was content to hold services in the courthouse without under-

taking to build a church edifice. McMurdy became an active partici-
pant in diocesan affairs and in 1857 succeeded Edward Berkley as
secretary of the annual convention. Almost certainly it was he who
prepared Jonathan Havens, the Mason County Campbellite minister,
for ordination to the diaconate in the summer of 1856. Early in 1857
McMurdy suffered a "domestic affliction," probably the death of his
wife, and not long afterward he turned over his school in Washington to his brother-in-law and removed to Frankfort. There he
established St. Ann's Hall, a Church school for girls, with the loyal
support of the Reverend Norton and Ascension Church. In 1860 he
undertook the presidency of reorganized Shelby College and assembled a remarkably good faculty, drawn chiefly from the clergy in
the Diocese. The war ruined this promising prospect, and he became a chaplain in the United States Army Hospitals in Washington, D.C., as will be noted in a later chapter.

Because the activities of Robert McMurdy constitute most of the
history of the Church of the Epiphany, it seems appropriate to
recapitulate his services to the Diocese as its diligent convention
secretary from 1858 to 1861 and as its first archivist. He undertook
to classify the considerable mass of material Edward Berkley turned
over to him: *Journals* of the Diocese for most but not all the years,
correspondence, press clippings, and the like. He located copies of
all the *Journals* save one—the lost *Journal* for 1829—and reduced
them to a "Synopsis of Thirty-One Annual Conventions" for presentation to the 1859 Convention. His fellow clergymen, especially
scholars like Dr. Craik, Dr. Norton, and the Reverend John Austen
Merrick, were so impressed with the value of McMurdy's investiga-
tions that he was requested to publish the "Synopsis" as part of the
Journal for 1859. He did so, adding also an equally valuable chart
setting out "Church Property in the Diocese" that contained notes
from the Bishop's files about "defunct" parishes. McMurdy's reports
as secretary to the conventions of 1859 and 1860 outlined a plan for
setting up the archives of the Diocese in a special alcove in the
theological seminary library at Shelby College. In 1860 he introduced a resolution in which the convention requested the rectors of
all churches to prepare historical sketches of their parishes, beginning with Christ Church, Lexington and Christ Church, Louisville,

which were to be ready by the following convention. Only James Craik accepted this challenge. His lively recollections, titled "Historical Sketches of Christ Church, Louisville, Kentucky," were published in 1862. Other parish histories did not appear until long after McMurdy's time, but his influence on the preservation of diocesan and parish records was far reaching.

Within about a year after the Reverend McMurdy's departure from Washington, Judge Beatty died. The small parish, without a rector or a church building and now without its most influential member, soon ceased to function. It appears on the diocesan assessment list for the last time in 1860. The last warden on the record is Peyton R. Key. Its members made their way back to the church in Maysville, which had been enjoying a fine period of growth during the decade of Epiphany's existence.

The Gothic building designed by the Bishop for the Church of the Nativity was begun very early in 1849 and was in use by February, 1850, although not yet entirely completed. Even though it did not include all the ambitious features that B. B. Smith had planned, it was admirably built.[12] The excellent Gothic exterior remains essentially unchanged today. The original interior that Bishop Smith planned was not Gothic, however, but plain and old-fashioned in the meetinghouse style. The sanctuary was the same width as the nave and not recessed. The altar was a table with a marble top. Across the "front" of the church was a gallery occupied by the choir. The small marble font, made by two parishioners who were stonecutters, stood on a rosewood pedestal in the chancel.

The use of Gothic architecture in the Maysville church emphasized the increasing popularity of that style for the larger Episcopal edifices being erected in the Diocese during Bishop Smith's administration. For several decades the American High Churchmen had been advocating Gothic churches because such settings were suited to catholic worship; and B. B. Smith might well have disapproved of them for the same reason. Surprisingly, he ignored the doctrinal connotations of the Gothic style and chose it for its beauty and

---

[12] Bishop Smith's original plans called for a spire, a peal of bells, and "a front window with the Nativity in stained glass," none of which were completed (*Church of the Nativity: the Hundredth Anniversary*, p. 7).

traditions. His convictions often seemed to be at cross-purposes with each other.

The new Church of the Nativity took its place among the handsome houses of worship being built by the various denominations in growing Maysville. Colonel David Lindsey, Judge E. C. Phister, James and William Wormald, Jesse Turner, Colonel Anderson Taylor, and William Wadsworth were among the many parishioners who redeemed their pledges to the building fund. The ladies held successful fairs. Further contributions were needed, however, both from within and without the Diocese. Mr. Chadbourne's successor, Mr. John Ufford from Virginia, reported the receipt of contributions during his first seven months from three Louisville churches —Christ Church, St. Paul's, and St. John's—and from Christ Church, Lexington and St. Paul's, Henderson. A "lady in Virginia" sent a gift of one hundred dollars.

After two years Mr. Ufford left, and his place was taken by Deacon Hugh Miller Thompson, whom the Bishop considered to be "a youthful, energetic and, we trust, . . . a devoted and successful minister." He lived up to the Bishop's expectations, and had the satisfaction of seeing his church consecrated on February 26, 1854. It may well have been his enthusiasm that induced the parish to begin at once to acquire an organ, and about the first of the following year, a "fine toned organ of Louisville manufacture" was purchased. Traditionally the first pipe organ in Maysville, it was used for half a century, until 1898. Hugh Thompson was gone in less than two years, to accept a call to the Diocese of Wisconsin and to begin a career that led to his election as Bishop of Mississippi.

The Maysville parish's problem was no longer that of paying off a debt. It was, as the Bishop expressed it in his address to the convention in 1856, "the delay and difficulty attending the choice and acceptance of a Minister to this interesting Parish." In 1854 the Reverend William Harlowe, one of the Bishop's ordinands, came for a year. After his leaving for a parish in Tennessee, the parish was ministered to by the Reverend George Alexander Crooke, A.M., for about two years, during which period he conducted services and Sunday school faithfully, presenting several persons for confirmation. In 1858 the Reverend Francis B. Nash, an early grad-

ANTEBELLUM EXPANSION ALONG THE UPPER OHIO   209

uate of the seminary in Lexington, came back to the Diocese from a parish in Illinois, and began what might well have been a most fruitful rectorship. When the war shattered community life in Maysville in the spring of 1861, the Church of the Nativity had reached a total of 49 communicants, fifty scholars in the Sunday school, six persons confirmed, and generous contributions to projects outside the parish. F. B. Nash resigned as rector that summer, and his place was filled at once by the Reverend Frank Gregg, who served for six years, sustaining and enlarging the life of the parish during that difficult time. An account of Gregg's part in wartime appears in the chapter devoted to that era. He made a large contribution toward establishing the Church of the Nativity as one of the important Episcopal churches on the upper Ohio River.

11 New Parishes in *Mid-Century*

In the northern belt of the Bluegrass country lies Harrison County, adjacent to Bourbon and Scott, and like them settled soon after the Revolution for its good farming land. The chief town, Cynthiana, was chartered in 1793 and became the peer of Paris, Georgetown, and other county seats. Stores, mills, newspapers, factories, and churches were established. As early as 1800, Harrison Academy was in operation. The Presbyterians, Methodists, and "Christians" all erected their own places of worship. When the Reverend Amos Glover Baldwin, an Episcopal priest from western New York, visited Kentucky in 1820 on behalf of the Domestic and Foreign Missionary Society, he reported that a Reverend William Wall officiated occasionally at Cynthiana. Apparently there were no immediate results from these meetings.[1]

The first Episcopal parish in the county was organized at Leesburg, a prosperous community nine miles southeast of Cynthiana. It was situated at the crossing of well-traveled roads, and until the coming of the railroads bid fair to be a sizable town. By 1830 it had its own tavern, post office, Masonic lodge, mills, and cotton factory. Episcopal services were held there for a year or so beginning in November, 1834, by Deacon Edmund Davis, one of the first graduates of the Episcopal Theological Seminary in Kentucky. He resided near Leesburg until his return in 1835 to his native England. The Reverend Amos Cleaver then came over from Paris occasionally to hold services, but the group was held together chiefly by two laymen, William Hearne and his brother James. William, owner of the cotton factory and a man of influence in the surrounding country, was a communicant of St. Peter's Church in Paris. By the spring of 1836 he had organized a half dozen families of Episcopal persuasion into a parish at Leesburg called Christ Church, which was admitted to the Diocese at the stormy convention in May. William Hearne served as its first lay delegate on that occasion and at the 1837 meeting, remaining steadfastly loyal to Bishop Smith on every crucial vote. Meanwhile, he and James Hearne were largely responsible for the erection of a "small, but very neat and judicious church edifice," which was not completed until along in 1839. During the years it was being built, the parish had services twice a month by the Reverend Charles Crowe, A.B., University of Dublin, a recent graduate of the theological seminary who was teaching intermittently in Cynthiana and Lexington. After his return to Ireland some time before 1844, the Reverend Amos Cleaver again came to Leesburg occasionally. But while neighboring towns were growing, Leesburg remained a crossroads community and the Episcopalian congregation dwindled. The Hearne brothers sold the modest church building, for which they had furnished most of the funds, and some years later contributed the proceeds to the church in Cynthiana.[2]

Regular services were begun in Cynthiana in early 1837 by Charles Crowe and James S. Greene, another Irish seminarian, who were residing in the town in order to "hold school in the academy building."[3] Since these zealous young candidates for Holy Orders had not yet been ordained to the diaconate, they held "lay readings" and organized a group that applied to the annual convention in May for admittance to the Diocese as St. Paul's Church. This somewhat hasty organization was an effort on the part of Bishop Smith's loyal theological students to get votes for his defense at the forthcoming convention. In nearby Bath County three other students, N. N. Cowgill, Edward F. Berkley, and F. B. Nash, effected a similar organization which applied to be admitted as Ascension Church in Owingsville. Meanwhile the anti-Smith partizans were equally diligent, and even more successful, in fostering new parishes during

---

[1] William Henry Perrin, *History of Bourbon, Scott, Harrison, and Nicholas Counties, Kentucky* (Chicago: 1882), pp. 278–293; *et passim*. For Leesburg, pp. 323–327.

[2] For the parish at Leesburg, see parochial reports in the *Journal of the Diocese of Kentucky* for 1836, 1841; for disposal of the church building see *Journal* for 1859, Appendix X, "Church Property in the Diocese," footnote on "Defunct Parishes" by Bishop Smith.

[3] Perrin, *op. cit.*, p. 278.

their controversy with the Bishop. They succeeded in blocking the admission of both the Cynthiana and the Owingsville groups. St. Paul's in Cynthiana and Ascension Church in Owingsville, along with St. Mark's in Bourbon County and other "ghost parishes" of this era, dropped out of sight and of the memory of men save for future historians.

After the convention in May, 1837, N. N. Cowgill, a youth from Pennsylvania who had graduated at Transylvania, took over the academy in Cynthiana and also continued to hold "lay readings" in the churches of other denominations or sometimes in the court-house. When Bishop Smith ordained Cowgill in December he sent the young deacon out to begin a lifetime of heroic missionary work in the small parishes all over Kentucky.[4] Charles Crowe officiated in Cynthiana occasionally at this time. Edward Berkley, who became the minister at Christ Church, Lexington in 1838, faithfully visited the people at Cynthiana through the years, and when G. G. Moore became the rector of St. Peter's in Paris, he adopted Cynthiana as one of his primary mission fields. Nowhere was the missionary zeal of the parish clergy of that day more fully demonstrated than in their concern for the Episcopal families of Cynthiana.

These years of devoted service bore fruit in the winter of 1846–47, when the Church-minded people of the community, in a sudden burst of conviction and enthusiasm, banded together to organize a parish. The various accounts of the founding stress various phases of the event, but, pieced together, they tell the story of what amounted to an "Episcopal revival" in Cynthiana.

According to the official report of the Reverend G. G. Moore, he began on November 4, 1846, to hold regular monthly services in Cynthiana "in addition to several successive services" at different times with the Reverend Mr. Berkley of Lexington. That continued "until the 6th of January when a Parish was duly organized" and he himself was invited to the rectorship.[5] Bishop Smith, in an official address delivered years later, credited G. G. Moore as "the chief

[4] *Journal of the Diocese of Kentucky* for 1876, p. 90: Obituary of Nathaniel Newlin Cowgill.
[5] *Journal of the Diocese of Kentucky* for 1847, p. 28.

instrument" of the founding of the Cynthiana church, "nobly seconded" by Edward F. Berkley.[6]

We gather additional information about the founding from the church's own excellent historical records.[7] We are told that about 1845 Dr. George H. Perrin, a prominent physician of the town, was induced to "look into the claims of the Church." We do not know who induced him to do so. It may have been the preaching of Moore and Berkley, or it may have been the doctor's friend, William Hearne, of Leesburg. At all events, Doctor Perrin read Cooke's *Invalidity of Presbyterian Ordination* and Chapman's *Sermons* and the writings of Bishop Ravenscroft. "Becoming convinced of the Evangelical and historical character of the Church and of her Apostolic Order he espoused the cause with greatest zeal and on the first day of December, 1846, he and his wife were baptized by immersion." The officiant was the Reverend G. G. Moore and the setting was the Licking River.

According to the parish history Bishop Smith persuaded Doctor Perrin to organize a parish in Cynthiana, and so the planning most likely was done between the time of his baptism and the organizing meeting, which was held on the Epiphany. Thus it was truly the church of the Advent season, and it may well have been B. B. Smith who suggested that it be so called. Smith once referred to the name as being "singularly appropriate" and a "charming historic record" of the "sudden awakening" that brought about its founding.[8]

In April, 1847, the Bishop visited the new parish to confirm a class of eleven persons presented by Mr. Moore. Their names were recorded as follows: George H. Perrin, Arabella Perrin, Agnes Coleman, J. A. Pritchard, Sarah Musser, Prudence Gruell, William Thompson, Sarah Thompson, John Trimble, John B. Gruell and (on the following day) Eliza Trimble. The parish now had fifteen communicants, plus their families and numerous regular attendants

---

[6] *Journal of the Diocese of Kentucky* for 1859, p. 36.

[7] Parish Register (1847-ca. 1910) of Church of the Advent, Cynthiana, Kentucky, pp. 6–9: "History," written in 1880 and attributed traditionally to the Reverend George A. Weeks, formerly rector of the parish. See also research notes on the history of the parish made by Mrs. Charles Kuster; and Perrin, *op. cit.*, pp. 292–293.

[8] *Journal of the Diocese of Kentucky* for 1859, p. 36.

at services. At the convention in May it was admitted to the Diocese, being represented in that body by Dr. Perrin and William Hearne as lay delegates. G. G. Moore resigned the rectorship of the Paris and Cynthiana churches the following year, and services at Cynthiana were irregular for several years thereafter. At last in 1852, through the aid of Bishop Smith, who was ever soliticious of the welfare of the Cynthiana Episcopalians, the parish obtained a rector of its own, the Reverend Carter Page, and entered upon a more active and fruitful era.

Carter Page, a priest from the Diocese of Virginia, was residing near Russellville, Kentucky, in 1850, and, as he reported to Bishop Smith, was "associated" with his brother, Deacon James J. Page, the missionary in charge of several small parishes in that area.[9] Bishop Smith, who had ordained James J. Page, sent Carter Page in December, 1851, on a preaching mission to Cynthiana that resulted in his taking up his duties as rector of the Church of the Advent in February. He was not only a popular preacher but an "able teacher of the classics" in the local Harrison Academy. His avocation as a teacher relieved his parishioners of the responsibility for his support.

Before the end of 1852 the parish resolved to build its own church, and shortly afterward a good half-acre lot, on Walnut Street facing Mill, was purchased. Generous pledges by Dr. Perrin, William Thompson, and others warranted drawing up plans, which proved to be a slow procedure. The Reverend Mr. Page's parochial report to the convention that met on May 31, 1855, sums up the progress to that date: ". . . the Church edifice, about which we have been so long talking and hoping, is at last under contract. The corner stone was laid by the Bishop, on the 6th of May. The building is to be of stone, and in accordance with a model furnished by the Bishop, and at the estimated cost of $4,500.—$3,500. of which has already been subscribed."

The Bishop's model has not survived, and early accounts of it differ as to whether it was made of wood or cardboard, but they agree that it was a replica of Stoke Pogis Church in England and

---

[9] For Carter Page's activities in the Diocese of Kentucky see his parochial reports in the *Journal* for 1850–72, with some years missing.

that the model influenced the style of the edifice. The church is in the form of a Latin cross, the nave being seventy-five feet long and the transept sixty-six, with a seating capacity of about three hundred. The plan called for a square bell tower, sixty feet high, beside the west end of the nave, and for high, narrow Gothic windows. The work was done by local artisans, supervised by knowledgeable parishioners, who ordered the woodwork made in Cincinnati and had it hauled overland. Carter Page's report in the spring of 1856 notes that although $4,500 had been spent the building remained "without pews, unplastered, and unpainted." A year later, however, he reported most of these deficiencies remedied, thanks to generous gifts from some of the parishioners and, he modestly added, himself. Services were held in the church beginning at Christmas season, 1856, including regular, well-attended ones for the "colored population."

The Cynthiana Episcopalians and their rector were perfectionists, and the work of completing the beautiful little church went on for another three years. The triple windows above the altar were designed of clear glass with a red border. The tower was finally completed. The grounds around the church were enclosed, graded, and ornamented, a rather advanced step at the time. It was a small parish to have achieved such an ambitious goal, with only seventeen communicants and their families, and a Sunday school of about forty. The same family names appear regularly in the register through the years, giving a special character to the parish.

Mr. Page's academy suffered financially during the war years, and he gave up his regular services at the Church of the Advent in about 1862, although no one took his place until about a year after the close of hostilities. He became principal of St. Matthew's School in Jefferson County, near Louisville, where he remained for nearly ten years before his removal to Missouri. He was remembered with affection by the people in Cynthiana, and when the altar windows were replaced with handsome stained glass ones about 1900, one of them was dedicated to his memory.

After Carter Page's departure it was Dr. Perrin more than any other one person who held the parish together during the war and

the following decade. He was not only an able and generous warden of the church's secular affairs but he became a respected exponent of Anglican theology. Well-known in the Diocese, he succeeded in having at least occasional services at the Church of the
Advent during the lean years of Reconstruction. In particular, he
was instrumental in getting the aid of the Reverend Silas Totten,
D.D., the distinguished principal of Christ Church Seminary, established in Lexington in 1866. Dr. Perrin was responsible in no small
measure for the excellent Churchmanship of the Church of the
Advent from its beginning to his death in 1891 at the age of 96
years, eight months, and ten days, as his burial notice in its register
reads. In contrast to the Reverend Carter Page, who had a part only
in the antebellum days of the Cynthiana church, Dr. Perrin's influence extended almost to the end of the century. Another of the altar
windows is a memorial to him.

ST. JOHN'S CHURCH, VERSAILLES

In 1830 Versailles, county seat of Woodford County, was a proud,
well-established town of about a thousand population. The deed
books in the courthouse were inscribed with grants and transfers of
ample tracts of fertile land signed by some of the most influential
early settlers in Kentucky. Located about ten miles west of Lexington, the community was only a few hours ride by stage from
Frankfort or Harrodsburg or Georgetown. There were a few Episcopalians in the area from an early date since about 1817 the
Reverend James Elliott "officiated occasionally" in the county. The
Reverend Amos Cleaver came to Versailles to survey the prospects
for establishing his school and a church there before he decided to
locate them in Paris instead. The Reverend B. B. Smith visited the
place even before he and Bishop Meade stopped in Versailles on
their official tour in 1832. In 1838 Bishop Smith assigned Deacon
Charles Crowe, a young Irish seminarian, "to attend the Versailles
station (where there were some Episcopalian families)." These
Woodford County families probably attended services occasionally
at Christ Church, Lexington. Nothing tangible resulted, however,
until John N. Norton became the rector of the Church of the

Ascension, Frankfort in 1846. The organization of a mission in Versailles was one of the first objects of his missionary zeal.[10]

According to a fictional account of his first services in Versailles which Norton published a decade later, he was asked to come by an Episcopal lady of the town who arranged for the meeting to be held in the court house and also for the Methodist choir leader to set the tune for the psalm and hymn. A goodly number turned out, but the Reverend Mr. Norton and the lady thought there were no other Episcopalians present. They were agreeably surprised when a reverent manly voice joined with them in the responses. The stranger who came forward afterward proved to be John Amsden, who had recently settled in the town with his wife and young family. It turned out that he had been "born, baptised, and confirmed in the Diocese of Western New York,[11] and he and Norton proved to be congenial co-workers in the new enterprise, maybe in part because they had both been reared in the same Church tradition. It was Amsden more than any other one person who searched out six communicants in the vicinity and gathered them and their families and a few other interested people to attend the services conducted during 1847 and 1848 by Mr. Norton and Mr. Berkley of Lexington and Dr. Craik of Louisville.

On the evening of June 29, 1847, at the conclusion of divine services, Mr. Norton was invited to preside over a meeting of citizens who resolved, on motion of John Amsden, the secretary, to organize a parish, to be called St. John's, under the doctrine and cognizance of the Protestant Episcopal Church. The first vestry was composed of Presley O'Banion, John Amsden, Joseph C. Carter, J. D. Helm, James A. Pleasants, Caleb D. Henry, Henry C. Brad-

[10] Parish Register of St. John's Church, Versailles, Kentucky, 1817–1937 (begun by the Reverend John W. Venable and containing his historical sketch of its beginnings, as published by him in *Spirit of Missions,* September, 1854.) Also *Journal of the Diocese of Kentucky* for 1838 and ff; and MS history of St. John's in Archives of Diocese of Lexington, University of Kentucky Library. A fictional account of some events in the early history of the Versailles parish appears in John N. Norton, *Rockford Parish; or, The Fortunes of Mr. Mason's Successors* (New York: 1856), pp. 65–68, 77–81, 134–137, *et passim.* "Rockford" is Frankfort; "Bedfordville" is Versailles; "Mr. Patterson" is J. W. Venable; and so on.

[11] Right Reverend Thomas U. Dudley, Bishop of Kentucky, in *Journal of the Diocese of Kentucky* for 1894, pp. 68–69.

ford, George T. Cotton, and Joseph B. Kincaid. At least one of them was not an Episcopalian, even by preference, but this fact is not surprising in a time when new churches were encouraged by prominent citizens as a matter of civic pride. Messrs. O'Banion and Amsden were the first wardens.

For the first two years or thereabouts the new group had the services of a missionary, the Reverend F. H. L. Laird, from the Diocese of Indiana, who divided his services between it and another small group at nearby Georgetown and meanwhile supported himself by conducting a school at Versailles. During his stay, work was begun on a church building and the wardens were able to report to the convention of 1851 that the "Church edifice, Gothic structure, 62 by 28 feet, of Brick, has been enclosed." They also reported having raised over a thousand dollars in their own county and having received more than four hundred dollars in contributions from the churches in Louisville, Lexington, and Frankfort. After Laird left to join the teaching staff at Shelby College, the indefatigable John Norton conducted services at regular intervals. It took two years more to finish the building and pay off the debt, but Norton continued to come and also he sometimes sent his assistant at Ascension, Deacon John W. Venable.

John Wesley Venable was the first of the many candidates for Holy Orders whom Norton called as his assistants in order to train them for their sacred profession. The program of theological studies at Shelby College, which had been set up after the closing of the Lexington seminary, was irregular and inadequate. Additional preparation for the candidates was provided by parish rectors like Norton, Berkley, and Craik.

Venable had already been of great service to the Church in Kentucky before he was admitted as a candidate for Holy Orders by Bishop Smith in late 1848 or early 1849. He had been an active member during its first three years of the little group that organized Trinity Church, Covington, serving in all the capacities open to a dedicated laymen, even at times as a layreader. He had in all likelihood attended one of the Cincinnati churches previously. After leaving Covington in 1846 he continued to support himself with his brush and pencil as an art teacher in the Louisville area. In

1850 he attracted the attention of Mr. Norton, under whom he prepared for ordination to the diaconate on June 22, 1851, and to the priesthood on January 15, 1854. In addition to his duties as Norton's assistant Venable was at times on the faculty of Shelby College. During the session of 1852–53 he was instructor in Drawing and Painting, and the next year he also served as professor of Belles Lettres, and Mental and Moral Philosophy. Both he and Norton were scholarly men blessed also with creative ability. Norton was a prolific writer, while some of Venable's delicate drawings and water colors still adorn the walls of homes in Versailles. His beautiful handwriting in the parish records of the Versailles and Georgetown parishes looks like medieval script. Norton's influence upon his assistant as well as Venable's own temperament inclined him to be a High Churchman, albeit more in reverent practice than in theological debate.

In 1853, at the invitation of the vestry of St. John's, Mr. Venable became its rector. At about this time he married Sarah Farnsworth and they moved to Versailles. His description of his church in 1853 calls it a "neat edifice" that seated 250 persons and was "tastefully fitted up for proper services." It possessed a six-hundred-dollar organ, the gift of Miss Margaret Logan, confirmed long before in New Jersey.

All was ready for the consecration of the building on the morning of Sunday, December 17, 1853, and both Craik and Norton were on hand to assist with the ceremonies. After the crowd had begun to fill the pews, a messenger arrived with word from Bishop Smith that he was prevented from coming on account of illness. Since many of the eager congregation had never seen the Bishop, it was decided to postpone the announcement of his absence until after the congregation had had the benefit of a sermon. Dr. Craik offered to preach the one that he had delivered the previous Sunday in his own church. In any event, he startled his hearers when he read his text from John 8:24: "If ye believe not that I am he, ye shall die in your sins."[12] St. John's Church was consecrated on May 10, 1854, by Bishop Smith with appropriate ceremonies.

---

[12] For this story, disguised as fiction, see Norton, *Rockford Parish*, pp. 134–137.

From their beginning, the Venable years at St. John's were good years, both spiritually and in practical enterprises such as the purchase of a lot adjoining the church property to the north, and a ladies fair to raise money to enclose the church with a "substantial fence." In the latter successful enterprise, the Versailles ladies were generously aided by those of Christ Church, Lexington and Christ Church, Louisville. Even more valuable than such practical accomplishments was the permanent hold the new church had taken upon the spiritual life of its members. Confirmations were frequent, considering the small community from which St. John's drew. Nathaniel Hart was the first confirmand; another early one was the wife of John Amsden. In his parochial report for 1857, the year of the ladies fair, J. W. Venable's greatest "cause for congratulation" was not material gain but the fact that of all the religious bodies in the town, only the Episcopalians had been privileged to maintain regular services. In addition to morning prayer on Sundays there were often afternoon services for the "country members," and the principal festival days of the Church were faithfully observed. This emphasis on corporate worship, so firmly established in its early days, has continued through the years to give depth to the life of St. John's parish.

After becoming resident rector of the church at Versailles, Venable continued to preach frequently outside his parish in accordance with the 1847 resolution of the diocesan convention. When the Central Convocation was organized in 1857 to promote diocesan missions, he participated actively and began in January, 1858, to hold regular services in Harrodsburg in addition to his own parish responsibility. His work there for the next five years constitutes an important chapter in the history of St. Philip's Church, Harrodsburg. Then he was given charge of the group that was organizing at Georgetown, and for the next twenty years he carried the double load of two parishes—Versailles and Georgetown. During the stresses of the war and the discouragements of the Reconstruction era in the state, he performed his duties as a gentle, steadfast parish priest. Apparently without worldly ambition, he was one of the most beloved of all the rector-missionaries in the antebellum Diocese of Kentucky.

ST. PHILIP'S CHURCH, HARRODSBURG

When the Reverend Gideon McMillan took charge of the newly organized Trinity Church, Danville at the beginning of the year 1830, there were a few Episcopal families at Harrodsburg, an old and influential town about ten miles to the north, and also a scattering of interested persons in the surrounding area. Harrodsburg, oldest permanent settlement in the state, had at that time about a thousand inhabitants, the same size as Danville, and already had congregations of several other denominations, some of whom alternated Sundays at a Union Church Building. McMillan elected to make his home out in the country from Danville, and he soon took the whole region for his parish, covering the countryside on horseback. Many years later people remembered how on a ferry over the Kentucky River he bade a man stop swearing and threatened to throw him overboard if he uttered another oath. After one look at the stout, impulsive McMillan, the man stopped.

In the spring of 1831 McMillan reported to the convention regarding the progress of his Danville flock and added: "Besides . . . I have preached nearly a fourth part of the time in Harrodsburg, and sometimes in Lancaster. My services are frequently called for in these and other places."[13] He continued to hold services in Harrodsburg in the courthouse or the Union Church or even in homes. When Bishop Meade in the summer of 1831 preached there to "a good congregation," it was probably in the Union Church. McMillan was hopeful about the prospects and continued to officiate at stated times until his death from cholera in July, 1833. Nearly thirty years later the builders of St. Philip's Church in Harrodsburg placed a memorial tribute to him as the first Episcopal missionary in the town.

McMillan's successor did not continue this missionary work because he was a busy schoolmaster as well as rector. There would have been no objection from the people of Trinity, Danville, as they

---

[13] *Journal of the Diocese of Kentucky* for 1831, p. 8. For the early history at Harrodsburg see the *Journals* for 1831 and ff.; Neva L. Williams, *The History of St. Philip's Episcopal Church, Harrodsburg, Kentucky* (Prepared for Harrodsburg Historical Society, April, 1948).

had given their express consent to McMillan's extraparochial labors. But rector-missionaries like Gideon McMillan are rare, and Harrodsburg had to get along for a generation with only intermittent Episcopal services. Bishop Smith came sometimes on his visitation rounds, as in 1834. There are reports of visits by James Craik and Edward Berkley in 1849, and there must have been numerous other services in Harrodsburg through the years of which no record was kept. The Danville Episcopalians maintained their contact with the Harrodsburg group and in 1856–57 the Reverend M. F. Maury, somewhat restored in health, held regular monthly services for it.

So matters stood when the diocesan convention of 1857 delegated the missionary work within the Diocese to regional convocations. The Central Convocation, organized immediately, began to operate efficiently under the direction of the Reverend John West, brought in temporarily from the Diocese of Massachusetts to promote the plan. Harrodsburg was one of several places selected for a concentrated effort to establish a parish. Many factors were favorable for it: the prosperous, cultured community; many years of unorganized missionary effort; the cooperation of the church in Danville; and the central location of the town for the visits of the rector-missionaries who were to minister to the new parish in its beginning stages. West himself worked to arouse local interest. Maury continued to hold services, and in January, 1858, Venable undertook to come every two weeks. On February 12 a group was incorporated as St. Philip's Episcopal Church "to form a parish and erect a house of worship." The incorporators were the Reverend M. F. Maury, Benjamin C. Trapnall, Thomas C. Mitchell, Henry H. Farnsworth, Joseph McGrorty, and William Cole.

Services were held in the courthouse. It was the policy of the convocation plan for new parishes, however, to strike while the iron was hot and to start building a church edifice at once. West evidently thought the iron in Harrodsburg was hot enough by the fall of that year, when he set the quarterly meeting of the convocation, composed of the clergy and a few laymen of the region, in Harrodsburg on October 28. These meetings were usually designed to hear reports of missionary progress and other routine business, but this one was also a local fund-raising campaign for the new church building. The account of it in the secretary's report is worth quoting.

This was the most missionary-like Convocation that we have had since our organization. Here we had no church or chapel, and we held services in the courthouse, using the Judge's platform and desk for a chancel and pulpit. On the Sunday preceding, the notice of the meeting was given in all the churches of the village, Baptist, Methodist, Presbyterian, and Christian. This, however, owing perhaps to the rainy weather, did not give us very large congregations. The subscriptions for a church were commenced the day before we met, the General Agent (Reverend John West) being on the ground before us, and we were agreeably surprised on our arrival at the announcement that it already amounted to $1,900. Before Convocation adjourned they counted their subscriptions at $3,500 . . . Nothing could reasonably be imagined more encouraging than this.[14]

"It is a red-brick cruciform building," writes Rexford Newcomb, a modern architectural historian, "with an apse at the rear and a spire-crowned octagonal tower at one corner. Triple lancet windows pierce the front wall of the nave. The beams, pew, and interior woodwork are of walnut. The baptismal font is of English china, and some of the glass came from Italy."[15] He counts it one of the best examples of pure Gothic, exterior and interior, of its size in the middle part of America.

Bishop Smith's guidance and aid in the building of St. Philip's Church have become a legend. The most authentic witness as to what he did is contained in a letter written many years later by Mrs. Sarah Smedley Fife, who was a very young communicant when the church was built. Her memories are clear.

The Bishop put his whole soul and every energy that he was possessed of in this work. He made a model of the entire church out of wood—perfect in every part. He whittled it out with his knife, much of the interior of the model as well as the furniture was done by him at the fireside of the church people. When he would visit them of evenings as soon as

[14] *Journal of the Diocese of Kentucky* for 1859, p. 24.
[15] Newcomb, *Architecture in Old Kentucky* (Urbana: 1953), p. 149.

seated—would spread out his handkerchief on his knees, take out his piece of wood and knife and commence work, talking the while in so interesting a way of what he had seen and heard while "abroad" that even the children were spellbound, and when he would suddenly stop talking and hold up a miniature chair, table or some other piece of furniture intended to be copied by the workman all were surprised to find how quickly time had flown. He would explain the use of what he had carved out and the place in the church so all could understand. He superintended everything himself. Windows were his especial care, he raising the money to pay for the most of them himself. The carpet for the chancel—we could not afford one anywhere else—he had made in "New York" so that we could have a churchly pattern.[16]

According to the legend cherished at St. Philip's, the little model was lent a few years later to the parish in Georgetown to guide them in erecting their church and was never returned.

The work of building proceeded slowly, not only because the fine workmanship took time and patience, but because the gathering war clouds made it difficult to raise money to complete the plan. J. W. Venable told the story in his report to the convention that met in May, 1861: "We succeeded, last fall, in getting our beautiful Church edifice under cover, but were then forced to suspend work upon it, for want of funds. . . . At length, to our great joy, one of the vestry-men (not a member of the Church) proposed to complete the building at his own expense, and then take a joint note from the Vestry . . . This proposal was accepted, and the work of completion is now going on. Should no interruption occur, we hope to have the church ready for occupation by the last of June." Shortly after the close of the convention, Bishop Smith "dedicated" St. Philip's Church in a sort of wartime substitute for a proper consecration after the payment of all debts. But by this time men in uniform, both blue and gray, were riding hard across the length and breadth of Kentucky. The stained glass windows were hardly in place before the backwash of a great battle all but overwhelmed the beautiful church and hallowed it with the prayers of a soldier-bishop.

[16] Sarah Smedley Fife to "Mr. Cooley," September 30, 1901 (Archives of Diocese of Lexington, University of Kentucky Library).

CHURCH OF THE HOLY TRINITY, GEORGETOWN

There is good reason for including the parish at Georgetown among the antebellum churches of the Diocese. Monthly services were being held there as early as 1847. The parish was admitted by the annual convention of 1864, and the cornerstone of its handsome church was laid in 1867. The actual founding of this parish during the war years is evidence of the "favorable position" of the Episcopal Church in Central Kentucky at this time.

Georgetown is located in the rich "level land," about ten miles north of Lexington and some twelve miles due east of Frankfort. Settled in the Revolutionary period around an exceptionally fine spring and near a fort for defense against the Indians, it attracted an enterprising citizenry. In time it supported taverns and newspapers, and numerous factories that turned out hats, shoes, nails, firearms, and much else. The Reverend Elijah Craig, eminent Baptist preacher of the community, operated paper and grist mills as well as a notably good distillery. He also established a school sometime before 1790 and thus early made the town a center for learning.[17]

By 1846 Georgetown was a community of well over 1500 inhabitants and the home of thriving Georgetown College, a Baptist institution of higher learning, founded in 1829. Frequently professors associated with the college established preparatory schools in the town that drew pupils from a wide area. Colonel Thornton F. Johnson, a West Pointer from Virginia, founded the Georgetown Female Seminary in 1837 and also the Western Military Institute in 1846. Dr. J. E. Farnham, originally from Waterville, Maine, opened another female seminary in 1846. Among the numerous educators who flourished in Georgetown at this time there were a few Episcopalians who desired the services of their own church, and fortunately the diocesan convention of 1847 urged parish rectors to extend their ministry to neighboring communities. Word of the Georgetown group reached John N. Norton, a zealous young priest who had just been called as rector of Ascension Church in Frank-

[17] B. O. Gaines, *History of Scott County, Kentucky* (Georgetown, Ky.: 1904), pp. 11–14 *et passim*.

fort, and he lost no time in coming to them. He has left an account of his visits.

You ask for a brief sketch of my "missionary efforts" in Georgetown years ago. My attention was drawn to the place in 1847, as being an important one on account of the flourishing schools, and especially the *Military Institute,* which was located there. I well remember my first visit to Georgetown; having come thither, on the top of the stage, through a drenching rain, which left me with few dry threads. On Tuesday night, August 10th, 1847, I read service and preached in the Presbyterian meeting-house. We then had three communicants in the place: viz,—Colonel William F. Hopkins, of the Military Institute; Miss Susan Farnham, who taught in the Baptist (Female) Seminary owned by her brother; and Mrs. Elizabeth Threshley, a widow lady of great worth, the sister of Colonel Thornton Johnson of the Institute. I kept up those services on the first Monday night of each month for about three years, when the Military Institute was removed to Drennon Springs. During all this time the congregations were large and attentive, and many young persons from the various schools received their first impressions of the Church, which in after years brought them into her communion. We were very fortunate in a choir. Among those who became Churchmen were the children of a deceased Baptist minister, all of whom had his fine musical taste, and sang the chants, etc., with great spirit. Several persons, the fruits of those missionary efforts, were baptized and confirmed at Frankfort. They are now scattered over the whole land, and some of them have proved the instruments of no little good. If I could have spared the time for pastoral visiting, much more might have been done.[18]

Norton's missionary work at Georgetown in 1847–1850 laid the foundations for the future parish. From that time forward a small group of faithful people met at intervals, sometimes only for "lay readings" and sometimes for services by visiting clergy. From 1850 to 1863 the visitors included Dr. Norton; the Reverend F. H. L. Laird, assigned to them as a missionary in 1847–1849; the Reverend Carter Page, rector of the church at Cynthiana; the Reverend Charles H. Page while he was at St. Matthew's near Louisville; and the Bishop, who made annual visitations.

[18] John Nicholas Norton to John W. Venable, May 9, 1865 (Copy in Parish Record Book I, June 1862–January 26, 1958) of Church of the Holy Trinity, Georgetown, Kentucky. This Record contains the basic facts about the history of the parish; see also a brief MS history by the Rev. Canon William D. Smith, its present rector.

The little group was greatly strengthened in 1851 by the addition of the Clarke brothers and their families, staunch Episcopalians from Newark, New Jersey. John and Henry Clarke were the sons of an English-born carriagemaker who built the excellent carriage presented by the citizens of Newark to the Honorable Henry Clay in 1844. They likewise were successful carriagemakers, despite the fact that John lost his left hand in the accidental discharge of a gun when he was twenty. They soon set up their factory in Georgetown and subsequently acquired also a quarry and a planing mill.

The Clarke brothers had been confirmed at Trinity Church in Newark, one of the great parishes in the East, and they brought confidence and enthusiasm to the meetings in Georgetown. John served as a lay reader. A little choir was organized, which rehearsed at his residence. The gatherings at the courthouse or in schoolrooms began to be better attended. As early as April, 1861, John W. Venable, rector at Versailles and missionary to Harrodsburg, reported to the Central Convocation of the Diocese (in charge of its missionary projects) that Georgetown was "a place urgently desiring the Church" and urged that steps be taken to provide occasional services by clergymen.[19] The beginning of the war interfered with these plans, and not until the following year was Venable able to offer help. At that time the church at Harrodsburg became temporarily inactive, and he opened up correspondence with the Clarkes.

The first week in January, 1863, he wrote to them offering to hold regular monthly services in Georgetown. He must have received a prompt reply, because on Sunday, January 11, he officiated at services in the courthouse that were well attended. Under his direction, the group organized a Sunday school and began to form a parish. In March, 1864, twenty-five persons signed a petition for admittance into union with the Diocese as the Church of the Holy Trinity. Several family groups were included: six Clarkes, four Bealls, three Webbs, two Whites, two Kearneys, two Pullens. Seventeen of the signers were women. The parish was admitted by the convention in May, 1864; and in August elected a vestry composed of the following: Henry Clarke, senior warden, Gustavus Schultz, junior war-

---

[19] *Journal of the Diocese of Kentucky* for 1861, p. 16.

den, John Clarke, Tyson Beall, J. Stoddard Johnston, T. B. Elliott, W. F. Pullen, and Ben Alvin Duvall.

Undoubtedly the Clarkes were chiefly responsible for the new parish's desire to build its own house of worship immediately, even in the midst of civil strife. Their Churchmanship had a background of Gothic architecture and ceremony in Newark which they wished to recreate for Holy Trinity Church. Their enthusiasm was shared by the other parishioners, who wanted for Georgetown an edifice on a par with the excellent Episcopal churches in nearby rival communities. The ladies held a benefit fair not long after the cessation of hostilities which raised six hundred dollars toward the purchase of two lots on one of the principal streets. The first contribution to the building fund was ten dollars sent to John Clarke by his friend, Jeremiah C. Garthwaite, of Newark, a zealous worker in Grace Church, of which the Reverend George T. Chapman had been the first rector.[20] Pledges from parishioners were generous; the Clarkes promised fifteen hundred dollars in labor.

The new church was to be a small Gothic edifice built of local stone, and according to all accounts, including those of his daughter, John Clarke drew up the plans and specifications.[21] The choice of Gothic architecture was not extraordinary in view of the Bishop's admiration for it and the Gothic buildings erected recently at Cynthiana and Harrodsburg. A tradition still persists in the Diocese that when the Georgetown Episcopalians started their plans they borrowed the small wooden model which the Bishop had carved for the Harrodsburg church and never returned it.[22] The model has indeed disappeared, but if it was ever sent to Georgetown it had small influence upon John Clarke's design. Holy Trinity differs from St. Philip's in basic ways: the materials used, the interior ceiling arches, and the effect of the windows. These two edifices, together with Advent in Cynthiana, form a group of small Episcopal Gothic churches that are of especial interest in the architec-

[20] Edward F. Bataille, *Grace Church in Newark,* p. 15 ff.
[21] Laura Clarke; MS regarding the building of Holy Trinity, written for Big Springs Chapter, D. A. R., April, 1921; and *Journal of the Diocese of Kentucky* for 1867, pp. 31–32, for Bishop George D. Cummins' account. Also Flem Smith Collection of papers about the building (Records of Holy Trinity Church, Georgetown, Kentucky).
[22] Williams, *History of St. Philip's Church, Harrodsburg, Kentucky,* p. 5.

tural development of central Kentucky because of their individual features.

In addition to being the planners of Holy Trinity Church, the Clarke brothers were literally its builders. Not since the early days when saintly Amos Cleaver hauled the bricks for St. Peter's through the streets of Paris had such zeal been displayed. Under the Clarkes' supervision, the stones for the foundation were excavated on the building site, and they themselves helped lay the foundation for a building seventy-two feet long, designed to seat three hundred and twenty-five persons. The cornerstone was laid in November, 1867. The walls rose slowly and were at last roofed over, but the tower at the northern angle of the nave and transept and also the basement were left unfinished while the brothers labored to complete the interior woodwork. At the end of the business day in the carriage shop they and their craftsmen had their suppers and then returned to work until midnight for the church. Ceiling arches, doors, pews, and the altar and chancel fittings—all these were designed and fashioned and carefully polished. With his good right hand John Clarke did the carving on the chairs, desk, table, and chancel rail. People must have come at times to watch the work in progress or else how would John's small daughter have remembered a half century later that the rails for the chancel and choir were made of white pine drygoods boxes? When all was finished and carefully fitted into place late in 1869 the church acquired a handwrought look, like the work of medieval craftsmen, a look it has retained through the years.

During this period of building Mr. Venable ministered faithfully to the parish, which was still small but growing slowly along with the stone church. As was his wont he inaugurated meticulous records, beginning with a brief history of the parish, all inscribed in his copperplate handwriting. To help pay the cost of building the church he solicited contributions from the large parishes in Louisville, Lexington, and Frankfort with heartening results. He received generous gifts from Philadelphia as well.[23] His good taste and knowledge of art undoubtedly influenced the builders in their ar-

[23] John W. Venable to James Craik, January 15, 1870 (James Craik Papers); also *Journal of the Diocese of Kentucky* for 1868 and 1869. Parochial reports from Church of the Holy Trinity.

rangement and decoration of the interior. The design for the center window with its floriated cross beneath the symbols for the Trinity —the All-Seeing Eye, the Lamb, and the Dove—may well have been his.

In June, 1869, a devastating fire swept through part of the business section of the town, sparing the new church but postponing the payment of some of the money pledged to it. Not until June 23, 1870, was the church consecrated by the Right Reverend George David Cummins, Assistant Bishop of the Diocese of Kentucky, in the presence of a large gathering from all over the central part of the state. At the consecration services the rector proudly presented a class of seven for confirmation, and the next day, being St. John's Day, young Deacon Walter Tearne, son of Trinity Church in Covington, was advanced to the priesthood and Holy Communion was celebrated. The little stone building was now truly the house of the Lord.

The stalwart generation that established Holy Trinity Church during the tumultous sixties flourished quietly under the ministry of the Reverend Mr. Venable until 1882, when he resigned to become rector of Grace Church in Hopkinsville. With his leaving, an era ended for Episcopalians in Georgetown.

CHURCH OF THE ASCENSION, MT. STERLING

When the diocesan convention of 1847 passed a resolution recommending that all rectors of established parishes conduct regular services where missions might be organized, there was an awakening which first bore fruits in the new parishes at Cynthiana (1847) and at Maysville (1848). Other towns in the same northeasterly direction were also promising prospects: Mt. Sterling, Flemingsburg, Winchester, and Richmond. Of these, Mt. Sterling became the next focus of interest.

It was a town of about eight hundred inhabitants, located at the eastern rim of the rich bluegrass plateau and on an old, well-travelled route from the Ohio River down to Cumberland Gap, familiar to the Indians long before the white settlers used it. Because the region was exposed to Indian attacks in the early days, it was settled later than some of the other good land. As county seat of Montgomery, it profited from the courthouse revenue of a territory that originally reached to the Virginia line and contributed to the formation of many additional counties. Its prosperity also derived from good crops and cattle. The settlers in Mt. Sterling, of the same stock as those in the rest of central Kentucky, included a number of families who remained Church-minded in the midst of Methodist and other denominations.

The first regular Episcopal services in Mt. Sterling were conducted by the Reverend John Austen Merrick, a zealous, scholarly High Churchman from the Diocese of Pennsylvania, who assumed his duties as rector of St. Peter's Church in Paris during December, 1854. Very soon thereafter he began to make "monthly missionary visits at regular intervals" to Mt. Sterling, which was only twenty-three miles distant. He probably did so at the suggestion of Bishop Smith, who wanted very much to see a mission established there. Although at first Merrick found it to be "uphill, antagonistic work" he continued his visits faithfully.[24] In the autumn of 1857 the Reverend John West of Massachusetts, the newly appointed General Agent of the Central Convocation of the Diocese, began holding fortnightly services in a rented upstairs room on South Maysville Street. Tradition says that in bitter cold weather a faithful couple, William C. and Caroline Davis Magowan, would fill the back of their carriage with coal and kindling, drive in from their home in the country, and build a fire in the bare little room before the congregation arrived.[25] Early in 1858 John West assisted the group in organizing the Church of the Ascension, which was admitted to the Diocese that year. In the meantime, services were held from time to time by the rectors from Lexington, Versailles, and Paris.

The new parish made excellent progress under the leadership of its wardens, William C. Magowan and William Foster, and other able laymen such as Charles Holman, George Howard, Robert P. Wil-

[24] See *Journals of the Diocese of Kentucky* for 1854–69 for parochial reports, reports to the Central Convocation, and the Bishop's Annual Addresses for mention of Mt. Sterling.

[25] Brief unpublished history of Church of the Ascension, Mt. Sterling, by Emily Turner Greene (Mrs. J. Oldham). Another valuable unpublished sketch of the parish by Larry Whitt, present Choir Director, is also in the church archives.

liams, George Gist, and J. T. Williams. A large lot across from the courthouse was purchased with funds, it is believed, that were willed to the parish by Mrs. Mary Howard Fleming, daughter of George Fleming. On the lot already stood a small brick building, which was remodeled for church services and drew praise from the Bishop as a "small, neat chapel." It was arranged also for use as a school. The parish was very desirous of having a resident minister, and so, in conjunction with the still newer group at nearby Flemingsburg, they called the Reverend Jonathan N. Haven as rector at a salary of eight hundred dollars a year. He was mature and experienced, having spent several years as a minister of the Christian Church in Mason County before being ordained to the Episcopal priesthood in April, 1869. Within a year the parish numbered "seventy souls." With pardonable pride he made the following report to the 1860 annual convention regarding the church at Mt. Sterling.

When the Rector took charge of this Parish, fifteen months ago, there was but one Communicant in it; now there are 11. Then the congregation was from 6 to 30; now the Church is too small to hold the congregation. Then there was no Sunday School; now, including pupils and teachers, there is an average of 30. Then there was no Bible Class; now there is one of 20 members. There is a good choir.

The Parish has commenced building a Parsonage upon the Church lot. Upon the whole, the Parish is in a flourishing condition.

Within a few months, however, he removed to Troy, Ohio, and the "neat and comfortable Parsonage" was occupied by his successor, Deacon Frank M. Gregg. Gregg was an unusually promising young clergyman who had been trained as a candidate for Holy Orders in Louisville. His new parishioners had the satisfaction of witnessing his ordination to the priesthood in their own church on April 21, 1861. To their regret he was called in September to the rectorship in Maysville left vacant by F. B. Nash. Services were held in Mt. Sterling during the following year by the indefatigable Reverend Charles Page, who, after retiring as teacher and army chaplain, became a missionary to a dozen churches and localities in the area. He preached 155 times that year but was unable to continue his travels on account of wartime conditions.

About 1862 the Reverend S. D. Tompkins, another teacher-missionary, held services and also conducted a school in the Church of the Ascension. His stay was short because the Federal troops took over the church for use as a "camp" and hospital. As a garrison town for the Union forces Mt. Sterling was repeatedly attacked by the Confederate cavalry raiders. In March, 1863, and again in July, 1864, there was fighting through the streets of the town and much destruction of property. Many residents left the town during these years. Mr. Tompkins departed when he was compelled to give up the use of the church building and shortly settled in Catlettsburg in order to resume his teaching and preaching there. In his report to the annual convention in 1865 he commented on his departure from Mt. Sterling: "When I left Mt. Sterling there were only four communicants in that place, the others having left in consequence of the difficulties arising from the raids."

The Union authorities used the Episcopal church in Mt. Sterling either for its troops or as a post office for over four years without any renumeration to the parish for rent or damages. Mrs. Henrietta Williams, one of the original members, recalled to the end of her days how the little group of Episcopalians were "completely debarred" from their cherished house of worship and compelled to watch in silence as its pews and furniture were burned for firewood. They must have had meetings somewhere for prayer and fellowship, with occasional services by some clergyman. When the building was released a year or so after the end of hostilities the group set about to restore it for services. The women gave "little suppers" to raise money. The cost to put it back in order was more than a thousand dollars.[26]

On Thursday, November 7, 1867, a small but thankful congregation gathered in the newly restored Ascension Church for a service conducted by the Right Reverend George D. Cummins, recently elected Assistant Bishop of the Diocese of Kentucky. On his first

[26] Transcripts of the recollections of Mrs. Henrietta Williams and other Mt. Sterling citizens regarding Ascension Church during the Civil War are preserved in the National Archives, as cited in Chapter XIV, Footnote 12, of this volume.

visitation he was evidently impressed by the devotion and courage of this remnant of a once promising parish. Soon afterward he assigned the Reverend Charles Stewart to be missionary to Mt. Sterling and Cynthiana.

Mr. Stewart's stay was short and the post was vacant for about two years. In 1870 the place was filled by Deacon Walter Tearne, who had been brought up in Trinity Church, Covington. He was a son of the Diocese, dedicated to its own missions. During his six years as rector the stouthearted church in Mt. Sterling was strengthened by the addition of new members from among the newcomers who were constructing the railroad and developing coal and timber prospects in the nearby mountain region. Ere long Ascension Church would be able to realize the hope of its antebellum founders in the erection of a beautiful Gothic church on their original lot.

ALL SAINTS CHURCH, FLEMINGSBURG

Fleming County, a part of Mason until 1798, was settled by intrepid people from Virginia and Pennsylvania who pushed up into the Licking Valley and the hills beyond to build stockades called "forts" for protection against Indian raids. Flemingsburg, the county seat, is only seventeen miles south of the Ohio River, and since pioneer days an important road leading from the river down to Cumberland Gap has passed through the town. In about 1850, when the Episcopalians were desirous of establishing missions in this "northeast middle part of the state," they were naturally attracted to Flemingsburg, then a community of about eight hundred. It was about the same size as Mt. Sterling and had much the same social and economic pattern.[27] A good many Fleming County citizens were prosperous enough to build "commodious, comfortable homes" in town and on the good farms nearby. Among such families were the descendants of Colonel John Fleming, for whom the county and town were named, and the household of Samuel Stock-

[27] Collins, *History of Kentucky* (1874), Vol. II, pp. 230–236; William Wilson Hume Clay, *Fleming County, Kentucky, 1773–1860,* M.A. Thesis, University of Kentucky, 1963; Dan T. Fischer, *Condensed History of Fleming County, Kentucky* (Flemingsburg, Ky.: 1908). Also Harriet D. Grannis (Mrs. J. Kidwell) to Rebecca Smith Lee, October 23, 1968 (re Ashton family).

well, one of the developers of the town. Samuel's wife, Charlotte Ashton, inherited her Episcopal faith from forebears who had been prominent members of Christ Church, Lexington.

In such a community there were numerous churches. The Methodists (1787), Presbyterians (about 1799), Baptists (about 1800), Christians (1839), and Roman Catholics (1850) were all well established by mid-century. In the spring of 1859 Bishop Smith assisted the Episcopalians in Flemingsburg "at the organization of a new parish . . . by the name of All Saints Church." The first wardens were Leander M. Cox and Samuel Stockwell. The group consisted of more than fifty "souls" from about a dozen families. Only three persons were communicants: C. F. Mitchell, Mrs. John Fleming, and Mrs. Charlotte Stockwell. All Saints Church applied for admission into union with the Diocese at the convention in May, 1859, and although it was not formally accepted until the following year it was welcomed cordially. It was arranged that the Flemingsburg parish should share the services of the Reverend Mr. Jonathan H. Haven, who was the rector at Maysville and made his home there.[28]

Mr. Haven was impressed with the prospects at Flemingsburg, and with good reason. Within a year's time the "number of souls" had increased to 86 and the communicants to five. A church edifice was under construction which was to cost $2500, of which $2000 had already been subscribed within the parish. Plans were under way for a rectory. A melodeon had been acquired at a cost of $150, and the choir and congregation were "well sustained," in the opinion of Mr. Haven. He even let it be understood that he intended to move his residence to Flemingsburg in the near future, but in the summer of 1860 he moved to Ohio instead. His leaving was a real loss to the Diocese. His young churches had done well under his leadership and thereby aided the convocation plan for diocesan missions.

Haven's place was filled immediately by Deacon Frank M. Gregg, an able young man who attracted good crowds to the services, organized classes for the children, and encouraged the Ladies' Sewing Society to have a fair and supper that raised $520 for the building campaign. The new building was located on Water

---

[28] *Journal of the Diocese of Kentucky* for 1857 and later is the source for most of the available information regarding All Saints, Flemingsburg. See also William Wilson Hume Clay, *op. cit.,* p. 114.

Street, in the center of town, near several other churches which it was intended to rival if not surpass. An influential trustee was Samuel Stockwell, who had been one of the builders of the excellent Federal style courthouse nearby. All Saints Church, too, was a square building set back a little from the street, with thick red brick walls, and no doubt was intended to have an imposing tower and spire.

The outbreak of the war stopped the construction work, and the handsome walls with pointed, churchly windows stood unfinished throughout those troublous times. The Reverend Mr. Gregg continued to hold services on a limited schedule in Flemingsburg, although in 1861 he gave up his post at Mt. Sterling to become the wartime rector of the church at Maysville. His successors at Maysville after the war continued to visit Flemingsburg, but work on the building was not resumed. When the Right Reverend George D. Cummins, newly elected Assistant Bishop of the Diocese, paid his first visit to Flemingsburg on March 11, 1867, he conducted services in the Presbyterian church. The sight of the roofless walls of All Saints grieved and embarrassed him so much that in his convention address the following May he wrote: "It was one of the saddest sights I have yet beheld in the diocese to look upon a church edifice half built which had stood there in its desolation for six years." As a matter of fact, the building was about to be put up for sale, but he persuaded the remaining parishioners to make another effort to complete it and promised to try to raise outside funds. The unfinished church disturbed him deeply, and he endeavored year after year to get it completed. Finally, early in 1871, he "assumed the responsibility of finishing this building to take away the reproach from our Zion," and trusted that he might find others willing to aid him in the good work.[29]

To the convention in 1872 he was able to report with pride some good news:

November 7 and 8 I passed in Flemingsburg; preached twice and confirmed one person. Here I had the great pleasure of officiating in our own church-edifice, which, after standing for ten years unfinished, has at last

---

[29] *Journal of the Diocese of Kentucky* for 1871, pp. 56–57; also *Journals* for 1867 through 1872 in the Assistant Bishop's reports.

been completed. At one time it seemed impossible to save the church-building from being sold, but it is at last saved to the Church, and will, I trust, be a great blessing in the community.

The completion of the church proved, however, to be little more than a proud gesture of the aging generation that had established All Saints Parish. Services were held infrequently for the little group of twenty-five worshipers by rectors of other parishes until 1878–80, when the Reverend Joseph Tays, rector at Maysville, was appointed missionary at Flemingsburg also. His first official report in 1879 sums up the situation he found there:

There are no male members connected with the Mission, and scarcely any of the female members are in a condition to pay anything. And although the most kindly feeling is manifested towards us, yet from the fact that almost everyone is identified with some religious body, we have but little to expect from the present population. We hope, however, that with the completion of the railroad, there will be an influx of population, of which we hope to get our share. The congregations vary from fifteen to fifty-five. I have been treated in the most hospitable manner by the citizens.

The town did not have an influx of prosperity and new people at this time, as did its neighbor, Mt. Sterling. Older members of All Saints died, notably Mrs. Charlotte Stockwell, a founder and a pillar of strength. Mr. Tays transferred to the Diocese of Mississippi at the end of 1880. About a year later the Fleming County Court ordered the church property sold to satisfy an unpaid mechanic's lien that had rested on it from the beginning. The deed of sale, dated March 27, 1882, was signed by three surviving trustees and vestrymen of the church: Samuel Stockwell, William S. Botts, and John T. Fleming.[30]

The name of All Saints, Flemingsburg, appears intermittently on the parish roster and assessment lists in the *Journal* of the Diocese until 1884. The church building still stands in the business section of Flemingsburg and is used for commercial purposes. Its ecclesiastical origin is hardly discernible because of a large addition built across the front and many other alterations.

[30] Fleming County, Kentucky, *Deed Book No. 46,* pp. 405–406. See also *Journal of the Diocese of Kentucky* for 1882, p. 32.

12 *The Berkley Era at Christ Church, Lexington*

The resignation of Benjamin Bosworth Smith as rector of Christ Church, Lexington in October, 1838, marked the end of his eight years of service in the parish. It had been a troubled time that saw the organization of the Diocese, the establishment of the Episcopal Theological Seminary, and the struggle for power between the Bishop and a group of his colleagues. Christ Church, meanwhile, had been involved overmuch in diocesan matters and neglectful of its own parochial life. The choice of the Reverend Edward Fairfax Berkley as the new rector was indeed providential. Although young, he had a practical turn of mind and was a natural diplomat and peacemaker. After the Bishop removed his residence to Louisville in 1841, Berkley became the accepted leader of Episcopalians in and near Lexington, and the moderator of many confrontations between them and the Bishop in the years to come.

Christ Church, Lexington, at the close of 1838 was in a depressed and diminished state, with less than fifty communicants. Many of its leading laymen had removed from the town or for personal reasons were not attending church. Having recently accepted the resignations of Bishop Smith as rector and of Edward Winthrop as assistant, the vestry met at the home of the Rev. John Ward on the day after Christmas for the purpose of choosing a new rector. Several clergymen from outside the Diocese were considered and rejected. The vestry agreed, in consequence of the grave importance of selecting a man who might bring peace and union to the strife-torn parish, to defer calling a permanent rector at this time. They resolved, instead, to engage temporarily the services of the Rev. Edward Berkley,[1] who less than two weeks before had been ordained to the diaconate in Christ Church[2] and who was well known to the parish. Certainly their choice met with Bishop Smith's approval and may have been made at his suggestion, an indication that the reorganized vestry handled the situation with good judgment.

Edward Fairfax Berkley was born in Washington, D. C. on September 20, 1813. He was baptized in Christ Church there and confirmed in the same church in 1831 by the Bishop of Maryland. The early death of his father made it necessary for him, the oldest son, to go to work to help his mother support his five brothers and sisters. Accordingly, at the age of eleven years, he entered the printing office of Davis and Force in Washington. One of his duties was to deliver each morning, except Sunday, to the four government departments of State, Treasury, War, and Navy, the *National Journal,* which was published by that firm. In the delivery of this paper, the boy met many prominent government officials and came to admire above all others the Honorable Henry Clay of Kentucky, who was Secretary of State in the Cabinet of President John Quincy Adams. The great statesman never failed to greet the paper carrier with a kind and cheering word.

In 1832, young Berkley entered Bristol College, on the Delaware River just above Philadelphia. The college had been established that very year to offer a collegiate education to young men interested in the ministry of the Episcopal Church. He remained there until the college closed in 1835.[3] It is highly probable that Bishop B. B. Smith visited Bristol College on his 1835 eastern trip, designed to interest students in the Lexington seminary. At any rate, Edward Berkley went thence to Lexington that same year and entered the seminary. From the very beginning he proved a helpful aide to Smith, who considered him one of his favorite "sons in the Gospel," upon whom he counted to be "ministers for life in this dear, this needy land."[4] As a student, Berkley operated the seminary's Griswold Press, and for a time he acted as agent for the local Bible Society in charge of its depository on Short Street.[5]

The Rev. Mr. Berkley noted in his paper-backed account book that he accepted the temporary rectorship of Christ Church on

---

[1] Christ Church, Lexington, Kentucky, Minutes of the Vestry, December 26, 1838.

[2] *Journal of the Diocese of Kentucky* (1839), p. 9. Also Christ Church Records, Edward F. Berkley Account Book.

[3] For biographical data on Berkley's early life, *The Church News,* Diocese of Missouri, XXVI, No. 303, p. 94 (March, 1895).

[4] B. B. Smith to Edward F. Berkley, May 2, 1839, in the Berkley Papers, Filson Club, Louisville. Indexed by Alex Galt Robinson.

[5] *Lexington Intelligencer.* August 25, 1837, p. 7.

January 2, 1839 at a salary of $900 per annum and "commenced" his labors as a minister of the parish on the following Sunday.[6] He was a big, handsome fellow, endowed with excellent presence and a fine speaking voice. He conducted the services with dramatic force, in contrast to the Bishop's unexciting delivery, a change which pleased his parishioners and no doubt accounted in part for the hundred-dollar raise in salary when they decided in April to retain him, although still in deacon's orders, as their permanent minister. The raise was most welcome at this time, and a few weeks later he married Sarah Anne Slaughter Maury of Bath County, sister of his fellow seminarian, Matthew Fontaine Maury,[7] who had recently become rector of Trinity Church, Danville. Of the seven children of Mr. and Mrs. Berkley, six (five daughters and a son) were born during their residency in Lexington, and all were baptized in Christ Church. The Berkleys lived in the rectory on the corner of Third and Mill during most of their stay in Lexington.

Blessed with common sense and understanding of human nature, Berkley joined with his parishioners in their wish to renovate the church building, which had been allowed to get shabby in the past few years. Within a few months, three hundred dollars was raised for inside painting and whitening and for remodeling the church entrance, as well as five hundred dollars for a new bell and contributions for the local orphan asylum, which Christ Church members had been instrumental in founding at the time of the cholera. The attendance at services and the number of communicants gradually began to increase. Berkley became rector of Christ Church officially on Christmas Day, 1839, when he was ordained to the priesthood in his church by Bishop Smith. His rectorate of nineteen years is the longest in the history of the parish.

From the beginning of his ministry as a young deacon, Berkley endeared himself to all with whom he came in contact. Friendly, outgoing, deeply concerned with the problems and perplexities of his parishioners, he ministered to the aged, the sick, and the dying with deep sympathy and understanding. He very early showed concern for the inmates of the Eastern Lunatic Asylum and was

[6] Christ Church Records, Berkley Account Book.
[7] B. B. Smith to Edward F. Berkley, May 2, 1839, Filson Club.

rejoiced when one inmate, to whom he had often ministered, returned to sanity.[8] The young people of his parish loved and respected him as a father. He was extremely popular among his fellow clergymen throughout the Diocese. He baptized many of their children and buried a number of them as well, so high was the infant mortality rate at that period. A few months after his own marriage he had the pleasure of marrying his sister-in-law, Elizabeth Maury, to his good friend, the Rev. Francis B. Nash, rector of St. Peter's Church, Paris.[9] He ministered to the slaves and free colored servants of his parishioners with the same tender understanding which he manifested to all sorts and conditions of people, baptizing their children, nurturing them in the Christian faith, presenting many of them for confirmation, marrying and burying them.[10] He was extremely interested in the blind, so much so that he employed a blind organist at Christ Church, Mr. William D. Hulett, a gifted musician who was greatly esteemed by the entire congregation. He never forgot the orphan waifs of the community and was zealous that his parish give generously to the support of the Orphan Asylum.

The young rector did not confine himself exclusively to his parochial duties, but almost immediately entered into the affairs of the Diocese with the same zeal and definiteness displayed at Christ Church. During his entire ministry in Lexington he served on all the most important committees. He acted as secretary of the diocesan conventions for a period of fifteen years and was a member of the Standing Committee, a trustee of the Episcopal Theological Seminary, and a member of the Sunday School Committee for almost as long. Over and over again he was elected a delegate to the General Convention. Perhaps the high esteem in which he was held by his fellow clergymen was due to his uncanny ability to hold a middle course in diocesan disputations. He was always close to the Bishop and to the Bishop's cortege, yet was also respected and importuned for advice by those not in sympathy with B. B. Smith.[11]

[8] Christ Church Records, Berkley Account Book.
[9] *Ibid.*, Berkley Diary.
[10] *Ibid.*
[11] Berkley Papers, Filson Club.

His Churchmanship never seemed to be an issue. Since he did not take sides, it is impossible to align him with any clerical clique. Because he did not publish any writings, his Churchmanship is mere guesswork. He conducted the Church services in an impressive and tasteful manner and he adhered to the *Book of Common Prayer* and to the canons of the Church.

Surely it was by ordinance and not by accident that Berkley was chosen rector of Christ Church during the crucial decades of the 1840's and 1850's. A clergyman of decided opinions who expressed them freely would not have been effectual and very likely would have proved entirely inadequate to mediate the differences of his parishioners. Lexington, during the period of Berkley's ministry at Christ Church, was a bustling community of some 8,000 inhabitants, of whom a little more than half were white. His ministry spanned a period marked by extremes—in politics, religion, economy, even in climate.

It was an age of great political excitement, with frequent meetings attended sometimes by as many as 12,000 persons, many from neighboring towns. Henry Clay was the undisputed leader of the Whig party, and the citizenry turned out to cheer the famous statesman whenever and wherever he spoke. Clay had long been a pewholder and supporter of Christ Church, often attending services there, and was well known to its young rector, who had been delighted to find his old friend of earlier days in his congregation. One Sunday in November, 1840, the rector of Christ Church had ascended the pulpit and, looking down upon the congregation, was both pleased and flustered to behold the President-elect of the United States seated beside Mr. Clay. General William Henry Harrison was in Kentucky on private business and while a guest at "Ashland," had accompanied his host to church. Berkley could not resist the impulse to preach a patriotic sermon on so grand an occasion, and this he did. It was a stirring sermon, patriotic but hardly spiritual. A few days later, while walking the paths of "Ashland" with his old friend, he received a gentle but effective reproof. "When I go to church," said Mr. Clay, "I wish to hear something of the way by which a poor sinner, struggling with the ills and the evils of the present life, may be able to reach and enjoy the blessings of the better land."[12] Berkley henceforth made it a point to preach only the Gospel of Jesus Christ.

It was a period of great religious fervour too. Berkley followed with great interest the debate on baptism and other subjects in 1843 between Elder Alexander Campbell of the Reformed or Christian Church and the Reverend Nathan L. Rice of the Presbyterians.[13] During the three weeks of heated argument, moderated by his friend, Mr. Clay, Berkley, bundled warmly against the cold November wind, walked the short distance from his church to the Main Street Christian Church to listen attentively to the controversy. The mode of baptism would have mattered little to the Episcopal minister as long as it was with water in the name of the Holy Trinity.

Likewise, the slavery issue was white hot in the early forties. There were angry and fierce contests between the abolitionists and proslavery advocates, and Christ Church contained its share of both. Robert Wickliffe, a vestryman, distinguished lawyer, and one of the largest and wealthiest slaveowners in Kentucky, was the leader of the proslavery element and waged unceasing warfare against both abolitionists and those who favored gradual emancipation, such as Henry Clay. The columns of the Lexington *Observer and Reporter* were filled with vitriolic debates between the two factions. Lexington was the storm center of the ever increasing controversy. On a hot August day in 1845, a large number of Berkley's parishioners were included in the committee of sixty citizens of Lexington who proceeded to Cassius Clay's *True American* office, took possession of the press and printing apparatus, and shipped it by rail to Cincinnati. It is very probable that their rector was on hand in city court a few days later to hear the verdict of not guilty. John W. Hunt, George Norton, Thomas Marshall, Richard Higgins, Dr. J. Bush, and Thomas Waters were a few of his parishioners directly involved. Many others, if not themselves involved, were, like James Clay, closely connected. The fiery abolitionist, Cassius Clay, who lay abed with typhoid fever, was also well-known to Berkley for al-

---

[12] *The Church News,* Diocese of Missouri (March, 1895) Also see Elizabeth King Smith and Mary LeGrand Didlake, *Christ Church 1796–1946* (Lexington, 1946), p. 30, for slightly different account.

[13] The debate began on November 15, 1843, and lasted three weeks.

though he was not himself a communicant of Christ Church, his wife, the daughter of Dr. Elisha Warfield, was a lifelong member.

At the end of three years as rector of Christ Church, Berkley could write in his report to the convention that his parish had been "the subject of many mercies."[14] The number of communicants had increased from below fifty to over a hundred, less than a dozen short of the communicant strength of the largest parish in the Diocese, St. Paul's, Louisville. The rector had begun a series of doctrine classes "with the view of pressing the truth upon the consciences of the people in his charge," and so happy were the results that the class was soon compelled to move to a larger meeting room. "These people," he stated, "have been brought to feel the exceeding sinfulness of sin so deeply that there are a number already looking forward to another visit from the Bishop, for the purpose of ratifying their Baptismal vows in the Holy Rite of Confirmation."[15] The Sunday school was prospering too, numbering about eighty students and fifteen teachers. The vestry, therefore, decided to erect in the rear of the church a lecture and Sunday school room, and the congregation contributed $1,000 for the purpose. Here the rector continued to hold his doctrine classes; here was housed the one-thousand-volume parish library; here in May, 1843, was held the Fifteenth Annual Convention of the Diocese of Kentucky.

The new lecture room added greatly to the life of Christ Church Parish, but the church building proper, which had been considered unsafe by many from the day of its erection in 1814, had become obsolete. It was therefore determined in December, 1845, that the old church be razed and a new and much larger building be erected on the same site. The rector and vestry contracted with a local architect, Major Thomas Lewinski,[16] to draw up the plans and specifications for a commodious church. Lewinski, a Polish émigré, had moved from Louisville to Lexington in 1842 and was then at the height of his popularity as an architect. Earlier in 1845 he had

---

[14] *Journal of the Diocese of Kentucky* (1842), p. 15.
[15] *Ibid.*
[16] For biographical sketch of Lewinski see: Clay Lancaster, *Ante Bellum Houses of the Bluegrass* (University of Kentucky Press, 1961) pp. 134–135.

designed "Mansfield," the Greek Revival home of Thomas Hart Clay, just beyond "Ashland" on the Richmond Pike, as well as a Greek Revival villa for James B. Clay, another son of Henry Clay, closer to town,[17] and was currently at work on the McChord Presbyterian Church, in the same block on Market Street as Christ Church. Lewinski worked on the plans for Christ Church throughout 1846, assiduously keeping account of the hours spent thereon each day. It was not unusual for him to devote eight or nine hours daily to this one project. From time to time he met with the building committee, and in late summer received instructions to reduce his original drawing. More long hours followed before he was able to write in his diary on October 12, 1846, "Finally closed specifications, delivered up the document and closed accounts—an epic in my career."[18]

Lewinski, who functioned strictly as an architect, had been associated in several projects with a young builder, John McMurtry,[19] who was related to him by marriage, and to him went the building contract for the Gothic Revival church on Market Street. McMurtry was a native Lexingtonian, who in 1833 at the age of twenty-one had become an apprentice to Gideon Shryock, the town's most prominent builder. The young apprentice had subleased a contract from Shryock for completing part of the work on Morrison College and he had a growing number of handsome residences to his credit. Ten years before he had made his first attempt at using Gothic motifs as well as his first attempt at church architecture, but St. Peter's Roman Catholic Church on North Limestone was not a particularly attractive building. He must have welcomed the opportunity to build Christ Church as well as to build the other Gothic church, the McChord Presbyterian, on Market Street. These two churches certainly helped establish the designer-builder team of Lewinski-McMurtry as among the foremost in America.

At eleven o'clock on the morning of March 17, 1847, a large crowd assembled on the corner of Market and Church Streets to

[17] Clay Villa is on Forest Avenue, near East Main Street.

[18] Account Book of Major T. Lewinski, 1845–1847, copied by Samuel Wilson, 1936, in Wilson Collection, University of Kentucky.

[19] For biographical sketch of McMurtry see: Lancaster, *Ante Bellum Houses*, pp. 116–117.

witness the laying of the cornerstone. The dedicatory address was delivered by the Reverend James Craik, rector of Christ Church, Louisville. A series of religious services, in honor of the occasion, began the night before and continued through the following Sunday in the City Hall.[20]

For over a year, while the church was abuilding, the congregation met elsewhere in the city, notably in the Chapel of Morrison College at nearby Transylvania University, and baptisms, confirmations, weddings, and funerals were likewise held either in the homes of parishioners or at Morrison College. It was for this reason that one of the most memorable baptisms in the history of Christ Church took place, not in the church but in the parlour of a private residence. The Rev. Mr. Berkley baptized his good friend, the Honorable Henry Clay, in the parlour of "Ashland" on June 22, 1847, in the presence of a few close friends, at the same time administering the holy rite to his daughter-in-law, Mrs. Thomas Hart Clay, and four of her children.[21] Thus at the age of seventy, the illustrious statesman, who had long professed an interest in the Church, became a member through baptism and a month later received the Holy Rite of Confirmation at the hands of Bishop Smith in Morrison College.[22]

The new church building was completed in May, 1848, and on Friday the nineteenth of that month the first service was held. The number of communicants stood at one hundred and twenty-five, and the rector reported that "this parish has the promise of greater prosperity than it has ever before enjoyed."[23] The whole cost of the building, including organ, bell and lamps, was $20,000.[24] The *Lexington Observer and Reporter* devoted several columns to a description of the new Christ Church, terming it "one of the most chaste, beautiful and perfect specimens of the plain Gothic which has been erected in the Western country, reflecting great credit alike upon the liberality of the congregation, the skill in art of the architect and

[20] *Lexington Observer and Reporter,* March 13, 1847, p. 3.
[21] Christ Church Records, Berkley Diary, p. 29.
[22] *Ibid.,* p. 50. Date of Clay's confirmation, July 18, 1847.
[23] *Journal of the Diocese of Kentucky* (1848), p. 20.
[24] *Ibid.*

contractor, and the exquisite taste and indefatigable attention of the building committee."[25]

Indeed, the congregation, the Diocese, and the entire community had reason to be proud of the new church. The proportions, though not large, were remarkably just, the building in exterior dimensions measuring fifty-nine by ninety-four feet. For a building in brick, it was one of the most massive and substantial of the period. The tower rose to a height of ninety-five feet and was surrounded by alternate cast-iron finials of Kentucky workmanship, six and eight feet in height. Ornamental finials also surmounted the buttresses along the sides. The building was colored with a wash of water, lime, and sand and at a short distance gave the appearance of stone.

Inside, the church manifested the same care and good taste. The height of the nave was thirty feet, with a ceiling of intersecting arches, coinciding lengthwise and transversely with the six window lays. There was a simple beauty in the side windows, the three lancets into which each was divided being filled with glass of a grave neutral tint, with a narrow border of brilliant blue and crimson, while the finials were of a more elaborate pattern, corresponding with the finish of the chancel window, of stained and painted glass and graceful and appropriate in design. The chaste and sombre effect of the interior was greatly heightened by the sober neutral tint of the walls and ceiling, in blocks as of stone. The floor of the church was of ash, and the woodwork of white pine, painted in imitation of oak. The chancel, which was raised two feet above the floor of the nave, was covered with an appropriate Gothic carpet, and the aisles with Venetian carpeting corresponding in colors with the pew linings and windows. The pews were lined and cushioned uniformly with a beautiful pattern of crimson moreen, in bold relief to the sober and chastened effect of the whole interior. A bell of very grave tones, an uncommonly large organ, manufactured by Henry Erben of New York, and a chaste and beautiful font, contributed by the children of the Sunday school, added greatly to the overall effect.[26]

[25] *Lexington Observer and Reporter*, May 24, 1848.
[26] *Ibid.*

The church was open for divine service and preaching twice on Sundays and once on principal holy days, as well as every Wednesday evening for worship and a lecture. The children were publicly catechized in the church on the first Sunday afternoon in each month.[27] On the second day of June, 1849, a year after its completion, the new Christ Church was consecrated to the glory of God by Bishop Smith.

By no means confining himself to parochial duties, Edward Berkley was becoming more and more involved in the missionary work of the Diocese. He had preached monthly in Maysville in 1846 and had assisted in the important work of organizing a parish there. He had preached in Versailles and Georgetown, at the request of the Reverend John Norton, with an eye to organizing parishes in these places. Throughout 1847 and 1848, he traded pulpits with various clergymen in the Diocese, feeling, with Dr. Craik, that this was an important aspect of diocesan life. He received calls from several parishes in the Diocese as well as some from without, but his work at Christ Church was not yet finished.

The excitement of the early forties had in nowise abated towards the middle or by the end of the decade. The War with Mexico had deeply affected the people of Kentucky, with a goodly number of its sons dead, wounded, and imprisoned. The death of Henry Clay, Jr. at Buena Vista had cast a gloom over the entire state. Cassius Clay received a hero's welcome upon his return from Mexico, and his political past was forgiven or temporarily forgotten. Early in 1849 the House of Representatives of Kentucky voiced its opposition to the abolition or emancipation of slavery in any form or shape whatever, but the issue remained one of the leading topics of public, private, and newspaper discussions, and there were an increasing number of clashes between those who held opposing views. Henry Clay's unequivocal declaration in favor of gradual emancipation, printed in newspapers throughout the country, was severely condemned by the Southern press. Cass Clay once more took up the abolitionist banner and harangued his cause from every available

---

[27] *Journal of the Diocese of Kentucky* (1849), p. 21.

stump, and more than once wielded his bowie knife in defense of his stand.

In the midst of this turmoil, Lexington was visited once again with the dreaded disease which sixteen years before had wiped out many of its citizens. In virulent form, the cholera swept like wild-fire through the city. A mass exodus by the wealthier citizens to distant spas began, some fifteen hundred white persons leaving the city. Those who remained battled the disease as best they could, and among these was the rector of Christ Church. During the long hot summer he ministered to his flock, baptizing a few and burying many, holding regular services in the new church on Sundays and on special days.[28] With the arrival of autumn, the great scourge left the city, but it returned from time to time during the next five years with renewed onslaughts.

The congregation of Christ Church had been worshipping in the new building less than two years when it became apparent that a mistake in seating capacity had been made. In his address to the Convention of 1850, Bishop Smith stated, "Were its size only a little more commensurate with the wants of the place, there would be almost everything to commend and be grateful for, in the completion of the third Church upon the same spot within the lifetime of some, who shared in the struggles of the earliest effort."[29] The rector was soon lamenting that there were so few free sittings for the poor, "a class of the population upon whom, it is believed, an excellent influence might be exerted, if we had church accommodations for them."[30] The necessity of enlargement increased as the congregation grew. "In its whole history here," wrote Berkley, "there never was such a tendency towards the Church as at this time."[31] Demands for pews, which the church was unable to supply, continued. Early in 1852 the church slightly increased its accommodations by installing eight new pews in the only space remaining open for the purpose. Edward Berkley continued to plead, though

[28] Christ Church Records, Berkley Diary.
[29] *Journal of the Diocese of Kentucky* (1850), pp. 21–22.
[30] *Journal* (1851), p. 19.
[31] *Journal* (1852), p. 25.

to no avail, for the enlargement of the church building: "If we sincerely love the Saviour and the Church, and desire to see her in the highest prosperity, there will be no hesitation in providing the comparatively small sum, which the fulfilment of this demand will require," he stated.[32]

On June 29, 1852 word reached Lexington that Henry Clay had died in Washington, D.C., that morning, plunging the town, and indeed the rest of the nation, into mourning. His good friend and rector, Edward Berkley, was engaged in writing his parochial report for the forthcoming diocesan convention when he received the sad intelligence. The report reflects his sense of loss.[33]

While I am now writing, the deep tolling of the bells around me, and the gloom which covers our city, remind me of the loss, which is suffered at large by the country, but which falls peculiarly upon us, as a congregation, of one who felt a lively interest in our Church affairs. Henry Clay will never again mingle his voice with the people who worship in the Church he loved, nor will his wise counsels ever again be heard in the promotion of her aims and ends. He is gone from us to a better Church in a better world, whilst this memorial shall remain of him here—that he was as simple and sincere in his religion, as he was great in wisdom, and mighty in his intellect.

On July 10, Mr. Berkley officiated at Clay's funeral at "Ashland," where were gathered a concourse of some thirty thousand people, four times the population of the town. Scarcely had the last of the funeral procession left Clay's home when the body arrived at the Lexington cemetery.[34] Berkley noted in his record book, "Honorable Henry Clay of Ashland—by far the grandest demonstration that was ever made in Kentucky in behalf of any public man."[35]

Edward Berkley continued in good works in his parish, diocese, and community and became more and more endeared to those whose lives he touched. His wife and growing family entered with him into the social life of Lexington, but he was never too busy or

[32] *Journal* (1853), p. 3.
[33] *Journal* (1853), p. 25.
[34] Robert Peter, *History of Fayette County, Kentucky, With an Outline Sketch of the Blue Grass Region*, William Henry Perrin, ed. (Chicago, 1882), p. 355.
[35] Christ Church Records, Berkley Diary.

too weary to go to the aid of an aged, sick, or needy parishioner, indeed to anyone of any denomination who needed him. The lunatic asylum continued to concern him, although in the fifteen years or more of his residency in Lexington vast improvements had been made there. He made frequent visits to the county jail, to comfort the prisoners. On a hot August day in 1854, he conducted the funeral of the first white man hanged in the county in probably fifty years, having conducted the victim's funeral eight months previously.[36]

Edward Berkley left an imprint on Christ Church Parish which has never been effaced. The church building today is basically the church built during his rectorate, and the moderate, conservative Churchmanship which is its hallmark is nowhere better exemplified than in its fifth rector. It is, however, the Diocese, itself, which owes him the greatest debt of gratitude, for, more than any other man in its history, he deserves the title of peacemaker. This was clearly shown in the case of Bishop Smith.

Although Bishop Smith was cleared of the charges brought against him in 1837, he never regained the confidence of many who had previously been his co-laborers, nor did he ever quite recapture the enthusiastic following of his people. There was, of course, peace on the surface, but it was a nebulous peace, born of the necessity of presenting a front to the outside world. Into this super-charged state of affairs had come Edward Berkley, considered by many to be "the Bishop's boy." He soon proved otherwise, yet he never lost the love and respect of the Bishop. They had their disagreements, and there were times when the young rector was sorely tried in remaining loyal to his superior. He managed to do so, however, and at the same time to retain the respect of those who most violently opposed Smith. During almost the entire 1850's, the Bishop's popularity was at low ebb. His relationships with his clergy were marked by wrangling and out-and-out disagreement and distrust. Two parties had by now emerged in the Diocese. Dr. Craik was accepted leader of the High Church party, referred to openly as "the high Craik"

---

[36] *Ibid.*, August 13, 1854. The funeral of William Weigart, executed in Fayette County the day before for the murder of Samuel C. Cushing. Berkley held Cushing's funeral on December 30, 1853.

party,[37] and aligned with him were many who considered themselves "Evangelicals" but were dissatisfied with the Bishop. Two such were Berkley's brother-in-law, M. F. Maury, and his good friend, F. B. Nash. Maury felt that Smith was endeavoring to remove him from Danville so that he himself might move there,[38] and Nash felt that the Bishop had been extremely unfair to him, insisting that he fill in gaps in the Diocese which he found it difficult to get anybody else to fill and so help to glorify his episcopate. "In its practical workings," Nash stated, "our Episcopacy in many important particulars is very poor stuff."[39] During the early fifties, it will be remembered, Bishop Smith and Dr. W. J. Waller, president of Shelby College, engaged in a feud concerning financial matters. So violent were the feelings between the two men and so vituperative their attacks on one another that those who thought the Bishop was in the wrong pressed for a second trial against him. Characteristically, Berkley managed to stay out of this dispute, but he was barraged with letters from both sides. N. N. Cowgill wrote him that the 'high Craik party' wished to get rid of Smith, stating "They think if they can get him to resign, they can get a man of their own." Cowgill feared Berkley might "go over with them" and urged him to sustain Smith "as being the head of the Evangelical interest."[40] He received letters from Dr. Craik, too, with whom he always remained on the friendliest terms and for whom he had great respect. Berkley remained the "peacemaker."

The Diocese at large therefore felt strongly the loss of Edward Berkley when in the fall of 1857 he left the state for another ministry. On September 30 of that year he resigned the rectorship of the parish which he had served for nearly nineteen years. He wrote, "The hand of Providence placed me here as your minister and that hand seems now to point me to another field." His letter of resignation was a sad one. He continued, "This is the only parish with which I have ever had any ministerial connection. Educated theologically in your midst, ordained to the sacred ministry in your

---

[37] The Reverend N. N. Cowgill to Edward Berkley, January 27, 1854, Filson Club.

[38] *Ibid.* Also see B. B. Smith to M. F. Maury, October 14, (no year given but it was probably 1854).

[39] F. B. Nash to Berkley, April 1, 1853, Filson Club.

[40] Cowgill to Berkley, January 27, 1854, Filson Club.

presence, and having had the oversight of your spiritual interests for so many years, with scarcely a jar to disturb our harmony of action, you may be assured that I take this step with very painful emotions."[41]

Berkley left Lexington on November 19 to take charge of St. George's Church, St. Louis, Missouri, at a substantial raise in salary.[42] His family remained in Lexington, at least through April of the following year. He made occasional visits to them during this period, and whenever in the city, he preached at his former parish and on several occasions performed the Holy Rite of Baptism. On one such occasion he baptized Thomas Hart Clay, the son of his old friend, whose wife and children he had baptized along with Clay in the parlor of "Ashland" eleven years before.[43] This service took place shortly after the Reverend James Morrison, who succeeded Berkley as rector, assumed his duties, for the following day the former rector received a note from his successor in which the latter expressed his gratification at the baptism of Mr. Thomas Clay.[44]

The Berkley era at Christ Church was finished. The State of Kentucky stood on the precipice of a fratricidal war, and the next few years would determine its course. And too, they would determine the course of the Episcopal Church in the United States of America and of Christ Church Parish in Lexington, Kentucky.

[41] Berkley Papers, Filson Club, First Copy of Resignation of Berkley from Christ Church, Lexington, September 30, 1857.
[42] Christ Church Records, Berkley Diary, p. 25.
[43] *Ibid.,* April 12, 1858, p. 32.
[44] The Reverend J. H. Morrison to Edward Berkley, April 22, 1858, Christ Church, Lexington Records.

13 *The Diocese in 1859*

The year 1859 is a good point at which to survey the position attained by the Diocese of Kentucky during the thirty years since its organization and to note the areas in which it had made its greatest progress. After an uphill start, the Episcopal Church in the Commonwealth had now reached a plateau where the outlook was good.

Fortunately, the basis for such a summary is available in the *Journal of the Thirty-first Annual Convention of the Diocese of Kentucky* compiled in 1859 by the Reverend Robert McMurdy, secretary of the convention. McMurdy, a well-educated teacher with a genuine interest in records, expanded the size and scope of the *Journal* with complete rosters and elaborate charts, and with historical information, making it a preliminary history of the Diocese to that date.

Some of the statistics, although lacking from certain parishes, give a bird's-eye view of the situation in 1859.

Bishop and clergy canonically resident; 29
Parishes; 31
Communicants; 1,936
Confirmations; 304
Baptisms; 443
Sunday school Teachers; 301
Sunday school Pupils; 2,354
Contributions exclusive of clergy support; $51,049.41
Value of church property; $317,850.00

A somewhat more detailed roster of the parishes, compiled from the *Journal,* shows even more clearly the generally good condition of the Church in the state.[1] Of the thirty-one parishes, twenty-three were being served by permanent rectors. In three instances one rector served two "united" parishes. The eight vacancies included four in the western part of the state, two in the Louisville area, and two in the eastward area. Louisville and its immediate environs had six flourishing churches and three small new ones in the area. The far-reaching western section claimed six well-established parishes and three weaker ones. The region that would one day become the Diocese of Lexington contained ten well-established parishes and three less flourishing ones. There were twenty-nine ordained clergy residing in the state, of whom twenty were parish priests. The others were the Bishop, two military chaplains, three teachers, and several who no longer officiated actively.

[1] PARISH STATISTICS BASED ON JOURNAL for 1859 Belmont Furnace, St. Paul's Church (1855); Rev. John C. Tennent. Communicants 6. No property. Bowling Green, Christ Church (1845); vacant. Communicants 10. Property, $800. Columbus, Christ Church (1843); Rev. N. N. Cowgill. Communicants 16. Lot, $300. Covington, Trinity Church (1840); Rev. Thomas W. Ralston. Communicants 100. Brick church, $6,000. Cynthiana, Church of the Advent (1847); Rev. Carter Page. Communicants 14. Rural Gothic brick church, $7,000. Danville, Trinity Church (1829); Rev. M. Fontaine Maury. Communicants 40. Brick church, $6,000. Elizabethtown, Christ Church (1843); Rev. John C. Tennent. Communicants 19. Brick church, $1,300. Flemingsburg, All Saints Church (1859); Rev. Jonathan H. Haven. Communicants 5. No property. Frankfort, Church of the Ascension (1837); Rev. John N. Norton. Communicants 222. Gothic brick church, $25,000. Harrodsburg, St. Philip's Church (1858); vacant. Communicants 23. Lot, $3,000. Henderson, St. Paul's Church (1833); Rev. Daniel H. Deacon. Communicants 58. Gothic brick church, $15,000. Hickman, St. Paul's Church (1843); Rev. N. N. Cowgill. Communicants 9. Building $2,000. Hopkinsville, Grace Church (1832); vacant. Communicants 60. Brick church, $7,000. Jefferson County, St. Matthew's Church (1840); Rev. George Beckett. Communicants 10. Brick church, $1,700. Lexington, Christ Church (1794); Rev. James H. Morrison. Communicants 198. Norman brick church, $35,000. Louisville, Christ Church (1822); Rev. James Craik. Communicants 239. Norman brick church, $23,000. Louisville, Grace Church (1855); Rev. Francis H. Bushnell. Communicants 91. Early English brick church, $10,800. Louisville, St. Andrew's Church (1857); Rev. John S. Wallace. Communicants 29. Brick church, $8,000. Louisville, St. John's Church (1847); Rev. Joseph S. Large. Communicants 160. English brick church, $8,000. Louisville, St. Paul's Church (1836); Rev. Francis M. Whittle. Communicants 298. Gothic brick church, $70,000. Maysville, Church of the Nativity (1845); Rev. F. B. Nash. Communicants 41. Gothic brick church, $8,000. Mt. Sterling, Church of the Ascension (1858); Rev. Jonathan H. Haven. Communicants 5. Brick church, $2,000. Newport, St. Paul's Church (1844); Rev. P. H. Jeffries. Communicants 82. Brick church, $3,000. Paducah, Grace Church (1846); Rev. Willard Presbury. Communicants 50. Plank church, $4,000. Paris, St. Peter's Church (1831); Rev. John Austen Merrick. Communicants 51 ("of whom 4 are slaves"). Roman style brick church, $3,000. Pewee Valley. St. James' Church (1858); vacant. Communicants 10. "Completed Methodist church and thus purchased right for 2 Sundays." Princeton, St. John's Church (1840); vacant. Communicants 8. Property, $3,000. Shelbyville, St. James' Church (1858); vacant. Communicants 10. Lot, $400. Smithland, Calvary Church (1837); vacant. Communicants 12. Frame church, $1,200. Versailles, St. John's Church (1848); John W. Venable. Communicants 38. Brick church, $4,000. Washington, Church of the Epiphany (1848); vacant. Communicants 10. No property.

The Bishop's address to the convention summed up the recent expansion in the Diocese from an historical viewpoint.

After some years of repose, shall I call it (or depression and stagnation), about the year 1847, in the Northern and Eastern section of the Diocese, there was a sudden awakening and marked expansion, a charming historical record of which may be noticed in the singularly appropriate names, for that purpose, of the Church of the Advent, Cynthiana, the Church of the Nativity, Maysville, and the Church of the Epiphany, Washington.

Our next *Journal* will bear evidence of another season of growth, after nearly as long a period of inaction or repose: St. Philip's Church, Harrodsburg, the Church of the Ascension, Mt. Sterling, and perhaps, also, All Saints Church, Flemingsburg, will apply to be received into union with this Convention.

The chief instrument, in the former case, was the Rev. Mr. Moore, of St. Peter's Church, Paris, nobly assisted by the Rev. Ed. F. Berkley, of Christ Church, Lexington.

In several of the recent instances the impulse, if not given by the Rev. Mr. West, has been ably seconded and followed up by him, cheerfully sustained as he had been by Convention and the neighboring clergy.[2]

John West's final report to the convention before his return to Massachusetts made mention of missionary visits he had paid also to Pewee, Lagrange, Owensboro, Ashland, Winchester, Richmond, and Nicholasville. He had traveled more than eight thousand miles during his twenty months in Kentucky. He well deserved the Bishop's praise as a large contributor to the growth of the Diocese. So, likewise, did the rectors and members of the two oldest churches in Louisville, who had fostered the establishment of four staunch parishes in the metropolitan area within the past fifteen years.

Another sign of progress manifested at this time was the improved financial condition of the parishes and of the Diocese as a whole. With the exception of four small sums still in arrears, all the church buildings were reported to be free of debt. The parishioners were for the most part inclined to be parsimonious about paying the rector's salary but they gave generously, sometimes sacrificially, to acquire and adorn their houses of worship. The parishes now ac-

---

[2] *Journal of the Diocese of Kentucky* for 1859, p. 36.

cepted responsibility for very modest support of the episcopate, and at this convention assessed themselves $1,745 during the forthcoming year, apportioning the assessments according to the strength of the several parishes. The Bishop's salary was apparently paid somewhat irregularly, and at this time seems to have averaged about $1,500 a year. This amount was, of course, inadequate and unrealistic, but it was an improvement over the income paid him in earlier years. In addition to meeting their parochial and episcopal obligations, the larger churches that could afford to do so donated frequently to calls from outside. For the year ending in May, 1859, the parishes in Kentucky reported these contributions: $514.44 to foreign missions; $2,321.96 to domestic missions; $3,889.40 to diocesan missions. An interesting report was rendered by St. Peter's Church, Paris for that year, during which its people gave almost exactly as much for missions as for parish needs.

Another advance in the field of financial responsibility was the adoption at this convention of a specific form of deed designed to prevent alienation of any parish property or the diversion of it from the primary use and ownership for which it was intended. This important legal precaution had been advocated by James Craik ever since his coming to the Diocese. To emphasize the importance of legal safeguards, McMurdy presented a tabulated chart titled "Church Property in the Diocese," listing the buildings owned by all active parishes, together with dates of acquisition and estimated valuation. To the chart he added notes regarding the disposition of any buildings owned by "defunct parishes," information which he obtained from Bishop Smith's recollections.[3]

There was one phase of the finances of the Diocese which was in only fair condition in 1859, although conditions were more promising than had sometimes been the case in the past. The fund obtained from the sale of the theological seminary building and grounds in Lexington was administered by four trustees, elected annually at the convention. Their duties consisted of investing the

---

[3] See *Journal of the Diocese of Kentucky* for 1859: Appendix X, "Church Property in the Diocese"; Appendix XI, "Synopsis of Thirty-one Annual Conventions of the Diocese of Kentucky." Also *Journal* for 1860: Appendix IX, "Addendum to Synopsis of Thirty-one Annual Conventions Published in *Journal* of 1859."

funds, disbursing the income for the training and education of candidates, and keeping a watchful eye on the valuable theological library that was lodged at Shelby College. A shadowy continuation of the seminary was maintained there as an adjunct to the liberal arts college.

Shelby College had presented many problems since its acquisition by the Diocese in 1841. These difficulties varied under a succession of presidents. Dr. Robert B. Drane, prominent clergyman from Wilmington, North Carolina, served during 1843–1844, and was succeeded by Deacon Joshua D. Berry of New Hampshire, who was ordained to the priesthood during his term in 1844–1845. Both were capable educators, but neither remained long enough to produce permanent results. In 1847 the Reverend William J. Waller, M.D., began an association with the institution that lasted, with interruptions, for twenty years (1847–1852; 1854–1859; 1862–1868).

Dr. Waller was dedicated and generous, but he was also dictatorial. He raised money on his personal credit for a handsome building and other facilities on the campus; however, when tuition receipts did not reimburse him to enable him to satisfy his own creditors, he virtually took possession of the college. The 1854 convention, wishing to save Dr. Waller's personal fortune from ruin, authorized the loan to him of the seminary fund on the security of his notes for the interest and principal. Even so, he and the Bishop quarreled acrimoniously over the management of the college, and Waller threatened another presentment. That calamity was averted by the astute diplomacy of Judge Adam Beatty, lay delegate at the 1855 convention from the Church of the Epiphany, Washington.[4] Dr. Waller and the Bishop soon renewed their combined efforts to improve Shelby College. Dr. Waller appears to have maintained the payment of interest on the seminary fund, and eventually he paid off the principal. In 1859, however, he offered his resignation as president of the college, saying that he had restored it once more to prosperity and now wished to "engage again in parochial labor, the noblest profession known among men."

[4] *Journal of the Diocese of Kentucky* for 1859, pp. 54–55, and for 1865, pp. 29–31, for Dr. Waller's account of his relations with Shelby College. Also Maysville, Ky., *Express-Extra*, September 26, 1855, for his controversy with Bishop Smith and Judge Beatty.

Waller's post was filled by the appointment of the Reverend Mr. McMurdy, who had given up his parish and school in Washington and was principal of a girls school in Frankfort. The new president made ambitious plans, and there was good reason for his optimism. On the twenty-acre campus stood the "college office" and nearby was the observatory with its Fraunhofer telescope, one which, according to the college prospectus, ranked fourth in the nation for magnitude. The library of the old Episcopal Theological Seminary of Kentucky, enlarged by a few later additions, was better than most small colleges of the day could boast.

McMurdy drew his faculty principally from the diocesan clergy. It speaks well for the educational standards set by the Episcopal Church of that day that he was able to enlist seven professors, including himself, who were well equipped by talent and academic training. Three of them held doctorates, and the other four the degree of A.M. McMurdy himself and Norman Badger were listed on the regular teaching staff. Visiting lecturers included B. B. Smith, John Norton, James Craik, J. Austen Merrick, and Francis B. Nash. The range of their scholarly competence more than matched that of the famous faculty of the Episcopal Theological Seminary in its prime in Lexington, and this fact must have been a matter of pride to Benjamin Bosworth Smith. The *Journal of the Diocese of Kentucky* for 1860 shows the following clerical members of the Shelby College faculty.

Rev. Robert McMurdy, A.M.
  President and Professor of Mental and Moral Philosophy
Rev. Norman Badger, A.M.
  Professor of Languages
Rev. J. Austen Merrick, D.Ph. (Visiting Lecturer)
  Professor Oriental and Biblical Literature;
  Ecclesiastical History
Rt. Rev. B. B. Smith, D.D. (Visiting Lecturer)
  Astronomy and Cathedrals; Relation of Classical and
  English Literature to Christianity and Free Institu-
  tions
Rev. James Craik, D. D. (Visiting Lecturer)
  (*Subject to be announced*)
Rev. John N. Norton, A.M. (Visiting Lecturer)

Bishop Berkley, the Christian Philosopher
Rev. F. B. Nash, A.M. (Visiting Lecturer)
History, in connection with the American Government

Amid the gathering clouds of war, the new president's term of office was short. He left in 1862 to serve as a chaplain in the Union hospitals in Washington, and Dr. Waller came out of his busy retirement to guide the college for its remaining years. McMurdy's efforts to broaden the cultural offerings of Shelby College had, however, contributed much to the prestige and influence of the Church.

Interest was increasing in Church-guided education for children and young girls. Three parishes at this date reported their parochial schools with a total of 219 pupils. There were also private schools that were closely affiliated with the Church, among them being the Misses Smith's Female High School in Frankfort, conducted by the Bishop's daughters, Elizabeth and Virginia; Miss Belle Peers' School for Young Ladies, found in Louisville, whose preceptress was the daughter of the Reverend Benjamin Orr Peers; and St. Ann's Hall in Frankfort, under the supervision of the Reverend Mr. McMurdy. Dr. John Ward's famous academy in Lexington was now closed because of his advancing years.

Charitable enterprises and good works for the needy received generous support from Kentucky Episcopalians at this period even more than did education. A shining example was the Protestant Episcopal Orphans Asylum in Louisville, founded in 1837, and endowed by John Bustard and others to provide for sixty children. Ascension Church in Frankfort established an Orphans Home in 1858 for ten little girls. In practically every parish the women were organized in societies to sew for the poor, visit the sick, and care for the children. As the Ladies Benefit and Relief Society, or the Ladies Benevolent Society, or the Dorcas Society, they were frequently praised in the parochial reports.

In the gradual development of the Church in Kentucky, one of its notable aspects was a concern for the spiritual welfare of the colored people in the community. The parish records contain baptisms, funerals, marriages, and a few confirmations of Negroes. Benjamin

Bosworth Smith began his mission to them very soon after coming to Kentucky. When Bishop Meade visited Lexington in 1831 he noted in his journal that he had "preached one evening to the colored people in a meeting-house where the Rev. Mr. Smith is accustomed to officiate for them." When he became bishop, Smith often appealed officially to his people on behalf of their colored brethren, notably at the 1835 convention, when he recommended Sunday schools "to look after the souls of those young persons of the colored race who are, or may be, committed to your care." It was at about this time that Henry Caswall and his zealous theological students at the seminary conducted such a flourishing Sunday school for Negro children that some conservative citizens in Lexington protested that the children were being "educated" beyond their station.

Throughout the antebellum period, many other Episcopal clergymen in Kentucky ministered to the colored persons in their communities. During the prosperous days of the little church at Smithland, Deacon A. A. Willis conducted well-attended Sunday afternoon services for them. In the late 1840's and early 1850's the Reverend Charles Page, native of Virginia, varied his duties at St. Matthew's Church on the outskirts of Louisville by preaching regularly to "African congregations" in the area. Soon after John Norton became rector of Ascension Church, Frankfort in 1846, he organized a successful Negro Sunday school, recruiting the prominent ladies of his parish as teachers. During one church year he baptized twenty-two colored children, and during his whole priesthood carried on a personal ministry to them, undergirded by philanthropic gifts from Mrs. Norton and himself. In Paris, heart of a rich, slaveholding section, John Austen Merrick in 1856 had shepherded sixty-one colored children into the Sunday school at St. Peter's Church. In the year 1859 he baptized five colored persons and counted four colored communicants as members of the parish.

These well-known instances of the concern among antebellum Episcopalians in Kentucky for the black population appear in the *Journals* and other contemporary records, and there were undoubtedly many others which were not put on record. In maintaining this attitude that the salvation of the Negroes was part of the task of domestic missions the clergy took the lead, but they apparently had the support of their parishioners for the most part or at least encountered no disruptive opposition. It is a case in point that the enemies of B. B. Smith during his trial and other later controversies at no time based their attacks upon his well-known antislavery views and his humanitarian interest in the colored race. By 1859 this broad view toward the welfare of the race was evidenced in a project undertaken by Dr. Waller after his resignation from the presidency of Shelby College. With the approval of the Bishop and at least the tacit consent of the Louisville Churchmen, he organized among the colored people of the community a mission parish that was their own, with a colored vestry and, *Deo volente,* in the course of time a priest of their own race.

Another matter, unrelated to missionary work among the colored people, did bring about differences within the Diocese, especially among the clergy. This was the cleavage between High Churchmen and Evangelicals, so-called, in matters of faith and order. These differing viewpoints and the many gradations between were agitating the national Church as early as the rectorships in Lexington of John Ward and George Chapman, both of whom were High Churchmen of the Hobart following. Neither of them, however, made Churchmanship a controversial issue within the ranks of Kentucky Episcopalians, who were few in number and hard pressed to defend themselves against the charges of the nonliturgical Protestants who flourished around them. Dr. Cooke, a High Churchman by conviction, evidently ignored the whole matter when he acted for the vestry of Christ Church, Lexington in issuing a call to B. B. Smith, a well-known spokesman for the Evangelical party.

Conflict between High and Low Church factions in Kentucky appeared only as an undercurrent in the trial of Bishop Smith although his leading opponents were High Churchmen. After their departure from the councils of the Diocese, Smith was reinforced in his theological position by the arrival of the Reverend William Jackson, an eminent Evangelical who became rector of Christ Church, Louisville, and by the group of young parish priests just out of the seminary—Berkley, Maury, Deacon, Cowgill, and Nash —all of them trained in the Evangelical tradition. In the House of

Bishops, Smith was counted upon to vote with the more aggressive Evangelicals, such as McIlvaine of Ohio and Meade of Virginia.

B. B. Smith was basically a Protestant, deriving his theology and ecclesiastical polity from the early Anglican divines. Suspicious of any "medievalism" in doctrine or ceremony lest it lead toward Rome, he was naturally opposed to the Tractarian Movement. An exception to his distrust of medievalism was his genuine love of Gothic architecture in spite of its having become a High Church symbol. His concern seemed to be not so much opposing the Roman Catholics as justifying the Anglican position as the *via media* for other Protestants. A number of his published sermons indicate this view.

An example is a pamphlet titled *The Position of Episcopalians in Relation to Christians of Other Names* issued after his removal to Louisville.[5] It was a reply to charges made by several Louisville ministers that the Episcopal Church by its doctrine of apostolic succession "excluded" them from salvation, and that its belief in baptismal regeneration and the Real Presence at the Eucharist were relics of pre-Reformation Romanism. Smith defended apostolic succession as the only authorization for the Christian ministry; yet he offered the Church's Holy Communion to any Christian believer. Baptismal regeneration he declared to be the necessary step in order to attain "renovation." The efficacy of the Sacrament resided in man's faith and God's gift of the Holy Spirit, never in itself. Sermons and publications in which he set forth views like these were a genuine ecumenical attempt on his part to reach agreement with the other Reformed branches of Christianity. They must have been read fairly widely because through the years he ordained a good many members of those denominations, some already ministers, into the priesthood of the Episcopal Church.

Bishop Smith's Evangelical views were not shared by all his Diocese, beginning with some of his most influential clergy. During the previous fifteen years a number of able High Churchmen had begun their long terms as rectors of important parishes. James Craik arrived in Louisville in 1844. He came, it is true, from the Evangeli-

---

[5] Published in Louisville by Morton & Griswold, 1850.

cal stronghold of Virginia, but having become an Anglican through reading the Church Fathers, he based his belief on the principles of the catholic church of antiquity. He opposed equally the "corruptions of the medievalists and the rationalism of the modern Protestantism."[6]

Two years after Craik's coming, Ascension Church, Frankfort called young John Norton, who had recently graduated from General Theological Seminary during the height of Tractarian influence there. Several of his more extreme classmates joined Bishop Kemper's High Church movement in the west, but Norton chose instead to shepherd a small Kentucky parish and to lead it into a sacramental way of worship. He kept in touch with the High Church leaders, and his parish's annual contributions usually included a gift to Kemper's seminary at Nashota House. The Diocese of Kentucky itself produced a priest with High Church leanings in John W. Venable, who was trained as a candidate by Norton in Frankfort.

Another dedicated High Church rector of the period was John Austen Merrick from Pennsylvania, who came to St. Peter's Church, Paris in 1854. He proved to be more of a ceremonialist than either Craik or Norton. With some difficulty he induced the Bishop to "institute" him as rector of the parish, a ceremony that had not heretofore been performed in the Diocese of Kentucky. A year later the Bishop, surprisingly, gave his approval and architectural advice for the renovation of the interior of St. Peter's to render it more suitable for worship in the High Church manner. A larger "chancel arrangement," a credence, a "proper communion table," and an episcopal chair were among the improvements.[7]

These examples of varied types of Churchmanship serve to show the wide latitude in such matters that prevailed in Kentucky in 1859. Whether from tolerance or timidity, Bishop Smith maintained at this time an attitude of permissiveness toward his clergy in this regard, making no attempt to impose his own views as did Meade

---

[6] Johnston, *Memorial History of Louisville,* II, p. 144. This is Bishop Thomas U. Dudley's definition of James Craik's Churchmanship.

[7] *Journal of the Diocese of Kentucky* for 1855–1865. John Merrick's parochial detailed reports document the first extensive ceremonialism in the Diocese.

and McIlvaine. The Diocese functioned in this area under a policy of laissez-faire that worked well so long as neither party became aggressive.

This summary of the state of the Diocese at midcentury has intentionally stressed its assets and achievements. Its mistakes and shortcomings have been recounted with a good deal of candor in the foregoing chapters as part of the history of the Anglican communion on the American frontier. By 1859 the Episcopal Church in Kentucky had taken its place among the important religious bodies, with influence and status far beyond its relative size.

14 The Church in Kentucky During the Civil War

The position of the Episcopal Church in Kentucky during the war-torn sixties reflected the attitude of the Commonwealth itself, and must be viewed in that context to be understood properly. The state's geographical location along the Ohio River from the Alleghenies to the Mississippi made it a borderland between North and South, not so much separating as connecting the two. Kentucky contained elements of both. Settlers and investments had come from all parts of the older East, and before the middle of the nineteenth century Kentucky's own emigrants had fanned out over Indiana and Illinois and Missouri, establishing strong ties with the Middle West. Influenced by these diverse backgrounds and contacts, Kentuckians came to be individualistic people. No single influence molded their thinking, as was the case in more homogeneous sections. Therefore they made a practice of tolerating opposition among their kinsmen and neighbors by working out a compromise even if sometimes an acrimonious one.

As time passed, there arose a great many differing views about religion and politics and especially concerning the "peculiar institution" of slavery. Where the land was fertile enough to support extensive farms profitably there were large slaveholders and strong sentiment for the institution. Where the land was poor, especially in the mountain area, there were few Negroes and general disapproval of slavery. In the rest of the state the ownership of slaves was not an economic factor but a convenience in securing servants. From the early days, however, there was some antislavery sentiment on moral and humanitarian grounds. A few masters freed their slaves, sometimes assisting them to emigrate to Liberia under the auspices of the American Colonization Society, to which many prominent Kentuckians belonged. Several routes of the Underground Railway for slaves escaping to free territory cut northward across the state to Maysville and Smithland and other points on the Ohio.

The Episcopal parishes in Kentucky included adherents of all these dissident views. Robert Wickliffe, wealthy landowner of Lexington, was the leader of the proslavery Democrats in the Legislature. Adam Beatty, Whig lawyer of Mason County, aided his friend, Henry Clay, in framing the political compromise between the free and the slave states. James G. Birney, son of one of the organizers of Trinity Church, Danville, became convinced in 1833 that Kentucky was "the best site in our whole country to take a stand against slavery" and undertook to publish an antislavery journal, *The Philanthropist,* in his home town.[1] No parish stood as a unit on the issue.

Episcopal clergymen in Kentucky were less outspoken about slavery than some of their parishioners. Their personal convictions usually were influenced by the section in which they had been reared. Some followed Kentucky custom and owned a few household servants. Others, like B. B. Smith, refrained from the practice without making an issue of their disapproval. In this attitude they were following the lead of the national Episcopal Church, which as a matter of policy remained aloof from any political involvement.[2] American Anglicans during the Revolutionary War period had learned a hard lesson regarding the penalties assessed against a religious body for political reasons, and the founders of the Protestant Episcopal Church in 1789 established it to function loyally under the authority of the state but separate from it. It is understandable that the Diocese of Kentucky produced no antislavery crusader like the famous Presbyterian minister-politician, Dr. Robert Breckinridge, of Lexington, who became the "Old War Horse" of Lincoln's party.

The fact that the Episcopal Church in Kentucky and the nation abstained from political agitation about slavery should not be construed to mean that they were indifferent to the welfare of the colored people. Like all the antebellum churches, Protestant and Roman Catholic, they had concern for the salvation and morals of

---

[1] For Robert Wickliffe see William H. Townsend, *Lincoln and the Bluegrass* (Lexington, Ky.: 1955), pp. 108–109 *et passim;* and for the Birneys in Danville see William Birney, *James G. Birney and His Times* (New York: 1890), *passim.*

[2] Walter Brownlow Posey, *Frontier Mission. A History of Religion West of the Appalachians to 1861* (Lexington, Ky.: 1966), p. 348 *et passim.* An invaluable study despite the brief treatment accorded the Episcopal Church in Kentucky.

the slaves, and sometimes for their physical well-being also. The Episcopalians, like the Roman Catholics, usually kept this missionary work within the parish framework instead of setting up separate churches for the Negroes. Parish priests in the Diocese of Kentucky administered the rites of baptism, marriage, burial, and sometimes confirmation to colored persons who requested it or who were looked after by their masters. Negroes attended the regular services and Sunday schools in some parishes, being seated in the gallery or pews reserved for them. Elsewhere, special preaching services and Sunday schools were arranged for them. Bishop Smith began conducting services for colored people soon after his arrival in Lexington in 1830, and throughout his long episcopate he pleaded their cause in his annual addresses to the diocesan conventions. It is probable that all the parishes did missionary work among the Negroes. The records show that much was done at Frankfort under John Nicholas Norton, at Cynthiana under Carter Page, at Paris under John Austen Merrick, and at Louisville under Dr. William Waller, who established St. Mark's Church for Negroes. St. Mark's had a troubled career, but it was the harbinger of later successful missions.[3]

Slavery was the underlying cause of conflict between the sections of the nation but when the crisis came the chief divisive issue between Kentuckians was not slavery but secession from the Union. As the first state west of the mountains to be admitted to the new nation, Kentucky had avowed its loyalty in its motto, "United we stand. . . ." In 1850, with dissension already rife, the legislature had instructed that the block of native marble sent to be placed in the Washington Monument should be inscribed ". . . Kentucky will be the last to give up the Union." Even after some of the Southern states had seceded, a group of prominent Kentuckians joined in submitting to the United States Congress a set of proposals designed to solve or at least to postpone once more the clash over slavery. These Border, or Crittenden, Resolutions were the most disinterested and earnest attempt made at that critical time to prevent civil strife, but the hour was too late for compromise.

[3] For St. Mark's, see *Journal of the Diocese of Kentucky* for 1860, p. 23; for 1861, p. 37; for 1865, p. 20.

At this juncture Kentucky declared its intention of remaining neutral in the conflict and forbade the armies of either side to penetrate its borders. Confederates and Unionists were both actively recruiting in the state, and both armies were camped just across the state line in all directions, waiting for any provocation that would justify invasion. What seemed a justification came to both sides in late August, 1861. General Leonidas Polk, C.S.A., lately Bishop of the Episcopal Diocese of Louisiana, moved his troops into Columbus, Kentucky, a strategic location on the Mississippi River, and almost simultaneously General Ulysses Grant, U.S.A., took possession of Paducah, an even more strategic point at the junction of the Tennessee and Ohio Rivers. All hope for the state's neutrality vanished as its territory was occupied by armed forces.

The Commonwealth was compelled to declare its allegiance, one way or another. On September 16 a called session of the Legislature voted, over the protest of Governor Beriah Magoffin and other Southern sympathizers, to censure the invasion by the Confederates and to affirm the state's loyalty to the Union. Kentuckians as individuals were left to decide whether to remain with the Commonwealth and the Union or to give their support to the Confederacy. The elite State Guard, comprising about ten thousand well-trained young men, went over to the Confederate command almost in a body. John Hunt Morgan's cavalry and thousands of other volunteers did likewise. Fully as many men or more enlisted in the Union forces. Civilians gave aid and comfort wherever their sympathies lay.[4]

The decision of the Commonwealth to remain in the Union rendered unnecessary any affirmation by the Diocese of Kentucky of its allegiance to the Protestant Episcopal Church in the United States of America. Only the dioceses in the seceded states faced the critical decision as to whether they should or could remain a part of the Church in the United States. Most of the Southern bishops interpreted the principles on which the American Church had been

---

[4] For Kentucky's position during the War, see Nathaniel Shaler, *Kentucky, Pioneer Commonwealth* (Boston: 1888), pp. 231, 257, *et passim;* Samuel M. Wilson, *History of Kentucky* (Chicago: 1928), II, pp. 309–359; J. Merton Coulter, *The South During Reconstruction, 1865–1877* (Baton Rouge, La.: 1947), *passim.*

founded to mean that "the secession of the state separated the diocese from the Church in the United States." The Protestant Episcopal Church in the Confederate States of America was organized in the summer of 1861 and eventually involved all the dioceses of the eleven seceded states.[5]

Close ties connected Kentucky Episcopalians with the newly organized Confederate Church. Many of its bishops were well-known in the state, especially Meade of Virginia, Otey of Tennessee, Cobbs of Alabama, and Polk of Louisiana. A number of the clerical delegates to its three conventions had been connected at some time with the Diocese of Kentucky. Among them were Aldert Smedes from North Carolina (the clergyman whom Bishop Smith did not call as assistant at Christ Church, Lexington in 1836); William T. Leacock from Louisiana; Willard Presbury from Mississippi (New England graduate of the seminary); R. D. Drane from North Carolina (former president of Shelby College); J. Thomas Pickett from Mississippi (who left the parish at Paducah in 1861); and others. Fellowship with the Southern Church was maintained by Bishop Smith, and after the death of Bishop Otey of Tennessee he performed episcopal offices for the stricken parishes at Nashville and Clarksville.[6]

The Diocese contributed some of its clergy to the North during the hostilities. Among them were F. B. Nash to Illinois, Henry M. Frost to Vermont, Jonathan Haven to Ohio, and Robert Lewis to New York. Charles Page had long been a United States Army chaplain for Federal troops stationed at the Newport Barracks and soon Norman Badger, George Currie, and J. F. Roberts were enrolled to work in hospitals near Louisville and Cincinnati. Robert McMurdy enlisted as a Union chaplain.

The departure of Robert McMurdy from Kentucky was a distinct loss. After serving a short time as president of Shelby College (1860–1861) he resided in Frankfort, assisting at Ascension Church

[5] Edgar Legare Pennington, "The Organization of the Protestant Episcopal Church in the Confederate States of America," *Historical Magazine of the Protestant Episcopal Church,* XVII (1948), pp. 303–338; also William A. Clebsch, ed., *Journals of the Protestant Episcopal Church in the Confederate States of America.* Centennial Edition in Facsimile (Austin, Texas: 1962).

[6] *Journal of the Diocese of Kentucky* for 1865, p. 20.

and working on the records and archives of the Diocese. In May, 1862, he became a chaplain in the United States General Hospital at Alexandria, Virginia, serving until the summer of 1865. He was connected later with the Dioceses of New York, New Jersey, and Western Michigan, but never served again in Kentucky.[7] He deserves to be remembered in the Diocese in which he was ordained, not only as a priest but as its first archivist.

The Diocese of Kentucky was also diminished when John Austen Merrick was dismissed to the Diocese of Minnesota some time early in 1865, leaving St. Peter's Church, Paris in a flourishing condition in spite of war's hardships. He had long been interested in the missions for the American Indians located in Minnesota, and he was also attracted by the High Church movement flourishing there among the disciples of Bishop Kemper. His own parochial reports from 1855 to 1864 constitute the fullest evidence of the spread of that movement in antebellum Kentucky. His departure seems to have had no connection with the issues of the war.

Two beloved clergymen whose influence helped to unite the Diocese in all its crises died in the early part of the war. The Reverend John Ward ended his long career in the spring of 1860, breaking almost the last link with the old Episcopal Society in Lexington. He had served the Church for nearly fifty years with wisdom, kindness, and generosity. He and his wife, who was a wealthy woman, left large legacies to Christ Church, Lexington.[8]

Another force for harmony was lost when Matthew Fontaine Maury, shepherd of the flock at Danville and "founder" of the new parish at Harrodsburg, died in the early months of 1862. He defied ill health long enough to lead his own people in rebuilding their church after a disastrous fire on February 22, 1860, and to know that the beautiful new edifice at Harrodsburg was under roof. With his Virginia kinsmen serving in the Confederate Navy, he may well have been a Southern sympathizer. At all events, he did not live to

[7] Hospital Muster Rolls of U.S.A. General Hospital, Alexandria, Virginia (National Archives). See also Registrar, Diocese of New York, to Rebecca Smith Lee, April 1, 1968.

[8] See John Ward's will, a model for such benefactions, in Fayette County, Kentucky. Will Book No. X, p. 335 (February 6, 1860).

see the tide of war sweep into his own neighborhood and all but engulf the parish churches to which he had devoted his life.

The traditional policy of the Episcopal Church to remain aloof from wartime issues was admirably exemplified by John Nicholas Norton at Ascension Church, Frankfort. In his fifteen years as its rector he had made it famous for piety and good works in the Diocese and the whole western Church. When the community and his parishioners were divided as with a sword, he made the beautiful church a "haven of rest" for all the town's citizens. From him they heard no "excited, harsh or partisan comment." Ascension Church has never been more influential or dedicated than during Dr. Norton's wartime ministry.

The Church's policy of aloofness did not deter some of the diocesan clergy who were interested in the issues of the day from expressing their individual convictions. One of them played a prominent part in preventing Kentucky from seceding. Dr. James Craik, at the request of prominent citizens, delivered an address before the House of Representatives in the capitol at Frankfort on December 19, 1859, titled "The Union: National and State Sovereignty Alike Essential to American Liberty" that strongly influenced future legislation.[9] He was, following the tradition of early nineteenth century Virginia, "a slave-owner and opposed to the forcible abolition of slavery, but a devoted Union man and opposed to the secession movement of the Southern states." He retained his ties with both sections and became one of the effective mediators of the postwar period.

Bishop Smith, despite his well-known antislavery and pro-Union convictions, was moderate and conciliatory during the war. At its outbreak he composed special prayers for use by the parishes in his Diocese to give "natural expression to the Christian feelings of the time." They were widely used and long remembered. He was an early admirer of Abraham Lincoln and in 1861 praised him because ". . . common sense and high principle, in times like these, are

[9] James Craik, D.D., *The Union: National and State Sovereignty Alike Essential to American Liberty* (Louisville, Ky.: 1860). See Johnston, *The Memorial History of Louisville,* II, pp. 595–596, for biographical sketch of Craik by the Rt. Rev. Thomas U. Dudley, Bishop of Kentucky.

much more to a man than mere ability or high diplomatic training."[10] Later on B. B. Smith supported the reforms of the Emancipation Proclamation and the educational work of the Freedmen's Bureau and various benevolent organizations in the North devoted to schools for the emancipated slaves. His efforts on their behalf were then, as they had always been, directed mainly toward their religious and educational welfare.

For nearly four years Kentucky was a battleground, and most of its sizable towns were at one time or another occupied by either the Federal or Confederate troops.[11] Along the Ohio at Paducah and Louisville and Cincinnati were concentrated the massive Union armies that eventually fought their way to Fort Donelson, Chickamauga, and Atlanta. Up from Tennessee the Confederates launched at least one formidable invasion of Kentucky, and John Hunt Morgan's cavalry raided the state almost at will. All sections endured hardships, but some communities escaped destruction and actually prospered during the war years, among them being Louisville, Lexington, Frankfort, and the Covington-Newport area. Louisville, as the logistic headquarters for the Federal forces, boomed into a large commercial city during the period. Quite naturally, the fortunes of the parishes followed those of the communities, and in the area of the future Diocese of Lexington the Episcopal Church endured the ordeal of war with remarkable stamina. No parish was lost; none was split by internal dissension; and only one church building was seriously damaged in conflict. Several of the smaller parishes that lay directly in the path of the armies suspended services until after the war. In Cynthiana, headquarters for Union troops in the region and scene of three battles, the Church of the Advent was dormant from 1862 to 1865. Mt. Sterling and Flemingsburg were, like Cynthiana, collision points where raiding graycoats fought the Federal troops from house to house through the streets of the town. The sturdy little Episcopal Church in Mt. Sterling was occupied by the Federal forces from 1862 to 1864

[10] Benjamin Bosworth Smith to Harriett Staples Smith, December 2, 1861 (Bishop Smith Papers, Church Historical Society).
[11] Collins, *History of Kentucky,* II, pp. 80–165, presents a detailed account of the war in Kentucky.

as a camp and hospital, its pews and fences being used for firewood. Although the parish members were divided in their loyalty, the church officially "gave no aid to rebellion"; and therefore fifty-five years later it received payment of its claim for use and damages by the United States Government.[12]

The critical year for the military control of Kentucky was 1862. In July General John Hunt Morgan made his "First Kentucky Raid," sweeping a thousand miles through the heart of the Commonwealth, capturing seventeen towns, some of them by sharp fighting. In the autumn General Bragg's Confederate army came up from Tennessee in a full-scale invasion, with General Leonidas Polk, former Bishop of the Diocese of Louisiana, and General Edmund Kirby-Smith directing much of the advance. The Confederates seized Lexington and swept as far north as the environs of Covington and Newport and the vicinity of Louisville and Frankfort. The real hardships of war began now among the civilian population of the area, affecting their local government, schools, and churches.

On October 8 the opposing armies met near Perryville, a village between Danville and Harrodsburg, in one of the most desperate engagements of the entire war. The result was indecisive, and both sides withdrew cautiously from the battlefield to recoup their losses, leaving it strewn with dead and dying. There were nearly ten thousand casualties, and the nearby towns were filled to overflowing with wounded soldiers. Churches were used for hospitals, among them Trinity in Danville and St. John's in Versailles. John Venable and the other clergymen ministered to Northern and Southern men alike.

The newly completed St. Philip's at Harrodsburg was not converted into a hospital because its stained glass made it too dark for that purpose. The beautiful lancet windows from Italy, the first in

---

[12] Mack C. Eckhoff to Mrs. Owen S. Lee, October 4, 1968: reference to War Warrant No. 16712 for $825.00, dated April 4, 1917, to Vestry of Ascension Protestant Episcopal Church of Mt. Sterling, Ky. (filed in Records of U.S. Accounting Office, Record Group 217). See also National Archives Microfilm Series Re "Ascension Church, Mt. Sterling claim vs. U.S. Government" in Records of U.S. Court of Claims, Record Group 123, Washington National Records Center, Suitland, Md.

UPPER LEFT: The Reverend
Jacob Shaw Shipman, Rector
of Christ Church, Lexington
(1861–1877). *Courtesy of
William B. Floyd.*

UPPER RIGHT: The Reverend
James Craik, Rector of Christ
Church, Louisville (1844–
1882). *Courtesy of Mrs.
Charles Ewell Craik.*

RIGHT: The Reverend John
Nicholas Norton, Rector of
the Church of the Ascension,
Frankfort (1846–1870);
Assistant Rector of Christ
Church, Louisville (1870–
1881). *In Richard L.
McCready, The Church of
the Ascension (Frankfort,
Kentucky, 1939).*

MID-CENTURY
LEADERS OF THE
EPISCOPAL CHURCH
IN KENTUCKY

The Right Reverend George David Cummins, Assistant Bishop of Kentucky (1866–
1873). *Courtesy Church Historical Society
Archives.*

The Right Reverend Thomas Underwood
Dudley, second Bishop of Kentucky, consecrated 1875. *Courtesy of Miss Rowland Durrett.*

The church building occupied in 1895 by St. John's Parish, Covington. *Archives of Trinity Church, Covington.*

St. Thomas' Church, Beattyville, begun in 1894. *Archives of the parish.*

The first church building acquired for St. Andrew's Mission, Lexington, in 1880. *Courtesy of the Bishop of Lexington.*

Christ Church,
Richmond,
erected in 1887.
*Archives of the
parish.*

The first building of Emmanuel Church, Winchester, built in 1888. *Courtesy of the Bishop of
Lexington.*

Calvary Church, Ashland, built in 1898 on the
site of the first church which was destroyed by
fire. *Archives of the parish.*

St. Mary's Church, Middlesborough, built in
1891. *Archives of the parish.*

St. John's Church, Lexington. *Sketch by the Reverend William K. Hubbell, reconstructed from contemporary records.*

Chapel of the Good Shepherd, South Broadway, Lexington, erected in 1888. *Archives of the Church of the Good Shepherd, Lexington.*

The Right Reverend Lewis William Burton, first
Bishop of Lexington, consecrated in 1896. *Courtesy of
Hendree Milward, grandson of Bishop Burton.*

the community, were deemed so valuable that the authorities were persuaded to place a guard on the premises to protect them.[13] Thus it came about that this parish church was the scene of one of the most moving episodes of the war in Kentucky.

One of the officers in Polk's command was Dr. Charles Todd Quintard, chaplain of the First Tennessee Regiment, who had been a prominent physician before being ordained to the Episcopal priesthood. After the battle Dr. Quintard, in his double capacity as surgeon and priest, worked without rest for two days and nights, pausing only to pray with the dying. He removed his shirt for bandages, contracting a cold in the chill weather. On the third day he received a message from General Polk requesting the doctor to accompany him to the church in Harrodsburg. They went, just the two of them, as Dr. Quintard remembered years later.

. . . I obtained the key and as we entered the holy house, I think we both felt that we were in the presence of God. General Polk threw his arms around my neck and said, "Oh, for the blessed days when we walked in the house of God as friends! Let us have prayer!"

I vested myself with surplice and stole and entered the sanctuary. The General knelt at the altar railing. I said the Litany, used proper prayers and supplications, and then turned to the dear Bishop and General and pronounced the benediction from the service for the sick. The Bishop bowed his head upon the railing and wept like a child on his mother's breast. Shortly after this service General Kirby-Smith begged that he might go to the church with me, so I returned and he, too, was refreshed at God's altar.[14]

General Polk was killed at the Battle of Pine Mountain, Tennessee, on June 16, 1864. Dr. Quintard became the second Bishop of the Diocese of Tennessee and a dynamic leader of the postwar Church in the South. General Kirby-Smith, an educator and a layreader, was associated in 1868–1869 with Western Military Academy (Newcastle) and St. James College (Shelbyville), both Episcopal schools

[13] Neva L. Williams, *The History of St. Philip's Episcopal Church, Harrodsburg, Kentucky* (Harrodsburg, Ky.: 1948), pp. 5–6.

[14] Arthur E. Noll, ed., *Dr. Quintard, Chaplain, C.S.A., Second Bishop of Tennessee. Being His Story of the War, 1861–1865* (Sewanee, Tennessee: 1905), Microcard No. 973–982, University of Kentucky Library.

in the Diocese of Kentucky, and subsequently was on the faculty of the University of the South for many years. Rarely ever has a small parish church furnished sanctuary for men of such stature as did St. Philip's in the autumn season of 1862.

The Kentucky counties along the Ohio River confronted the power of the North even earlier than those in the interior. Up the river from Louisville, the chief centers of such contacts were the Covington-Newport area and Maysville. Their own business and social interests had always been closely connected with those of their Ohio neighbors, and now they had only to look across the river to see the military might as well as the economic power of one of the great free states of the Union.

In all the nation few communities so epitomized the clash of convictions and interests that led to civil conflict as did Maysville and Mason County. Many large landowners in the area depended upon slave labor. Yet there were many business and professional men in town, some with Northern backgrounds, who had little love for the institution. For years there had been a nearby station of the "Underground Railway" for slaves escaping across the river into free territory. A conspicuous example of the situation here is the family of Colonel Thomas Marshall Key, landed slaveowner, and his wife from a prominent Cincinnati family, who lived in Washington on the outskirts of Maysville. Naturally they sent their daughter to a girls' institute in Cincinnati and, of course, entertained one of her instructors, Miss Harriette Beecher, when she came to visit them. She also paid visits to other Kentucky homes where there were slaves, and it may be that all she used in her famous novel from the visit to the Keys was the sight of a slave sale. *Uncle Tom's Cabin* was published a decade too early to record the fact that sons from the Key household were loyal to the Union and served in the Federal army.[15]

Episcopalians in Mason County were divided like everyone else. There were Nelsons and Wadsworths fighting for the Union, while Dukes and Lashbrooks were in the Confederate army. Many families had men in both uniforms. In early 1861 the town of Maysville

[15] J. Winston Coleman, *Mrs. Stowe, Kentucky, and Uncle Tom's Cabin* (Harrogate, Tenn.: 1946).

came under Federal martial rule, and was subject to attacks by Confederate forces. In the confusion of the summer of 1861, Nativity's rector, the Reverend F. B. Nash, resigned and left the Diocese. His place was filled immediately by young Frank M. Gregg, recently ordained to the priesthood. He had been in charge of the parishes at Flemingsburg and Mt. Sterling, and even after moving to Maysville continued to minister to the Flemingsburg people. Gregg was not discouraged by wartime conditions and actually increased the number of communicants during the war from 49 to 60, no small gain under the conditions. Seventy-five pupils were enrolled in a parochial school that by 1865 all but supported the parish. In addition he managed to preach in Aberdeen, Ohio, across the river. He was a faithful wartime rector.[16]

Wartime conditions in Covington and Newport were notably different from those in Maysville. Indeed, they were unique in the state. Although the Kentucky side of the river near Cincinnati was under Federal control from the beginning of the war and was fortified against the Confederates in September, 1862, the Southern forces halted a few miles south of Covington and withdrew without attempting to capture it or cross the river. No military engagement of consequence took place in this northernmost tip of the state. In spite of unrest and some harassment of Southern sympathizers, the two Kentucky communities continued to share in Cincinnati's activities and growth. A suspension bridge across the river was constructed during the hostilities and opened for use in 1866. Churches and other institutions on both sides of the river prospered as a consequence.

It was at this time that Trinity Church, Covington carried out its first great period of expansion and achievement. In 1860 the Reverend George Currie, a native of Scotland, was just beginning a successful rectorship of eight years, during which he was supported by an able vestry. His parishioners were moved to express their approval of him twice by raising his salary in spite of the precarious times. Currie was known as a Union sympathizer, but because he still retained his British citizenship he was able to avoid bitter

---

[16] *Journal of the Diocese of Kentucky* for 1862–1865, parochial reports.

partisanship. He won the esteem of all by ministering to soldiers of both sides in the local hospital. Bishop McIlvaine, who was his personal friend, recommended him highly to President Lincoln for an appointment as chaplain in the local army hospital, declaring that Dr. Currie "in the midst of secessionists has maintained a faithful stand."[17]

His popularity with his own parish derived in part from the fact that its leaders included a good many loyal Union men such as John P. Baker, an influential businessman in Cincinnati who resided in Covington, M. M. Benton, a native of New York who was the town's first mayor, and the Honorable John W. Stevenson, who had recently represented the district in the United States Congress.

Currie's career at Trinity is best remembered for an eloquent sermon he delivered from his own pulpit on Easter, April 16, 1865, just after the assassination of Lincoln. His sincere if rhetorical tribute to the dead President is noteworthy for the "words of calmness and discretion" in which he urged Unionists not to accuse the South of the murder. His address so moved his hearers that he was requested by a committee of eleven citizens, mostly from outside his parish, to publish it. He consented to do so.[18]

St. Paul's, Newport, faced the same problems during the war that existed for the Trinity parish. Debt-free and harmonious in 1860, the parish lost only a little ground in the following five years under the Reverend P. W. Jeffries. Its obligations within and without the parish were regularly met. The rector apparently took no public stand in politics, but it is likely that he and his parishioners were tolerantly Unionist in their sympathies.

One of the most prominent laymen in the Diocese of Kentucky during the mid-nineteenth century was John White Stevenson of Trinity Church, Covington. A Virginian, whose forebears included distinguished clergymen and statesmen, he became a successful lawyer in Covington. As congressman in 1861, he was known for a

---

[17] Charles P. McIlvaine to Abraham Lincoln, October 24 (no year). (Bishop McIlvaine Papers, Church Historical Society).

[18] J. H. French, John W. Baker, and others to the Reverend C. George Currie, May 1, 1865; and C. George Currie to the Committee, May 20, 1865 (Archives of the Diocese of Lexington, University of Kentucky Library).

speech of allegiance to the Union in which he charged the extreme Republicans with responsibility for the impending conflict. Caught in the stalemate of neutrality, he did not become politically prominent again until he attended the Union Convention in Philadelphia the same year that he was a lay delegate to the important General Convention of the Episcopal Church. As Kentucky's governor and senator during the next decade Stevenson did much to restore the South to the Union.

Stevenson, like James Craik and many another Churchmen, illustrates the withdrawal of Kentucky Union sympathizers from the national Republican (Union) Party during the late years of the war. The Commonwealth had attempted to prevent civil strife by every means at its command; yet during much of the war it was treated by the Union military command as if it were seceded territory. Federal officers left in charge of towns and districts taken by force were often harsh and even brutal. This oppressive treatment, together with the social upheaval following the Emancipation Proclamation, prompted Kentuckians to make common political cause with the South. Later historians have sometimes remarked that Kentucky joined the Confederacy after Appomattox.

In this summary of the wartime condition of the parishes in the future Diocese of Lexington we must give attention to the Lexington community, a citadel of custom and at the same time a center of the winds of change. Since the turn of the century, many of its wealthy residents had been large slaveowners, although a much larger number of citizens owned only a few Negroes in order to live more comfortably. Here the Colonization Society flourished in its early years as the Whig hope for getting rid of the problem of slavery easily. And here, too, Henry Clay's turbulent kinsman, Cassius Marcellus Clay, in the summer of 1845 succeeded in publishing his antislavery weekly, *The True American,* for a few weeks until forced to discontinue it by an orderly crowd of some of the town's leading citizens.

By 1861 Lexington was even more divided on the question of secession. Ties of family, friendship, church, and political party were broken. Henry Clay's sons and grandsons served in both armies, North and South. Old Dr. Breckinridge had a son in the

Union army and two with the Confederacy. President Lincoln's Lexington brothers-in-law wore gray. The social structure of the community was fragmented. The result was a kind of neutrality.

Christ Church was affected by these antagonisms. In 1858, when Edward F. Berkley's long, harmonious rectorship came to an end, the parish called the Reverend James Horace Morrison, D.D., of Pemberton, Virginia. His portrait at this time shows a man of about forty with a stubborn jaw and a worried look in his eyes. Historians of the parish say he was "an austere and reserved man, one of profound convictions and great learning." Immediately upon his arrival contracts were let for a large addition to the church building, but as war clouds gathered, construction had to be stopped for lack of funds. "Morrison's folly," as some called it, was boarded up to keep out the weather. When Morrison tendered his resignation on July 12, 1861, he complained of being blamed unjustly for the building problems and he also complained of "certain unkind remarks about him that were untrue.[19] Since he was "an ardent Southerner," he may have resigned because of Kentucky's decision to remain in the Union. He was officially dismissed to the Diocese of Virginia.

The minutes of the vestry meeting that chose a new rector in September do not state what qualifications the vestrymen had in mind or make any mention of politics.[20] The families of the parish were ranged on opposing sides, and even within their own ranks there were rifts. Defending the Confederacy were the Hunts, Morgans, Bullocks, Prestons, Wickliffes, Dudleys, and many others. For the Union were the Goodloes, Warfields, Bruces, Macalesters, and many more. The kind of rector Christ Church needed was a tolerant man who could minister to the needs of people, sorely divided themselves, who might yet unite in an undivided church. The parish found him in the Reverend Jacob Shaw Shipman, a young New Yorker whose connections in Kentucky were impeccable.

Shipman, a native of Niagara Falls, New York, graduated with honors from Hobart College and in 1857 was ordained to the

[19] For Morrison's resignation, see Minutes of the Vestry of Christ Church, July 12, 1861; also Smith & Didlake, *History of Christ Church, 1796–1946,* pp. 31–32.
[20] Minutes of the Vestry of Christ Church, September 17, 1861.

priesthood by Bishop DeLancey of the Diocese of Western New York. He was a moderate High Churchman like John Norton, who had come from the same background. Shipman was rector of the largest parish in Mobile, Alabama, when that state seceded and the Diocese of Alabama joined the Confederate Church. He resigned his rectorship at that time and probably came directly to Kentucky to visit relatives in the state. A sister, Mary, had recently been married to Judge George Canning Drane, of Frankfort, and was a teacher in the Sunday school at Ascension Church. A brother, Paul R. Shipman, had for nearly ten years been assistant editor of the pro-Union Louisville *Journal,* owned by George D. Prentice, famous editor for Clay's Whig Party in its prime.[21] With such a background Jacob Shipman came well recommended to the vestry of Christ Church.

When the new rector assumed his duties in October, 1861, he found the city under military rule, with batteries of artillery parked on Cheapside and Union soldiers camping in the courthouse yard hardly a stone's throw from his church. Citizens were required to take the oath of allegiance, and if known to be Southern sympathizers might be arrested on flimsy pretexts. Not until the following spring was he able to rouse enough enthusiasm in his parish to resume construction on the church addition. Nevertheless, Christian faith and courage prevailed, and the money was raised. Individuals gave or lent generous sums; a providential payment from the John Ward estate was made available; and there seems to have been a loan from the theological seminary fund. In March, 1864, when it was possible to meet in the beautiful, redesigned church, with added transepts and organ space, it did not seem too large. The parish now numbered well over four hundred communicants, together with their families. A few years later Bishop Smith declared publicly that Shipman was "the only man in America who, when every Protestant church in Lexington was divided during the war, could have held this church together."[22]

[21] For Paul R. Shipman see Johnston, *Memorial History of Louisville,* II, p. 65.

[22] Smith & Didlake, *The History of Christ Church, 1796–1948,* pp. 32–33, 35–36; also *Journal of the Diocese of Kentucky* for 1861–65, parochial reports from Christ Church, Lexington.

On April 9, 1865, General Lee surrendered at Appomattox, signaling the collapse of the Confederacy. Americans faced the awesome problems of reunion, of reconciling the opposing factions of all its divided institutions. The need for restoring unity among Christians was obvious. As an eminent historian has put it, "It might well have been supposed that the churches . . . would have quickly healed their breaches. . . . But the only divided denomination which immediately decided to forgive and forget was the Episcopal Church."[23] In this prompt reconciliation between Northern and Southern Episcopalians the Diocese of Kentucky played a prominent part.

The surrender and Lincoln's assassination were fresh in the minds of each of the forty-one delegates and visiting clergy who gathered at St. Paul's Church in Louisville on May 24, 1865, for the Thirty-seventh Annual Convention of the Diocese. Of the twenty-four parishes, half were represented by their clergy, and thirteen lay delegations were present. Of the eight visiting clergy invited to attend the sessions, four were chaplains in the United States Army. One new parish priest had just been transferred from the Confederate Diocese of Georgia.

Bishop Smith's address to the convention was unusually optimistic. Within the past few days he had consecrated the parish church at Owensboro, and he could report with satisfaction that St. Mark's Mission for colored people in Louisville was conducting a day and night school. The high point of the address was an appeal to those whom the convention would elect as deputies to the forthcoming General Convention for them to "receive with open arms" any Southern bishops or laity who might return to take their seats in that body.

In response to the Bishop's appeal the convention unanimously adopted the following resolution:

Resolved 1st—That the sentiments expressed in the foregoing extract from the Bishop's Address are—especially in the present crisis of the Church and the country—a very noble illustration of the true spirit of Christ;

---

[23] E. Merton Coulter, *The South During Reconstruction, 1865–1877* (Baton Rouge, La.: 1947), pp. 331–332.

eminently worthy of a Bishop in the Church of God, and have the cordial approval of this Convention.

Resolved 2nd—That this Convention disapproves of uncharitable sermons, addresses, and Church newspaper articles, against the Bishops, Clergy, and Laity of the South, as tending inevitably to greatly impair if not to destroy the truly Christian policy enunciated in the extract from the Bishop's Address.

To represent the Diocese in the General Convention in October an eminent group was elected, headed by Dr. Craik, who had served as a deputy since 1846. He had presided with great diplomacy over the House of Clerical and Lay Deputies at the stormy meeting in 1862. The others in the delegation were: The Reverend Messrs. Francis Whittle of St. Paul's, Louisville, John Norton of the Church of the Ascension, Frankfort, Jacob Shipman of Christ Church, Lexington; and of the laity A. H. Churchill of Elizabethtown, William Cornwall and W. F. Bullock, both of Louisville, and John W. Stevenson of Covington. For knowledge of jurisprudence and ecclesiastical polity this group of deputies has rarely been equaled in the history of the Diocese.[24]

Bishop Smith's statement and the Kentucky convention's resolution favoring the reunion of the American Church at the 1865 General Convention were all the more important because they appeared early. In June the Presiding Bishop asked the Northern bishops to join in an invitation to the Southern deputies to take their places in the General Convention, but a majority of them refused to do so. Bishop Hopkins then extended the invitation personally.[25] Some of the Confederate bishops were also dubious about an immediate reconciliation and did not accept the invitation. Nevertheless, delegations from North Carolina, Tennessee, and Texas presented themselves at the General Convention and were admitted. During the three weeks of debate over the terms of their admittance, Kentuckians were leaders in the party of reconciliation.

[24] *Journal of the Diocese of Kentucky* for 1865, *passim.*
[25] Edgar Legare Pennington, "The Organization of the Protestant Episcopal Church in the Confederate States of America," *Historical Magazine of the Protestant Episcopal Church,* XVII (1948), pp. 305, 338. For an objection to the Presiding Bishop's proposal see Rt. Rev. Charles P. McIlvaine to Rt. Rev. John Henry Hopkins, July 1, 1865 (Bishop McIlvaine Papers, Church Historical Society).

As was to be expected, the House of Clerical and Lay Deputies elected Dr. Craik as its presiding officer, confident that under his direction law and order would prevail. In making his committee appointments, he utilized the talents of his Kentucky colleagues to good advantage. He named Norton on the "State of the Church," Shipman on the "Consecration of the Clergy," Cornwall on "Missions," and Churchill on both "Prayer Book" and "Cooperation with the Canadian Church." On this last committee, Judge Churchill had an opportunity to observe one of the prominent figures of the convention, the Reverend George D. Cummins, Rector of Trinity Church in Chicago. Cummins was a loyal supporter of the Union but had strong ties in Virginia and Maryland. He became the spokesman of the party of reconciliation when, early in the meeting, he introduced and eloquently defended a resolution recognizing and welcoming the Southern delegates. The resolution read:

Resolved: That this House offers its profound gratitude to God that we have among us our brethren, the Clerical and Lay Delegates from the Dioceses of Tennessee, North Carolina, and Texas, and that we recognize their presence in our midst as a token and pledge of the future and entire restoration of the union of the Church throughout the length and breadth of the land.

It was adopted.[26]

A few less conciliatory Northern delegates protested and offered critical resolutions, but on the whole reconciliation prevailed. The convention accepted two bishops the Confederate Church had consecrated and a new diocese it had created. With genuine Christian charity, it authorized the consecration during the meeting of Dr. Charles Todd Quintard, late a chaplain in the Confederate Army, as the second Bishop of Tennessee. Dr. Craik was given a vote of thanks by the House of Deputies for his able conduct of the long and sometimes argumentative sessions. His response, printed in full in the minutes, emphasized the unity of the clerical and lay deputies in arriving at the great decisions of the meeting. The Episcopal

[26] *Journal of the General Convention of the Protestant Episcopal Church in the United States of America,* MDCCCLXV, pp. 38–39 *et passim.*

Church, he declared, depends not only upon the clergy but upon "the essential priesthood of all its members."[27]

This meeting was the most rewarding General Convention that Bishop Smith had experienced for thirty years. He had not been influential in the councils of the national Church during the decades since his trial, but on this historic occasion he stood vindicated by the statesmanlike leadership of the Kentucky deputies and by the wartime record of his Diocese. His episcopal report was proud and optimistic.

Although this Diocese suffered severely during the unhappy civil war which brought so much misery upon our land, the conservative character of the Church has preserved her in no small degree from the distractions and divisions which have impaired the strength and influence of other religious bodies; and the return of peace finds her occupying a most favorable position for reaping an abundant harvest.[28]

The ministry of the first Negro ordained in the Diocese of Kentucky was presented by the Bishop to the annual convention of 1868.

The Rev. J. S. Atwood, of St. Mark's Church in this city, is from the island of Barbadoes, where, in connection with the Codrington College, he received a good classical education, and has since been connected with the Divinity School in West Philadelphia. He is doing well in his parish, where he has a flourishing Sunday School. The Day School is one of the best in the city . . . .

Three other young men from Barbadoes have just reached this country . . . two, Mr. Straker and Mr. King are daily expected in this city—the former to be associated with the Rev. Mr. Atwood and the latter to open a school in Lexington[29] (Footnote: There has been, for a year, a prosperous school in Lexington, under Miss Kendall, a well educated colored person from Boston, recommended to the Bishop by the Rev. Dr. Huntingdon, who is about to take charge of an orphan asylum, under the care of the ladies of Christ Church, who are already conducting a Sunday school of 300 scholars.) with the encouragement and oversight of the Rector of Christ Church.

[27] *Ibid.*, pp. 140–141.
[28] *Ibid.*, p. 237.
[29] See *Journal of the Diocese of Kentucky* for 1860–1869, *passim*, especially the Bishop's Addresses, parochial reports of St. Mark's, and committee reports.

In all, from the Avery Fund, Pittsburgh; the American Church Missionary Society, New York; and the Ladies Branch of the Pennsylvania Freedmen's Aid Society these various charities have reason to expect aid for the work amongst the colored people in this Diocese, for the current year, of about $2,500.00 . . . .

The parochial reports of these years from Frankfort and Lexington show these parishes joining in work for colored people, aided by funds from the Northern states. These funds diminished after a few years, however, and the parishes ceased to undertake secular schools for colored children. Deacon Atwell went to the Diocese of Virginia in early 1869, and Lay Reader Straker's efforts were not successful, but St. Mark's was the forerunner of a permanent mission for Negroes founded by the Reverend John N. Norton after his removal to Louisville. The labors of the Reverend Jacob Shipman and the ladies of Christ Church in Lexington contributed to the establishment of a church for colored people several decades later.

The war years were marked by several other significant missionary enterprises. Like St. Mark's Mission they were short-lived but indicative of a broadening outlook on the part of the Diocese. One project was the establishment of the first parish in the "Iron Country" up the Ohio River at the Virginia (now the West Virginia) line. The earliest services in this region were held by clergymen from the Diocese of Ohio, with the advice and consent of Bishop Smith, who favored interdiocesan visitations. As early as 1857–1858 the rector of Christ Church in Ironton, Ohio, preached regularly to groups at Ashland and Catlettsburg, and in late 1860 the Reverend Henry Blackaller, also from the Diocese of Ohio, began once more to hold services in both towns, using the church buildings of other denominations. He aided the group at Catlettsburg to organize as the parish of St. John's Church, and to apply for admittance at the convention in May, 1861. He was rightly encouraged at the large numbers who attended services, but they dwindled as the war spread through the area. To the 1862 convention Mr. Blackaller sadly reported: "In September last our young and promising Junior Warden was shot while acting as major in the 5th Virginia Regiment, and the amiable secretary of the Vestry left us and is lieutenant colonel in the same regiment, and others who were intending to unite with us have gone to the War." Mr. Blackaller often preached to the soldiers and attended the sick and wounded in the temporary hospital and in private houses, praying with them and giving them tracts, which he also sent to the large hospital in Ashland. Unfortunately, by 1862 the Diocese was already hard put to furnish salaries for missionaries or aid to missions. Mr. Blackaller departed and the next rector, the Reverend Samuel D. Tompkins, who came in 1865, supported himself chiefly by conducting a successful parish school, with thirty-five pupils. For a time St. John's prospered, and its rector ministered sometimes over at Ironton, thus returning in kind the good offices of the Diocese of Ohio. But many of the parishioners moved away and without assistance it could not have a church edifice of its own. After Samuel Tompkins left at the end of 1867, the parish never again had its own rector, although it survived for about five or six years. It contributed to the establishment, a few years later, of a strong church at Ashland.

Another type of missionary expansion in the 1860's is exemplified by St. John's in the Wilderness, a mission established in 1866 among the rural people of the Benson Hills region, five miles west of downtown Frankfort. It was one of the many missionary and educational projects of Ascension Church under the leadership of John Nicholas Norton. His parochial report to the convention in May, 1867, tells of the beginnings of the mission.

The Mission of St. John's in the Wilderness, organized in September last, is accomplishing great good; and the Rev. Robert W. Summers and his self-denying wife keep up a Sunday school, day school, an orphans home, besides the regular service every Sunday. We hope that the liberality of Churchmen will enable them to worship in a comfortable chapel before the return of cold weather.

Already, through the gifts of Frankfort people, a large log building housed Mr. and Mrs. Summers and served as school and temporary chapel. A "neat chapel" was erected within the year. Robert Summers, a teacher turned preacher, was made deacon in March, 1867, and priest in November, 1868.

A high point in the history of St. John's in the Wilderness was

Saturday morning, April 18, 1868, when Assistant Bishop Cummins came to consecrate the newly completed chapel. He was greatly impressed with this mission to win the rural people to the Church.

I consecrated the Church of St. John's in the Wilderness, five miles distant from Frankfort in the midst of a rude and wild country, almost inaccessible by carriages . . . I found a new frame church, holding two hundred people, a school house for day and Sunday schools with fifty scholars, a home for the Missionary, and an asylum containing already twelve orphan girls. Although it was a working day the church was filled with the people of the region around it . . . The music was led by the wife of the Missionary and the older girls of the Asylum . . .[30]

The mission prospered under Mr. and Mrs. Summers. The *Journal* of the Diocese for 1870 lists it among the parishes, although it had not been formally admitted. Despite its having twenty-two communicants and large attendance at services, St. John's in the Wilderness was never self-supporting. Summers pointed out this fact in his 1870 parochial report: "The fostering care of the Reverend Dr. Norton over this mission is about to be withdrawn by his removal to Louisville. To render it prosperous it will require that continued stream of benefaction which has flowed in from friends far and near, and upon which the school at Nashota has lived and prospered." This reference to Nashota suggests that Norton and Summers looked upon the Episcopal community in the Benson Hills as resembling Bishop Kemper's labors in remote Wisconsin. Significantly, the following year Robert Summers and his wife moved to the still more remote Missionary District of Oregon.

The mission was then placed in charge of Thomas B. Hubbell, lay reader and teacher, who carried on the work faithfully, setting up other small missions—"Six-mile" and "Benson"—in nearby neighborhoods.[31] Other laymen served after his departure, notably W. H. Hampton, later ordained to the priesthood. Nevertheless, even before the death of Dr. Norton in 1881, these missions were dwindling, and in a decade they disappeared. They were well remembered for the good works done in them. The community of St.

[30] *Journal of the Diocese of Kentucky* for 1868, p. 34.
[31] *Journal of the Diocese of Kentucky* for 1871, p. 70, and for 1872, pp. 54–55.

John's in the Wilderness appears on the county precinct maps until the end of the century.[32] John Nicholas Norton's short-lived rural missions illustrate the fact that the Church in Kentucky has flourished chiefly in sizable towns and cities.

To return to the state of the Diocese at the close of hostilities, the outstanding administrative problem was that Bishop Smith's active service was coming to an end. When he participated in the reconciling General Convention of 1865 he was in his seventy-first year, a veteran of nearly half a century in the priesthood. He was, moreover, next in line of succession to Presiding Bishop John Henry Hopkins, who was a little older than he. They had been consecrated to the episcopate together by the saintly Bishop White thirty-three years earlier. For some time B. B. Smith's precarious health had made it difficult for him to visit the outer reaches of the Commonwealth, and it was becoming increasingly clear that he needed an assistant bishop. The return of peace to the land and the encouraging outlook for the Diocese seemed to justify this forward step.

[32] Map, "Frankfort Gas House and Market House Precinct" (Franklin County Records, Frankfort, Ky.).

15 George David Cummins, Evangelical Bishop

The election of an Assistant Bishop of Kentucky was the main order of business at the convention of 1866, held in St. John's Church, Louisville, May 20—June 1. Bishop Smith pointed out in his address "the imperative need of an assistant," necessitated by his advanced age and infirmities which kept him from the full performance of the duties of his office.[1]

A committee of ten, composed of five of the clergy and five of the laity, was appointed by the chairman and proceeded to the election. The names of the Reverend James Craik and the Reverend Francis McNeece Whittle, both Louisville clergymen, were proposed, Dr. Craik later withdrawing his name and supporting Whittle. The latter, the rector of St. Paul's Church, was thrice chosen by the clergy and thrice rejected by the laity, resulting in no little ill feeling on the part of the clerical order. To promote harmony in the convention, the laity proposed the appointment of a conference committee, composed of six of each order, to whom the whole subject was referred.[2]

At the final session of the convention, the committee of conference, after careful consideration, recommended the Reverend George David Cummins, D. D., rector of Trinity Church, Chicago. The spokesman, Judge W. F. Bullock, delegate from St. Paul's, Louisville, stated, "We were all willing to surrender for ourselves and the party we represent all personal feelings and private ideas," and urged that unanimity govern the meeting.[3] Cummins was nominated by Whittle and seconded by Dr. Craik, after which the convention proceeded to ballot. The Illinois clergyman received twenty-one of the twenty-three clerical votes, and the laity confirmed his election with only one dissenting vote.

George David Cummins was a prominent member of the Evangelical or Low Church party and for many years had been quite outspoken against the growing tide of High Churchism. In 1866 the Evangelicals in the Diocese of Kentucky were strong enough to elect as Assistant Bishop a man of their own persuasion.

The Reverend Dr. Cummins was in Paris, France when he first read in a New York journal an announcement of his election as Assistant Bishop of Kentucky, shortly thereafter receiving the official announcement from the Standing Committee of the Diocese of Kentucky. Many letters from all over the Diocese, including several from Bishop Smith, urged him to accept, as did letters from many other American bishops.[4] One letter in particular, from a presbyter of the Diocese of Kentucky, may have influenced his decision. The writer was the Reverend George D. E. Mortimer, rector of St. Paul's Church, Newport.

There are three parties in the Church here—the Virginia Churchmen, the Evangelical High Churchmen, and the Sacramentarian High Churchmen. All, however, united upon you. I am confident that by the blessing of God you can harmonize these conflicting interests. Moreover, your ecclesiastical sentiments are admirably adapted to this Diocese. Kentucky is the daughter of Virginia, both in ecclesiastical polity and theology and in political sentiment. A conservative, evangelical Churchman (as I know you to be) can at this time, as a bishop, wield a mighty influence for good by the blessing of God.[5]

Dr. Cummins accepted by letter from France on July 7. Among the many congratulatory letters he received was one from Bishop Charles P. McIlvaine, one of his closest Evangelical friends. The Ohio bishop stated that because of ill health he might not be present for the consecration, but he hoped that the solemnity would be "free from any of the novelties that disturb our peace."[6]

On November 15, 1866, Dr. Cummins was consecrated a bishop in the Church of God, in Christ Church, Louisville, by the Right

[1] *Journal, Diocese of Kentucky*, 1866.

[2] *Ibid.*

[3] *Ibid.* At least half of the first committee was from Louisville. The second committee had one Louisville clergyman, a post chaplain stationed in that city, and two laymen from the largest parishes in Louisville, St. Paul's and Christ Church. All the rest were from other cities. It is obvious that the conference committee was appointed to end a controversy among the Louisville delegates. Of the fifty lay delegates listed on opening day, twenty represented the six Louisville parishes. The new committee obviously despaired of settling the dispute in regard to Whittle and started all over again.

[4] Alexandrine Macomb Cummins, *Memoir of George David Cummins, D.D., First Bishop of the Reformed Episcopal Church* (New York, 1878).

[5] *Ibid.*, p. 249.

[6] *Ibid.*, p. 264.

Reverend John Henry Hopkins of Vermont, Presiding Bishop of the Protestant Episcopal Church in the United States, assisted by Bishops Smith, Lee of Iowa, Talbot of Indiana, Clarkson of Nebraska, Quintard of Tennessee, and Kerfoot of Pittsburg. He became the eighty-first in order of succession of American bishops.

George David Cummins was born in Smyrna, Delaware, on December 11, 1822. His father and paternal grandfather were Episcopalians, but his mother, the daughter of a Methodist minister, the Reverend John D. Durborow, remained in that communion all her life and endeavored to rear her children in that faith. Cummins was only fourteen years of age when he entered Dickinson College in Carlisle, Pennsylvania, and it was here during a revival that he joined his mother's church. He graduated *cum laude* in 1841 and became a Methodist circuit rider. When twenty-one, however, he joined the Episcopal Church, in his words, "then so simple in her ritual,"[7] and was confirmed in Wilmington, Delaware, by Bishop Alfred Lee, under whom he subsequently studied for Holy Orders. He was ordained deacon in 1845 and priest in 1847. Three years of close association under the tutelage of one of the most evangelical of the American bishops, coupled with his early Methodist training, at least partially explain his Churchmanship. Shortly after his ordination to the priesthood in 1847, he became rector of Christ Church, Norfolk, Virginia, the largest parish in the state, and in June of that same year married Alexandrine Macomb of Virginia. He received frequent calls during the 1850's, during which he was rector of St. James's Church, Richmond; Trinity Church, Washington, D.C., and St. Peter's Church, Baltimore.

Although a Union sympathizer, Cummins evidently assumed a rather neutral position in 1861 and, with his wife, spent the whole of 1862 abroad, returning in 1863 to become rector of Trinity Church, Chicago. He attained prominence at the General Convention of 1865 in Philadelphia, where he introduced an earnest resolution, welcoming the Southerners back into the Episcopal Church, the resolution passing by almost unanimous vote. In defense of the Southern Church, Dr. Cummins made the most eloquent and mov-

[7] *Ibid.*

ing speech of the entire Convention.[8] There can be little doubt that it was his picture of the glory of the Church in good and happier days, that "she was the last to break the bonds of union," and his pleas to "give her the everlasting honor of being the first Christian body to restore the bonds of union," that clinched the acceptance of the Southern bishops back into the Church. Doubtless the fact that George David Cummins was not a Southerner, not trained in the doctrine of states' rights, and was in fact a clerical deputy from the state of Illinois and an avowed Unionist, added immeasurably to the attention his speech received. The Kentucky delegation was impressed with Dr. Cummins' stand in relation to the South, the precise stand of Kentucky and the border states, as well as with his oratorical skill, and these probably were large factors in his call to the episcopate in Kentucky.

The new Assistant Bishop was welcomed with open arms into a Diocese which, for several years, had been without the full services of a bishop. He chose, after some consideration, to make Louisville his seat of operation, obviously preferring a metropolitan ministry. The Diocese purchased a country home for him in Peewee Valley, sixteen miles from Louisville, and here at "Oak Lea" he and his family resided for several years, part of which time he enjoyed great popularity in Louisville and its environs.

Cummins was in appearance almost the exact opposite of Bishop Smith—a large man, arresting and histrionic where the Diocesan was spare and unassuming. He had a melodious voice, burning with eloquence, and "crowds ever thronged the place where he had been announced to preach and were held spellbound by the thrilling tones, the graceful diction and the vivid word-painting of the orator."[9] He made a most auspicious beginning in his new office, throwing himself into his episcopal duties with great fervor and zeal.

At the end of his first six months he had covered the length and breadth of the state, visiting all but three of the thirty-five parishes

[8] *Journal of the General Convention of the Protestant Episcopal Church in the United States of America,* 1865.
[9] The Right Reverend Thomas Underwood Dudley, "The Protestant Episcopal Church," in J. Stoddard Johnston, *Memorial History of Louisville from Its First Settlement to the Year 1896* (Chicago and New York, 1896), II, 149.

and missions in the Diocese.[10] His primary concern was the creation of a Board of Diocesan Missions, aimed at supporting weak missions and creating new ones, and he recommended at the 1867 convention that such a board be created and elected annually by the convention. He adhered to the convocational system of dividing the Diocese; he pointed out the need of an endowment fund for the support of the episcopate by individual contributions and outlined a feasible plan for obtaining funds; he expressed his concern for the newly emancipated colored population, urging that these persons be trained "in the sober Scriptural ways of our Communion." Each of his plans was greeted with enthusiasm and referred to special committees. It appeared that Cummins might indeed be a "mighty influence for good by the blessing of God."[11]

During the remainder of 1867 and greater part of 1868 all appeared well, Cummins continuing the good work of building up the Diocese, raising money both within and without its boundaries for mission work. However, many of his suggestions, which the year before had met with enthusiastic support, had not been carried out. In his address to the convention of 1868 he stated that even though the past year had seen marked progress in Kentucky, he was still far from satisfied with the results. "This Convention," he stated, "finds us, as did the last, with our greatest weakness still existing, an entire lack of organization."

For reasons not readily apparent, the Assistant Bishop was meeting with opposition in his Diocese. It was during 1868, according to Cummins, that a ritualistic[12] service was introduced for the first time into the Diocese of Kentucky and "the unspeakable trial" was placed upon him of being compelled to visit this church and take part in its services.[13] The church was Grace Church, Louisville.

When he accepted the episcopacy in Kentucky, Cummins was

[10] *Journal, Diocese of Kentucky,* 1867, p. 36.

[11] Cummins, *Memoir,* p. 249. Previously quoted from letter, George D. E. Mortimer to Cummins, June 6, 1866.

[12] The term "ritualistic" or "ritualism" is an unfortunate one when used to mean "ceremonialism." Ritual is the form of conducting worship; a rite is a prescribed form of conducting a ceremony. The simplest Prayer Book Office is ritualistic. Except where quoting, the present writers will refer to advanced ritual as ceremonialism.

[13] Cummins, *Memoir,* p. 510.

certain that he was coming to a Diocese much like Virginia in its Churchmanship. He knew Bishop Smith to be a Low Churchman who was unalterably opposed to ceremonialism, and he was of the impression that most of the clergy and practically all of the laity held the same views as the Bishop. He found it hard to understand how "ritualistic" services, such as those at Grace Church, could be tolerated in an evangelical environment. He began to realize that some of the men he had counted as his supporters, such as Craik, Shipman and Norton, although themselves not advanced ceremonialists, were decidedly at odds with him in the matter.

Dr. Craik, who was one of the most influential Churchmen of his time and the leader in the Diocese of Kentucky as well as in the general councils of the Church, held decided convictions, believing with all his heart the principles of the One, Holy, Catholic and Apostolic Church of antiquity. He adhered strictly to the Book of Common Prayer, and was "equally outspoken against the corruptions of the medievalists and the rationalism of modern Protestantism." "When he spoke, his word was law, his opinion was the end of controversy to the great congregation of Christ Church, Louisville" and to many Episcopalians throughout the state.[14] Dr. Shipman and Dr. Norton were at one with Dr. Craik on Church principles, although Norton "perhaps held even higher views of the sacraments."[15]

It is a matter of no little difficulty in any age to designate a man's Churchmanship, so varied are the issues which align him with one party or the other. It is especially hard during the years in which George David Cummins was Assistant Bishop of Kentucky. The period from 1860 to 1875 was marked by more party strife and internal dissension than any period in the history of the American Church. One writer called it "a veritable ecclesiastical war, a reflection of the war of secession."[16] Two types of Churchmanship dominated, "Evangelicalism" and "High Churchmanship," but between the extremes of these two parties were many gradations and there were numbers of devout Churchmen of the *via media* who did not

[14] Dudley, in *Memorial History of Louisville*, II, 145.
[15] *Ibid.*, p. 145.
[16] Greenough White, *An Apostle of the Western Church* (New York, 1900), p. 219.

fit readily under either label. Some, in fact, while claiming to be of one party, were more in sympathy in some areas with the opposite party. Nowhere was this so true as in the border state of Kentucky.

It is necessary to point out for clarification that the older school of "Low Churchmanship" of the eighteenth and early nineteenth centuries had largely disappeared and had been replaced by the "Evangelicals." The members of the older school of Low Churchmen had been orthodox in their theology, but tolerant of a considerable variety of opinion so long as there was no departure from essentials. Bishop William White was such a Churchman.

The "Evangelicals," the nineteenth century's Low Churchmen, were much less conservative. They accepted the episcopacy as a matter of expediency rather than necessity; they regarded the sacraments more as matters of form and ceremony than means of grace; they were willing to abridge or change the liturgy; they believed the Bible to be the sole rule of faith based on personal interpretation; they attached great importance to revivalistic and evangelical preaching, giving precedence to pulpit over altar; they abhorred ceremonialism in worship, branding it innovation; and they often held joint worship services with Protestant denominations. It was the party of at least half of the Kentucky Episcopalians.

There were in the nineteenth century in America two schools of High Churchmanship, to which this book will refer as "Evangelical High Churchmanship" and "Sacramentarian High Churchmanship."

The first and older was the more conservative or moderate wing. This type prevailed in America even before the founding of the Protestant Episcopal Church. It was born in Connecticut, and the Church's first bishop, Samuel Seabury, was an adherent. It was often called "Connecticut Churchmanship." After the Revolution, it spread into New York. The undisputed leader of the High Church party in America during the first half of the nineteenth century was John Henry Hobart (and his successor, William H. DeLancey), so much so that the type for which he stood was often called "Hobartian Churchmanship." Hobart's watchword was "Evangelical Truth and Apostolic Order," and the name by which this early High Churchmanship was known in many parts of the country, including Kentucky, was "Evangelical High Churchmanship." James Craik and Jacob Shipman were Kentucky examples. An Evangelical High Churchman was one who believed, among other things, in the divine origin of the Christian ministry under the Episcopal form; who believed in the Real Presence of Christ in the Holy Communion; who believed that all things necessary to salvation are found in Holy Scripture, yet depended upon tradition and patristic teaching for guidance and instruction; who had great attachment to the liturgy of the Church, to form and decorum, yet did not rule out fervor, zeal, and evangelical preaching. The Evangelical High Churchman was not a ceremonialist, for to his mind High Churchmanship had nothing whatever to do with ceremonialism. He believed that the Episcopal Church had all things necessary for salvation.

The second type of High Churchmanship, "Sacramentarian High Churchmanship," came to America on the crest of the Oxford Movement as a result of the publication of the famous *Tracts for the Times*. Although the *Tracts* did much to revive Catholic truth as well as spiritual life in America, they stirred up the wrath of the Evangelicals and sharpened hostility between High and Low Church, pointing up as they did the fundamental differences. This was the prevailing type of High Churchmanship from about 1835 to 1850. A Sacramentarian High Churchman believed in the Real Presence of Christ in the Eucharist; considered the Eucharist a commemorative sacrifice and the principal service of the Church; believed salvation depended upon an Apostolic ministry; reverenced tradition and patristic teaching; countenanced religious orders within the Church, used prayers for the dead, opposed any sort of fervor, revivalistic meetings, and evangelical preaching; did not object to lights, incense, songs, and adoration as means whereby to enhance the beauty of worship. The Reverend John Nicholas Norton and John Austen Merrick were representative of this type in Kentucky.

It will be seen that doctrinally there was little real difference between the two types of High Churchmanship, merely a shift of emphasis. The latter, however, was more amenable to extremism, innovation, and excess in the direction of Romanism. Thereby, there came into the Church what one writer calls the "lunatic fringe," the genuine Romanizers.[17] It was this "lunatic fringe" which drove some High Churchmen into the arms of the Evangelicals and others into an attitude of indifference.

During the War between the States, party factionalism ceased for a time within the Church, but no sooner were the North and South reunited than it broke out anew and waxed hotter than before, raging furiously until 1875. It was, therefore, at its height during the incumbency of George David Cummins as Assistant Bishop of Kentucky.

Now that a "ritualistic" service had been introduced into the Diocese of Kentucky, the Assistant Bishop became more and more outspoken in his stand against such "errors," and had he possessed the authority, "ritualism would have been put down in Kentucky."[18] Now both High Church parties were determined that the authority of a diocesan bishop would never be his. Since his arrival, Cummins had been, in effect, the acting Bishop of the Diocese, and he was, as a matter of fact, assuming all of the duties of a diocesan. Bishop Smith, while still attending diocesan conventions, had from year to year taken less and less an active role because of age and infirmities and, upon becoming Presiding Bishop of the Protestant Episcopal Church in the United States on January 9, 1868,[19] was spending almost all of his time in the East. However, he was still Bishop of Kentucky and, even in absentia, had the final say as to the Diocese.

In October, 1868, the Assistant Bishop attended the General Con-

---

[17] George E. DeMille, M.A., *The Catholic Movement in the American Episcopal Church* (Church Historical Society, 1941), p. 129. "Finally, there was the lunatic fringe, the genuine Romanizers, who were avowedly working for reunion with Rome, who were willing to accept all Roman doctrine except papal infallibility, who despised manners and customs distinctly Anglican."

[18] Cummins, *Memoir*, p. 295.

[19] Bishop B. B. Smith became Presiding Bishop upon the death of the Right Reverend John Henry Hopkins, by virtue of his seniority. He had been consecrated bishop in 1832, along with Hopkins, Charles P. McIlvaine and George W. Doane. Hopkins was the first upon whom the hands of the consecrating prelates were laid, thereby giving him precedence. Smith was the second. Therefore, on the death of Hopkins, Smith was the oldest in episcopacy by a few moments, giving him precedence over the other two. The selection of the Presiding Bishop by seniority was the mode in the American Church for many years.

vention in New York City. He was extremely outspoken within the House of Bishops and left no doubt in the minds of any who heard him speak that his stand was "firmly on the old evangelical basis now and ever and to keep this Church upon the platform of the Reformation."[20] If he had confined his remarks to the convention itself he would not have received such censure from the High Church party. Instead, he availed himself of every opportunity to speak before the three great Evangelical societies, the American Church Missionary Society, the Evangelical Knowledge Society, and the Evangelical Education Society, and to preach on their behalf in numerous New York churches. His subject was ever the same, the Protestantism of the Protestant Episcopal Church and a defense of the principles of the English Reformation, which according to Cummins were "now so imperilled in the Church, both in England and America." His eloquence and fearless advocacy of "evangelical truth" put him much in demand as a spokesman for the Evangelicals and aroused the indignation of the High Church party.

One incident, which was especially disheartening to Cummins, occurred on October 10 at a Board of Missions meeting held in the Church of the Transfiguration in New York City. In his journal he wrote, "You may judge my feelings when, upon entering the church, I saw before me in the chancel an altar, with a superaltar, and on it in the center a brass cross three feet high, and two brass candlesticks of the same height on either side, with candles in them, but unlighted. And just in front of the altar was the venerable Bishop McIlvaine, within a few feet of what he had all his life so earnestly protested against."[21] The incident was doubly hard for Cummins to bear because, of all the Evangelical bishops with the possible exception of Alfred Lee, McIlvaine was closest to him. Only the morning before, he had jubilantly entered in his journal that Bishop McIlvaine had arisen in the House of Bishops and objected to the surpliced choir of boys at the daily service at Trinity Chapel, resulting in the withdrawal of the choir.[22]

[20] Cummins, *Memoir*, p. 288.
[21] *Ibid.*, p. 289.
[22] *Ibid.*, p. 289.

Bishop Cummins came away from the General Convention feeling that little had been accomplished concerning questions vital to his party. A canon on ceremonialism, strongly desired by the Evangelicals, had not materialized, the only action taken being the appointment of a committee of the House of Bishops to consider the whole question and report to the next General Convention. Likewise, a committee, appointed to consider Prayer Book revision, which would allow the use of alternate forms for such terms as "regeneration" in the Baptismal Service, reported that it was "unwise and inexpedient to attempt any such changes."[23] Cummins wrote in his journal before leaving New York, "This convention will prove an era in my life and may decide the whole future of my career."[24]

The Assistant Bishop's course at the General Convention antagonized many leading men in Kentucky, as he himself had anticipated.[25] When he returned to Kentucky he soon found out that he could no longer count on the support of many men he had considered his allies.

This was particularly manifested within the Board of Missions, of which Cummins was ex officio president.[26] Some of his fellow board members felt that Cummins was "stocking the diocese with his own men and that he thought it the duty of the diocese as represented in the Board of Missions to support them." This first became apparent in his appointment in 1869 of a missionary to Lebanon, an appointment in which the board had no voice.[27] Dr. Craik objected for the board because of "the very defective views of the missionary in regard to the Church and to the policy to be pursued in Kentucky in intercourse with other religious bodies." When at a meeting of the board on January 2, 1869, Dr. Craik confronted Cummins with the question of that body's responsibility in regard to the appointment of missionaries, the Assistant Bishop made it plain that he

[23] *Journal of the General Convention,* 1868.
[24] Cummins, *Memoir,* p. 300.
[25] *Ibid.,* p. 297.
[26] The Board of Missions was elected annually by the convention. It was composed of members of both orders with the Assistant Bishop at its head. It was created in 1867 at Cummins' request.
[27] This was the Reverend Isaac Gibson.

would "appoint the very persons he pleased" and that he thought it a strange proceeding that while he was supporting and befriending so many High Churchmen, such as Venable, Curtis, and Weller,[28] he himself should be criticized for appointing one man "on his own side." This, according to Craik, was the first time Cummins had ever avowed that "he was on one side and some of us on the other." The rector of Christ Church, Louisville, made it plain that the Board of Missions should not be an auxiliary to the American Church Missionary Society. The board, according to Craik, was alarmed because Cummins and some of his followers were at this time making concessions to Protestant denominations in Kentucky, using their buildings for worship and holding joint services. "To put the Church upon a simple equality with all the denominations," stated Craik, "is to place her far below them all, for in every particular of numbers, power, and social influence they are all far above her, and she has nothing but her Divine Charter by which to appeal to men and induce them to forfeit all these advantages for the sake of a small and despised Communion." The result of the meeting of the Board of Missions was that the Bishop had all the rights he claimed, but the Diocese was not bound to support that policy beyond the appropriations already made.[29]

In the episcopacy of Bishop Cummins, 1869 might well be considered the climactic year, for his action at this time, both within and without the Diocese of Kentucky, left no doubt as to his complete obsession against all High-Churchism, both in matters of doctrine and in ceremonialism. His life was, in truth, fraught with vexation, so fiercely did he struggle against the ceremonial trend in the Church, wavering at times from the Augustinian principle he so often quoted of "unity in essentials, liberty in non-essentials, and charity in all things." To Bishop Cummins ceremonialism seemed completely alien to the Protestantism of the Church. He opposed

---

[28] J. W. Venable, rector of St. John's, Versailles; Judson Curtis, rector of Christ Church, Bowling Green; and R. H. Weller, rector of the Church of the Nativity, Maysville.

[29] James Craik to John Cowan and Dr. George Cowan, January 4, 1869. The original and unpublished letter is in the possession of Mrs. Charles Ewell Craik of Louisville.

such things as processional crosses, frontals, candles on the altar, and all but the simplest vestments, and reacted furiously against such "innovations" as incense, crucifixes, and reverencing the cross. He avoided the use of the word "catholic" except in the universal sense; altar, Eucharist, and priest were words he never used, substituting holy table, Lord's Supper, and minister or pastor.

While outwardly it appeared to be ceremonialism to which he was most opposed, it soon became apparent that his obsession had deeper roots, as he began to indict the Church's doctrines. The Doctrine of Baptismal Regeneration probably received his severest opprobrium, and the Baptismal Office in the Prayer Book, now came under his attack. The term "regeneration," or the verb or adjective thereof, is mentioned four times in the Baptismal Office. Regeneration, as held by the Episcopal Church, is the spiritual rebirth which is effected in the soul by Christian baptism.[30] Of the many subjects of controversy in the Episcopal Church during the lifetime of Cummins, that which centered around baptismal regeneration was probably the most crucial. Indeed, it had shared the center of the stage in the Evangelical—High Church battle for almost two centuries. During the eighteenth century in England, the century of the Evangelical Revival, it had been one of the basic areas of disagreement because it hit hard at the Doctrine of Justification by Faith, at the very heart of the Evangelical system. The Reformers all but eradicated it from the Church of England; in America, in the proposed Prayer Book of 1785, the words "to regenerate this infant by Thy Holy Spirit" had been deleted. Cummins leaned heavily on this fact, stating that it was on the basis of this proposed Book that the American Church was judged a true daughter of the Church of England and its first bishops were consecrated.[31] In the nineteenth century in England, the century of the Anglican Revival, the Oxford Movement once more brought the controversy over baptismal regeneration to the forefront, defending its Catholic interpretation.

[30] *Book of Common Prayer,* Articles of Instruction, p. 292, "a death unto sin and a new birth unto righteousness." Articles of Religion, p. 606, Article XXVII, "A sign of regeneration or new birth." Catechism, p. 581, "a death unto sin and a new birth unto righteousness."

[31] Cummins, *Memoir,* pp. 330–347.

To the Catholic Christian, regeneration means an act of God on behalf of the creature; it is an actual change of state, a conversion; the life of God in the soul begins with Holy Baptism; baptism and regeneration are inseparable. To the Evangelical, regeneration is a change of character, not of state. Infant baptism is a dedication of the child and a declaration of the universal availability of the salvation wrought by Christ, which is prior to any individual response. It does not, however, make the child "regenerate"; he is not renewed or converted by the Holy Ghost. This must be brought about later in response to profession of faith. This was the view of baptismal regeneration which Cummins held. In a letter to his good friend, Bishop G. T. Bedell of Ohio, Cummings stated that he, himself, could use the term "regenerate" in a thoroughly evangelical sense with no hurt of conscience, but that there were many clergymen in the Church who felt that they must take this term and other terms, not as the Reformers understood them, but as their plain literal language teaches, and in no other sense. He pointed out that he felt it to be "the duty of the Church towards her children troubled by conscience to grant them the liberty of omitting the word 'regenerate' from the Baptismal Office or that the Church should formally declare that regeneration was not synonymous with renovation, sanctification, conversion, or any other term by which the renewing of the Holy Ghost might be designated."[32]

Another doctrine to which Cummins strongly objected was the Doctrine of Sacerdotalism, and he expressed regret that "two or three generations of clergymen in this country have been trained in the belief that the term 'priest,' applied to a minister of this Church, means that he is a sacerdos, a priest ordained to offer a commemorative sacrifice in the Eucharist, and to stand between Christ and the soul as the only divinely appointed channel through which grace can be conveyed and the benefits of Christ's death imparted."[33] To the Assistant Bishop, the Lord's Supper was "a precious feast of remembrance"—nothing more. He did not believe in the Real Presence of the body and blood of Christ in the elements

[32] *Ibid.*, pp. 331–341.
[33] *Ibid.*, p. 332.

of the Holy Communion, and the validity of the Sacrament did not depend on its administration by an apostolically ordained priest.[34]

Many of Bishop Cummins' beliefs were at this time held by other Kentucky clergy, some of whom supported him all along the way. It seems only fair to state, too, that at this time and for some years afterward, Cummins was firmly convinced that the "errors which had crept into the Protestant Episcopal Church must be fought against within her pale."[35] He looked to the older Evangelical bishops to instigate this action and became thoroughly disappointed by what he considered their passive attitude.

A really serious breach between Cummins and those, both within and without the Diocese of Kentucky, who held different views, came early in 1869, when he received an invitation to "take a prominent part" in the establishment of a new Society for the Promotion of Evangelical Religion in the Northwest, to be organized in Trinity Church, Chicago, his former parish. He was invited by its rector, the Reverend E. Sullivan, but the Bishop of Illinois, the Right Reverend Henry John Whitehouse, an inflexible High Churchman who was well aware of the nature of Cummins' Churchmanship, asked him not to take any part in the organization of the meeting, which he regarded as a movement designed to disturb the peace of his Diocese.[36]

On receipt of Bishop Whitehouse's letter, Cummins wrote to several of his Evangelical friends asking for advice on the matter. Bishop McIlvaine answered immediately, stating that, while he wished the society had been connected with one of the general Evangelical societies, he thought Cummins had every right to go. He pointed out that if he did not go, he would be admitting the schismatical nature of the society and would also give credence to Whitehouse's claim that he had a right to forbid a clergyman to go into his diocese for any cause.[37] Several other bishops and clergymen advised Cummins not to go, warning him of possible grave consequences. The Reverend Charles Edward Cheney, rector of Christ

[34] *Ibid.*, p. 422.
[35] *Ibid.*, p. 295.
[36] Archives of Church Historical Society, Box VII, Envelope 1; "1869 Correspondence between Cummins, Smith and Others."
[37] *Ibid.*, McIlvaine to Cummins, 1869.

Church, Chicago, and one of the organizers of the questionable society, wrote that he had proposed that the society be made an auxiliary to the Church Missionary Society, but his proposal had not met with success, especially among the lay members of the organization.[38] He stated that the organization much desired Cummins' presence, but in view of the determined opposition of Bishop Whitehouse, he did not feel at liberty to insist that Cummins "go against his own convictions of what courtesy towards another bishop or the good of the cause demands." Cummins decided to postpone the visit for the present and informed the Reverend Mr. Sullivan, who wrote that this was perhaps the wiser course.[39]

Before Cummins had replied to Whitehouse's first letter, he received a second and stronger one, stating that if Cummins should come into his Diocese, as rumored, "to act, accredited by the American Church Missionary Society or its kindred organizations, the exercise of such agency will raise questions still more serious, probably, in other jurisdictions as well as my own."[40] In reply, Cummins told Whitehouse that he had decided not to come for the original purpose of helping organize the society in question, since it was not to be an auxiliary to any of the three general societies, but that he had promised to visit Chicago on February 21 to preach and ask for offerings in behalf of the American Church Missionary Society and the Evangelical Education Society and that he intended to fulfil his promise.[41]

On February 11 Whitehouse wrote a still harsher letter, saying that he had forwarded full copies of the correspondence to Bishop Smith and had protested to him "against the Assistant Bishop of Kentucky assuming, in virtue of a traveling agency from the American Church Missionary Society, the right to act without consent within the jurisdiction of another bishop, or contrary to his expressed wishes." Said he, "I now respectfully present to you my protest against your assumed authority and your contemplated visit

[38] Cummins, *Memoir,* p. 309. Charles Edward Cheney to Cummins, January 23, 1869.
[39] *Ibid.,* p. 311. The Reverend E. Sullivan to Cummins, January 29, 1869.
[40] Archives of Church Historical Society, Whitehouse to Cummins, February 1, 1869.
[41] *Ibid.,* Cummins to Whitehouse, February 3, 1869.

at the time indicated."[42] Whitehouse also enclosed a copy of a resolution by the Standing Committee of the Diocese of Illinois protesting against a visit by Cummins.

It is probable that Cummins did not consult his own Bishop at all about his intended visit to Chicago, and doubtless Smith first heard about it when he received Whitehouse's letter of February 11. Just before Cummins left for Chicago on February 18, he received a hastily written note from Bishop Smith, and from Chicago he answered, "I just didn't want to mingle you in the controversy, especially as you have never been identified with the American Church Missionary Society or the Evangelical Education Society."[43]

The news of Cummins' invitation to preach in Chicago and of Whitehouse's request that he refrain from coming received wide publicity, as did his actual visit to the city. The Chicago affair aroused much feeling, both for and against Cummins. It incensed the High Church party more than any of his actions heretofore, but the Evangelicals seemed to support his course completely. Among these were Bishops McIlvaine and Alfred Lee. Yet, when Cummins wrote McIlvaine in regard to taking part in a series of similar Evangelical meetings in other cities, the Ohio bishop advised against such action on the basis that, while the Chicago meeting was to meet a crisis, he should avoid seeming to go out of his way to attend other meetings of societies where they would be offensive.[44] Bishop Lee suggested that Cummins attend only meetings of the societies held in cities where he knew the bishops would be in sympathy with his action.[45]

Cummins did, indeed, preach in behalf of the Evangelical societies in several cities, notably Baltimore, Philadelphia, Washington, D.C., and again at Trinity Church, Chicago early in July.[46] When

[42] *Ibid.,* Whitehouse to Cummins, February 11, 1869.

[43] *Ibid.,* Cummins to Smith, February 20, 1869. The American Church Missionary Society was organized in 1859 and proposed to carry on work entirely under its own direction both at home and abroad. At this date it was under the control of Evangelicals. After the strife of parties had begun to subside, it became an auxiliary of the Domestic and Foreign Missionary Society. See Manross, *A History of the American Episcopal Church,* p. 262.

[44] Cummins, *Memoir,* pp. 327–328; McIlvaine to Cummins, March, 1869.

[45] *Ibid.,* pp. 328–329; Bishop Alfred Lee to Cummins, March 27, 1869.

[46] *Journal, Diocese of Kentucky,* 1870, p. 40.

again, later that month, he was asked by the vestry and congregation of Trinity to return and fill the pulpit during the absence of the
rector, he accepted. Again he received a letter of protest from the
Bishop of Illinois, forbidding him to visit that Diocese "to officiate in
any manner within its bounds."[47] Upon the insistence of the vestry,
Cummins decided to go, and he preached there twice on Sunday,
July 25, and he and his wife were guests of one of the vestrymen.
Whitehouse brought proceedings to enforce the canon which forbade any minister of the Church to officiate within another minister's parish without his consent,[48] but the House of Bishops refused
to consider it.

So ended the Chicago affair, but the enmity between the Bishop
of Illinois and the Assistant Bishop of Kentucky was never resolved.
It was enhanced by the deposition by Whitehouse of the Reverend
Charles Edward Cheney, Cummins' friend and the rector of Christ
Church, Chicago, for omitting the phrase in the Prayer Book Office
for infant baptism which ascribes regeneration to the act.[49]

Shortly after his first controversy with Whitehouse in regard to
his attending the meeting of the new Evangelical society in Chicago
in February, 1869, Cummins received an overture in regard to a
separation from the Protestant Episcopal Church. This overture
came from a former clergyman of Kentucky, the Reverend Mason
Gallagher,[50] then residing in Paterson, New Jersey. In a lengthy
letter, he presented to Cummins the reasons why a number of
presbyters and laymen sought to start a reformed Episcopal Church,
adding, "It appears that the Lord has indicated that you are the

[47] Cummins, *Memoir*, pp. 363–364, Whitehouse to Cummins, July 20, 1869.

[48] Manross, *A History of the American Episcopal Church*, pp. 295–296. This canon
was an imitation of the primitive and medieval canons against "intrusion," but the
effort to adapt it to this country, where there are no definite parish boundaries, was
not a happy one. For the purposes of the canon, a parish was defined as including
the whole community in which a church was situated; if there were more than one
church, the community was regarded as a joint parish, so that a visiting clergyman
had to receive the consent of all the ministers before officiating. In practice the canon
was used chiefly to prevent the Evangelicals from joining in the services of other
denominations.

[49] The Cheney case is one of the most celebrated in the American Church. See
Chase, plaintiff in error, v. Cheney (58 Ill. 509, 11 Am. Rep., p. 95).

[50] Mason Gallagher is listed in the *Journals, Diocese of Kentucky*, 1849, 1850, and
1851 as rector of Trinity Church, Covington; thereafter he is not listed. He had
come to the Diocese of Kentucky from the Diocese of Western New York.

bishop he has elected to effect the most important ecclesiastical reformation since that of the sixteenth century."[51] He continued, "What, my dear Bishop, is the work in Kentucky, with so ineffective and lame a Church; with your hands so tied; with the leading divines of your diocese opposing your principles; and with the prospect of the results of your years of labor being overthrown by a ritualistic successor?"

Cummins answered Gallagher on March 11, stating that he was still unable to believe that there was really ground for leaving the Protestant Episcopal Church and that no action should be taken without calling a congress of all Evangelical men—bishops, clergy, and laity—to discuss the subject. He continued, however, with an opinion that "a Protestant Episcopal Church, freed of all High Churchism, would be a mighty power, and by God's blessing a great success in this land; and it may be that God designs that such a Church shall be."[52]

From time to time Cummins received other letters, from both clergy and laity, in regard to taking part in a secession movement, but he did not consider them at this time. Back in Kentucky, he continued to carry on his work in the Diocese, but many had the feeling that his episcopal duties were becoming unpleasant to him and that he was becoming dissatisfied with his field of labor.[53] The feeling in some of the churches was very bitter toward him, and there were many complaints of his absence during the summer months and of his receiving payment.[54] The winter of 1869/70 was the last spent by Bishop Cummins in his own home and, in spite of his declining popularity in the Diocese, it was in a sense a happy one. His youngest daughter and his son George were with him much of the time, as was his beloved wife until her failing health necessitated her being hospitalized. His family ties were close and a great comfort to Cummins, but his happiness was short-lived. In the spring of 1870, "Oak Lea" was sold to the highest bidder, and he

[51] Cummins, *Memoir*, pp. 342–345. Mason Gallagher to Cummins, February 12, 1869.
[52] *Ibid.*, pp. 345–347. Cummins to Gallagher, March 11, 1869.
[53] *The Courier-Journal*, Louisville, November 11, 1873, p. 4. Interview with Mr. R. A. Robinson.
[54] Cummins, *Memoir*, p. 371.

lost the cost of improvements he had put on it.[55] His removal from his home in Peewee Valley was especially disheartening because there had been a belated offer, made at the diocesan convention of that year through the influence of friends, to purchase it as a permanent episcopal residence. Cummins went to live with his elder daughter and son-in-law in Louisville.[56]

From the standpoint of growth and strength, the state of the Diocese in 1870 was gratifying to the Assistant Bishop. The number of clergy stood at thirty-five, as did the number of church buildings, and the communicant strength was four thousand. There was evidence of renewed life in southern and southwestern Kentucky, with parishes in Henderson, Paducah, Hopkinsville, Bowling Green, Princeton, Eddyville, and Fulton County all steadily advancing in strength and influence. Plans were in the offing for church buildings in Richmond, Lebanon, and Lancaster, and in northern and eastern Kentucky there were encouraging tokens of progress. St. Peter's Church, Paris, was erecting a new building; Holy Trinity, Georgetown, was almost completed; and Trinity, Covington, was about to build a new church to meet the demands of the growing city. Christ Church, Louisville, had plans for remodeling, and Grace Church, there, was soon to be completed.[57]

In August, 1870, Cummins accepted the temporary rectorship of St. James' Church, Peewee Valley, "to enable the vestry to complete their new and beautiful building," a charge he held for a little over a year.[58] This church, near his former home, "Oak Lea," was very dear to Cummins and he considered it his home parish.

The Assistant Bishop was finding more and more time to preach and speak before Evangelical societies outside the state. In June, 1870, he preached in St. John's Church, Cincinnati, and made an address in behalf of the Evangelical society, presided over by his good friend, the Right Reverend Gregory Bedell of Ohio. That same month he preached the baccalaureate sermon before the graduating class of Kenyon College. In September he preached in Christ

[55] Journal, Diocese of Kentucky, 1870, p. 23.
[56] Cummins, Memoir. His daughter had married Thomas Chalmers Peebles, M.D., of Dublin, Ireland, who practiced medicine in Louisville.
[57] Journal, Diocese of Kentucky, 1870, pp. 48–49.
[58] Journal, 1871, p. 50.

Church, St. James' Church, and Trinity Church, Chicago, and in October, in Baltimore, New York, New Hampshire, Rhode Island, Pennsylvania, and Washington, D.C.[59]

Bishop Smith was still attending diocesan conventions and visiting the Diocese on special occasions, but at the convention of 1872 the aged Bishop requested that he be granted a leave of absence from the Diocese until after the next General Convention. The committee[60] to which this matter was referred, headed by Dr. Craik, granted Smith's request, but with the understanding that he would continue the administration of the Diocese in general by correspondence, and in any special emergency requiring his presence, by personal visitation. They thereby made it plain that no judicial authority was to be conferred on the Assistant Bishop, even though the entire load of episcopal duties was his. This was not what Bishop Smith had in mind, for the month before he had written Cummins of his intention to live out of the Diocese for the few remaining days of his life, of relinquishing $1,000 per year of his salary, and of devolving the administration of the Diocese and all its work upon the Assistant Bishop.[61]

In his address before the 1873 convention, Cummins pointed with pride to the progress of work throughout the Diocese during the past convention year. In the city of Louisville this was particularly apparent, for St. Paul's Church had been remodeled and practically rebuilt; a new edifice for Calvary Church was abuilding; the Church of the Advent had been erected; and the Church of Our Merciful Saviour for colored people was completed, making twelve churches in all, where seven years before there had been but five. In Harrodsburg, St. Philip's Church, having liquidated its indebtedness, had been consecrated, as had St. James', Peewee Valley; in Paducah, Grace Church was being built. Almost all of the parishes and missions were supplied with rectors.[62] The Assistant Bishop's

[59] *Ibid.*, pp. 49–51.
[60] Journal, 1872, pp. 187–188. The committee was composed of three clergymen and two laymen: Dr. Craik, the Reverend E. T. Perkins, rector of St. Paul's, Louisville, and the Reverend Jacob S. Shipman, rector of Christ Church, Lexington; Messrs. M. M. Benton, J. R. Hallam, both of St. Paul's, Newport.
[61] Cummins, *Memoir,* pp. 405–406. B. B. Smith to Cummins, April 16, 1872.
[62] *Journal,* 1873, pp. 43–44.

address was heartening and hardly indicative of the factional friction within the Diocese.

Bishop Smith did not attend the 1873 Diocesan Convention held in Christ Church, Lexington, and the Reverend Dr. Shipman read his written address to the convention. There was more than a note of sadness in the address as the Bishop reminisced about his past forty-odd years as Bishop of Kentucky. He lamented that most of the clergymen ordained in Kentucky had found fields of labor in other dioceses. His reason for opposing "any advances in ritual" in Kentucky, he explained, was that "the unlettered thousands, whom the Church is trying to reach, are repelled by advanced ritualism, accustomed as they are by education and habit to a more simple form of worship." He pointedly alleged: "Our simple, full Scriptural worship disdains the meretricious aid of tinsel ornaments, and groans under the burden of a gorgeous ceremonial."[63] It was almost as if the Presiding Bishop, though hundreds of miles away, sensed what subject would be the focus of attention at the convention.

The tone of the convention, as attested by the numerous press notices, was anything but calm, with the two party factions strongly aligned against one another. However on May 27, the convention opened peacefully enough, as described in the *Lexington Daily Press*.

The scene at this time was in some respects striking. It reminded one slightly of the pictures one sees of the conventions of the first reformers, when Luther and Melancthon and John Knox guided their councils, except that their spirit and fire were wanting. Bishop Cummins, wearing a dark silk robe, sat within the railing of the sanctuary, beside him a small table upon which were his papers, behind him the altar, covered with a scarlet cloth, on which were handsomely embroidered the words, "Holy, Holy, Holy." Standing upon the altar was a magnificent floral cross, the base of which was one mass of flowers, the shaft and arms dotted with white roses. It was one of the most beautiful designs of the kind we ever saw. Outside the sanctuary railing sat the secretary at another small table, and in the body of the church sat the delegates, priests, and laymen.[64]

[63] *Ibid.*, pp. 29–33.
[64] *Lexington Daily Press,* May 28, 1873.

The next day, however, there appeared in the same newspaper some ominous headlines: High and Low Again, Romanism vs. Protestantism, A Hot Speech from the Bishop, and there followed a story of the second day's proceedings which could not have failed to illuminate that day's reader as to the strife in the Episcopal Church in Kentucky. "The majority of the members are unquestionably opposed to all ritualistic novelties," it stated. "The President, Bishop Cummins, is avowedly their enemy, and the election of Dr. Perkins,[65] a well-known opponent of the new fangled ceremonies, to deliver the opening sermon on these innovations foreshadowed the probable action of the Convention. . . . The beautiful floral cross was removed out of sight, the table of the Lord's Supper having no other decoration than the embroidered scarlet cloth." [66]

The event which, more than any other, precipitated Cummins' abandonment of the Communion of the Protestant Episcopal Church took place in New York City on October 12, 1873. Cummins, who was in the city for a meeting of the Evangelical Alliance, officiated in a joint celebration of the Lord's Supper in a Presbyterian Church, at the invitation of the minister, Dr. John Hall. Participating in the service, in addition to Cummins and Dr. Hall, were Dr. William Arnot of Edinburgh, and Professor Dorner of Berlin. The affair was highly publicized in both the religious and secular press, and letters pro and con filled many columns of daily newspapers. Bitter invective was directed at Bishop Cummins, not only by High Churchmen but even by some Evangelicals, who deemed his action ill-advised and inexpedient. In defending his action, Cummins stated, "It was a practical manifestation of the real unity of 'the blessed company of all faithful people' whom God

[65] The Reverend Edmund Taylor Perkins, D.D., rector of St. Paul's Church, Louisville. He was a Virginian by birth, a graduate of Virginia Theological Seminary, ordained deacon, 1847, priest, 1848. He was missionary-at-large in the Confederate Army, and the Confederate Government appointed him chaplain-at-large to the Confederate Army. After holding several cures in Virginia, he accepted a call to St. Paul's, Louisville, succeeding the Reverend F. M. Whittle. An active supporter of the American Church Missionary Society, the Evangelical Education Society, and the Evangelical Knowledge Society. See *The Biographical Encyclopedia of Kentucky* (Cincinnati, 1878), pp. 590–591.
[66] *Lexington Daily Press,* May 29, 1873, p. 4.

hath knit together in the mystical Body of His Son, Jesus Christ."[67] No canonical proceedings were instigated against Cummins for this act, but the wide controversy which it caused made him feel that his liberty within the Episcopal Church was too limited.

On November 10 from New York, Cummins wrote Bishop Smith in Hoboken, New Jersey, an official letter of abandonment, with a summary of his reasons: (1) He felt a conscientious objection to officiating in certain churches in the Diocese of Kentucky "where the services are conducted so as to symbolize and to teach the people doctrines subversive of the truth as it is in Jesus, and as it was maintained and defended by the Reformers of the sixteenth century." (2) He had lost hope that "this system of error now prevailing in the Church of England and in the Protestant Episcopal Church in this country, can be or will be eradicated by any action of the authorities of the Church, legislative or executive." He stated that he thought the only remedy to be the "judicious revision of the Prayer Book, eliminating from it all that gives countenance directly or indirectly to the whole system of sacerdotalism and ritualism." (3) He was dismayed by the storm he had aroused by communing with members of other denominations, referring specifically to his participation in the Communion service in Dr. John Hall's church in New York. He stated, "As I cannot surrender the right and privilege to meet my fellow Christians of other churches around the Table of our dear Lord, I must take my place where I can do so without alienating those of my own household of faith." He ended by saying, "I have an earnest hope and confidence that a basis for the union of all evangelical Christendom can be found in a Communion which shall retain or restore a primitive Episcopacy and a pure Scriptural Liturgy, with fidelity to the Doctrine of Justification by Faith only."[68] At the same time, Cummins sent printed copies of this letter through the mail to the Reverend E. T. Perkins, a mem-

[67] Archives of Church Historical Society, Box 81, "Collection of George David Cummins," Bishop Cummins' letter of Abandonment of the Communion of the Protestant Episcopal Church, November 10, 1873, to the Right Reverend B. B. Smith.
[68] *Ibid.*

ber of the Standing Committee of Kentucky, and to many persons throughout the United States, and published it in the newspapers.

The Kentucky newspapers made much of the affair, and the Louisville *Courier Journal* ran lengthy articles discussing it and reporting detailed interviews with prominent clergy and laity of the Diocese. Opinions were divided among the clergy. Some, such as the Reverend Dr. Norton and the Reverend Mr. Tschiffely, rector of Grace Church, Louisville, believed that it was the best thing Cummins could have done. Dr. Norton stated, "My candid opinion is that it has relieved the Church from the painful necessity of presenting the Bishop for trial for breaking his consecration vows." On the other hand, the Reverend Dr. Perkins and the Reverend Dr. Shields, rector of St. Andrew's, Louisville, stated that their feelings were of deep regret and concern for the peace of the Church. However both of these Evangelical Churchmen thought that Cummins had acted unwisely and could have done more good by fighting error within the Protestant Episcopal Church.[69]

The laity, too, expressed varying opinions. Mr. William Cornwall, described by the *Courier* as one of the most prominent members of Christ Church, Louisville, when asked his opinion as to Cummins' withdrawal, stated, "I think the Church will probably gain by it." He also gave Canon 8 (Of the Abandonment of the Communion of the Church by a Bishop) as the canon which was applicable to Bishop Cummins' case, the canon being quoted in full by the paper. Mr. R. A. Robinson, a member of St. Paul's Church, Louisville, stated that Cummins' withdrawal had caused profound regret in many Episcopal circles. He was of the opinion that the cause of his withdrawal was "merely a culmination of the little differences which have for years existed between him and the Church rather than a result of any censure or dissatisfaction on the part of the Church for his action during the sitting of the Evangelical Alliance."[70]

In another article, the *Courier* stated, "Since the withdrawal of Bishop Cummins, no little exultation has been expressed by mem-

---

[69] *The Courier Journal,* Louisville, November 15, 1873, p. 4.
[70] *Ibid.*

bers of other denominations who predicted that a serious and speedy division of the Episcopal Church would result from the Bishop's action and a new church would be organized, the motive power of which would be the spirit promulgated by the Evangelical Alliance." The paper published an extract from a letter received from the East by a member of the Kentucky Standing Committee, stating, "The Bishop acted by himself and against the protest of Evangelical men. Even the most radical oppose his course and will give his movement no support."[71]

Upon receipt of Cummins' letter of abandonment, written on November 10, Bishop Smith immediately wrote Cummins a touching letter, full of amazement and sorrow, in which he said, "Can it be possible that you have formed such a determination after duly weighing the gravity and the magnitude of the consequences of a step without precedent in the history of our beloved Church?" In imploring him to reconsider, Smith expressed the hope that "this painful subject will not be brought before the public,"[72] but George David Cummins had already burned his bridge behind him.

Cummins almost immediately met with a few like-minded clergymen and laymen in New York and at Passaic, New Jersey, to discuss his action. He then prepared a circular letter, which he distributed freely throughout the country and published in the press. In this circular he set forth the chief features of the proposed Prayer Book of 1785, which he stated was to be the official book of the new Episcopal Church, organized to "embrace all who hold the faith once delivered to the saints, as that faith is maintained by the reformed churches of Christendom." It stated that the organizational meeting would take place on December 2, 1873, at Association Hall in the city of New York.[73]

The day after he distributed the circular letter, Cummins an-

---

[71] *Ibid.*, November 21, 1873, p. 4.

[72] Archives of Church Historical Society, "Cummins' Collection," B. B. Smith to Cummins, November 13, 1873.

[73] Cummins, *Memoir*, pp. 421–422, Circular Letter, dated November 15, 1873. Also see *The Lexington Dollar Weekly Press*, December 24, 1873, p. 1. Story and platform of new church are given; also resolutions which were adopted at the meeting.

swered Bishop Smith's letter, stating that his mind was made up and that "he had long anticipated the possibility and probability of his act."[74]

News of Cummins' break and subsequent action, along with the publicity attached, caused deep concern in the Diocese of Kentucky and brought prompt action. The Standing Committee[75] met in Christ Church, Louisville, on November 18 and, upon the evidence of a printed copy of Cummins' letter of abandonment to Bishop Smith, and acting in accordance with Canon 8, Title II,[76] did certify to Bishop Smith that the Right Reverend George David Cummins, D.D., had abandoned the Communion of the Protestant Episcopal Church.[77] Whereupon, the Presiding Bishop, having received the certificate, gave due notice on November 22, 1873, to Dr. Cummins of his pending deposition.[78]

Cummins received letters from friends and strangers alike, urging

[74] Archives of Church Historical Society, Cummins to B. B. Smith, November 16, 1873.

[75] The Standing Committee was at this time composed of James Craik, E. T. Perkins, and W. H. Platt of the clergy, and the Honorable W. F. Bullock and William Cornwall of the laity. The copy of the certificate of the Standing Committee on the abandonment of Cummins was an act of four-fifths of the committee. It is signed by all but the Reverend W. H. Platt, rector of Calvary Church, Louisville, as noted by Cornwall, secretary, in the certificate.

[76] Canon 8, Title II, "If any bishop, without availing himself of the provisions of Section 16 or Canon 13 of Title I, abandon the Communion of this Church, either by open renunciation of the doctrine, discipline, and worship of this Church or by formal admission into any religious body not in communion with same, it shall be the duty of the Standing Committee of the Diocese to make certificate of the fact to the senior bishop, which certificate shall be recorded and shall be taken and deemed equivalent to a renunciation of the Ministry by the Bishop himself. Notice shall then be given to said bishop, by said bishop, receiving the certificate, that unless he shall within six months, make a declaration that the facts alleged in said certificate are false, he will be deposed from the ministry of this Church. And if such declaration be not made within six months as aforesaid, it shall be the duty of the senior bishop, with the consent of the majority of the House of Bishops, to depose from the Ministry the Bishop so certified as abandoning, and to pronounce and record in the presence of two or more bishops, that he has been so deposed. *Provided*, nevertheless, that if the Bishop so certified as abandoning, shall transmit to the senior bishop, a retraction of the acts and declarations constituting his offense, the Bishop may, at his discretion, abstain from any further proceedings." (Section 16 of Canon 13, Title I, to which reference was made related to the resignation of a bishop). The above quoted was the canon under which Smith deposed Cummins. It was amended at the 1874 Convention because of certain defects in it.

[77] Archives of Church Historical Society. Standing Committee of the Diocese of Kentucky, Certificate of November 18, 1873—dated May 25, 1874.

[78] *Ibid.*, B. B. Smith's notice to Cummins.

him not to act hastily and expressing the hope that he would change his mind during the six-month period of grace. Among these letters was one from his old and dear friend, Bishop Alfred Lee.[79]

The six-month clause in Canon 8, Title II, became a source of consternation on the part of Bishop Smith and many other clergymen and laymen, because of the fear that before he could be deposed, Cummins, still clothed in the episcopal office, might consecrate other bishops and organize another Episcopal Church. This led Smith to consider another canon, which would allow for a trial and deposition at a sooner date. He thereupon consulted with several bishops on the subject of the best procedures to pursue.[80] A series of letters and wires between Smith and the Standing Committee of the Diocese of Kentucky followed, the committee stating its opinion that Canon 8, as first proposed, best covered the case.[81]

Bishop Smith, however, had taken it upon himself, as Presiding Bishop, to summon a number of bishops to meet with him at Grace Church, New York City, for the purpose of deposing Bishop Cummins.[82] Accordingly, six bishops, who were most accessible to New York City, met there on November 29 and discussed the legality of presentment charges against Cummins. Bishop Smith wired the Standing Committee of Kentucky, requesting a presentment for trial under Canon 9, Title II,[83] and the secretary, William Cornwall, complied with his request. On December 1, the following proclamation was sent forth: "Notice has been received from the Standing Committee of the Diocese of Kentucky that a presentment for trial of George David Cummins, D.D., has been prepared; First, for

[79] *Ibid.,* Alfred Lee to B. B. Smith, December 5, 1873.

[80] *Ibid.* Correspondence included letters from Bishops Bedell of Ohio, Alonzo Potter of New York, Whittingham of Maryland, Williams of Connecticut, and M. A. DeWolfe Howe of Pennsylvania.

[81] *Ibid.* Letter from William Cornwall, Secretary of the Standing Committee of Kentucky to B. B. Smith, November 25, 1873, stating that Kentucky is considering action under Canon 8.

[82] *Ibid.* Letters from B. B. Smith to various bishops, November 26, 1873, summoning them to a meeting at Grace Church, New York City, on November 29, 1873.

[83] The canon dealt with the offenses for which a minister is liable to presentment and trial. In Cummins' case, they were 3 and 5, (3) Violation of the Constitution or Canons of General Convention. (5) Any act which involves a breach of his ordination vows. On being found guilty, "he shall be admonished, suspended or degraded, according to the Canons of the Diocese in which the trial takes place, until otherwise provided by the General Convention."

violation of the Constitution and Canons of the General Convention; second, for breach of his consecration vow. Be it known, therefore, that any Episcopal act of his, pending these proceedings, will be null and void; and it is hoped that respect for law and order on the part of all members of this Church will restrain them from giving any countenance whatever to the movement in which Dr. Cummins is engaged."[84] Smith then wired Cummins informing him of the action of the Standing Committee.[85]

The publication of this proclamation precipitated a storm of controversy as to the applicability of Canon 9 to the Cummins case. The Presiding Bishop received letters from throughout the United States, expressing opinions pro and con.[86] Most of his fellow bishops were against presentment, and it was generally conceded that Bishop Smith had acted hastily and ill-advisedly in introducing Canon 9 and preparing a presentment for trial.

There were certainly misgivings among the Standing Committee of the Kentucky Diocese. More letters kept the mails hot between Louisville and Hoboken. Cornwall wrote that the Standing Committee had sought the advice of legal counsel.[87]

By this time, realizing that he had acted hastily and ill-advisedly, Bishop Smith also sought legal advice. He wrote to Judge Murray Hoffman of Flushing, Long Island, the most distinguished American canonist of that time, and laid the entire matter before him. On December 11, Hoffman answered, strongly advising Smith to adhere to the proceedings under Canon 8, and at the end of six months to at once take measures to get the consent of a majority of the bishops to proceed to depose. He pointed out that in the long run this would occupy less time than would be spent in reaching a sentence upon a trial.[88]

[84] Archives of Church Historical Society. Letter (Notice), Copy in B. B. Smith's hand. Notice of Presentment under Canon 9, December 1, 1873.

[85] Ibid., December 12, 1873. The wire stated, "I hereby formally and officially withdraw all such Episcopal authority as you have heretofore exercised under Canon 13th, Title 1st."

[86] Ibid. Correspondence included letters from Bishops H. N. Pierce of Alabama, and Joseph C. Talbot of Indiana, both of whom were against Canon 9; Bishops Whittingham of Maryland, and Atkinson of North Carolina, who supported action under Canon 9.

[87] Ibid. Cornwall to Smith, November 29, 1873; Cornwall to Smith, December 1, 1873.

[88] Ibid. Judge Murray Hoffman to B. B. Smith, December 11, 1873.

On the same day that Hoffman wrote, Dr. Craik also had a letter in the mail to the Presiding Bishop. It was a lengthy letter reviewing the case as it appeared to the Louisville churches, in which he stated that the specifications against Cummins prepared by Cornwall were necessarily hasty and too inaccurate for use. He made it plain that he and the Honorable William F. Bullock, also a member of the Standing Committee, had agreed throughout the proceedings that there should be no trial. He stated that he did not think that Dr. Cummins "either morally, intellectually, or ecclesiastically was worth the cost, trouble, and vexation of a trial under the extraordinary Canon." (Canon 9, Title II). Craik further stated that the Standing Committee had been under the impression that Smith, himself, had a "strong repugnance for that mode of proceeding" and they had supposed that all danger of a trial was past. "It is a pity," said Craik, "that your own better judgment was overruled by some of your brethren in the Episcopate."[89]

Bishop Smith, after receiving Judge Hoffman's opinion, again wrote to Dr. Craik, informing him that the Long Island judge was in complete agreement with Craik's views on canonical law. The Louisville clergyman answered Smith on December 24 and again implored him not to "bestow the favor of a trial on the unmitigated charlatan but to depose him by the noiseless action of Canon 8."[90]

The upshot of the whole controversy over Canon 9, Title II, was that no such presentment was attempted, all legal advisors recognizing the fact that Cummins, having by his own volition separated himself from the Protestant Episcopal Church, was no longer amenable to its laws.

Meanwhile, on December 2, Bishop Cummins and certain ministers and laymen, formerly connected with the Protestant Episcopal Church, had assembled in the Y.M.C.A. building in New York City and formally organized the Reformed Episcopal Church. The Declaration of Principles, as drafted by Cummins, declared the new church's belief to be in the Bible as the sole rule of faith and practice; in the Apostles' Creed; in the divine institutions of the sacraments of Baptism and the Lord's Supper; and in the doctrines of grace, substantially as set forth in the Thirty-nine Articles. The

[89] *Ibid.*, Dr. James Craik to B. B. Smith, December 11, 1873.
[90] *Ibid.*, Craik to Smith, December 24, 1873.

church recognized and adhered to episcopacy, not as a divine right, but as an ancient and desirable form of church polity; it retained a liturgy which was not imperative or repressive of freedom in prayer; accepted the Book of Common Prayer, as it was revised, proposed, and recommended for use by the Convention of the Protestant Episcopal Church in 1785, with full liberty to alter, abridge, enlarge, or amend it provided that the substance of the faith was kept entire. The new church condemned and rejected the following as errors and strange doctrines: (1) that the Church of Christ exists only in one order or form of ecclesiastical polity; (2) that Christian ministers are "priests" in another sense than that in which all believers are a "royal priesthood"; (3) that the Lord's Table is an altar, on which the oblation of the body and blood of Christ is offered anew to the Father; (4) that the presence of Christ in the Lord's Supper is a presence in the elements of bread and wine; (5) that regeneration is inseparably connected with baptism.[91] The Right Reverend George David Cummins was elected Presiding Bishop, and among the members of the Standing Committee appeared the names of the Reverend Charles Edward Cheney, D.D., of Illinois, and the Reverend Mason Gallagher of New Jersey.[92] Dr. Cheney was nominated Bishop of the Northwest and was duly elected. He was consecrated a bishop of the Reformed Episcopal Church by Bishop Cummins on December 13, 1873 in Christ Church, Chicago, for Cheney took his parish with him into the new church.[93]

Cummins and Cheney forthwith toured the United States founding reformed churches, ordaining, and confirming. This was before the six-month waiting period allowed Cummins had expired, and there were those in the Protestant Episcopal Church who felt that these ordinations and confirmations were valid, according to the canons of that Church, in spite of the Presiding Bishop's proclamation of December 1 to the contrary.

Bishop Smith, in accordance with the advice of most of his fellow bishops and the Standing Committee of Kentucky, resolved that the

---

[91] Cummins, *Memoir,* Platform of the Reformed Episcopal Church, pp. 432–434.
[92] *Ibid.,* p. 438.
[93] *Ibid.,* p. 439; 456.

best course was to quietly await the termination of the six-month waiting period, and then to officially depose Cummins. In order to effect this, in accordance with Canon 8, he needed a vote of the majority of the House of Bishops. The canon, however, did not specify whether this meant a majority of bishops in session, or whether their written votes would suffice. Ever anxious to avoid a confrontation of his peers, Bishop Smith decided to take the votes of the individual bishops by letter. To do this, he requested that a Court of Preliminary Inquiry be chosen by lot and a summation of its findings be circulated to individual bishops in the United States.[94] Accordingly, a three page folder was mailed from Louisville by the Court of Inquiry on May 25, 1873, and a request by Bishop Smith for "consent" of the bishops to the deposition of Cummins, to be given by June 25, 1874, the six-month expiration date.[95]

The reaction of the bishops was anything but noiseless. Many of them objected strenuously to the mode of ascertaining their votes, by mail rather than in orderly session in the House of Bishops, but there were those who approved of the measure on the basis of the publicity concomitant to a meeting of the House of Bishops. Bishop Alfred Lee was one of the latter, stating that Cummins "had ceased to be a nine day wonder and this would bring him again into notice."[96] This good friend of Cummins had all along sought to save his former protégé, by personal contact with him, by numerous letters in his behalf, by an open letter addressed to Cummins at the request of his friends, reviewing Cummins' break and refuting it, and a last-ditch effort was to be made in June, pleading with Bishop Smith to proceed slowly in regard to sentencing Cummins.[97]

[94] Archives of Church Historical Society. Blue sheet in B. B. Smith's hand, written memo of persons chosen by lot. The Court of Inquiry was composed of Dr. Craik and the Reverend W. H. Platt of the clergy, Col. S. Churchill and William Cornwall of the laity, representing Kentucky, and four of each order from the states of Ohio, Virginia, and Illinois inclusive.

[95] *Ibid.* Printed three-page folder, May 25, 1874.

[96] *Ibid.* Letter disapproving of Smith's action came from Bishop Talbot of Indiana, April 2, 1874; Letter from Bishop Bedell, April 25, 1874, stating that he is of the opinion that consent can be given by the bishops "only when acting as a House," but that there are many bishops who agree with Smith that consent of individual bishops is all that is required; Bishop Alfred Lee to Bishop J. Williams, April 4, 1874, approves Smith's action.

[97] *Ibid.,* Bishop Lee to Smith, June 9, 1874.

Bishop Smith received letters from laymen, as well as clergymen, expressing their views in regard to the vote by the bishops. One of these, which should have carried weight with Smith, was from Judge Hoffman, strongly counseling him to summon the House of Bishops and advising him to give Cummins another chance to retract.[98] This latter portion of Hoffman's advice Smith heeded and followed, but in vain.[99]

On June 24, 1874, in the vestry room of St. Peter's Church, New York City, Benjamin Bosworth Smith, Bishop of Kentucky and Senior Bishop of the Protestant Episcopal Church in the United States, with consent of a majority of the members of the House of Bishops and, in terms of Canon 8, Title II, did pronounce George David Cummins, D.D., deposed, to all intents and purposes, from the ministry of this Church, and from all the rights, privileges, powers, and dignities pertaining to the office of a bishop in the same.[100] In accordance with the canon, requiring that the pronouncement be made in the presence of two or more bishops, it was witnessed by Alfred Lee of Delaware, William Bacon Stevens of Pennsylvania, and M. A. DeWolfe Howe of Central Pennsylvania.

So ended the Cummins case from the standpoint of the Protestant Episcopal Church in the United States, but not quite from the standpoint of that Church in the Diocese of Kentucky. Before continuing with the account in regard to Kentucky, let us note briefly what happened to the Reformed Episcopal Church that was founded by Bishop Cummins.

For a time, it prospered. Cummins and Cheney continued to organize reformed Episcopal churches throughout the United States and Canada, and set the machinery in motion for union with the "Free Church of England," likewise a schismatic organization in that country. The Reformed Church, which had begun in 1873 with but eight clergymen and a score of laymen, had within two years grown to number fifty-two clergymen and fifty congregations, consisting of a considerable number of laymen.[101] George David Cum-

---

[98] *Ibid.*, Judge Murray Hoffman to Smith, March 27, 1874.
[99] *Ibid.*, Smith to Cummins, June 12, 1874.
[100] *Ibid.* Notice of Deposition of Cummins. Thirty-six bishops gave their consent.
[101] Cummins, *Memoir*, p. 486.

mins, having served as Presiding Bishop of his new church for less than three years, died at Lutherville, Baltimore County, Maryland, on June 26, 1876, at the age of fifty-three.[102] Even after the death of its founder and guiding light, the church grew for a time under the leadership of Presiding Bishop Cheney, but it was never destined to attain renown, either numerically or ecclesiastically. The Reformed Episcopal Church stands one hundred years later as one of the smallest religious sects in the United States, numbering sixty-five churches and 7,085 members.[103]

In Kentucky, the subject uppermost in the minds and hearts of Churchmen during the winter of 1873 and spring of 1874 was, quite naturally, the Cummins affair. The press and Church periodicals kept it in the news; it was harangued from pulpit and rostrum, bandied about on the street and at home; its pros and contras discussed socially and intellectually. Party feeling ran high, and the strife-torn Diocese showed the marks of internal dissension. "Bitterness of feeling, severity of censure, and wide alienation between brethren"[104] were the order of the day.

Feeling was intensified, especially in the Louisville area, by the withdrawal of the rector, the Reverend Joseph S. Malone, and a portion of the congregation of Emmanuel Church to join the Reformed Episcopal Church, and the ensuing battle over the title of the church property.[105] Fortunately the courts protected the title of the trustees of the Protestant Episcopal Church to the property,[106] which was later sold and the money invested in the erection of a new church for Zion Parish, Louisville.

---

[102] Memorial Tablet in First Reformed Church, New York City. Cummins is buried in a cemetery near Baltimore.

[103] *The World Almanac*, 1969, p. 220.

[104] *Journal, Diocese of Kentucky*, 1874.

[105] *Journal of the Proceedings of the Special Session of the Protestant Episcopal Church in the Diocese of Kentucky*, November 11-12, 1874, p. 11. Also see *Journal*, 1875, p. 68. Malone was deposed from the ministry of the Protestant Episcopal Church, November 27, 1875.

[106] Louisville Chancery Court, No. 28,399, *Charles H. Pettet and Wm. McCready, Trustees of Emmanuel Protestant Episcopal Church of the Diocese of Kentucky, in the City of Louisville. . . . Plaintiffs, VS. Wm. A. Meriwether, et al., acting as Emmanuel Reformed Episcopal Church. . . . Defendants.* Also see: Court of Appeals of Kentucky, *W. A. Meriwether & c., Appellants VS. Chas. H. Pettet & c., Appellees.*

With no assistant bishop and with the Diocesan out of the state during most of this period, the administrative reins fell upon a few clergymen, any one of whom might well have borne a crozier. Dr. Craik was, in effect, acting bishop, but Dr. Shipman, Dr. Norton, and Dr. Perkins were all powers in the Diocese.

The concern of these men and of all the clergy and laity soon turned to the election of a successor to Dr. Cummins. It was therefore resolved at the diocesan convention, meeting in Calvary Church, Louisville, in May, 1874, "that when this Convention adjourn, a recess be taken until after the General Convention, and shall meet at the call of the Bishop, he giving at least thirty days notice thereof, the meeting to be held in Calvary Church, Louisville."[107]

[107] *Journal, Diocese of Kentucky,* 1874.

16 *Eastward Parishes after the War*

During the seven-year episcopacy of the Right Reverend George David Cummins, missionary expansion within the Diocese of Kentucky continued and showed, at least for a time, great promise. The Assistant Bishop was vitally interested in the cause, and under him the convocational system of dividing the Diocese for missionary work, inaugurated by Bishop Smith some years earlier, was reinstated and enjoyed some five years of effective operation. Had Bishop Cummins' interest in the Diocese of Kentucky and its mission work continued, a different story might be told. Certainly the Church would have expanded throughout the state at least a decade earlier.

A goodly number of new missions, however, did spring up, particularly in the northern and central portions of the state, which in 1895 became the new Diocese of Lexington.

ST. JOHN'S, BELLEVIEW-DAYTON

During the early years of the 1870's, the population of Newport, on the Kentucky side of the Ohio River opposite Cincinnati, had increased to about 18,000. Dayton, the new name given in 1866 to the two consolidated villages of Jamestown and Brooklyn, a mile and a half east of Newport; and Belleview, a new town incorporated in 1870, also to the east and separated from Newport by Taylor's Creek, had shared in the larger city's rapid growth. Campbell County, in which all three are located, had, in addition to its factories and rich productive bottom lands, a very desirable residential area in the verdant hills overlooking the beautiful Ohio.

Prior to 1871, Episcopalians residing in Dayton and Belleview attended divine service at St. Paul's, Newport. In the early spring of that year, however, a new and larger church was abuilding in Newport, and the communicant strength was such that a mission had been established at Dayton. For a while, the rector of the parent church, the Rev. A. R. Walker, preached twice a month in the Evangelical Lutheran Church and later in the Odd Fellows' Hall there. Faithful lay workers conducted a flourishing Sunday school composed of about fifty scholars.

When, in May, Walker resigned because of impaired health, the Reverend Frederick Elwell became rector pro tem of St. Paul's.[1] A native of London, England, he had come to the Diocese of Kentucky in 1864 from Tennessee and was well known in northern Kentucky and Ohio, where as a missionary he had gathered together a congregation which had later become Emmanuel Church, Cincinnati. He had often assisted the rector of Trinity Church, Covington, and during 1868 had been in charge of that parish for six months between regular rectors.

On January 1, 1872, a new rector having arrived at St. Paul's, Newport, Elwell assumed the charge of the new mission at Dayton on a full-time basis. He was seventy years old, but energetic, dedicated, and determined that the mission should succeed and become independent. On March 22, 1873, the parish was incorporated and C. L. Gibson and W. R. Locke elected wardens and F. L. Cochran, A. E. Daisy and A. B. Burton, vestrymen.[2] The parish was named St. John's, and called the Reverend Mr. Elwell to be its rector. Two months later, at the diocesan convention, St. John's Church, Dayton, was received into union with the Diocese, and the rector reported that the foundations of a little church were laid and the superstructure under contract for immediate erection.[3] In a few months a small but neat frame building, topped by a wooden cross, stood on a lot on McKinney Street near Fairfield Avenue.[4] On May 4, 1873, Assistant Bishop Cummins visited Dayton and confirmed one person. Two years later, on May 26, the new Assistant Bishop, Thomas U. Dudley, preached in St. John's Church and confirmed two. He consecrated the church on Whitsunday, June 4, 1876.

During the next few years the membership of St. John's increased

---

[1] *Journal of the Diocese of Kentucky,* 1872, p. 53.
[2] *Forth Magazine,* April, 1948 (Lexington Edition), pp. v–vi.
[3] *Journal,* 1873, p. 59.
[4] This building is still standing at 507 McKinney Street, Dayton, Kentucky. It is presently used as a garage (Bob's Garage) and is owned by Mr. Robert Hoh.

slowly but steadily. The venerable clergyman went in and out among the people of the growing community, serving them fervently and devotedly. By 1879, one hundred and fifty souls were enrolled in the small parish. "We have great reason to bless the Great Head of the Church who has so encouraged our efforts and increased our numbers during the past year," the faithful Elwell reported.[5]

On Sunday, May 2, 1880, the Rev. Mr. Elwell was stricken by paralysis while administering the Holy Communion, lingering in a semiconscious condition until the following Friday, when he died. Under its first rector, who came to them after he had passed the allotted three score years and ten, St. John's Parish had been organized and the church building erected. His rectorate of eight years was among the most successful in the history of the parish.

The Rev. Christopher L. Pindar, formerly of the Diocese of Southern Ohio, succeeded Elwell as rector and remained for about two years before assuming charge of the mission at Hickman. The Rev. Lawrence Guerin took charge in 1883 and, during his five years as rector, St. John's remained in a healthy condition, with a membership of about one hundred and twenty-five souls, about sixty of whom were listed as communicants. The towns of Dayton and Belleview were growing rapidly and the rector reported "a larger attendance upon the services of the Church and a growing appreciation of its benefits."[6]

Upon Guerin's resignation and removal to the Diocese of Missouri in 1888, the little church was once again placed under the charge of the rector of St. Paul's, Newport. The Reverend Reverdy Estill began to hold weekly Sunday services in Dayton, with a monthly Celebration of the Holy Communion. St. John's had once more become a mission of the Newport parish, a status it would retain until 1896. By then it was a part of the new Diocese of Lexington. In 1899, the present stone church was erected at the corner of Eighth and O'Fallon Avenues in Dayton, across the street from Belleview. It is known as St. John's Church, Belleview-Dayton.

[5] *Journal*, 1879, p. 53.
[6] *Journal*, 1887, p. 80.

SAINT GEORGE'S, LEBANON

In Lebanon, the county seat of Marion County, on the principal branch of the Louisville and Nashville Railroad, the Church established a mission in 1867. This mission was admitted into union with the Diocese of Kentucky the following year as St. George's, Lebanon. The Reverend E. W. Gilliam, rector of Trinity, Danville and St. Philip's, Harrodsburg, was placed in charge. He officiated in Lebanon twice a month to a small but interested congregation of about a dozen persons. He was followed during the latter part of 1868 by the Reverend Issac Gibson, who had become the general missionary for the Central Convocation. Of him, Assistant Bishop Cummins said, "At Lebanon he (Gibson) ministers to the largest Protestant congregation in the town, and is winning many to love our services."[7]

Bishop Cummins visited the mission on March 7, 1869, preaching morning and night in the Methodist Church, where the regular Episcopal services were held on alternate Sundays, and "was delighted to find the growing favor with which our Church is regarded in this community." The following May, he reported to the convention: "I regard the opening here of our Church as a very important and auspicious one, and trust soon to hear of the inauguration of measures towards the erection of a church edifice in this place."[8] Cummins visited Lebanon again the following year, this time preaching in the Presbyterian Church. The Reverend Anselan Buchanan was now in charge here. By the spring of 1871, several women active in the mission had secured $450 toward the erection of a church building and Mr. Buchanan was endeavoring to raise more from outside sources. Regular bimonthly services were conducted on the first and third Sundays, the missionary being assisted by the Reverend W. I. Waller and G. C. Waller of Louisville. A suitable lot was secured and deeded to Bishop Cummins as trustee, and the first payment of $150 was made, leaving two additional $100 payments due.[9]

[7] *Journal*, 1869, p. 40.
[8] *Ibid.*, p. 42.
[9] *Journal*, 1873, p. 49.

In October, 1872 the Reverend Henry T. Sharp became mission-ary-in-charge. Bishop Cummins continued his vital interest in the mission and in November of that year visited there for three days, preaching in the Methodist and Presbyterian churches and confirming four persons. It was, however, his last visit to St. George's, for he soon thereafter left the Protestant Episcopal Church.

The new Assistant Bishop, Thomas Underwood Dudley, visited St. George's Mission on March 9, 1875, the month after he arrived in the Diocese, and preached in the Methodist Church, once more loaned for the occasion. The next day he confirmed one lady and administered the Holy Communion in the morning, baptized one infant in the afternoon, and again preached in the evening. He found the "few communicants of the Church in Lebanon faithful and devoted" and felt that the prospects were good if a suitable house of worship could be erected.[10] In 1893, however, when the Reverend M. M. Benton, General Missionary of the Diocese, visited Lebanon, he found only one communicant and saw no necessity to continue services there.[11] There was never an Episcopal church building in the town.

GRACE MISSION, LAWRENCEBURG

The first Episcopal services ever held in Anderson County were conducted by a lay reader at Lawrenceburg, the county seat, on the second Sunday in January, 1867.[12] Lay readers continued to hold monthly services until March 24 of that year, when the Reverend Stephen A. Scearce was ordained to the diaconate and placed in charge of the station. There was but one Episcopalian in the town at the time but, according to the young deacon, "The best people of the county took a deep interest in the undertaking and a parish was duly organized on Palm Sunday."[13] The mission was first called the Good Shepherd. The officers, elected on April 14, were Messrs. James Saffell, senior warden; J. H. D. McKee, junior warden;

---

[10] *Journal,* 1875, pp. 71–72.
[11] *Journal,* 1894, p. 126.
[12] *Journal,* 1867, p. 53.
[13] *Ibid.*

George Mathews, Robert B. McKee, Wade H. Dawson, James A. McBrayer, William S. Hickman, and John Witherspoon.[14] On May 12 Bishop B. B. Smith baptized two and confirmed seven persons.[15]

In his parochial report for 1867, Mr. Scearce wrote, "A cabinet organ has been purchased, a choir formed, a Sunday School organized, and public worship celebrated twice on the second Sunday in each month."[16] Prospects were bright. An Episcopal school for females was started under the direction of an efficient man, the grounds for a church building and rectory donated, and a class prepared for confirmation.[17] The vestry, meeting in the court house on June 22, 1867, planned to erect a church building as soon as practicable.[18]

The Reverend Mr. Scearce resigned in February, 1868, and became assistant at Christ Church, Louisville. He was succeeded by the Reverend William Flynn, who conducted services on the second Tuesday of each month until January, 1870. In that year Lawrenceburg was assigned to the Convocation of Lexington, and the Reverend Roland Brent became missionary-in-charge, moving to the parish in May. He began holding services morning and evening each Sunday in Lawrenceburg, with very encouraging prospects, and regular afternoon services at Rough and Ready, where there was not a church or Sunday school of any denomination. He held occasional services at Salvisa and other points in the county. At this time the missionary work in Anderson County was supported by "two earnest friends of the Church," the Missionary Board not having taken over support of the mission there. "If the Church is in earnest, if she wishes to evangelize, here is a field which challenges her admiration and love," wrote Brent in his 1872 parochial report.[19]

Bishop George David Cummins was much interested in the Anderson County missions and looked to their permanent establish-

[14] H. H. Sneed, Parish histories, Diocese of Lexington Archives, University of Kentucky Library, Box 120.
[15] *Journal*, 1867, p. 23.
[16] *Ibid.*
[17] *Journal*, 1868, p. 52.
[18] Sneed, History of parishes.
[19] *Journal*, 1872, p. 47.

ment. He visited the Good Shepherd Mission on September 7 and 8, 1872, preached three times, and baptized five children.[20]

Roland Brent continued his labor during 1873. Upon his resignation in June there followed a long period in which the Lawrenceburg mission was without any clerical supervision at all. During this time the zeal of one layman, Mr. McKee,[21] kept the mission alive. He conducted lay services and maintained the Sunday school. In May, 1875, when Bishop Dudley first visited the mission to preach and confirm, he credited the "faithful McKee" with preparing the candidates for the rite.[22]

More than a decade was to pass before Lawrenceburg again came under the jurisdiction of the Board of Diocesan Missions. The Reverend William H. Hampton, assistant rector of the Church of the Ascension, Frankfort, began holding services there in 1886 with good results. Bishop Dudley visited the mission and confirmed six persons. A guild and Sunday school were organized. Upon Hampton's resignation in 1887, the Reverend Edwin A. Penick, rector of the Frankfort parish, took charge for a short period.

During the next eight years no services were recorded as held in Lawrenceburg, but perhaps the faithful laymen held occasional services. The Mission of the Good Shepherd was a thing of the past.

In 1894 the mission at Lawrenceburg was revived and reorganized and became known as Grace Mission. It prospered once more under the regular ministrations of the Reverend Wiley Jones Page, rector of St. John's Church, Versailles. He resigned, however, the next year and when Grace Mission became a part of the new Diocese of Lexington there was no missionary-in-charge there.

ALL SAINTS' MISSION, NICHOLASVILLE

The important town of Nicholasville, the county seat of Jessamine County, is in the heart of a rich country on the terminus of the

---

[20] *Journal*, 1873, p. 35.

[21] *Journal*, 1875, pp. 75–76. Dudley mentions only the last name. Doubtless he is one of the two McKees of the vestry.

[22] *Ibid.*

Kentucky Central Railroad. It first claimed the attention of the
Episcopal Church as a mission station in 1871. That year the Reverend Silas Totten, rector of Christ Church Seminary in Lexington,
was holding services in the town two Sundays in each month. His
congregation varied between twenty and sixty persons, twelve of
whom were communicants of the Episcopal Church. For the most
part, services were held in the Jessamine Female Institute, which
was kindly provided and kept warm in winter at the expense of the
principal, Mr. G. A. Butler.[23] Assistant Bishop George David Cummins was particularly interested in the town of Nicholasville at this
time and hoped that a mission might be organized there with some
hope of permanency. He preached in the town in December, 1871,
and confirmed two persons.[24] He confirmed two more in the spring
of 1872 in Christ Church, Lexington, and baptized four infants.

Dr. Totten reported to the 1873 convention that, although there
was no organized mission in Nicholasville, there were thirteen
communicants who attended the services and whose names were
not registered anywhere. He continued to serve as often as every
other Sunday until his death in 1874. The death of Dr. Totten and
the departure from the Episcopal Church of the Assistant Bishop
within the span of a few months dealt a mighty blow to the little
congregation in Nicholasville. For almost twenty years thereafter,
there seems to have been no Episcopal service held in the town.

In 1893 the Reverend Mortimer Murray Benton, General Missionary of the Diocese, visited Nicholasville on a missionary trip which
included Brandenburg, on the Ohio River in Meade County, and
Hawesville, in Hancock County, holding a service in each place.
Noting that there had been no services of the Church in Nicholasville for many years, he reported that he had received urgent requests for a return visit. Acting on Benton's report, the Board of
Missions appointed the Reverend Wiley Jones Page, who had become rector of St. John's Church, Versailles, on February 1, 1894, to
include Nicholasville and Lawrenceburg in his charge, granting
him a stipend of $350.[25] He remained only a short time, and once

[23] *Journal*, 1872, p. 54.
[24] *Ibid.*, p. 37.
[25] *Journal*, 1894, p. 119.

again services in Nicholasville ceased. It was not until after the formation of the Diocese of Lexington that a mission was established in the town.[26]

CHAPEL OF THE REDEEMER, LUDLOW, AND THE MILLDALE MISSION

As the largest and most prosperous parish in northern Kentucky, it was natural that Trinity Church, Covington, should be parent to a number of missions. Two such, which fall within this period, were the Chapel of the Redeemer, Ludlow, and a mission at Milldale.

In 1867 a mission was organized at Ludlow, a rapidly growing village a mile distant from Covington.[27] It was called the Chapel of the Redeemer and was placed under the charge of a candidate for Holy Orders, Walter Tearne. The Reverend C. George Currie, rector of Trinity Church, preached there from time to time, administered the sacraments, and held cottage meetings. Subsequent rectors continued to hold services there, usually in the Baptist Church. By 1883 the mission was prospering and felt ready to pay for its own resident minister, and by the next year it was an organized mission, now under the Diocese. It was called Trinity Mission. Before long, however, it reverted to unorganized status and as such it entered the Diocese of Lexington in 1895.

In 1869 a mission was established in South Covington at Milldale[28] (now Latonia), and a chapel was opened for services the following year on February 13. It was maintained by the rectors of Trinity Church. Bishop Cummins, and later Bishop Dudley visited it several times. The mission flourished for a time, proving the need for a larger mission in the town, and in 1890 it was sold in order to build a larger chapel in another location.

[26] *Journal of the Diocese of Lexington,* 1899. The Reverend Henry H. Sneed began holding services on the first and third Fridays in each month, the first being held on February 18, 1898. See also *Journal,* 1900. On May 23, 1900, All Saints' Mission was organized and services held in the Odd Fellows' Hall, rented for the purpose.
[27] Trinity Church, Covington, Archives.
[28] *Ibid.*

17 Beloved Bishop, Thomas Underwood Dudley

Bishop Smith was not on hand for the special convention, November 11–12, 1874, when the clerical and lay deputies again assembled in Calvary Church, Lousiville, for the purpose of electing an Assistant Bishop of Kentucky.[1] There was tense excitement in the air. Still smarting from the recent Cummins fiasco, all were wary lest the wrong choice be made once again. Churchmanship, as might be expected, played the leading role.

Three candidates for the office were nominated: the Reverend Jacob Shaw Shipman, rector of Christ Church, Lexington; the Right Reverend William Hare, Missionary Bishop of Niobrara, Indian Territory; and the Reverend Thomas Underwood Dudley, rector of Christ Church, Baltimore, Maryland.

By far the most popular candidate among the clergy was Dr. Shipman, who had been in the Diocese for fourteen years and was respected for his piety and forebearance. He was also popular among the laity, but he had made powerful enemies. Shipman was the choice of the High Church party and, although he was not an extreme partisan in any sense of the word, all High Churchmen, evangelical, sacramentarian, and the few extremists in the Diocese, rallied to his support to block the election of Bishop Hare, an avowed Evangelical. The third candidate, Dr. Dudley, was little known in Kentucky except by the handful who had comprised the delegation to the General Convention held recently in New York City, all of whom were favorably impressed by him.

Speaking strongly in favor of Dr. Shipman was Dr. Craik, who expressed himself as decidedly opposed to the election of an assistant bishop from among strangers. Bishop Hare's chief advocate among the clergy was St. Paul's rector, Dr. Perkins, probably the leading Evangelical presently within the Diocese. In his support of Hare, he leaned heavily on the great advantage of prior episcopal experience, and carefully pointed out that the Missionary Bishop entertained "no extravagant Church notions." Dr. Dudley had been nominated by the rector of Nativity Church, Maysville, the Reverend R. C. Foute, but it was a layman from northern Kentucky who threw his powerful influence behind the Baltimore clergyman. Senator John W. Stevenson, delegate from Trinity Church, Covington, had been associated with Dudley on the Church's Indian Committee in 1871 and testified to "his orthodoxy and great earnestness in the cause of Christ." Both Stevenson and Dudley were natives of Virginia, both had attended that state's university, and, although Stevenson was twenty-five years Dudley's senior, he was acquainted with his family and background. The Senator referred to Dudley's record in an artillery company in the late war, pointing out that the hardships, privations and exposure in the camp indicated his physical capacity for labor and afforded him large experience in his knowledge of men.[2] This brought forth a scathing rebuke by one of Hare's supporters in objection to the airing of Dudley's war record for the purpose of strengthening his prospects.[3]

On the afternoon of the second day the House finally proceeded to the election of an assistant bishop, and the balloting consumed the entire afternoon session. The first twelve ballots of the clergy were a close race between Hare and Shipman, never varying more than one vote and often tied at twelve to twelve, but of the twenty-seven votes cast, fourteen were necessary for a choice. Dudley received at most five votes, and this on the twelfth ballot. The deadlocked convention adjourned until 8:00 o'clock that night.

During the interval the laity held an informal meeting, and when the convention adjourned it was informally declared that a vote revealed eighteen in favor of Dudley and fourteen for Shipman. The clergy, having been informed as to the direction the wind was blowing, resumed their voting. On the sixteenth ballot, Dr. Dudley received fourteen to Dr. Shipman's thirteen. His name was then referred to the laity for their action, and of the thirty-one votes cast,

[1] *Journal of the Special Session, Diocese of Kentucky,* 1874.
[2] *The Courier-Journal,* Louisville, November 13, 1874, p. 4.
[3] *Ibid.* The rebuke was by the Reverend C. H. Shield, rector of St. Andrew's Church, Louisville.

he received twenty-two yeas and nine nays. Thomas Underwood Dudley's nomination as Assistant Bishop of Kentucky was confirmed and his election declared unanimous.[4]

In reporting the election, the press, particularly the Lexington papers, conjectured freely as to the reasons for Dr. Shipman's defeat. They attributed no little importance to Senator Stevenson's support of Dudley, stating that his "name and character gave great weight to his utterances in behalf of Dr. Dudley and doubtless turned the scales in his favor."[5] The *Lexington Daily Press* suggested as a contributing factor certain enemies in high places. Five years previously Shipman had preached a sermon in Christ Church, Lexington, in which he forcibly denounced betting on horseracing, stating that racetracks were immoral places which no Christian should attend. He had incurred the wrath of many leading members of his congregation who regarded the exhibition of horses for speed as an innocent recreation, and had brought down upon himself the bitter denunciation of all racing associations in the state. Now, five years later, the incident had not been forgotten, and, suggested the newspaper, it had cost him the assistant bishopric of Kentucky.[6]

The decisive factor in Shipman's defeat, however, was more probably that he was the choice of the High Church party in Kentucky, and the Evangelicals were determined that he not be elected. There were those who believed that Hare had been merely a red herring and that Dr. Dudley was the real choice of the Evangelicals. "As such," stated the *Lexington Press,* "Dudley achieved a triumph over the gentleman who represented high, though not too high, Church views."[7] More likely, in the light of later events, Dudley was simply a compromise candidate between the two parties.

[4] *Ibid.,* November 13, 1874, p. 4. Also, *Journal,* 1874, p. 13.

[5] *Lexington Daily Press,* November 21, 1874, p. 1.

[6] *Ibid.,* November 8, 1877, p. 2. Also, *Lexington Weekly Press,* November 14, 1877, p. 2. In reporting a call which Shipman had received to a New York parish, the Lexington papers ran a story on him, stating, "The opposition excited by that sermon was so great and so long continued that it was believed by many to have resulted in the defeat of Dr. Shipman for the position of Assistant Bishop of Kentucky. There was no doubt that many gentlemen, largely interested in the turf, boasted that his defeat was due to their indirect influence on the Convention which elected the present assistant bishop."

[7] *Lexington Daily Press,* November 21, 1874, p. 1.

There can be little doubt that had Jacob Shipman been elected assistant bishop, he would have served effectively and with the esteem of virtually all Kentucky Churchmen, but neither can there be any doubt of the divine guidance and heavenly aid to those who chose the Reverend Thomas Underwood Dudley. His episcopacy of twenty-nine years marked an era of prosperity in the Diocese, and the power of his presence was felt far and near.

The Rev. Dr. Dudley was consecrated bishop in Christ Church, Baltimore, on January 27, 1875, by the Right Reverend Benjamin Bosworth Smith, assisted by the bishops of Virginia, Pennsylvania, Huron (Canada), and Oregon and the assistant bishops of Virginia and Maryland. During the month following his consecration, in obedience to the claims of domestic duty, he remained in the city of Baltimore, officiating chiefly at Christ Church, where he had been rector for the past seven years. On February 1 he received a letter from Bishop Smith, in which the aged prelate handed over to him "all the ecclesiastical authority over the Diocese" which was possible for him to do, in accordance with the canons and usages of the Church while remaining senior bishop. "This much I can do," he wrote, "and I do it with the utmost cheerfulness; but I cannot give the wisdom, firmness, conciliation, and other graces which you will need for the faithful performance of those sacred duties, but counsel, moral support, and fervent prayers shall not be wanting to you on the part of your faithful friend and senior bishop."[8]

The new Assistant Bishop arrived on February 27 in Louisville, where he was greeted with the warmest cordiality and genuine welcome. The very next morning, the third Sunday in Lent, he preached in St. Paul's Church to an overflow congregation, supplemented by members of other parishes in the Louisville area who came for the occasion of the new Bishop's first appearance in the Diocese of Kentucky. A commanding figure, manly and dignified, with brilliant dark eyes and an intellectual, benign expression, Bishop Dudley dominated St. Paul's pulpit, preaching an eloquent sermon in a magnificent voice, full of subtle power. After the sermon he expressed his gratitude at his election as Assistant Bishop

[8] *Journal, Diocese of Kentucky,* 1875, pp. 70–80.

but made it plain that he had left a peaceful, happy home not to any preference that he himself had felt for such a change, but that he had taken the step in obedience to the will of the Master. He preached again that night to an equally large congregation in Christ Church, Louisville.

Bishop Dudley spent the first two weeks in the city which was to be his home and the seat of his episcopacy, officiating in the several churches and becoming acquainted with his flock in the largest city in the state. On the last day of March he accepted the nominal rectorship of Calvary Church, stating, "This, as every other rela-tion I sustain, must be wholly subordinate to my relation to the Diocese of Kentucky."[9]

During his first three months in Kentucky, the Assistant Bishop traveled extensively, visiting more than three-fourths of the par-ishes and mission stations, becoming acquainted with clergy and laity alike. It soon became apparent to all who heard him preach or had any contact with him that a dedicated, zealous, untiring leader had come among them.

Before proceeding with the story of Bishop Dudley's fruitful episcopate in Kentucky, let us review the background which so admirably fitted him for the duties of a missionary bishop.[10]

Thomas Underwood Dudley was born in Richmond, Virginia on September 26, 1837, the son of Thomas Underwood Dudley, a prominent merchant, and Maria Friend Dudley. He was bound by ancestry to his native state by ties which were never broken, nor did he ever lose his soft Virginia accent or loyalty to his birthplace. He received his early education in private schools and at Hanover Academy, and on October 2, 1855, at the age of nineteen, enrolled at the University of Virginia, where he was both a good student and a good fellow. His warm personality and ready wit endeared him to fellow students and faculty alike, and one classmate described him as one of the most delightful companions, noting that "he could

[9] Ibid., p. 74.
[10] National Encyclopedia of American Biography (New York, 1891–1940), III. Also, Henry Codman Potter, Reminiscences of Bishops and Archbishops (New York and London, 1906). Also The Bishop's Letter, Memorial Edition (Louisville, February, 1904), XIII, no. 8.

sing a good song and was inimitable as a story teller."[11] After graduation, with a degree of Master of Arts in 1858, he was for awhile professor of Latin and Greek at his alma mater, during which time he married Fannie Berkeley Cochran of Loudoun County, Virginia. At the outbreak of the War Between the States, he entered the Confederate Army in an artillery company, but was afterwards transferred to the commissary department, attaining the rank of major and serving until the surrender. After the war, he studied law in Middleburg, Virginia under John Randolph Tucker, but soon gave it up to become a candidate for Holy Orders and entered the Theological Seminary of Virginia in January, 1866. As in college, so in seminary, he was exceedingly popular as well as scholarly. A fellow student, later Bishop of West Virginia, described him as "by far the best furnished man that we had." He was a special favorite of Dr. William Sparrow, president of the seminary, and from this learned man he formulated many of his theological ideas.[12] On June 28, 1867, he was ordained to the diaconate by Bishop John Johns in the seminary chapel, and was placed in charge of a parish in Harrisonburg, Virginia. He was ordained to the priesthood by Bishop Whittle on June 26, 1868, also in the chapel of the Virginia Theological Seminary, and shortly thereafter began his six-year rectorate at Christ Church, Baltimore. His wife having died, leaving him with four young daughters, he married in 1869 Virginia Fisher Rowland of Norfolk, Virginia, by whom he had three children. His second marriage also terminated with the death of his wife, and in 1881 he married Mary E. Aldrich of New York. Their son and daughter brought to nine the number of Dudley's children. In 1874, St. John's College, Annapolis, conferred on him the degree of Doctor of Divinity, and that same year he was a deputy to the General Convention, serving on several important committees, notably the Committee on Amendments to the Constitution. It was at this Convention in New York that he so favorably impressed the Kentucky delegation.

Dudley was thirty-eight years of age when he was elected Assistant Bishop of Kentucky, with a reputation for wisdom, conviction,

[11] Potter, *Reminiscences of Bishops and Archbishops*, p. 166.
[12] *Ibid.*, p. 173.

and eloquence. He came as Bishop into a Diocese riven by party strife, a house divided against itself. "Rumor has it that when the young Bishop arrived in Kentucky, some one, determined to have a 'line upon' him and his policy, asked him whether he was 'high' or 'low'; to which he replied, 'Sir, I am high, low, Jack and the game!' "[13] The Bishop's estimate of his policy was typical of the man, for Dudley deplored factionalism in the Church, deeming himself neither "high" nor "low." A perfect summation of his Churchmanship and one of which he would have approved heartily was pronounced a few years ago by the oldest living Episcopalian in Louisville, an eminent Churchwoman, who when asked the question, "What kind of Churchman was Bishop Dudley?", replied without hesitation, "He was a real Churchman."[14] One would have to search long and hard for a more fitting epitaph.

Clues throughout his writings substantiate this claim. From these it is immediately apparent that Thomas Underwood Dudley was extremely difficult to label, that he did not fit readily into any category as regards his Churchmanship. Most certainly he was not the Evangelical some believed him to be when elected Assistant Bishop; nor could he be called a High Churchman. From the vantage point of nearly a century, he looms large as a "real Churchman," neither "high" nor "low" nor "broad" in the connotation of wavering or not holding decided views, but *"in medio tutissimus ibis,"* he stood for the best of Anglicanism. Like Dr. Craik, Shipman, Norton and Merrick, he believed with his whole heart the principles of the One, Holy, Catholic and Apostolic Church of antiquity. He was firmly convinced of the "supreme value and ordinary necessity of the Apostolic ministry," believing that such a ministry was the bond of the Church's continuous life, and that the Lord's "abiding presence would be with the office and not the officer"; that "personal excellence was not the warrant for ministerial authority."[15] Yet he rejoiced with true Christian charitable-

[13] *Ibid.,* p. 178.
[14] Interview with Mrs. Spalding Coleman, Louisville, October 6, 1965.
[15] Thomas U. Dudley, *The Christian Ministry,* The first course of lectures delivered on the Reinicker Foundation for the session of 1899–1900, at the Theological Seminary in Virginia. Pamphlet reprinted from the *Protestant Episcopal Review* of April, May, and June, 1900.

ness "for the great company of Christian men and women who have been born anew of water in the name of the Triune God, and just as certainly 'renewed of the Holy Ghost,' because the fruits of the Spirit are manifest in them." "Hold the truth, the whole truth as the Church teaches," he admonished, "but hold and speak it in love as the Church commands." [16] Bishop Dudley was esteemed and popular, not only within the Church but also among all the denominations, for although he ever asserted the apostolicity and catholicity of Anglican orders, he showed forebearance and tolerance towards all and firmly believed that "the Omnipotent cannot have tied Himself exclusively to His own appointed means." [17] A priest of the Diocese of Kentucky wrote of him, "If he could not quite say of the 'Campbellites,' who (like the fish, probably named after them, the 'new lights') were quite abundant in Kentucky, that they, with him, belonged to the 'army' of the Lord, he could at least say and feel that they belonged to the 'navy'." [18] The Bishop could not, however, concur in any enterprise, and there were such afoot, "for the merging of all Christian bodies into one, after the fashion of a gigantic Young Men's Christian Association." "The Church is the Body of Christ," he maintained, "and the project is, it would seem, that the body shall be formless as a jelly fish, a mass whose one function is pulsation, in which no organs have been developed, and so no function performed save only the meaningless and worthless movement of itself." [19] As to the exchanging of pulpits with non-Episcopal brethren, the question which had been brought so squarely before Kentucky Episcopalians less than a year previously, Dudley quoted, as his own feeling, the words of his good friend and former teacher, Dr. Sparrow, who stated, "We cannot; we must testify by our refusal, our sense of the value of our peculiarities." [20]

The Assistant Bishop was, in every sense of the word, a Prayer Book Churchman, and was known in all quarters for his strict adherence thereto. A fellow clergyman of the Diocese of Kentucky, writing some years later, stated, "I never knew the Bishop to take

[16] *Ibid.*
[17] *Ibid.*
[18] Potter, *Reminiscences,* p. 179.
[19] Dudley, *The Christian Ministry.*
[20] *Ibid.*

any liberties with the Prayer Book. On special occasions, of course, he exercised his *jus liturgicum;* but on ordinary occasions he stuck to the rubrics."[21] The Bishop, himself, stated, "In the interpretation of the rubrical directions of the Book of Common Prayer, strict construction is the only principle of safety and of absolute loyal obedience."[22]

If in any one particular Bishop Dudley might be classified as leaning toward an Evangelical, it was in the importance he attached to preaching. He admonished against the temptation to "push the pulpit away into a dark and gloomy corner, while the altar is made to blaze with light and color, and the preacher is merged more and more into the priest." He insisted that "the preaching of the Gospel of Jesus Christ is not an obsolete and nugatory ordinance, which we must continue merely because once commanded, but it is as necessary now as then." He ever contended that "preaching is the official, authoritative proclamation of God's redemption of man by the death of His Son, whom He has declared to be His Son with power by the resurrection of the dead." He urged "simplicity" and "directness" in preaching the Gospel as the Church received it, and warned against the minister preaching his opinions, or even the opinions of some great doctor of the past or of the present, but only Christ and Him crucified. The Bishop believed with all his heart that a priest was ordained to the ministry of the Word and the Sacraments, both-and, not either-or.[23]

His stress on preaching the Word in no way detracted from the importance of dispensing the sacraments, for he firmly believed these to be the divinely appointed means of grace and essential to the very being of the Church, and certainly not, as Cummins had held, merely matters of form and ceremony. As for the doctrine of sacerdotalism, he believed in priesthood as an essential idea in the very conception of the Church as the Body of Christ, but insisted that it never be forgotten that "the Church is the Priest, and that individual men are such only as her representatives and ministers."[24]

[21] Potter, *Reminiscences,* p. 185.
[22] Dudley, *The Christian Ministry.*
[23] *Ibid.*
[24] *Ibid.*

Bishop Dudley loved the beauty and dignity of the liturgy of the Church and felt that enhancements thereto were acceptable, but he was not a ceremonialist. He attached little importance to ceremony one way or the other. "These things may be good, may be evil, as they are helps or hindrances to devotion," he stated.[25]

The "real Churchmanship" of the Assistant Bishop was just what the Diocese of Kentucky most needed during the crucial years following the apostasy of Bishop Cummins. An extreme Churchman in either direction might have proved its undoing or at least set back its progress many years. No wonder he was beloved of both factions in Kentucky. He was veritably "a man for all seasons." And, too, he was all things to all sorts and conditions of men. Revered for his piety, admired for his steadfastness of purpose, his administrative ability, and scholarship, loved for his wit and charitableness to young and old, rich and poor, black and white, he soon gained the respect, not only of his own Diocese, but of the entire American Church.

Bishop Dudley immediately showed his earnest and unremitting advocacy of the missionary cause. "We are essentially a missionary diocese," he stated in his first convention address, "almost as much so as any one of the great missionary jurisdictions of the far West. Very much land remaineth to be occupied in the name of the Lord, and to do it there must be united strength applied through some agency which can best evolve and distribute our united force."[26] As a result, the Board of Diocesan Missions, which had functioned effectively during the years of its full existence but, for the past year or two, had ceased to exist, was revived. Also revived was the canon dividing the Diocese into four missionary convocations, which had fallen into disuse during Cummins' episcopacy.[27] Almost immediately the missionary outreach of the Diocese showed marked im-

[25] *The Courier Journal,* Louisville, May 28, 1875.
[26] *Journal,* 1875, p. 78.
[27] *Ibid.* The Board of Diocesan Missions would henceforth consist of the Bishop and the Assistant Bishop, three clergymen and three laymen elected annually by the convention from the city of Louisville and vicinity, and the deans of each convocation as ex officio members, together with one layman elected by each convocation. It would be the duty of the board to raise funds for carrying forth the missionary work of the Diocese and to receive and disburse same, and each parish would contribute an amount equal to one-third of the assessment for the Bishop's Fund.

provement. The Board of Missions expressed gratification at the zeal, energy and wisdom of the Assistant Bishop in advising their plans and administering the missionary work of the Diocese. "To him, under God," it was felt by the board, "was due the signal and unexpected success of that work."[28]

Bishop Dudley's interest in the missionary cause in Kentucky did not wane, and throughout his entire episcopacy he maintained that the extending of the Gospel of Jesus Christ was the cause for which the Church was founded. The Board of Diocesan Missions continued, however, to operate on a limited budget. At times, nearly all the parishes and mission stations would be staffed by clergymen; at others, numerous points would be vacant. Various schemes for missionary extension were tried. Bishop Dudley appointed a diocesan evangelist to visit struggling missions, to hold services from time to time, and to keep alive the hope and interest in such places as were without clerical supervision. Although the first such evangelist remained in office only a few months, he proved the desirability of maintaining such an officer, and a number of those who followed did much good. The Bishop appealed to the laity to concern themselves with the furtherance of the missionary cause, and appointed lay readers in many parishes and missions. The Bishop and the board were both extremely reluctant to abandon any point which the Church had ever occupied, but there were times when it seemed expedient to do so temporarily in order to support a clergyman at a more hopeful spot. For the most part, the missionary outreach improved each year. By 1880 the Church was firmly established throughout the state, from the important trade center of Hickman in the far west to mountainous Lee County in eastern Kentucky. There were still, to be sure, important centers where the Church had not yet been planted but it was already making strides in those directions. There was within the Diocese an aura of peace and good will among Churchmen, even among those who held widely divergent views, an atmosphere which continued to prevail amid changing times and faces.

An important and urgent aspect of the missionary work in the

---

[28] *Journal*, 1876, pp. 18–19.

Diocese, and one which ardently concerned Bishop Dudley, was the Christian education of the Negro and the Church's ministry to the many thousands of these people within the borders of the state. Both Bishops Smith and Cummins had been deeply interested in the evangelization and instruction of the former slaves, as had other clergy in the Diocese. Back in 1859, Dr. W. J. Waller had founded St. Mark's Mission in Louisville, and in 1871, the Reverend John Nicholas Norton had founded and entirely financed the Church of Our Merciful Saviour there. Another Negro mission had been founded in the early years of Dudley's episcopacy, also in Louisville, but the Mission of the Good Shepherd had waged a constant struggle for its existence and had never been fully organized. At the 1879 diocesan council, as the convention had begun to be called that year, Bishop Dudley had appointed a special committee to consider Church work among colored people, composed of three clergymen and two laymen.[29] In his report to the council, the Rev. Mortimer Murray Benton, longtime rector of the Church of the Advent, Louisville, and chairman of the committee, advocated the holding of services for the Negroes in each parish in the Diocese, the organizing of schools for their religious instruction, the training of them in industrial pursuits, and training in household duties by Christian women. The committee stressed, however, that "to be successful in this there must be no patronizing, no treating them as dependents, no inviting them to 'our Church', but teach them that they are welcome in Christ's Holy Catholic Church, in which there is no respect of persons."[30] The report was adopted.

By the next year the Church of Our Merciful Saviour was a flourishing mission with thirty communicants, under the charge of a colored lay reader, William H. Smith, who soon became a postulant for Holy Orders. Several important and necessary improvements were made during the year, some by the members themselves, others through the generosity of the founder, the Reverend Dr. Norton. Various Louisville clergymen officiated from time to time

[29] *Journal*, 1879, p. 22. The clergy: the Reverend M. M. Benton, chairman, rector of Trinity Church, Danville; the Reverend John N. Norton, Louisville; the Reverend John S. Gibson, Owensboro. Messrs. Clinton McClarty, Calvary Church, Louisville; John Esten Keller, Christ Church, Lexington.
[30] *Ibid.*, pp. 37–38.

and dispensed the sacraments. Eighty-seven scholars were enrolled in the Sunday school, staffed by four teachers. The Bishop, at the request of Mrs. Norton, who kept the mission under her financial care after the death of her husband, took it under his personal supervision in 1885–1886 while it was without a missionary in charge. The other Louisville mission, the Good Shepherd, was put under the charge of the Reverend William Floyd, formerly of the Diocese of Pittsburgh, and was regularly organized in 1883. Upon the missionary's resignation, it remained vacant for a time and finally ceased to exist. The building was taken over in 1885 by St. Andrew's Church, and the rector, the Right Reverend Charles Clifton Penick, formerly Missionary Bishop of Cape Palmas, Africa, reopened the mission with the title of St. Luke's, with most encouraging results. By the end of that year there were seventy-five communicants and one hundred more souls, and weekly services were being held.

In 1880 a Negro mission had been founded by Christ Church, Lexington, through the efforts of the rector, the Reverend Thomas Allen Tidball, and a layman, A. J. Campbell, also with good results. Weekly services were held, with either Mr. Tidball or some other clergyman officiating, until the fall of 1882, when St. Andrew's, as it was called, was put in charge of a Negro priest, the Reverend Hannibal S. Henderson, formerly of North Carolina, who began work there in July, 1884.[31]

Three Negro missions to minister to the thousands of that race in the state was a very small beginning. The parishes had made token efforts in answer to the Bishop's appeal, and in a few instances services were held by the parochial clergy. The Bishop felt strongly that more should be done. He continued to plead for support from all the parishes, begging that they gather congregations of colored people and establish Sunday schools for them. He pointed out the need of educating and ordaining Negro clergymen, believing this to be the best way ultimately to incorporate them into the Church. Bishop Dudley was far ahead of his time in his firm conviction of the rights of the Negro, and he never missed an opportunity to

[31] *Journals*, 1880–1885 inclusive.

express his belief that the Church of Jesus Christ was not for one nation or race or color, but for all men. "Immortal souls, they are inheritors with us of the fallen nature of the first Adam, and entitled to share with us in the redemptive work and blessing of the second Adam, the Lord from Heaven,"[32] he believed and constantly reiterated. In view of the traditions of the past and of the social complications arising, the Bishop realized that the greatest difficulty would be to persuade the Negro to come into the Church, instead of building his own "City of God." "I cannot agree," he stated, "that a separate Church shall be established for this people, that they must be excluded from the fellowship with men of other races, and dwell apart, for that were to contradict the fundamental idea of the Catholic Church of Jesus Christ."[33] At the Bishop's suggestion, a canon was enacted in 1883 providing for the annual election of a board to have special charge of mission work among the Negroes,[34] and to excite more interest within the Diocese. The work in the Louisville and Lexington Negro missions continued, and at Henderson a Sunday school flourished and a day school was now in operation, taught by a Negro woman. Donated land was available for the erection of a chapel there. In other parts of the Diocese, virtually nothing was being done, however, and it was finally determined that the Board of Diocesan Missions for Colored People was superfluous and that one Board of Missions was sufficient.[35]

Bishop Dudley never lost his consuming interest in the evangelization of the Negro, and for the rest of his life he worked actively for the advancement of the race. For years he served as chairman of the National Church's committee for evangelistic work among Negroes, and in 1885 he set forth his views in an essay, "How Shall We Help the Negro?" published in *The Century*.[36]

Of all the mission stations in the State of Kentucky, the one closest to the heart of Bishop Dudley was Lee County, in the mountains of eastern Kentucky. None loved and honored him more than the Churchmen and people of that county, where he labored

[32] *Journal*, 1883, p. 82.
[33] *Ibid.*, p. 83.
[34] *Ibid.*, p. 56.
[35] *Journal*, 1890, p. 48.
[36] *The Century*, June, 1885, XXX.

and planned and builded. The stories of Bishop Dudley's efforts in the Cumberland Mountains are legend as well as legion. His remarkable adaptability enabled him to be as much at home in the humblest log cabin as among his peers in the House of Bishops, and many was the time he spent the night on the floor of a rustic hut or shared the bed of a rugged mountaineer.

A story is told of his visit to a mountain hamlet one day. As he was admiring a fine horse ridden by, a strapping blacksmith, grimy and aproned, emerged from a nearby smithy and said, "They tell me that you'se the Bishop of Kaintuckee. I don't know nothin' 'bout what that may be, but I seen you a lookin' at that hoss, and I wants to shake." The Bishop shook and had a chat, and that night took supper with his new friend. Eventually he baptized and confirmed him and his household. Some years later at a diocesan convention, the Bishop received a telegram from the warden of the Lee County mission, informing him that his friend, the blacksmith, had died the night before, and that his last words were, "Tell the Bishop that I love him."[37] The blacksmith's words eloquently express the feeling of all those mountain people whom he baptized and confirmed over the years, of those for whom he often expressed sincere affection and who returned to him unmeasured love and reverence.

One of the problems within the Diocese which plagued Bishop Dudley, as it had Smith before him, was the transience of the clergy, particularly in the mission field. No sooner would a mission be well established and on its way to becoming self-supporting than the missionary in charge would receive a call to a vacant parish or would remove to another diocese. The larger and more influential parishes did not have this problem to such a degree, some of the parochial clergy remaining for a decade or more. During Bishop Dudley's nine years as Assistant Bishop of Kentucky, many changes took place in the ranks of the clergy. Among the more notable losses was that caused by the resignation in December, 1877, of the Rev. Jacob Shaw Shipman, rector of Christ Church, Lexington, for the past sixteen years. This was the man who was almost elected Assistant Bishop of Kentucky instead of Dudley, and there was not

[37] Potter, *Reminiscences,* p. 183.

in the Diocese a more esteemed clergyman. A few years previously, Shipman had been elected Bishop of Fond du Lac in northern Wisconsin, but such protest had arisen among his congregation that he had declined the honor,[38] remaining at Christ Church for two more years, continuing his excellent ministry there and participating with his usual efficiency in diocesan affairs, as well as in the national councils of the Church. Many of his more controversial sermons received wide notice, as had the sermon which played a role in his defeat by Dudley for Assistant Bishop in 1874. Not only was he beloved and respected by the members of his own parish but by the entire community. In an election held by the Lexington Public Library early in 1877 for the most popular minister in the city, he easily won, with more than two hundred votes over his nearest opponent.[39] It was, therefore, an occasion for great sorrow when he accepted a call to become rector of Christ Church, New York City. Bishop Dudley was offered the rectorship of Christ Church, Lexington, to hold with an assistant rector, but, although willing to accept the position, he felt that he could not act in the matter without the consent of the convention, which would not meet until May. The Lexington parish felt that it was not feasible to postpone the matter until then, and in March called another rector, the Reverend Thomas Allen Tidball, of Portsmouth, Virginia, to fill the vacant office.

Two conspicuous losses to the Diocese during this period were caused by the deaths of the Reverend John Nicholas Norton in January, 1881, and of the Reverend James Craik in June of the following year. The Diocese had no more faithful workers and the Church no more loyal sons than these two. For thirty-three years Dr. Norton had labored in Kentucky, and Dr. Craik for more than three-fourths of the entire existence of the Diocese. The passing of the triumvirate of Shipman, Norton, and Craik ended an era in the history of the Diocese. Many good and loyal clergymen would follow in their footsteps in the years ahead but, perhaps, none would be more fitted for the great work they did in Kentucky.

On May 31, 1884, in New York city, the Right Reverend Benja-

[38] *Lexington Weekly Press,* July 4, 1875, p. 2.
[39] *Lexington Daily Press,* February 3, 1877, p. 4.

min Bosworth Smith departed this life, and Thomas Underwood Dudley thereupon became officially Bishop of Kentucky. No visible change in diocesan policy was apparent, for he had been the Bishop in all save name since his consecration to the episcopate in 1875. It was, however, the mid-mark in his ministry as Bishop of the Diocese of Kentucky. The confidence lost during the Cummins' years had been regained, and the Church in Kentucky was stronger than ever before in its history.

The extent of territory covered by the State of Kentucky had given rise as early as 1882 to consideration of division, thereby creating a new diocese, but financial support for the episcopates of both dioceses was not guaranteed and the proposal failed. Some years later the election of an assistant bishop was considered, but no action taken. Bishop Dudley continued as the one Bishop of the one Diocese of Kentucky for another decade.

Louisville had long been the center of diocesan influence and the hub of diocesan activity. Here the Bishop made his home, here were the largest and strongest parishes—St. Paul's, Christ Church, Calvary, St. Andrew's—and flourishing St. John's, Advent, Zion, Trinity and Grace, the High Church bastion. Here were located virtually all of the diocesan institutions and orphanages—the Church Home and Infirmary, the Home of the Innocents, the Orphanage of the Good Shepherd, the John N. Norton Memorial Infirmary, and the Girls' Orphanage. Here, too, was opened in 1886 Trinity Hall, a diocesan high school for boys. The two Negro missions, Our Merciful Saviour and St. Luke's, continued to minister effectively to members of that race. The Bishop was finding his work more and more concentrated in the Diocese's largest city, but his interest in the mission field throughout the whole state never lessened.

Between 1885 and 1895, missions in the eastern half of the state increased in number, at times surpassing those in the western half. Emmanuel Church, Winchester, and Calvary, Ashland, begun in 1886, were completed and opened for services in 1888 and 1889 respectively. In the latter year, St. Stephen's Mission was erected at Sideview in Montgomery County, under the auspices of the rector of the Church of the Ascension, Mt. Sterling. A new and much larger church had been built in Richmond in 1887, and the prospects of Christ Church there were considerably brighter. In the brand new boom town of Middlesboro, in mountainous Bell County, the Episcopal Church moved promptly and established St. Mary's Mission in the summer of 1890, and the following February a beautiful little church was formally opened for worship. The mission in Lee County, which had long been the most successful in the entire Diocese, continued to prosper. The Episcopal Academy, sometimes called Dudley High School, was built in the winter of 1887 and 1888 and prospered for a number of years, and in 1894 the cornerstone of St. Thomas' Church, Beattyville, was laid by the Bishop. Both school and church, named for Thomas U. Dudley, attest to the esteem in which he was held by the people of Lee County. By 1893, Christ Mission, Somerset, and Grace, Lawrenceburg, had been organized, and the next year services were being held in Nicholasville.

Missionary expansion was hardly less notable in the western portion of the Diocese during this period. There were organized missions in Fulton, Grahamton, Russellville, and Guthrie, and a new mission in Henderson, called St. Clement's. Besides these, services were maintained in unorganized missions in Shelbyville, Anchorage, Kuttawa, and Madisonville.

Never before in the history of the Diocese had so many points been occupied as in the early years of the 1890's, and new fields were continually being opened. Largely responsible for the increase in the missionary outreach were the diocesan missionaries or evangelists, appointed by the Bishop. The system of utilizing general missionaries had first been tried, it will be remembered, in the mid-1870's, but it was not until the spring of 1892, when the Reverend W. G. McCready was appointed, that it achieved any permanency. So successful was he that at the council of that year enough money was pledged to pay the salaries of three such missionaries, each being assigned a portion of the Diocese by the Bishop. Under the successful ministrations of such diocesan evangelists as McCready, the Reverend Mortimer M. Benton, the Reverend W. H. Hampton, and the Reverend Lysander Rose, new missions were established, and vacant parishes and moribund stations revived.

In addition to the missions founded and maintained by the Diocese, there were a number of new missions and churches begun by the older parishes, especially in Louisville and Lexington. In the latter city in 1885, some thirty communicants of Christ Church, desiring free pews and a more ornate worship, withdrew and founded St. John's Church, meeting in a room on Main Street for several years. In danger of dying an early death, the parish rallied and in February, 1889, a lovely little church was erected on East Main Street.[40] Forty-seven communicants transferred from Christ Church to the new parish.[41]

Also in Lexington, on December 30, 1888, a new mission of Christ Church Parish opened on South Broadway.[42] The Chapel of the Good Shepherd grew rapidly, and soon there were from fifty to seventy-five pupils and ten teachers in the Sunday school.

A Protestant Infirmary[43] had also been opened in Lexington in 1889, the title of the property being held by the Women's Guild of Christ Church Parish. Of the eighteen managers, all women, seventeen were communicants of Christ Church.

Saint Andrew's, the Negro mission maintained by Christ Church, Lexington, had flourished during the ministry of the Reverend Hannibal S. Henderson, a Negro priest. He became missionary in charge in 1884, also serving as principal of a public School for Negroes until his death of pulmonary consumption in 1888. For awhile the mission languished, but the rector of Christ Church, the Reverend E. H. Ward, revived it and during the 1890's, under a colored deacon, it prospered once more.

In northern Kentucky, Trinity Church, Covington, the largest parish in the area, built in the fall of 1890 a chapel nearer the center of the town. St. John's Chapel was constituted a mission in February, 1894 and a number of communicants of Trinity transferred to the new mission.

In Dayton, another St. John's Church, which had attained parochial status back in 1873 during the rectorate of the beloved Rever-

[40] St. John's Church was located on a lot where the Mammoth Garage stands today at 333 East Main Street.
[41] *Journal*, 1889, p. 118.
[42] *Ibid.*, p. 118. The lot was the gift of Mr. John Q. A. Hayman.
[43] The Protestant Infirmary later became the Good Samaritan Hospital controlled by the Methodist Church.

end Frederick Elwell and flourished for a time, had fallen on hard times and since 1888 had been under the care of St. Paul's, Newport. The rector of that parish held regular Sunday afternoon services in the little wooden church building at Dayton [44] for a congregation of approximately sixty.

While missionary expansion within the Diocese of Kentucky remained of primary importance to Bishop Dudley, his interest in education was hardly less commanding, for he considered schools essential to missionary work. "I am convinced more and more thoroughly every year," he stated in 1893, "that schools, good schools, and cheap schools are perhaps the most effective agencies for the dissemination of Church principles, and so for upbuilding the Church in any commonwealth."[45] He expressed the hope that one day there would be a proper school in at least each convocational district of the Diocese. Already a beginning in this direction had been made. In Louisville, Trinity Hall, a boys' preparatory school, which had its ups and downs during the years of its existence, had been revived in the fall of 1893, and by the next year was in a most prosperous condition. Plans were underway for the organization of a school for girls in that vicinity. The mission school in Beattyville, now housed in a large schoolhouse, was called the "pride of the mountains." The Eastern Kentucky High School, established in Ashland in 1892, was filling a pressing need in that portion of the Diocese.

Every bit as vital was Dudley's interest in higher education. For years he had wished to reestablish the Episcopal Theological Seminary in Kentucky at Louisville but his efforts had not been successful. He was, however, successful in allocating the income of the seminary fund to provide preparatory instruction for four postulants for Holy Orders, under the tutelage of a professor of theology, the Reverend W. T. Elmer of Louisville.

In 1885 the Diocese of Kentucky accepted the invitation of the University of the South to join other Southern dioceses in the

---

[44] St. John's Church, Dayton, was located at 509 McKinney Street. The building, still standing, is now a garage. In 1899 the present stone church was erected at Eighth and O'Fallon Avenues, Dayton.

[45] *Journal*, 1893, p. 62.

government and conduct of that university. Bishop Dudley had long felt the importance of this step on the part of the Diocese of Kentucky and was disappointed when, in 1878, the first such invitation was declined for financial reasons. He had stated on more than one occasion that he considered it the bounden duty of the Diocese to accept. Throughout his life, Dudley maintained a love for Sewanee and did all in his power to further its aims. "Our University is the one chief hope of religious education;" he stated in 1890, "I mean of both religion and education as this Church understands them, in all our dearly loved South. Men die, but the Institution, if nourished and cherished by all who love the South and the Church, will live."[46] In 1894 Bishop Dudley entered upon his duties as the sixth Chancellor of the University of the South, a position he held until his death.

The beloved missionary could look back upon his works with satisfaction. He had brought to a faction-rent Diocese a new and badly needed concord, and had so enlarged the scope of its enterprise that now, like Ohio, its northern neighbor, it began to contemplate a division into two dioceses.

[46] *Journal,* 1890, pp. 68–69.

18 *Expansion Under Dudley*

During the two decades in which Thomas Underwood Dudley was Bishop of the Diocese of Kentucky, when that Diocese comprised the whole state, the Church enjoyed a greater degree of prosperity than at any time in its history. From the day in 1875 when the new Assistant Bishop took up the reins dropped by Bishop Cummins until he turned over all of eastward Kentucky to the Bishop of Lexington twenty years later, the Diocese had grown steadily, in both numbers and prestige. The number of communicants had doubled; there were more parishes and missions than ever before; and a larger number of clergymen were resident in the Diocese.

Bishop Dudley had set about from the beginning to establish the Episcopal Church in the state on a firmer basis through the establishment of more and more missions. In some of the places in mountainous eastern Kentucky and farther north on the Ohio River where he established missions, no Episcopal clergyman had ever set foot; in others, earlier attempts may have been made but without lasting result. It is with the missions, established during the 1875–1895 years, that this chapter deals. All bear distinctly the Dudley mark.

CHRIST CHURCH, RICHMOND

In the eastern portion of Kentucky on the waters of the Kentucky River lies Madison County, the largest in the Bluegrass Region. Its county seat, Richmond, was in the 1870's a thriving town of some sixteen hundred inhabitants in the center of a large cattle-producing area. Besides one of the handsomest courthouses in the state, a female academy, two hotels, a newspaper, three national banks and numerous business houses, it boasted six churches—Presbyterian, Baptist, Methodist, Reformed or Disciples of Christ, Roman Catholic, and African.[1]

Strange as it may seem, the Episcopal Church had not been

planted here in the county where the first recorded religious service in the state was conducted nearly one hundred years earlier by the Reverend John Lyth, but the Church did not earnestly move to the east of Lexington until nearly a half century after the organization of the Diocese of Kentucky in 1829.

Richmond was one of several towns in which the Church was especially interested back in 1859 when B. B. Smith first inaugurated the convocational system to propagate the Episcopal faith in Kentucky. In that year the Church made preparations toward organizing a mission there but the war curtailed virtually all Church extension in the Diocese.

During the incumbency of Assistant Bishop Cummins, the first of a succession of missionaries was assigned to Richmond. This missionary was the Reverend Isaac Gibson, missionary-at-large in central Kentucky. In 1869 he began to hold services once a month in Richmond. He found there a small group of Episcopalians, mostly women, who had somehow managed to hold the faith even without the services of a clergyman. In the fall of 1870 Cummins spent several days in the town, preaching twice. "I found the little flock of our Church people in this place composed almost entirely of zealous women, earnestly engaged in the work of securing funds to erect a small church," he reported to that year's convention.[2]

By the next year the ladies had purchased a lot for $500 and had raised a subscription of $1,000 toward the erection of a building.[3] During the next four years the little mission was much of the time without a missionary, for each of the two who were assigned the station remained only about a year. One of them, the Reverend Anselan Buchanan, explained, "There is no church at Richmond and no male communicant of the Episcopal Church."[4] Missionary expansion had all but ceased during the last year of Cummins' episcopacy, and most of the stations which had their beginnings during this period lay dormant.

Disheartened surely by the transience of its missionaries and the

---

[1] Collins, *History of Kentucky*, II, 493.
[2] *Journal, Diocese of Kentucky*, 1871, p. 52.
[3] *Ibid.*, p. 65.
[4] *Journal*, 1872, p. 48.

lack of pecuniary aid from the sorely afflicted Diocese, yet unde-terred, the little band of six women struggled on to add to the building fund. By 1875 they had succeeded in erecting a small frame church at the junction of Tates Creek Pike and West Main Street. Their names deserve to be remembered: Mrs. James Bennett, Miss Sallie Burnam, Misses Lucille and Nanette Crooke, Mrs. William Mullins, and Mrs. Edward Gunby.[5]

Christ Church Mission, Richmond, was organized during the episcopacy of Bishop Dudley. True, it had its beginnings earlier, due almost entirely to the faithful laymen in the town, but it was during the missionary expansion of the Dudley years that it became firmly established. He had been Assistant Bishop for less than six weeks when he made his first visit to Richmond in mid-March, 1875, to hold four services and celebrate the Holy Communion in the newly completed Christ Mission.[6] Three months later, on June 13, the Reverend C. R. Page, the new rector of Trinity, Danville, became missionary-in-charge. Upon his arrival he stated, "My heart was made glad in finding a beautiful little church erected by the untiring efforts of a few ladies, whose example thousands of our Churchmen will do well by imitating."[7]

With its own house of worship, there was every reason to hope that the little mission would prosper. There were by now ten families, eleven communicants and fifty "souls" on the register. After the resignation of the Reverend Mr. Page, the mission was under the charge of the Reverend Mortimer Murray Benton, rector of Trinity Church, Danville. During his three years there he held services in Richmond at least as often as once a month, celebrating the Holy Communion. He usually gave, in addition, a weekday to the mission. The first full-time missionary to be assigned to Rich-mond was the Reverend Robert Habersham Barnwell, newly ar-rived from the Diocese of Georgia, who served for about two years. A marked improvement was manifested in the mission. A Sunday school with eight teachers and fifty scholars, all members of other denominations, was in operation, two regular Sunday services were

---

[5] *Richmond Daily Register,* November 23, 1963.
[6] *Journal,* 1875, p. 90.
[7] *Journal,* 1876, p. 72.

held, and the missionary also found time to preach in nearby villages. Unfortunately the distance of the little church from the center of the town, together with the fact that there were no children in the congregation, rendered the Sunday school a failure, and the missionary removed to another cure. Another missionary followed and remained about a year, after which the mission was vacant for many months, but still the faithful laymen did not despair. In fact, they set about making plans for a new and larger church building nearer the center of town. Their faithfulness was rewarded the following winter with the arrival of the Reverend William Y. Sheppard from the Diocese of New Mexico and Arizona. For the first time the Board of Missions made a small appropriation for the missionary's support. Sheppard labored faithfully and successfully for a little over two years, preaching also at nearby Bybeetown and Concord. The number of communicants increased, and in 1887 a new and much larger building was erected at the corner of Lancaster Avenue and Water Street. The very eligible lot was the gift of the senior warden, Mr. J. Stone Walker, and the building was financed entirely by the communicants at no cost to the Diocese. Miss Lucille Crooke singlehandedly raised $900 for the building fund "without the circle" of Episcopalians in Richmond.[8] The new Christ Mission was consecrated by Bishop Dudley on June 19, 1887.

It was a handsome red brick building, square, with steep slate roof, four gables, and tower, surmounted by two crosses. Interiorly the ceiling conformed to the steep roof and was paneled in oak, the polished ash benches were trimmed in walnut, and the entire floor was covered with Brussels carpet. Four large and four small windows, set with cathedral glass, were among the "grandest in Central Kentucky."[9]

The Reverend Mr. Sheppard, according to Bishop Dudley, was by far the most devoted of the growing number of missionaries who had served the mission. He was beloved and revered in all the region round about. "Men," said the Bishop, "who believed in neither God nor devil believed in 'Brother Sheppard'."[10] Never in

---

[8] *Journal*, 1887, p. 59.
[9] *Richmond Daily Register*, clipping prior to 1900, date unknown.
[10] *Journal*, 1893, p. 47.

robust health, he utterly disregarded his own well-being to rush to the aid of anyone in need, whether or not of his own flock. It was indeed the hardest blow of all when in 1888 he left Richmond to assume the rectorship of the faltering Trinity Church, Danville, and the virtually dying St. Philip's, Harrodsburg, to infuse new life into both before his untimely death in 1892.

A succession of short-term missionaries migrated in and out of the little mission for the next five years, none of whom remained long enough to achieve any real results. Thus far in its history, Christ Mission had not been able to retain a clergyman for a long enough time to either build up its communicant strength or make a lasting impression upon those of other persuasions. The dogged faithfulness of its few laymen, still largely women, was all that kept it alive. In mid-1893 a new priest, recently arrived in the Diocese from Iowa, was in charge and the state of affairs in Richmond appeared to improve. Still at his post in December, 1895, the Reverend Lewis M. Wilkins was one of the seventeen clergymen who became canonically connected with the newly constituted Diocese of Lexington.

THE LEE COUNTY MISSION
ST. THOMAS', BEATTYVILLE; ST. PAUL'S, PROCTOR

Although the first Bishop of Kentucky, the Right Reverend Benjamin Bosworth Smith, had penetrated into the mountainous regions of eastern Kentucky as early as 1840, his business there was of an educational rather than a religious nature. He was at the time Superintendent of Public Instruction in the Commonwealth of Kentucky. Just how far back into the mountains the Bishop traveled on the tall, rawboned horse lent him for the purpose is not known, but his six-week journey must have acquainted him fairly well with the Cumberland Mountain area of his Diocese. A friend of his, who knew all about the region, remarked, "I never heard of any one's going so far back into the mountains without a pilot."[11]

---

[11] Benjamin Bosworth Smith, "Glimpses Backwards over two hard years of my Life from 1839 to 1841, whilst I was Superintendent of Public Instruction in the Commonwealth of Kentucky," B. B. Smith Papers (Insko Collection), Box 4, Church Historical Society.

While in Boston in 1845, Bishop Smith had succeeded in interesting a circle of ladies of St. Paul's Church there upon the subject of "the great moral and religious destitution of the mountainous regions of the Diocese of Kentucky." Moved by his story, the ladies contributed $200 for a special mission to that region, but the Bishop had never found a person "possessed of the amazing amount of missionary and self-sacrificing zeal" required for the task.[12]

Indeed, it was another thirty years before a clergyman of the Episcopal Church went as a missionary into the eastern Kentucky mountains. By then Bishop Smith had become Presiding Bishop and was making his home in New York, and the Right Reverend George David Cummins was acting Bishop of Kentucky. In the summer of 1871, however, the Reverend Walter Tearne, recently ordained rector of the Church of the Ascension, Mt. Sterling, added Richmond, Winchester, Owingsville, and "the whole region" thereabouts to his charge."[13]

Within the next few years, he penetrated into Menifee, Estill, and Lee counties, holding services in the more important villages. In the little town of Beattyville, in Lee County, he found three communicants of the Episcopal Church and by 1874 was holding regular services there on the fourth Sunday in each month.[14]

Lee was a new county, carved in 1870 from Owsley, Estill, Breathitt, and Wolfe counties. Located on both sides of the main Kentucky River and including a large part of the valleys of its South and Middle forks and their tributaries, Lee is nevertheless one of the smallest counties in the state. Its population in 1870 was 2,924. Beattyville, the county seat, on the north side of the river, was sparsely populated with one hundred and twenty-three inhabitants, and Proctor, opposite it on the south side of the river, had one hundred. They were remote villages where men farmed the rich valleys and hunted the woodlands, mined coal and cut timber on the mountains, and traded horses and guns. The women kept house and tended the children, cooked the meals in iron pots in rude fireplaces, washed clothes in river and streams, and had babies

---

[12] *Journal*, 1845, p. 16.
[13] *Journal*, 1871, p. 52.
[14] *Journal*, 1875, p. 90.

unattended except when a midwife, called a "granny," was summoned. The county roads were those laid out by the early settlers, dusty in summer and deep with mud in winter, some impassable except by foot.

Although B. B. Smith had dreamed of evangelizing in the eastern Kentucky mountains and Cummins had made a beginning, it was Dudley who firmly established and organized the mission in Lee County which, during all the years of his episcopacy, remained among the most important in the Diocese.

In the fall of 1875, the same year of his consecration, Bishop Dudley left his home in Louisville, accompanied by the Reverend Lewis P. Tschiffely, rector of Grace Church there, on a long trip to the Cumberland Mountains to visit the mission in Lee County. That night they spent in Richmond, and early next morning arrived by stage in Irvine, where they were met by the Reverend Mr. Tearne, who conducted them the rest of the way.[15] The three clergymen probably got as far as Miller's Creek before they had to set out on foot "to the Old Landing, up the Winding Stairs, passing the headwaters of Contrary Creek to the top of the ridge leading toward Beattyville." Tradition states that near Beattyville a mountaineer took pity on them and loaned them a mule, upon which they took turns riding. The Bishop was on the mule when they descended from the top ridge into Lower Stufflebean Creek and into Beattyville.[16]

The following morning, October 13, the three clergymen held a service in a schoolhouse in Proctor, and Bishop Dudley preached and administered the Holy Communion. That afternoon he had a conference with the men of both Proctor and Beattyville as to the establishment of a school and church. In the evening he preached to a large congregation in the courthouse in Beattyville, and confirmed one person.[17] Among the handful of Episcopalians in Lee County were Mr. Thomas Pryse, who had migrated from Wales in the late 1860's, and Mrs. Felix McGuire, who had come from the Big Sandy

---

[15] *Journal*, 1876, p. 47.

[16] Report by Miss Gladys Sale of St. Thomas' Church, Beattyville, given at Women's Conference, Cathedral Domain, May, 1965.

[17] *Journal*, 1876, p. 90.

region and had married a grandson of one of the first settlers. They were staunch Churchmen who would help the Bishop and clergy hold together the mission.

Bishop Dudley's visit to Beattyville and Proctor that October day in 1875 was the beginning of an association with the people of that area which was to be one of his chief concerns throughout his years in Kentucky. Very soon the Bishop was able to "secure on reasonable terms" the Mountain Inn in Proctor, a large, rambling frame hotel and tavern, the barroom of which became the chapel, other rooms being used for a mission school. The mission in Proctor was called St. Paul's Mission, Lee County. By 1877 there were nine families and thirty-six persons, fourteen of whom were communicants, in the mission. The work increased so rapidly and the demands upon "Father Tearne," as he was affectionately called, became so great that he felt compelled to resign the rectorship of the Mt. Sterling parish, also relinquishing Winchester and Richmond, in order to concentrate his efforts entirely in the mountain area. His mission now included the counties of Lee, Owsley, and portions of Estill. He held regular services at Proctor and Beattyville in Lee County, and Booneville and Cross Roads in Owsley, known as the St. Barnabas Mission. Occasional services were held at Pine Grove, Pleasant Grove, Royal Oak, Mount Hope, Buffalo, Old Landing, Vinks, Mount Tabor, and Canaan.[18] Bishop Dudley had only praise for Walter Tearne. "In labors he is abundant," he stated, "and he endures hardships as a good soldier of Jesus Christ." The poverty of the people of this area was so great that Tearne felt it necessary to relinquish his small salary for six months and rely solely on the stipend paid him by the Board of Missions. Parishes throughout the Diocese came to the aid of the Lee County Mission, from time to time sending clothing and food for the poor. Parishes in Lexington and Louisville began the custom of preparing Christmas boxes for the mountain children.

In August, 1877, Tearne was joined in the work by the Reverend Charles Harry Lockwood, ordained to the diaconate the month before, who came to assist him in the mission and to have charge of

[18] *Journal*, 1877, pp. 90-91.

the school. Harry Lockwood was a protégé of Tearne. When the War Between the States ended, he was a sergeant in the signal corps of the United States Army at Mt. Sterling. There, under Tearne's influence, he determined to enter the sacred ministry and went to Seabury Hall, Farribault, Minnesota, for his training. Lockwood proved a happy choice for the Lee County Mission, and under him the school flourished. He held daily services in the chapel of the school and also assisted Tearne in the several stations in Lee and Owsley counties, thus enabling the priest to penetrate into new territory, such as Jackson, Wolfe, and Breathitt counties.

In his 1879 report to the convention, Bishop Dudley announced that he had formally constituted the mission in Lee County by the title of St. Paul's Mission and that a woman communicant of Christ Church, Lexington, had purchased and given to the Church the property occupied for the past two years.[19] In June of that year, Walter Tearne resigned and transferred to the Diocese of Iowa, and Lockwood became the missionary-in-charge.

During Lockwood's tenure, the Church put down deep roots. He had a great love for people and in a quiet, unassuming way taught them about the Episcopal Church. His wife, a cultured and educated woman, gave piano lessons and taught the women fine sewing and new ways of cooking. With her two younger sisters, who were with her most of the time, she went about serving in the community. The mission house at Proctor was always open and alive with purpose, and many a wayward young person found help and guidance there.[20] With the assistance of Mrs. Lockwood, the mission school increased in scholarship and in numbers. Lockwood continued to preach in the courthouse in Beattyville, but before long began to realize the need of a chapel and mission school in that town. He rented a room above the main saloon for use as a chapel and secured other rooms on Main Street for the school. The Board of Missions, at the missionary's request, agreed to pay $500 salary for support of a teacher, and nineteen-year-old Lucien Lee Kinsolving of Virginia was employed as headmaster. The red-haired young man was an able teacher, charming and vivacious, and during his

[19] *Journal,* 1879, p. 49. The donor of the church property was Mrs. Julia W. Hunt.
[20] Miss Gladys Sale's report.

administration the school grew and prospered. After three years, Kinsolving resigned to become a candidate for Holy Orders and later became the first Bishop of Brazil.

During the winter of 1877/78 a large schoolhouse was erected in Beattyville; part of it was used as a chapel. It was known both as the Beattyville Academy and the Dudley High School. Kinsolving's successor, Mr. Robert Funsten, died after a year as headmaster, and Lockwood took charge of the school.

Early in 1878 Lockwood, persuaded by his wife's ill health and the desire to further opportunities for his children, resigned and accepted a call to the Diocese of Alabama. His entire ministry had been rendered in Kentucky, where for eleven years he had faithfully served the most remote outpost of the Diocese. His loss was severely felt, and for a while the Bishop and Board of Missions feared for the life of the mission.

The new headmaster of the Beattyville school, Preston L. Gray, conducted lay services there for a while, and during the summer of 1888 the Reverend D. I. Hobbs, a native son educated by Walter Tearne and recently ordained deacon, took charge of the mission until September, when Mr. Charles Samuel Walkley was appointed by Bishop Dudley. Walkley was ordained to the priesthood in the chapel in Beattyville, known now as St. Thomas' Chapel. He was in charge of the mission for just a little over a year, but during that time the mission prospered. Bishop Dudley confirmed ten persons at his visitation, and twenty infants and three adults were baptized during the year. St. Paul's Chapel, Proctor, was enlarged, and the attendance at Sunday school and services there kept up very well. In Beattyville, regular services were maintained with a fair attendance. The building was unattractive and ill-suited for holding divine services, and various attempts were being made to raise money for a new chapel.[21]

Coal and timber were bringing unknown wealth to Lee County. The town boasted a three-story brick hotel, and board sidewalks had been laid. The courthouse hummed with prospectors, lawyers, and litigants in land boundary cases. By the beginning of 1889, the

[21] *Journal*, 1889, pp. 99–100.

Methodists were holding regular meetings at the Beattyville court-house, and the Baptists a few months later inaugurated meetings at regular intervals. A Roman Catholic priest had been in town, view-ing the situation and looking for a site for a church. "Such things are perhaps among the necessary results of a railroad and more open communication," reported the secretary of the Board of Missions that year, "but they show us the paramount necessity of having a church building which will attract strangers and be a comfort and help to those already here."[22]

After Walkley's resignation and removal to the Diocese of Iowa in December, 1889, the Lee County Mission was without services of a clergyman for a year and a half. In February, 1890, it was hard hit by the "worst flood in the history of Lee County, "resulting in extensive damage to church property in both Beattyville and Proc-tor. The devastation brought about by the flood caused Bishop Dudley to choose a spot well above the high water mark as a site for the proposed new St. Thomas' Church, Beattyville. The Bishop and Board of Missions made every effort to supply the mission with clergymen during this time, but in their endeavor "to get only one who was peculiarly fitted for the important work," they were delayed.[23] Meanwhile the services of the church and of the Sunday school were regularly conducted for a time by Mr. Thomas Pryse, and afterwards by Mr. Joseph W. Chalmers, principal of the Episco-pal Academy at Beattyville.

In June, 1891, the Reverend J. E. H. Galbraith of Arkansas, having accepted Bishop Dudley's appointment, entered upon his duties as missionary in Lee County. Under his able ministry, attend-ance at services improved steadily in both towns, and the schools flourished. Although continuing to receive aid from throughout the Diocese and some from without, the mission gained in financial strength during the next few years. The greatest need was for a proper church building at Beattyville. The Girls' Sewing Guild had collected more than $200 to help furnish it when built.[24]

On June 21, 1894, the cornerstone of St. Thomas' Church was laid

[22] *Ibid.*, p. 100.
[23] *Journal*, 1890, p. 84.
[24] *Journal*, 1893, p. 107.

by Bishop Dudley. The occasion was his last official visit to Lee County; the next year the new Diocese of Lexington embraced the eastern half of the state, under the ecclesiastical jurisdiction of the Bishop of Lexington, the Right Reverend Lewis William Burton. The first service in the beautiful little stone church was held on August 30, 1896, the Church people from Proctor uniting with those of Beattyville in divine worship and in the reception of the Holy Communion at the hands of Bishop Burton.[25] In his parochial report that year, the Bishop of Lexington stated, "It is proper to make very grateful acknowledgments to the Right Reverend Bishop of Kentucky for furnishing all the money necessary in order to complete the church according to its original tasteful design, and to supply it with all the appurtenances and appliances for the orderly worship of our Church and the prosecution of its work. The church bears the name of St. Thomas in suggestion of this generous patronage and as a memorial of the twenty years Episcopate of the present Bishop of Kentucky over the undivided Diocese, in the course of which the Lee County Mission shared particularly in his earnest attention and free-handed support."[26]

EMMANUEL MISSION, WINCHESTER

As early as 1859 Bishop Smith and the Board of Diocesan Missions were interested in establishing the Church in Winchester. That year the Reverend John Austen Merrick, rector of St. Peter's Church, Paris, and the Reverend James H. Morrison, rector of Christ Church, Lexington, were appointed by the Central Convocation to visit Winchester[27] and report to the next meeting the prospects of establishing a mission station there. B. B. Smith was no stranger to Clark County, having traveled extensively in the middle and eastern portions of the state, and tradition has it that he had held the first Episcopal services in the Methodist Church there some years earlier. During the 1870's the Reverend Walter Tearne, rector of the

---

[25] *Journal, Diocese of Lexington,* 1897, p. 22.
[26] *Ibid.*
[27] *Journal, Diocese of Kentucky,* 1859, p. 25.

Church of the Ascension, Mt. Sterling, had held occasional services in the town, as had his successor, the Reverend J. S. Johnston.

It was, however, during the episcopacy of Bishop Dudley that the Church was formally established in Winchester. In October, 1884, the Convocation of Lexington was held there in the Baptist Church, borrowed for the occasion. The clergy present were Bishop Dudley, the Reverend Thomas Tidball of Lexington, W. G. McCready of Versailles, S. S. Pentz of Richmond, and Henry H. Sneed of Mt. Sterling. During the four-day meeting tentative plans were made for the establishment of a mission in the town. Early the next year the Reverend William H. Hampton, a young deacon appointed by Bishop Dudley, was holding services there, in the courthouse, the Baptist and Methodist churches, or the homes of interested persons. He reported an average attendance of seventy-five and the hope that a church might be erected.[28] In 1886 the Reverend Edwin A. Penick and the Reverend William G. McCready conducted a week-long mission in the Methodist Church, arousing much interest in the Episcopal Church.

In January, 1887, the Board of Diocesan Missions appointed the Reverend Henry H. Sneed to take charge of Winchester and hold four services each month. Sneed visited the town on March 10 and again on March 14 and took the first real steps toward establishing a permanent mission. He met with Mr. Francis Hubbard Dudley, a communicant who had long been interested in building a church in the town, and received from him the names of a number of persons who would give their support to Sneed. The missionary set about to find a place to hold services, and the courthouse was kindly offered to him by the county judge.

On the morning of March 27, 1887, Sneed left Mt. Sterling in the company of Mr. Harry Campbell, his daughter, Miss Ollie Campbell, and Dr. William D. VanAntwerp, all members of Ascension Church, and drove the fifteen miles to Winchester. At 11:00 A.M., Sneed held services in the courthouse and administered the Holy Communion to fourteen persons. Among those receiving were Mr.

[28] *Journal,* 1886, p. 31.

Dudley, Mr. and Mrs. Charles Baillie, Benjamin F. Buckner, Mrs. Chilton Allen, Mrs. Joel Frasier, Mrs. Louis A. Saarback, Mrs. R. L. Clinkenbeard,[29] and the Presbyterian minister's wife.[30]

Again on April 10, Easter Day, at 3:00 P.M., Sneed held services in the courthouse for a large congregation. He baptized Mr. Elcon Everett Harris, who had long shown an interest in the Church. By now services were held on two Sundays in each month and on two weekdays.

On Tuesday, April 19, Bishop Dudley visited Winchester and preached to a large congregation. He confirmed Mr. Harris, baptized the previous week, and Dr. Chilton Allen, who was baptized just prior to his confirmation. The need of a church building was apparent, and Mr. Dudley donated a lot on Hickman Street, just two blocks from the courthouse. Bishop Dudley and the Reverend Edwin Penick raised the money for the erection of a church building. Emmanuel Mission was officially constituted on March 3, 1888, and had the following officers: Francis H. Dudley, warden and treasurer; C. R. Baillie, clerk; and R. W. Jones, Dr. Chilton Allen, O. C. Ashbrooke, and J. H. Frasier, committee.[31]

On Tuesday, May 1, 1888, the new church was opened for worship. The Reverend Mr. Sneed celebrated the Holy Communion, assisted by Bishop Dudley. Trinity Church, Covington, had presented a very good pulpit and twenty-two well-cushioned pews. The Bible was presented by Mrs. Kimbrough of the Methodist Church, and the Communion set, used for the first time at this service, was the gift of Mrs. Joel H. Frasier.[32]

Sneed described the church as "simple and tasteful, plain and unornamented."[33] The neat little wooden church had a seating capacity of two hundred, and Sneed felt that it would answer the use of the congregation for some years. A Sunday school was organized on May 6 and classes were conducted weekly.

[29] Mrs. Charles C. Hendrick's, "History of Emmanuel Church, Winchester.", November, 1968.
[30] H. H. Sneed, "Parish Histories," prepared by Miss Kate Scudder, Box 120, Archives, Diocese of Lexington, University of Kentucky Library.
[31] Hendricks, "History of Emmanuel Church."
[32] Ibid.
[33] Journal, 1888, p. 60.

"I feel that the whole field is promising, that the Church is extending her borders, that the barriers of prejudice and ignorance are gradually giving way and that the people are beginning to realize in the Church a living witness, from the beginning till now, of the blessed truths of our salvation," stated the devoted Sneed the next year.[34]

In the summer of 1890 the church building was improved, a chancel and vestry room were constructed, and chancel furniture was ordered.[35] In just three years, under the charge of the faithful missionary, Emmanuel Mission had grown and prospered. There were but six communicants when he came, and now there were twenty-four; there were nine families, and the whole number of souls was fifty-one.[36]

In 1891 Sneed resigned the rectorship of Mt. Sterling and gave up Winchester as well, in order to begin a mission in Middlesborough. Although the rectorship was vacant throughout most of the following year, interest was maintained by means of missions sponsored by the General Missionary of the Diocese. The Reverend W. G. McCready once more conducted a successful mission in June, 1892.[37]

On August 1, 1892, the Reverend E. V. Evans assumed charge of Mt. Sterling and Winchester, dividing his time between the two. He resigned in June of the following year, and the Reverend William Hugh McGee, lately assistant at Trinity Church, Covington, became missionary-in-charge, remaining until 1894. Emmanuel Mission was without the services of a clergyman when it became a part of the new Diocese of Lexington in 1895, but the Reverend George Abbitt, from Richmond, Virginia, took charge in November, 1896, and remained four years.

CALVARY CHURCH, ASHLAND

The important and growing town of Ashland, on the Ohio River in the extreme northeastern corner of Kentucky, prior to 1885 had seen

[34] *Journal*, 1889, p. 101.
[35] *Journal*, 1890, p. 84.
[36] *Ibid.* Summary of Parochial Reports for Year Ending April 30, 1890.
[37] *Journal*, 1893, p. 75.

only spasmodic and seemingly futile attempts to establish an Episcopal Church with any hope of permanence. Both Bishop Smith in the 1850's and Cummins in the 1870's had realized the desirability of planting the Church in this rich mineral section of the state, but their efforts had not brought lasting results. In the nearby town of Catlettsburg, a mission called St. John's had been organized in 1860 and enjoyed a brief success for several years.

The first Episcopal service ever held in the region then covered by Greenup, Carter, and Lawrence counties was in Ashland on Easter evening, 1857, in the dining hall of a large, unfinished hotel. The congregation numbered two hundred persons. The officiating clergyman was the Reverend W. E. French, rector of Christ Church, Ironton, Ohio, who at the request of Bishop Smith had made "a slight missionary exploration of the Iron Region of Kentucky."[38] The policy of clergymen from neighboring dioceses assisting one another in filling mission stations and struggling parishes without rectors was not unusual in the West at this time. In the adjacent villages of Catlettsburg and Ashland, then in Greenup County,[39] he found six or eight decidedly Episcopal families and determined at once to hold services each Sunday afternoon at 3:00 o'clock. His visitations to the Kentucky Diocese continued for over a year, and his congregations remained large and attentive. On one visit he baptized four children, and shortly thereafter three adults made the short journey to Ironton to receive the Holy Rite of Confirmation at the hands of Bishop Bedell.

The Reverend Mr. French's flourishing mission in Ashland was visited that year by the Reverend John West, a temporary resident of the Diocese of Kentucky, who was at this time General Agent of the newly organized Central Convocation. He made a four-thousand-mile missionary journey through Kentucky in order to establish missions. In his 1858 report to the convention he noted that a

---

[38] "A Little History of the Church in Ashland," written in long hand on several sheets of paper by a communicant of Calvary, Ashland. No date, no name. Quoted from the old register-scrapbook combined of Christ Church, Ironton, Ohio, from a lengthy article by the Reverend W. E. French, rector, on "Missions in the Iron Regions," published in the *Western Episcopalian*.

[39] Boyd County was founded in 1860 out of parts of Greenup, Carter, and Lawrence counties.

mission had been organized at Ashland "under the most flattering auspices."[40] Missionary funds soon failed, however, and so did the first attempt to establish the Church in the Iron Region of Kentucky.

Still another Ohio clergyman, again the rector of the Ironton parish, the Reverend Henry Blackaller, interested himself in the towns across the river and in October, 1859, began holding services in Catlettsburg every other Sabbath in the Methodist Church building, kindly loaned to him for the purpose. In the spring of the following year, St. John's Mission was founded. The very next year, having already met the canonical requirements, it was admitted into union with the convention. Appropriations were made to keep up occasional services at Catlettsburg, now the county seat of newly formed Boyd County, as well as at Ashland, also now in that county. Reporting at the 1861 convention on the new parish of St. John's, the Ohio clergyman remarked, "A very hopeful indication of the final establishment of our Church here is that our services have been so acceptable that the house is usually nearly filled on Sunday morning, there being no services elsewhere, and more than half filled in the evening."[41] Mr. Blackaller also officiated every Wednesday evening and Sunday afternoon at Ashland, where there were eight communicants and as many families of the Church, holding services in the Presbyterian Church. During 1862 the Catlettsburg mission and the small congregation in Ashland passed through severe trials and were barely able to survive. The Reverend Mr. Blackaller continued to officiate for the remainder of the year and for a few months of 1863, often preaching to soldiers in the area and attending the sick and wounded in the temporary hospital and in private houses, praying with them and giving them tracts, which he also sent to the large hospital in Ashland. His primary concern was the lack of a suitable place of worship, but the Diocese was unable to supply any funds toward this end. For the remainder of the war, it could only struggle on with more faith and more self-denial, and pray and hope for better times.

During the latter years of the war, Catlettsburg and Ashland

[40] *Journal*, 1858.
[41] *Journal*, 1861, p. 36.

were not visited by Episcopal clergymen, but early in 1865 the Reverend Samuel D. Tompkins, having recently left Mt. Sterling, became rector of the Catlettsburg parish and opened a parish school there. For a while it appeared that the parish would survive, but in 1867, when Assistant Bishop Cummins visited there, he found it in a very feeble condition. That same year Mr. Tompkins gave up his charge. After remaining vacant for the next two years, the Catletts-burg station was supplied between 1870 and 1873 with a succession of missionaries from Ohio and West Virginia, but none officiated long enough to attain any lasting results.

The internal strife within the Diocese of Kentucky during 1873 and Bishop Cummins' subsequent departure brought a halt to missionary endeavors, and the Board of Missions ceased to function. St. John's, Catlettsburg, was one of the small parishes which never quite recovered from the lack of interest in the missions during this crucial period. By the time Bishop Dudley arrived in Kentucky early in 1875, it had become a defunct parish, and services in Ashland had also entirely ceased.

Bishop Dudley, however, almost immediately turned his attention to the woeful state of the diocesan missions, and it did not take long for his great zeal in this cause to make itself felt. The Board of Missions was revived and was soon infused with new vigor. A happier state of affairs had at last come to the Diocese of Kentucky.

It was, however, to be another decade before the new Assistant Bishop would be able to seriously consider the plight of the Church in northeastern Kentucky. He had visited Boyd County in the spring of 1877 and preached in the Methodist Church in Ashland, but he was not to return to the region until 1885. During that period he stated, "I have not been to Catlettsburg or Ashland because I think it is a vain thing for me to make a visit of two or three days when I have not the means to leave behind me a regular missionary."[42] Bishop Dudley ever contended that it was better to have no minister than one unsuited to the work of a particular parish. And so the work of the Church in the northeastern corner of Kentucky had to wait.

[42] *Journal,* 1878, p. 64.

Upon the death of Benjamin Bosworth Smith on May 31, 1884, Thomas Underwood Dudley became Bishop of Kentucky, and a year later he visited Ashland to confirm ten persons. The following spring he again visited the small congregation of twenty active communicants who, during the past year, had rented a vacant storehouse and fitted it decently with desks and seats and organ. There they conducted Sunday school and held occasional Church services. They had begun to despair, however, of ever having a regular minister. In his address to the convention of 1886, the Bishop stated, "Their poverty makes it impossible that they can support a man of experience and force, such a man as would be fitted to begin the work of the Church there; and I have promised that a man shall be sent there. Dear brothers, help me to fulfil my promise."[43]

Before another year had passed, Bishop Dudley had fulfilled his promise to the little flock of faithful Churchmen in Ashland. However, it was no experienced and seasoned clergyman whom he sent, but a young deacon, who had been assistant minister of the Church of the Ascension, Frankfort, for the past three years and who was to prove peculiarly well suited to his new charge. The Reverend William Henderson Hampton took charge of the new little mission, called Calvary Church after the Louisville parish of that name, in March, 1887, and was ordained as priest the next year. He held services for the congregation wherever convenient, usually in his own home, until 1889, when "On Easter morn," in the Bishop's words, "the faithful and indefatigable missionary was permitted to gather his little flock about the altar in the completed building to 'keep the feast.' "[44] At 7:00 o'clock on that happy morn, the Holy Communion was celebrated with great thankfulness and praise, and at the 10:30 service the church was crowded with worshipers. Three hundred people assembled in the church, the estimated seating capacity of which was two hundred and fifty. Again at the evening service the church was filled. The missionary reported at the convention the following month, "Since worshiping in our Church the congregations have increased fully one hundred per cent. The

[43] *Journal*, 1886, p. 70.
[44] *Journal*, 1889, p. 82.

outlook for the Church is bright and we have every reason to be encouraged."[45]

During the next few years the town grew and the Church grew —in numbers, usefulness, and in the esteem and affection of the people, under the wise guidance and faithful work of the missionary. By 1891, Calvary Mission had become, during the four years of its existence, "a power for good, recognized as such and felt by the entire community."[46]

During 1892 the church was closed for nine weeks due to the sickness of the missionary, and in October of that year the Reverend Mr. Hampton gave up the charge of the mission which he had established and maintained until it became one of the most successful of the Church's missions in the Diocese. Shortly thereafter he became one of the Diocese's general missionaries, and the next year left Kentucky to take charge of Christ Church, Ironton, Ohio.[47]

The Reverend Andrew Fleming, recently of Pittsburgh, became priest-in-charge of Calvary Mission in October, 1892, and served the congregation faithfully for six years. He also was headmaster of the Eastern Kentucky High School, afterwards the Ashland School for Girls. The school prospered for a number of years, but after the division of the Diocese in 1895, it became obvious that a change of location was necessary. A few years later it was transferred to Versailles, to become Margaret Hall.

Calvary Church, Ashland, which began as a small mission of the Diocese of Kentucky during the Dudley era, was to occupy a place of importance as one of the most active and dynamic parishes of the newly formed Diocese of Lexington. Nothing remains today of the small building which was the first church, for fire destroyed it in 1898, but the same spirit and zeal lives on in the beautiful Gothic structure which today is Calvary Church.

CHRIST MISSION, SOMERSET

An Episcopal service had never been held in Pulaski County before June 1, 1891, when the Reverend William Sheppard, rector of

---

[45] *Ibid.*, p. 98.
[46] *Journal*, 1891, p. 77.
[47] *Journal*, 1893, p. 75.

Trinity Church, Danville, preached in Somerset, the county seat. He found there half a dozen Episcopal families and established Christ Mission.

From the beginning, Sheppard felt strongly that interest here warranted the permanent organization of a mission and the building of a house of worship. In the spring of 1892 he reported to the council, "Place a good, earnest worker at Somerset and in a very short time we will have a strong mission."[48] The dedicated missionary preached often in other towns near Danville, such as Harrodsburg and Stanford. In the summer of 1892 he died after a brief illness and was succeeded at Danville by the Reverend Frank Cooley, who also assumed charge of the Somerset mission.

By 1894 Christ Mission had become an organized mission of the Diocese of Kentucky. The "whole number of souls" was twenty-seven and the communicants, twelve.[49] Cooley held services twice a month on Thursday and Sunday whenever able. "The faithful workers in Somerset are untiring in their zeal," he stated in his convention report in 1895. In the summer of that year Bishop Dudley preached in Somerset and confirmed two persons, noting that the prospects were bright.

Christ Mission became a mission of the new Diocese of Lexington in 1895, and Bishop Burton preached and administered the Holy Communion in the newly erected chapel in the spring of 1896.

SAINT STEPHEN'S MISSION, SIDEVIEW

In Sideview, a small rural village in Montgomery County, seven and a half miles from Mt. Sterling near the Bourbon County line, a Sunday school was organized in the summer of 1885 by the Reverend Henry H. Sneed, rector of the Church of the Ascension, Mt. Sterling. From this small beginning, interest in the Episcopal Church was aroused and, in July, 1887, Mr. Sneed began holding services twice a month in a neighborhood schoolhouse to a congregation of men and women who had never before heard a "liturgical service."

[48] *Journal*, 1892, p. 121.
[49] *Journal*, 1895, p. 145.

Interest in the Prayer Book services was such that the need of a proper church edifice was soon apparent to Sneed if the Church were to have any future there. The Board of Diocesan Missions approving the establishment of a mission there, Sneed set about gathering a congregation, and in November, 1888, a small "churchly building," designed to hold about one hundred and fifty persons, was erected and paid for. The first service in the new St. Stephen's Mission, as it was called, was held on the third Sunday in November, and there was a large attendance. Sunday school was open every Sunday and services conducted by Sneed every other Sunday. A stone font was presented by the women of a church in Exeter, New Hampshire, and a Communion set by the women of Trinity Church, Danville. Mr. Sneed reported to the 1889 convention, "The interest manifested by the people of this community, all of whom are outside the Church, save two, the readiness with which they join in the services of the Church which are rendered with a heartiness surpassing even some Church congregations, the increased attendance is evidence that the expenditure in building and furnishing the church has been wise."[50]

During October, 1889, a two-week mission was conducted in Sideview by the Reverend Mr. Sneed and the two general missionaries, the Reverend W. G. McCready and the Reverend William H. Hampton. During this mission, Mr. Sneed baptized nine persons, six adults and three children.[51] St. Stephen's was consecrated on April 18, 1890, by Bishop Dudley, and four persons were confirmed by him.[52] That year it became an organized mission of the Diocese of Kentucky.

Until the late summer of 1890 the little church at Sideview, under the loving care of its founder, H. H. Sneed, continued to prosper, even though only a handful of its congregation became Episcopalians. Of these the two most interested families were those of Mr. Corwin Anderson and a Mr. Haggs,[53] who generously supported the mission. In August the Reverend Mr. Sneed removed from Mt.

[50] *Journal*, 1889, pp. 100–101.
[51] Sneed, "Parish Histories."
[52] *Journal*, 1890, p. 66.
[53] Sneed.

Sterling at the request of Bishop Dudley and organized St. Mary's Mission, Middlesborough, giving up Sideview at the same time.

The little mission, although listed as organized through 1891, ceased to function. It was either closed or was occupied by other bodies of Christians until it was revived once more in the spring of 1897 as a mission of the Diocese of Lexington.[54]

ST. MARY'S CHURCH, MIDDLESBOROUGH

In 1888 the Louisville and Nashville Railroad entered mountainous Bell County and the industrial boom was on. Almost overnight, the new town of Middlesborough sprang up and spread over a good part of the Yellow Creek Valley. An industrial and mining town, it soon exceeded Pineville, the county seat, in population.

Before that year the little hamlet of Cumberland Gap, at the foot of the famous pass where the boundary lines of Kentucky, Tennessee, and Virginia meet, was an isolated spot in the heart of the Cumberland Mountains, accessible only by wagon-breaking roads and footpaths. It consisted of about half a dozen homes and a general store. Three years earlier, in 1885, a Scotch-Canadian timber and mineral expert, Alexander A. Arthur, while prospecting in the area, found evidences of great coal and iron ore deposits. He formed a syndicate to buy up some of the land in order to exploit the untouched natural resources. His plans to construct railroads, build a mile-long tunnel under Cumberland Gap, and create a mining and manufacturing city in the vicinity seemed too stupendous for the syndicate to undertake, whereupon Arthur went, the following year, to London, England, where he had some acquaintances in financial circles, and persuaded a number of distinguished Englishmen to join in his scheme. English mining experts were sent to the Cumberland Gap field to investigate and render opinions on the natural resources, and their favorable reports resulted in the formation of The American Association, Limited, a company designed to carry out the extensive plans proposed by Arthur. The necessary funds were supplied through the flotation of stock. Arthur bought

[54] *Journal, Diocese of Lexington,* 1897, p. 29.

from the prominent Colson family of Bell County almost the entire Valley, and from them and others nearly 100,000 acres of mountain lands.

Construction of the Cumberland Gap tunnel, directly beneath the famous Wilderness Road, and the building of extensive railroads, began. Coincident with the beginning of these works, the town of Middlesborough was born. Soon men of all trades and callings entered the Yellow Creek Valley; apparently men from every city and town in Kentucky and almost every state were represented. Many were rugged and boisterous speculators, not unlike the gold prospectors in the far West; many were adventurers. Among them were a host of Englishmen and some Scotsmen, who had followed Arthur's lead. There were artisans, clerks, and merchants, as well as a few scions of wealthy and aristocratic families to whom this was a great adventure. All of these made up the bustling new town, which until now had been a quasi-wilderness.

Gradually coal and iron mines were opened, coke ovens built, steel mills and blast furnaces put up, and other industries established. A large and luxurious hotel, the Middlesborough, and several smaller ones were erected. Within six months after the completion of the railroads and the tunnel under the Gap, Cumberland Avenue, the main business street, was lined on both sides for a dozen blocks with stores and office buildings, almost all of wood. From here the town spread out in all directions and now occupied half the Valley.[55]

The Episcopal Church moved vigorously into this rapidly developing area. In 1889, the Right Reverend Thomas Underwood Dudley, accompanied by the Right Reverend Charles Clifton Penick, formerly Missionary Bishop of Africa and then residing in Louisville, traveled to Middlesborough to look over the prospects of establishing a mission there. Very probably Bishop Dudley had been approached in the matter by one or more of the Englishmen residing in the area. At any rate, on June 23, the bishops held services

---

[55] Charles Blanton Roberts, "The Building of Middlesborough, A Notable Epoch in Eastern Kentucky History," *Filson Club Quarterly*, Vol. 7, No. 1 (1933), reprinted in *History of Bell County. Kentucky*, by Henry Harvey Fuson, II, 559 (New York, 1947).

and preached to a large gathering in a printing office near the corner of 19th Street and Cumberland Avenue, becoming convinced of the practicality of planting the Church in this growing town.[56]

At Bishop Dudley's request, the Reverend Henry Harrison Sneed, rector of the Church of the Ascension, Mt. Sterling, visited Middlesborough on August 17, 1890, and held services in the Baptist Church morning and evening; the next morning he presided at a meeting in the Middlesborough Hotel, attended by a large number of interested residents of the area, and the preliminary steps were taken toward organization of a mission, to be known as St. Mary's. Money was subscribed both for the support of the mission and for the building of a church, and the names of several men were recommended to the Bishop as a church committee. Shortly thereafter, Bishop Dudley appointed the following persons as officers of the newly constituted mission, to serve until Easter Day, 1891: C. M. Woodbury, warden; F. C. Fisher, clerk; George Heid Black, treasurer; and Messrs. Henry C. Hudgins, Charles H. Waring, C. W. Gronson, and Frank Watts, committeemen.[57]

On the last day of that month, at a service held in the Baptist Church, the Reverend Mr. Sneed formally instituted St. Mary's Mission, a goodly number being present. The missionary, meanwhile having resigned the rectorship of the Mt. Sterling parish, officially took charge of the new mission at this time, and two weeks later moved to Middlesborough and began his work. The church committee pledged him $1,000 and the Board of Diocesan Missions allowed him a $300 stipend. Nearly one hundred communicants were enrolled, and the committee made plans to erect at once a house of worship on a lot on Edgewood Road, deeded to them by The Middlesborough Town Lands Company, a subsidiary of the American Association. A three-room cottage was moved to the rear of the lot, and five rooms were added, so that it could be used by the missionary as a parsonage.

In the spring of 1890, a disastrous fire almost annihilated Middles-

[56] *Journal, Diocese of Kentucky*, 1891, p. 78.
[57] Courtesy of Mrs. Glenn Greene, formerly of Middlesborough. From a speech delivered by Mr. D. G. Hinks, now in possession of Mrs. Roy Hutchinson, Middlesborough.

borough. Out of the ashes arose a new city, safer and of more enduring material. Business flourished in the town, and many wealthy and important personages, including prominent London stockbrokers and an occasional duke or duchess, visited here. In November, 1890, the cornerstone of St. Mary's Church was laid by the Reverend Mr. Sneed, in the presence of a large gathering. It was formally opened for worship on the first Sunday in Lent, February 15, 1891, with full Morning Prayer and Holy Communion. A few months later Mr. Sneed attended the diocesan convention with a glowing report of success and the names of ninety-six communicants, sixty men and thirty-six women, on his register.[58] The church was consecrated by Bishop Dudley on October 4, 1890, the entire five-thousand dollar building cost having been paid.

The first officers of the mission, appointed in 1891, were: C. M. Woodbury, warden; C. W. Bronson, secretary; H. C. Hudgins, treasurer; and C. W. Waring, Frank Watts, Charles G. West, George McLaughlin, and General H. B. Hayward. Prominent among the early communicants was Mr. A. A. Arthur, who gave to St. Mary's its fine bell from Troy, New York, the altar, and the chairs.[59]

St. Mary's Church had been built and consecrated in the midst of a calamity which, though it originated in England, brought financial ruin to many citizens of the Kentucky town and doomed it to years of stagnation. News of the failure of the Baring Brothers' Bank of London, in which many of the English investors in the American Association lost heavily, reached Middlesborough in the latter part of 1890. Panic seized the town, and approximately one half the population vacated, many returning to England. Had not the Episcopal Church been established prior to this troublous period, it might not have come to Bell County.

Despite this period of extreme financial distress, the Church fared well. The Reverend Mr. Sneed devoted his full labors to his pastoral duties and won the love and respect of the whole community. There were now two services on Sunday, the Holy Communion being celebrated at 8:00 in the morning, and holy days were observed.

[58] *Journal,* 1891, p. 61.
[59] Sneed.

Early in 1892 Sneed completed a chapel at the Mingo Mines, just over the Tennessee line, with a capacity of one hundred and fifty persons, at which the Bishop remarked, "I believe that this chapel is situated in the Diocese of Tennessee but I have no fear that the Bishop of Tennessee will quarrel with us for having erected it."[60]

The Reverend Mr. Sneed accompanied his church into the new Diocese of Lexington in 1895, carrying on his good work there until the beginning of 1898, when he resigned to become rector of Holy Trinity Church, Georgetown, and missionary at Nicholasville and Lawrenceburg. Middlesborough, while never recovering the affluence of the 1888–1890 period, became some years later a normal, prosperous community, ringed by the beautiful Cumberland Mountains. Only the nomenclature of the streets—Cirencester, Glouchester, Dorchester, Exeter, Winchester—remains today to attest to its earlier English influence, as does the beautiful little church, reminiscent of those which dot the countryside of rural England.

SAINT JOHN'S CHURCH, COVINGTON

Among the new missions founded during the Dudley era fall a group which were parochial rather than diocesan. While they were not the first of this type in the Diocese (there were several in Louisville, one in Frankfort and two in Covington), they were the only ones founded in the eastward part of the Diocese during the Dudley years. The first of these was Saint John's Church, Covington.

The only mission of Trinity Church, Covington, to attain parochial status was St. John's Chapel, built in the fall of 1890 in Covington, during the ministry of the Reverend Frank Woods Baker.

In the spring of 1890 Mr. Baker presented to the vestry of Trinity Church a proposal that the property in Milldale be sold and the proceeds applied to the purchase of new property. A committee composed of Messrs. J. W. Baker, James S. Wayne, Sackett Mead, and William R. Benton[61] was appointed to select a site for the new

[60] *Journal,* 1892, p. 52.
[61] Sneed.

chapel. They selected three lots belonging to the Longworth estate, on the corner of Scott and Eighteenth Streets. In his parochial report the rector explained, "Trinity Church is situated nearest the Ohio River of all Protestant churches in Covington. As the growth of the city is back from the river, it became necessary for self-preservation to have a chapel further up-town."[62]

A debt of $6,100 was placed upon Trinity Church.

The first service held in the new chapel was on the day after Christmas, 1890. Officiating were the Reverend Mr. Baker; his brother and assistant, Dr. Walter Baker; and the Reverend Reverdy Estill, rector of St. Paul's Church, Newport. St. John's was a handsome wooden structure of modern English rustic architecture, with nine double windows in six colors and a triple chancel window. The furniture and organ had previously belonged to Milldale Chapel. Eighty-five communicants of Trinity Church withdrew and attended the new mission, the location being more convenient to their newer uptown homes.

St. John's was governed by a board of seven trustees, four of whom were elected by the vestry of Trinity Church, and three of whom were appointed by the rector of the parish from among those worshiping at St. John's. The original Board of Trustees were: John W. Baker, F. P. Woolcott, D. N. Comingore, and W. D. Spalding, from Trinity vestry; A. G. Simrall, F. M. McDonald, and J. F. Gedge from St. John's congregation.[63]

Services at St. John's were conducted by the rector of Trinity Church or his assistant. The Reverend William Hugh McGee became assistant rector of Trinity Church on October 1, 1891, having been ordained in St. John's Chapel the previous month. He was placed in charge of the new mission, and, although canonically assistant at Trinity, he was the first actual resident minister at St. John's. The Reverend Robert Gratton Noland became rector of Trinity that same year and officiated at the mission from time to time.

At first, St. John's adopted the system of renting its pews and continued that plan of collecting revenues until April, 1893, when

[62] *Journal,* 1891, pp. 96–97.
[63] Sneed.

by unanimous vote the trustees decided to make it a free church. The parent parish contributed funds to cover any deficit in the running expenses.[64]

The mission became so prosperous and so numerically strong that on January 30, 1894, Bishop Dudley consented to its separation from Trinity Church. The next month St. John's became an organized mission of the Diocese of Kentucky. The Reverend Mr. McGee having resigned, the Bishop appointed, in April, 1894, the Reverend William Worthington, newly arrived in the Diocese from Connecticut, as priest-in-charge. By the spring of the next year the mission had completed arrangements to pay Trinity Church $4,500 for the church property and had made the first payment of $400.[65]

St. John's Mission became St. John's Parish in 1895, and the first vestry was elected on April 15. It was composed of Messrs. A. G. Simrall, senior warden; James P. Weller, junior warden; Frank Gofton, clerk; F. K. Ransom, treasurer; and William Warner, J. F. Gedge, W. N. Hamilton, and Albert Brockman.[66] The Reverend Mr. Worthington accompanied St. John's into the new Diocese of Lexington. Seventy-nine families were among the 218 "souls" on the parish register.[67]

ST. ANDREW'S MISSION

St. Andrew's Mission, Lexington, founded by Christ Church in 1880, was the fourth mission established for Negroes in the state. Its founding was due largely to the efforts of the rector of Christ Church, the Reverend Thomas Allen Tidball, and a layman, A. J. Campbell, who, like Bishop Dudley, were vitally interested in the evangelization and education of the colored race.

A building on the corner of Fourth and Upper Streets, formerly belonging to the Disciples of Christ,[68] was purchased by Christ

[64] Ibid.
[65] Journal, 1895, p. 128.
[66] Sneed.
[67] Journal of the First Annual Council of the Diocese of Lexington, 1896, pp. 84–85.
[68] The Reverend Egerton E. Hall, "Saint Andrew's: An Opportunity," a paper reprinted from The Spirit of Missions (No issue or date given).

Church and completely renovated and fitted for Episcopal worship. The location was within easy reach of all its members. For the first year or two of its existence, St. Andrew's Mission was financed entirely by Christ Church, and services were conducted by Mr. Tidball or some other clergyman resident in Lexington. Mr. Campbell assisted with the Sunday school. Bishop Dudley made the first of his official annual visitations on May 1, 1881, and confirmed three persons. He took a special interest in St. Andrew's and held it up as an example of parochial missionary work among the Negro race, urging other parishes to emulate Christ Church.

In 1882 the Reverend J. B. McConnell became the first of a series of Negro deacons to take charge of the mission, also acting as principal of the Church Street colored school. A West Indian by birth, he was educated in Europe and for four years taught school in Memphis, where he was induced by Bishop Quintard to prepare himself for the sacred ministry. He came to St. Andrew's from Nashville.[69]

In 1884 the Reverend Hannibal S. Henderson, from the Diocese of North Carolina, assumed charge, and under him the mission flourished. His support was given chiefly by the General Missionary Society in New York, but Christ Church Parish and the Board of Diocesan Missions for Colored People, created in 1883 at Dudley's request, supplemented the appropriation. Henderson further increased his income by becoming principal of the Negro school. The little mission continued to make "slow but sure progress." He visited the North in 1885 and succeeded in getting $1,000 subscribed for payment of the debt on the church and for repairing the building.[70] He was respected by the entire community. His little church was crowded early on the morning of March 24, 1885, when the Reverend S. S. Pentz of Danville joined him in holy matrimony to Miss Ella T. Smith.[71] Henderson performed ten baptisms during that year, and Bishop Dudley confirmed seven on his spring visitation. The Sunday school, begun by Campbell, now numbered 101 scholars. Prospects were bright. Then tragedy struck, for on June 23,

[69] *Lexington Daily Transcript*, July 3, 1882, p. 4.
[70] *Journal, Diocese of Kentucky*, 1885, p. 84.
[71] *Lexington Daily Transcript*, March 25, 1885, p. 2.

1887, just three years after he had assumed charge, Hannibal Henderson died of pulmonary consumption.[72]

After Henderson's death the work at St. Andrew's languished for a time. Once again the rector of Christ Church, now the Reverend Edward H. Ward, conducted regular Sunday evening services, while Campbell once more took charge of the Sunday school. The congregation averaged thirty to fifty and the Sunday school, thirty.

In 1892 the second of the more notable Negro deacons assumed charge. During the ministry of the Reverend John G. Urling, transferred from the Diocese of Albany, St. Andrew's grew in numbers and slowly progressed. A day school was begun and soon numbered fifty-two scholars, most of whom were from Baptist and Methodist homes. Wrote the young deacon in his 1894 parochial report, "The progress of the work on the whole is encouraging, though that progress is slow taking into consideration the tremendous obstacles by which we are confronted from the gross ignorance of my colored Baptist brethren, and from the irrational notions which they entertain and instill in the minds of their ignorant followers respecting the Episcopal Church."[73] So highly regarded was Urling that the Standing Committee of the Diocese granted dispensation of time and candidature, and Bishop Dudley advanced him to the priesthood in May, 1894. It appeared that once again, with a dedicated and zealous minister in charge, the little mission would prosper and grow, but once more tragedy struck. On April 26, 1895, after only three years service, John Urling died suddenly from heart failure.[74]

Again the little mission suffered, and for nearly six months there was no service of any kind held there. The people were disheartened. Then on November 1, the Reverend Charles H. Thompson, D.D., a Negro priest from the Diocese of Georgia, took charge. There were nine families and fifty-seven "souls" connected with the mission, only twenty-one of whom were communicants. He found the building so dilapidated that he deemed it useless to try to gather a congregation there when Negro churches of other persuasions had neat, well-built houses of worship. He therefore had such repairs

[72] *Ibid.*, June 24, 1887, p. 2.
[73] *Journal*, 1894, p. 146.
[74] *The Press-Transcript*, Lexington, April 27, 1895.

and alterations made as necessary. The next month St. Andrew's became a mission of the new Diocese of Lexington, and the Reverend Dr. Thompson brought the number of clergymen canonically resident to seventeen.

THE MISSION OF THE GOOD SHEPHERD

The Mission of the Good Shepherd was established by Christ Church, Lexington, in July, 1888, and by the following December an "elegant" chapel had been erected on South Broadway and opened for services.

The rector of Christ Church, the Reverend Edward H. Ward, and the vestry had long realized the advisability of establishing a mission somewhere in Lexington and in 1887 a committee had been appointed to look into the matter of securing a lot. It was decided to build on East Third Street on the cemetery property owned by the parish, but the current lessee would not give his consent. Mr. J. A. Hayman, a prominent layman of Christ Church offered the use of a cottage which he owned at 302 South Broadway, and there on the third Sunday in July, 1888, the first service was held, the rector of Christ Church officiating. There were fifteen Sunday school scholars and a "goodly number" of adults.

There was at this time no church of any denomination in the vicinity, and many residents of the area were attracted to the little mission. It was almost immediately apparent that the small cottage could not long accommodate the congregation and that a chapel was a necessity. Mr. Hayman offered the vestry of Christ Church a choice of several lots which he owned, and one at 523 South Broadway was chosen. "Without the gift," stated Mr. Ward, "it is doubtful if the mission would have been commenced.[75] A committee composed of Messrs. James Jones, R. H. Fitzhugh, Charles Edge, Sidney Warren, Miss Mary Harrison and Mesdames Avery Winston, Dan Saffarans, and William Warren, canvassed the parish for subscriptions toward building a chapel and within a week reported that $1,000 had been pledged.

[75] *Lexington Daily Transcript,* July 28, 1889, p. 5.

On December 30, 1888, the Chapel of the Good Shepherd was formally opened by Bishop Dudley, who delivered an address to "a crowded house."[76] Hayman superintended the work from beginning to end. "From the painting of the first post to the erection of the cross upon the completed structure nothing escaped his attention, and to his good judgment we are largely indebted for the excellent character of the work," stated the rector.[77] The new Chapel of the Good Shepherd was a substantial wooden building with a very beautiful Gothic window in the front gable, one of many memorials. A fine Mason and Hamlin organ was another gift. By July, 1889, one year after its founding, the mission was in "most prosperous" condition. Services were held on Sundays and Tuesdays, with attendance varying from twenty to seventy-five. The Sunday school numbered ten teachers and from fifty to seventy-five scholars; its success was largely due to the energy and efficiency of Mr. James Jones, the superintendent. His good work was carried on by Mr. William Warren, who held the position for nearly forty years.

During most of 1889 the mission was under the charge of the Reverend William C. Barnes, assistant rector of Christ Church; the Reverend George A. Weeks followed him and was placed in charge for a few months. From 1891 to 1893 the Reverend Richard Lightburne McCready served as assistant rector of Christ Church, and for a large part of the time was in charge of the Good Shepherd. A native of Louisville, McCready had been ordained to the diaconate in 1891 by Bishop Dudley, having read theology under Dr. Ward in Lexington after his graduation from the University of Kentucky. He was much beloved, and the work of the mission progressed and flourished during his three years.

Although Ward held occasional services at the mission during the next two years, the affairs were efficiently conducted by earnest laymen and laywomen thereof. Services were held by lay readers on Sunday and Tuesday nights of each week, and the Sunday school was conducted on Sunday afternoon. The Brotherhood of St. Andrew, active in the mission, prepared candidates for confirmation.

The Good Shepherd remained a mission of Christ Church for

[76] *Ibid.*
[77] *Ibid.*

many years, and as such it entered the Diocese of Lexington in 1895.

In 1906 the little chapel was taken down in sections and rebuilt on a lot on East Maxwell Street near Woodland Avenue. It prospered and flourished in the new location and in 1916 was recognized by Christ Church as an independent congregation, becoming an organized mission of the Diocese of Lexington. Completely destroyed by fire in 1918, the Good Shepherd Church was rebuilt on a lot on East Main Street at Bell Court, the site of the present beautiful church, now one of the strongest and most vital in the Diocese.

ST. JOHN'S CHURCH

A new parish in Lexington, which was a variant of the pattern of mission establishment under the auspices of parish or diocese, was St. John's Church, organized independently by a group of laymen of Christ Church, Lexington. It was, however, not without precedent, for Christ Church had sustained a similar withdrawal back in 1837, when a number of its communicants founded St. Paul's Church. In both cases nearly all of those who withdrew later returned to Christ Church and again became faithful members.

In January, 1885 a number of laymen of Christ Church, Lexington, desiring free pews and a more "Catholic" worship, began a discussion of organizing a second parish in the city. Christ Church was at this time without a rector, the Reverend Thomas Allen Tidball having recently resigned, and there was a noticeable lack of unity in the parish.[78] The vestry felt that it should know the extent of the movement being "noised about" before calling a new rector. In March the Lexington newspapers ran a series of letters for and against the establishment of St. John's Church. Some were highly indignant over the proposed movement, feeling that there was "room enough and call enough and work enough" to occupy every true Churchman in the old parish as organized.[79] Others, calling themselves St. John's Church Workers, defended the movement and asked for the good will of Christ Church.[80]

[78] Christ Church, Lexington, Minutes of the Vestry, March 11, 1885.
[79] *Lexington Daily Press,* March 25, 1885, p. 4.
[80] *Ibid.,* March 26, 1885, p. 2.

By April 3 Bishop Dudley had given his official consent to the establishment of a new parish in Lexington, to be known as St. John's. On Easter Monday, April 6, fifteen male communicants of Christ Church met and elected the following vestrymen for St. John's: Messrs. A. J. Campbell, senior warden; A. I. Totten, junior warden; John Esten Keller, secretary; and Anderson Berry, John S. Wilson, William Farley, Alexander Gibbons, Edward K. Graves, Frank E. Johns, Harry L. Williams, Theodore Williams, and Dr. J. F. Edgar.[81] The Reverend Robert Elliott Grubb, a graduate of the University of the South who had been ordained to the diaconate the previous December, was called by the vestry, and with the approval of the Bishop took charge on the first day of May. A room in the Carty Building on the corner of Main and Mill Streets was rented and fitted for Church services, and on May 17 the first services were held. Seventeen families were included in the seventy-seven "souls" enrolled on the parish register.[82] The young deacon was ordained to the priesthood the following September.

It was an auspicious beginning, but at the end of seven months, services were discontinued due to the inability of the congregation to meet expenses. Mr. Grubb resigned and became Assistant Master in the Grammar School at his alma mater, although still canonically a resident of the Diocese of Kentucky.

For two years the parish was dormant. Then in April, 1888, a quorum of the original vestry met and determined to revive the services and begin anew. At a meeting on June 15, St. John's Parish was reorganized and plans made for the erection of a church building on a lot donated by John Esten Keller, one of the original founders. Keller was the mainstay of St. John's Church for many years. The grandson of Dr. Cooke, for whom he was named, and son of Dr. David Keller, both Catholic Churchmen, he not only gave the lot but paid the rector's salary as well.

On September 18, 1888, the cornerstone of the new church on East Main Street[83] was laid by Bishop Dudley in the presence of a

[81] *Ibid.,* April 7, 1885, p. 2.

[82] *Journal, Diocese of Kentucky,* 1885, p. 29.

[83] St. John's Church stood on a lot on East Main Street, opposite Rose Street, where the Mammoth Garage now stands. See: Insurance Maps of Lexington, Kentucky, Sanborn Perris, 115 (New York, September, 1896).

large gathering of clergymen and interested townspeople. The first rector of the new St. John's was the Reverend Samuel Johnson French from the Diocese of Milwaukee, who took charge on November 14, 1888. Father French was a High Churchman and the "services began on true Catholic lines and continued so."[84]

The first service in the new St. John's Church was held on February 24, 1889, at which time the Reverend Mr. French was instituted by Bishop Dudley. The Holy Eucharist was then celebrated by the new rector. According to the *Lexington Transcript,* "In the administration of the Lord's Supper there was a significance manifestly beyond the ordinary Protestant conception of a memorial service. The responses throughout were sung by the people and the rector's part was intoned."[85]

The red brick church building was of the pure Norman Gothic order, constructed on advanced Church principles,[86] with a seating capacity of about four hundred. A beautiful window in the front represented St. John the Evangelist with pen and eagle, and the window directly over the altar depicted the crucified Christ upon the cross. The seats in the church were free and unappropriated. There was a daily Celebration of the Holy Communion, and on Sunday there were numerous services.[87]

In speaking of St. John's at the May council, Bishop Dudley stated, "The liberality of one faithful man made St. John's a possibility, and others, many others, his co-laborers, have done what they could. The small debt which still encumbers the property is but a little burden to the zeal which has accomplished so much, and I doubt not that at no distant day St. John's will be given to the Lord."[88] There were now forty families and one hundred and thirty-four souls enrolled on the parish register. The Reverend Edward H. Ward, who had assumed the rectorship of Christ Church in May, 1885, reported that forty-seven communicants had

[84] *The Church Record,* "Historical Sketch of St. John's Episcopal Church" (New York, 1897), pp. 108–113.
[85] *The Lexington Transcript,* February 26, 1889, p. 1.
[86] *Ibid.*
[87] *Ibid.,* February 14, 1889, p. 4. Holy Communion at 7:30 A.M., Morning Prayer and Instruction at 10:00; Evening Prayer, 4:30; and sermon and conversation at 7:30 P.M.
[88] *Journal, Diocese of Kentucky,* 1889, p. 82.

transferred from his parish to the new parish.[89] There was still dissension in the older parish, and in 1890 there were more transferrals and three members of the vestry resigned from that body. Much of the lack of unity was over the matter of whether or not Christ Church should inaugurate the free pew system.[90]

St. John's Parish grew considerably during French's three-year ministry. The first Christmas in the new church was celebrated with great thankfulness, and for the first time in Lexington a "full choral Celebration of the Most Blessed Eucharist" was held on Christmas Eve.[91] The character of the services at St. John's is shown by a paper read by a layman to the vestry meeting, August 31, 1891. "I believe that here we are worshipping with forms and ceremonies which are in accordance with the spirit and letter of our Ordinal and without which the services at the Celebration of the Holy Eucharist and at the minor offices are mutilated, incomplete, and non-Catholic. I believe only in observing such ritual as is today called Catholic and is found in conformity with the tradition, usages, and doctrines of the Holy Catholic Church of the ages past and present."[92] A vested choir, the first in Lexington, was introduced on Easter Day, 1890.

In November, 1891, French resigned and removed to the Diocese of Central Pennsylvania, leaving the Reverend Pelham Williams, a wealthy Bostonian, in temporary charge for a period of six months. It was about this time that a number of families, prominent in the parish, removed from the city, and the withdrawal of financial support further weakened the parish.

The Reverend Roger Hanson Peters from the Diocese of California served from June, 1892, to February, 1895, and valiantly tried to rejuvenate the parish. The communicant strength had decreased to twenty-five families and 105 members, and within the next few years it decreased even more. The parish went from trouble to trouble and was never able to liquidate the building debt and be consecrated. Under the next rector, the Reverend John Sword, a

---

[89] *Ibid.*, p. 118.
[90] Christ Church, Lexington, Minutes of the Vestry, 1890. It was decided, after lengthy consideration, in 1893, that the pews should not be free.
[91] *The Lexington Transcript*, December 24, 1889, p. 4.
[92] *The Church Record*, pp. 108–113.

chapel was added and a side altar erected, largely through his generosity.

Sword resigned early in 1886, and in March of that year the Reverend E. A. Bazett-Jones from the Diocese of Milwaukee became rector. By then St. John's was a parish in the new Diocese of Lexington. It struggled for a few more years but was finally sold for a fraction of its worth [93] and was demolished in 1903.[94] Many in the congregation returned to Christ Church, but a number of families later became members of the Church of the Good Shepherd when it was established in Lexington's east end.

[93] *Lexington Morning Herald,* November 28, 1900, p. 5.
[94] *Ibid.,* May 31, 1903, p. 5.

19 The Parting of the Ways, 1894-1895

When the Protestant Episcopal Church was organized on the At
lantic seaboard, each diocese as a rule consisted of an entire state,
presided over by one bishop. However, in the populated areas of the
East, where the parishes became more numerous, as well as in the
West where the states were large, the bishops were unable to maintain the requisite spiritual oversight of their people in addition to
performing the administrative duties of the office. Some dioceses
sought to improve matters by electing an assistant bishop, choosing
him in the regularly prescribed manner but assigning to him no
direct jurisdiction.[1] Another means of obtaining more adequate
episcopal supervision was to divide the original diocese into two or
more smaller ones.

Both these methods, with variations, were employed during the
middle decades of the nineteenth century to solve the basic problem.
The frontier Diocese of Western New York was cut off of the rest
of the state soon after the completion of the Erie Canal. The
Diocese of Ohio provided an assistant bishop to aid Bishop McIlvaine, who opposed dividing his domain, but in 1874, shortly after
his death, Ohio took advantage of the General Convention's modified regulations regarding the creation of new dioceses to organize
the Diocese of Southern Ohio.

Kentucky granted the request of aging Bishop B. B. Smith in 1866
to relieve him of some of his duties by choosing George D. Cummins as Assistant Bishop and a few years later by electing Thomas U.
Dudley to the same office. Tennessee preferred the election of an
assistant bishop for Bishop Quintard to dividing the state. Meanwhile as early as 1868, Bishop Alexander Gregg of Texas headed the
movement to reduce the territory of his enormous Diocese. Six years
later, the Texans persuaded the General Convention to authorize
the creation of two new missionary jurisdictions within the original
boundaries of Gregg's Diocese.[2]

These changes made to preserve the historic role of the bishops as fathers-in-God to their clergy and as chief pastors to the people placed under their charge reveal how deeply the entire Church was concerned with the problem. The variety of changes suggests the opposing views as to the best way to solve it. Although sectional rivalries and personal ambitions sometimes affected the choice of solutions, the basic motive of both clergy and laity was to enable the bishops to keep in close and direct contact with their people.

Bishop Dudley was rounding out two decades of indefatigable effort in Kentucky when he made his first official request for assistance in meeting the responsibilities and challenges of his office. He made it clear that he was not asking this because of failing health or powers. He was a vigorous, dynamic man of fifty-seven when he addressed the Sixty-sixth Annual Council (Convention) on May 23, 1894, in Christ Church, Louisville. Actually the chief reason he needed assistance was his great success in enlarging and uplifting the Episcopal Church in the Commonwealth.

At this date the Diocese numbered thirty-six parishes, seventeen organized missions, and ten unorganized missions—a total of sixty-three. Fifty clergymen were canonically resident, of whom thirty-nine were attached to parishes and missions. Parochial reports—a little incomplete, as usual—showed a total of 5,662 communicants, 3,247 Sunday school scholars, 372 confirmations, and contributions of $110,606,64.[3] The parishes and missions were loosely organized

---

[1] See Powell Mills Dawley, *The Episcopal Church and Its Work* (Greenwich, Conn.: 1955), pp. 28–32, for the evolution of the two modern offices of "Suffragan Bishop" and "Bishop Coadjutor."

[2] Lawrence L. Brown, *The Episcopal Church in Texas, 1838–1874* (Austin, Texas: 1963), pp. 147–53.

[3] *Journal of the Diocese of Kentucky* for 1894, p. 53 *et passim*. The parishes were: Bowling Green, Christ Church; Columbus, Christ Church; Covington, Trinity Church; Cynthiana, Church of the Advent; Danville, Trinity Church; Dayton, St. John's Church; Elizabethtown, Christ Church; Frankfort, Church of the Ascension; Georgetown, Holy Trinity Church; Harrodsburg, St. Philip's Church; Henderson, St. Paul's Church; Hickman, St. Paul's Church; Hopkinsville, Grace Church; Jefferson County, St. James' Church; Jefferson County, St. Matthew's Church; Lexington, Christ Church and St. John's Church; Louisville, Church of the Advent, Church of the Ascension, Calvary Church, Christ Church, Grace Church, St. Andrew's Church, St. John's Church, St. Paul's Church, St. Peter's Church, and Trinity Church; Maysville, Church of the Nativity; Mt. Sterling, Church of the Ascension; Newport, St. Paul's Church; Owensboro, Trinity Church; Paducah, Grace Church; Paris, St. Peter's Church; Pewee Valley, St. James' Church; Uniontown, St. John's Church; Versailles, St. John's Church. Organized Missions were:

into convocations designated as Lexington, Louisville, Paducah, and Covington, which were actually conferences with little executive power.

The Board of Missions and two archdeacons worked directly and efficiently under the Bishop. The Woman's Auxiliary, in its tenth year, was active in the larger parishes, as was the Brotherhood of St. Andrew for laymen.

The Theological Seminary Fund (successor to the original Episcopal Theological Seminary in Kentucky Fund) now consisted of $27,000 invested in securities, the income being used chiefly to supplement the salary of the headmaster of Trinity Hall, a Church school for boys, recently established in Louisville by the Bishop. This school furnished "preliminary training" for four candidates for Holy Orders who would receive their theological instruction at the University of the South in Sewanee, Tennessee. Bishop Dudley, now chancellor of that institution, advocated concentrating support for Episcopal higher education in the South at Sewanee. The emphasis in his own Diocese for any extra-parochial giving centered in the group of notable charitable institutions in Louisville, including the Norton Memorial Infirmary and three orphan asylums, and in the Protestant Infirmary founded by the Woman's Guild of Christ Church, Lexington.

Bishop Dudley had indeed wrought mightily, and it seemed fitting that he should announce at this council of 1894 the establishment of a cathedral, the Bishop's Church that he had so greatly desired for sixteen years, here on the spot where he stood as he spoke. Only recently the vestry and parishioners of Christ Church, Louisville, had offered to deed their whole property to become the Cathedral of the Diocese. The situation was not altogether ideal as yet, he admitted, but the inauguration of a cathedral would bring

---

Ashland, Calvary; Covington, St. John's; Crescent Hill, St. Mark's; Fulton, Trinity; Grahamton, Holy Trinity; Guthrie, Christ's; Henderson, St. Clement's; Lawrenceburg, Grace; Lee County, St. Paul's; Lexington, St. Andrew's; Louisville, Epiphany and Our Merciful Saviour; Middlesborough, St. Mary's; Richmond, Christ; Russellville, Trinity; Somerset, Christ; Winchester, Emmanuel. Unorganized Missions were: Anchorage, St. Luke's; Eddyville, St. Stephen's; Kuttawa; Lexington, Good Shepherd; Louisville, Calvary Mission and St. Stephen's; Madisonville; Princeton, St. John's; Shelbyville, St. James'; and Stanford.

closer the time when the city of Louisville would become "the great central stronghold" of the Church of Kentucky.

The council to which Dudley announced the inauguration of the diocesan cathedral was composed of thirty-nine clerical and forty-eight lay deputies. Few of the laity from outlying parishes were present, but the eight principal parishes in the Louisville area were well represented in both orders. An important part of the assemblage consisted of such stalwarts from among the laity as William Cornwall and W. A. Robinson, of Louisville, who had respectively guided the legal and financial policies of the Diocese for a generation, and John L. Amsden, of Versailles, long-time spokesman for St. John's Church. Most of the clergy were comparatively new in the Diocese, but these lay deputies had listened to the annual addresses of three bishops.

In this setting Bishop Dudley requested the council to consider the plan he proposed for electing an assistant bishop in order to free their Diocesan for the building of a greater Church in Kentucky. The wording of his request provides a useful background to the events that followed it.

. . . I am, I believe, just as fully equal to all the demands made upon me by my office upon body and mind as I was twenty years ago, and yet I have reached the conclusion that it will be wise in the Diocese of Kentucky to elect an Assistant Bishop at this time. Why?' Because the opportunity is ever widening for the entrance of the Church into places where it has never been known; because a Bishop can be more effective as missionary than a Presbyter; because this great city is a mission field white to the harvest, and because the building up of a great stronghold here will be the mightiest means of conquering the outlying regions. Because here in this city a Bishop is needed the larger part of his time to be chief missionary, to direct and build up Church schools, to guide and to govern Church Homes and Hospitals, and because one man cannot do the work to be done here and at the same time visit as it should be visited this great Diocese. . . .

After thus setting forth the critical need for more episcopal leadership in Kentucky, Dudley went on to prove logically, according to his views, that it would be impossible to support a second diocese in Kentucky.

. . . But granting all this to be true, is not the proper remedy to divide the Diocese? And I answer yes, without doubt, if division be possible; but I hold that in our case division is not possible. Suppose division agreed upon, and the Kentucky River the line of demarkation. A moment's reference to the report of our Finance Committee will show that the Parishes and Missions east of that line have during the past year paid toward the support of the Diocese $1,610 out of a whole amount collected by the Treasurer of $4,619. Then, further, from the same report we learn that the Parishes and Missions east of that line contributed to the Diocesan Mission Fund the amount of $1,956 out of a whole amount collected by the Treasurer of $7,836. Would it be prudent or expedient to undertake to set up a Diocese with such feeble resources for the support of the Bishop and the doing of the Missionary work? . . .

After explaining the rulings of the General Convention in such matters, he stated just how he proposed to use the services of an assistant.

. . . Let the Diocesan assign to the Assistant the oversight of a certain portion of the Diocese, as has been done in the neighboring Diocese of Tennessee, and bid him work it as his own as far as is possible, without the surrender of jurisdiction which can not be made. So shall increased Episcopal service be obtained and so shall most speedily the region assigned to the coadjutor be builded up into self-sustaining independence. . . .

Dudley concluded his proposal by generously offering to meet the expense of an assistant bishop by surrendering fifteen hundred dollars a year from his own episcopal stipend, which, together with the salary currently being allotted to a diocesan missionary, would equal the amount being paid in other dioceses. In his enthusiasm for the project he felt that he was thus removing the only obstacle to its being carried out.

As a routine procedure, a committee of deputies, appointed to consider this part of the Bishop's address and to recommend some action by the council, brought in a recommendation that the council proceed to get the necessary consent from the other dioceses to elect an assistant bishop "on the ground of extent of territory."

The discussion that followed was long and heated. There was

strong opposition to the recommendation, especially from most of
the larger Louisville parishes and their rectors and from both the
Lexington parishes and rectors. The recommendation was modified
in the direction of deliberation and fiscal soundness, as follows: no
election was to be held for a year; the Standing Committee (all six
of whom resided in Louisville) was to ask the other dioceses for the
necessary permission; and a committee of ten, plus the Bishop, was
to be appointed to recommend to the next annual council the best
means of supporting an assistant bishop. This recommendation was
adopted by a substantial majority. Among the few "Noes" at the
end were John W. Venable, long since removed to Hopkinsville's
Grace Church, Dr. Charles E. Craik, son of Dr. James Craik, plus
the entire delegation from St. John's, Lexington. The Bishop had
won his point, but with no immediate or solid support for his plan.
His generous offer of half his salary was bypassed as being a dubious
precedent to set for the future. No actual step could be taken for a
calendar year. Nevertheless, he named the committee to make plans,
with obvious intent to be fair to all parties. The members were,
besides himself: the Reverend Charles E. Craik, rector of Christ
Church, Louisville; the Reverend R. G. Noland, rector of Trinity,
Covington (related by marriage to the Bishop's wife); the Reverend W. G. McCready, rector of St. Paul's, Newport, and leader in
that area; the Reverend E. H. Ward, the scholarly rector of Christ
Church, Lexington; and the Reverend P. A. Fitts, rector of St.
Paul's, Henderson, whose position in the matter was neutral. The
laymen appointed were W. A. Robinson, of Louisville; A. L. Terry,
of Louisville; J. L. Amsden, of Versailles; A. E. Richards, of Louisville; and J. E. Rankin, of Henderson.

In drawing up his blueprints for a cathedral-centered diocese, the
Bishop had failed to reckon with the centrifugal pattern of the
state's social and economic development and its historic regional-
ism. During the twenty years since his coming to Kentucky the city
of Louisville had continued its rapid growth as a wealthy commercial and manufacturing metropolis, a hub of river and railroad
transportation. Meanwhile, the rest of the state had changed very
little from its antebellum structure of small cities and communities,
located usually in good farming sections. The areas adjacent to

Lexington and to the towns on the upper Ohio remained prosperous and influential in their own right, with no tradition of looking to Louisville for leadership in any field. It is somewhat extraordinary that Dudley, who loved and was loved by all the people of his wide domain, should have overlooked at this critical time the local pride and traditional independence of his northern and eastern parishes.

When the deputies from these areas took back the news to their parishes that the Bishop's plan proposed to assign them to the supervision of the new assistant, their reaction was unfavorable. When the *Journal* containing the minutes of the council's proceedings and the text of the Bishop's address circulated among them, the unfavorable reaction crystallized into active opposition. It is not difficult, even at this later time, to understand why the proposal that was adopted by the council did not win approval in the Convocations of Lexington and Covington after they had an opportunity to consider its full implications.

Bishop Dudley's argument in his 1894 address for electing an assistant bishop consisted, as we have seen in the portions of it quoted already, of a series of neat syllogisms based upon assumptions which he himself sincerely believed to be true. Thus he assumed that the building up of Louisville as "the Church's stronghold" in Kentucky was the "mightiest means of conquering the outlying territory." Few Episcopalians in the "outlying territory" to the north and east agreed with that view. Likewise, they did not accept Dudley's assumption that a new diocese in their part of Kentucky would logically contain only the territory east of the full length of the Kentucky River, denying it a group of rich Bluegrass counties that belonged economically in the Convocation of Lexington. Most emphatically of all, they did not concede to the Bishop his assumption that their part of the Diocese had such "feeble resources" that it could not support a bishop of its own. So the thinking in eastward Kentucky tended to be that they should and could raise the money to become a new diocese with their own diocesan instead of having an assistant bishop assigned to them.

There is little documentary evidence to show by what precise steps the dissatisfaction with the 1894 council's adoption of Dudley's plan to elect an assistant bishop developed into an active movement for the division of the Diocese. Bishop Dudley sensed the dissatisfaction soon after the adjournment of the council, and hurt by implications of "sharp practices" in the voting, countermanded the council's instructions to the Standing Committee to carry out the plan. When delegations from the dissatisfied parishes called upon him, he told them that he was willing for them to put their plan for the division of the Diocese to a test at the next council. It is certain that the two meetings of the Convocation of Lexington during the following year were strenuous and acrimonious, although the report of them in the *Journal* for 1895 says only that "many questions of importance were discussed and much interest manifested." In an informal memoir of Bishop Dudley published a decade later, there is an account, furnished by the Reverend Robert Grattan Noland, of one of these meetings.[4] Noland tells how he persuaded Dudley to let him attempt to get the convocation to unite with the Bishop in proceeding under the terms of the resolution to elect an assistant bishop. Noland says he "was rapped down and cried down" by that body. He was naturally inclined to support the Bishop, but there is every reason to believe that his account of Dudley's genuine desire to achieve justice and harmony is accurate.

All in all, it seems best to accept Bishop Dudley's own frank and generous statement of what happened between the councils of 1894 and 1895, as he incorporated it in his annual address for 1895.

. . . You will remember that at our last Council I proposed as one mighty means of increasing our Missionary work that we should ask the consent of our sister Dioceses that Kentucky should elect an Assistant Bishop. I thought that it was possible for us to maintain such added Episcopal service because I thought the scheme which I proposed was one which could be carried out. Many of you differed from my view of the situation, and the resolution to take steps looking to the election of an Assistant Bishop was passed but by a small majority. Because I saw, as it seemed to me, that to proceed as we had resolved to do would work damage to the Diocese; because I saw, as I thought, that such procedure had produced and was likely to produce in larger measure a spirit of dissatisfaction and division, I took the responsibility to ask the Standing

[4] Potter, D.D., *Reminiscences of Bishops and Archbishops,* pp. 177–192.

Committee of the Diocese not to send out the letters of request to the other Dioceses. I thought that, inasmuch as the action of the Diocese was dependent upon my official consent, that it was competent for me to withdraw the consent I had given at any time before the action had been consummated. I have learned that some of my brethren have found fault with this action as being unwarranted because my consent having once been given, the Conciliar determination was complete; the Council was dissolved, and the final action of Bishop and Council could not be changed by him. It may be that the point is well taken. I shall not discuss the matter or seek to justify my action save only by the declaration that what I did was done with only the desire to preserve harmony in the Diocese.

Considering the Bishop's deep disappointment at the failure of his plan, this is a very temperate version of the criticism he had received. And if he had flouted the authority of the Council, his own authority had in turn been ignored. He puts it this way in his Address.

. . . The Committee appointed by the last Council to recommend the best plan for securing reliable and substantial means for the support of an Assistant Bishop was called together by the Bishop, the chairman, but a quorum of the members did not attend the meeting. To those present it was reported that a committee appointed by the Convocation of Lexington was canvassing that Convocational district to secure means for the erection of that district into a new Diocese, and the members of the Committee agreed that no action should be taken in reference to the matter committed to them until they should hear the result of the effort of the committee appointed at Lexington. Nothing further has been heard and no further meeting of your Committee has been had. Brethren, the whole matter is with the Council for such action as you may think best. Your Bishop would say to you now what he said last year, that if a division of the Diocese be practicable, that such division is the natural and proper remedy for our difficulties . . .

On May 29, 1895, when Bishop Dudley made this report to the council assembled at Calvary Church, Louisville, it was already a certainty that the advocates of division would bring the matter to a vote. Time was an important factor, because if a new diocese was to be erected soon, the matter must be passed upon by the General

Convention scheduled to meet in October or else wait for the next triennial meeting. The council at Calvary was well attended, with thirty-seven of the forty-nine canonically resident clergy present and more than the usual of the laity.

The floor leader of the division party was the Reverend William G. McCready, rector of St. Paul's, Newport. He was the son of a loyal Episcopal family in Louisville who had been accepted as a candidate for Holy Orders by Bishop Dudley during the Bishop's first year in the Diocese. His younger brother, Richard Lightburne McCready, currently rector of the Church of the Ascension, Frankfort, had been ordained priest only three days before the opening of this council. W. G. McCready had voted for the Bishop's original plan for electing an assistant bishop, but had since become an advocate of division. The younger McCready took no recorded stand on the matter. W. G. McCready's chief supporters were Densmore D. Chapin, the eminent rector of the Church of the Nativity, Maysville; young Frank Hallam, a Marylander, who had been rector of St. Peter's, Paris, for about three years; and F. H. Dudley, layman from Winchester. To all these men the Bishop, as presiding officer of the council, gave opportunity to present their proposal for division to the council.

During the afternoon session of the second day a committee composed of Chapin, Hallam, and F. H. Dudley presented a report which reminded the assembly that the eastern part of the Diocese of Kentucky now had only a thousand fewer communicants than the whole Diocese had had when Bishop Dudley arrived, and that it also had almost as many "clergy in active work" as the western part. The report assumed that "the fact of division, and at no distant date, is practically settled," and therefore recommended to the council that a committee be appointed to take steps to decide whether to divide at once or three years hence. The report did not go into such matters as which diocese the present bishop would "elect" to retain or the division of the funds now in existence.

While this report was waiting its turn to be considered, W. G. McCready and Hallam offered several resolutions to keep the question before the house: i.e., that the dividing line between the new dioceses be fixed along the line of counties southward from Boone to Wayne; and, equally thought-provoking, a recommendation that the present fund for the support of the episcopate be allotted entirely to the new diocese. Finally, to avert further controversy, S. K. Sneed, an influential layman from stalwart St. Paul's, Newport, offered a conciliatory proposal that a committee be appointed, consisting of six laymen and six clergy divided so as to have six members from each of the Convocations of Louisville and Lexington, with the Bishop as chairman, to which committee was to be referred the question of dividing the Diocese. The proposal spelled out the responsibility of the committee carefully: "If such Committee shall conclude that such division is expedient and advisable, and practicable, under the Canons of the Church, they shall so notify the Bishop, who, in that event, is requested to call a special meeting of the council, to convene in Louisville prior to the meeting of the General Convention."

Mr. Sneed's motion went on to specify that this committee would, in the event that a special meeting was called, present a plan for the financial support of both dioceses and a plan also for dividing the funds and properties of the Diocese of Kentucky between them. His proposal was adopted, apparently without dissension, since there was no record made in the minutes of the "Ayes" and "Noes."

The success of this plan depended, of course, upon the confidence placed by all parties in the men who composed it. Fortunately for the future of the Church in Kentucky, the men selected for the committee represented all factions and viewpoints and were, moreover, devoid of any personal ambition in making the decision. They were: the Reverend E. H. Ward, rector of Christ Church, Lexington; the Reverend R. Grattan Noland, rector of Trinity Church, Covington; the Reverend W. G. McCready, rector of St. Paul's, Newport; and Messrs. William H. Cox, Maysville; F. H. Dudley, Winchester; Virgil Hewitt, Frankfort—these from the Convocation of Lexington. From the Convocation of Louisville were the Reverend C. E. Craik, Dean of Christ Church Cathedral, Louisville; the Reverend J. G. Minnegerode, rector of Calvary Church, Louisville; the Reverend B. E. Reed, rector of Grace Church, Paducah; and Messrs. W. A. Robinson, Louisville; S. K. Sneed, Henderson; and A. E. Richards, Louisville.

Events moved forward rapidly. The committee decided that division of the Diocese was expedient, desirable, and practicable, and so notified the Bishop. At a special meeting of the council called by him in September, the committee's recommendation was adopted. Information was gathered regarding the need for division and the financial ability of the two areas to support separate dioceses in order to gain the consent of the General Convention in October for the creation of a new diocese. The consent was granted without delay.

In carrying on these negotiations, Bishop Dudley rendered full assistance. There was no doubt, of course, as to which diocese he would elect to retain as his own responsibility. Louisville had been his administrative headquarters and his home since his arrival, and he had long since become one of its most beloved and distinguished citizens. It seems likely that he acceded to the wishes of the eastern convocations for a separate diocese several months before the 1895 Council at which the open break was made. It seems even more likely that his chief Louisville supporters did not object to the division. They regarded the change not so much as a creation of two new dioceses—the view the Chapin-Hallam-F. H. Dudley report had expressed at the 1895 council—but as the breaking away of a "daughter diocese." It was agreed at the special meeting of the council that the Theological Seminary Fund (now valued at a par $27,500) should be combined with the Episcopate Endowment Fund (valued at $10,500) and divided between the two dioceses. It remained now to organize the new Diocese.

Assembled by the Bishop of Kentucky, the clergy and lay deputies of the new Diocese met in Christ Church, Lexington, at ten o'clock on the morning of December 4, 1895. It was appropriate that the meeting should be held here because a little more than sixty-six years earlier the Diocese of Kentucky had itself been organized on this same historic and sacred spot. Some of the lay deputies were lineal descendents of those earlier founders: Jacob Spears Keller was descended from Dr. John Esten Cooke; Dr. George Cowan from H. J. Cowan; and doubtless others as well. Once again the parishes of the region were meeting with their rectors to establish an episcopate.

The mood of the meeting was harmonious and cooperative. The many sharp rivalries and debates of the past year became less important now that the eastern area had won its new freedom. For all their victory, however, the delegates were saddened by their loss of Bishop Dudley's leadership. He had accepted the change with magnanimity and optimism. As he reminded them, he had ordained several of the clergy into the priesthood, and most of the lay persons in the new Diocese had received the blessing of confirmation at his hands. He was gratified that after he had summoned the meeting and organized it the body immediately requested him to have provisional charge of the newly created Diocese and to continue to preside over this Primary Council.[5]

The territory of the new Diocese had been defined as including the counties of Boone, Gallatin, Owen, Franklin, Anderson, Mercer, Boyle, Casey, Pulaski, and Wayne, together with all of the state lying to the eastward. From this wide area came accredited clerical and lay deputies of thirteen parishes and six missions. Seventeen clerical deputies (one not yet entitled to a vote) were present; and about forty-five lay deputies. Their names, like those of the founders of the Diocese of Kentucky in 1829, are a part of the chronicle of the Church in Kentucky.

PARISHES

Covington, St. John's: The Reverend William Worthington; Laity present: A. G. Simrall, J. F. Gedge, F. Gofton.

Covington, Trinity: The Reverend R. Grattan Noland; Laity present: D. N. Comingore, F. A. Rothier, H. C. Farmer.

Cynthiana, Church of the Advent: The Reverend Rolla Dyer; Laity present: J. T. Hedges, J. W. McGibben, L. C. Woolford.

Danville, Trinity: The Reverend Frank Earl Cooley; Laity present: Dr. George Cowan, B. F. Oxley.

Frankfort, Church of the Ascension: The Reverend Richard Lightburne McCready; Laity present: Grant Green, D. W. Lindsey, T. M. Turner, H. M. Duncan.

[5] *Journal of Primary Council of Diocese of Lexington* in 1895, *passim*. Also *Journal of Diocese of Lexington* for 1896, pp. 48–49: "Extract from the Address of Bishop Dudley to the Sixty-eighth Annual Council of Kentucky, relating to that part of the old Diocese now comprised within the territory of the Diocese of Lexington."

Georgetown, Holy Trinity: The Reverend Augustine J. Smith; Laity present: John A. Herring.

Lexington, Christ Church: The Reverend Edward H. Ward, D.D.; Laity present: John T. Shelby, T. B. Wood, Hamilton Scott.

Lexington, St. John's: The Reverend John Sword; Laity present: Jacob S. Keller, George A. Warren, A. M. Peter.

Maysville, Church of the Nativity: The Reverend Densmore D. Chapin, B. D.; Laity present: W. Wormald; T. J. Chenoweth, Omar Dodson.

Mt. Sterling, Church of the Ascension: vacant; Laity present: H. R. French, H. Campbell, Sr.

Newport, St. Paul's: The Reverend William G. McCready; Laity present: Henry Higgin, George P. Wilshire, J. W. Shanks.

Paris, St. Peter's: The Reverend Frank Hallam; Laity present: W. W. Forman, Lewis Hodges, J. Stewart.

Versailles, St. John's: The Reverend Alexander Culbertson Hensley; Laity present: J. N. Camden, Jr., J. L. Amsden, W. S. Taylor.

MISSIONS

Ashland, Calvary: The Reverend Andrew Fleming, A.M.; Laity present: George L. Bryant.

Dayton, St. John's: Laity present: W. M. Washington.

Lee County, St. Paul's: The Reverend John E. H. Galbraith; Laity present: M. F. Reed, Thomas Pryse, T. U. Dudley, Jr.

Middlesborough, St. Mary's: The Reverend H. H. Sneed; Laity present: C. M. Woodbury.

Richmond, Christ Church: The Reverend Lewis M. Wilkins; Laity present: Claude Smith.

Winchester, Emmanuel: Laity present: F. H. Dudley, E. H. Bagby, R. W. Jones.

Present but not entitled to a vote was a newcomer, the Reverend Charles H. Thompson, D.D., who had arrived on November 11 from the Diocese of Georgia to take charge of St. Andrew's Mission in Lexington. This mission, together with Christ Mission at Somerset and St. Philip's Church, Harrodsburg, did not become accredited to the new Diocese until the following June.

Under Bishop Dudley's skilful guidance, the business of organization proceeded quickly and without friction. As a gracious gift from

the Diocese of Kentucky came a book of records, containing certified copies of all proceedings and documents relating to the formation of the new Diocese.

The new organization was unanimously named the Diocese of
Lexington, and its chief officers were chosen without dissent from
among the distinguished elder statesmen who were present. General
D. W. Lindsey was elected chancellor; Jacob S. Keller, registrar; the
Reverend R. L. McCready, secretary; Theodore B. Wood, treasurer;
and as trustees of the important Episcopate Endowment Fund, J. B.
Taylor, John T. Shelby, D. N. Comingore, and General Fayette
Hewitt. The powerful Standing Committee included the Reverend
Messrs. Ward, Chapin, and W. G. McCready of the clergy, and
Messrs. F. H. Dudley, Grant Green, and Theodore Wood of the
laity. The many official posts were distributed among the relatively
small group of laymen, ranging all the way from J. L. Amsden,
dedicated vestryman of St. John's, Versailles, to the Bishop's son,
T. U. Dudley, Jr., who was located at Beattyville and active in the
mission there. F. H. Dudley, the advocate of division, was also
related to the Bishop.

Next to the election of a bishop for the new Diocese, the most
important item of business had to do with money. The council
chose representatives from the Diocese of Lexington to arrange
with their opposite numbers from the old Diocese about dividing
the securities in the Theological Seminary Fund, and appointed a
finance committee, made up of experienced older men. It was
necessary also to guarantee that Bishop Dudley would be reim-
bursed for money advanced toward the building of the church at
Beattyville. To some extent offsetting this friendly solicitude for
Bishop Dudley, the Reverend Mr. Hallam made a motion that the
word "Council" be deleted from the records of the new Diocese in
favor of the time-honored "Convention." Bishop Dudley had, as
everyone knew, introduced the term "Council" as part of his rhetorical style.

Meanwhile, nominations for the office of bishop were proliferat-
ing. All of the names put in nomination during the early sessions
were from the outside. The list reveals the diverse opinions of the
deputies.

The Reverend Reverdy Estill, D.D., rector of St. Paul's Church, Louisville, Ky.

The Reverend Frank Woods Baker, rector of St. Paul's Church, Cincinnati, Ohio. (rector, Trinity Church, Covington, 1886–1891).

The Reverend John H. Elliott, D.D., rector of the Church of the Ascension, Washington, D.C.

The Reverend Lewis W. Burton, rector of St. Andrew's Church, Louisville, Ky.

The Reverend E. A. Penick, rector of St. Paul's Church, Camden, N.J. (rector, Ascension, Frankfort, 1882–1894).

The Reverend G. A. Carstensen, rector of St. Paul's Church, Indianapolis, Indiana.

The Reverend W. B. Bodine, rector of the Church of the Saviour, Philadelphia, Penn.

The Reverend Stephen H. Green, Anniston, Alabama.

The Right Reverend Ethelbert Talbot, D.D., Bishop of Wyoming and Idaho.

The Right Reverend James S. Johnston, D.D., Bishop of West Texas (Formerly rector of Advent, Cynthiana, 1876).

Before the vote was taken, the names of the Reverend Messrs. Bodine and Green were withdrawn, but at the same time four new names were added to the list of nominees.

The Reverend Mortimer M. Benton, Archdeacon, Diocese of Kentucky, residing in Louisville.

The Reverend Richard L. McCready, rector of Ascension, Frankfort.

The Reverend Charles E. Craik, D.D., Dean of Christ Church, Louisville.

The Reverend Edward H. Ward, D.D., rector of Christ Church, Lexington.

The election was held at the close of the afternoon session on December 5, 1895. From the start, it was clear that the choice lay among three candidates, Burton, Estill, and Talbot. After the fifth ballot the Estill supporters switched to Burton, but not until the eleventh ballot was Bishop Dudley able to announce that the Reverend Lewis W. Burton had received a majority of both orders and was thereby elected the first Bishop of the Diocese of Lexington.[6]

Thereupon, the testimonials of the Bishop-elect having been duly signed, with prayer and a benediction by Bishop Dudley, the Primary Council adjourned *sine die*. It had accomplished its business efficiently and in a spirit of Christian charity that boded well for the future of the Episcopal Church in Kentucky. Bishop Dudley's benediction would continue beyond the consecration of the new bishop. The clergy and laity of the new episcopate had drawn the blueprints for its erection and soberly assumed the responsibilities of building and maintaining it. In their search for a leader they had laid aside personal ambitions or rivalries. They wanted a man of intellectual attainments and they needed a good administrator but above all they desired a "chief pastor" whose Christian spirit would light the way for them. They had observed Lewis William Burton during his years in Louisville, and they had reports of him from other dioceses in which he had served. They were sure that in electing him as their Bishop they were choosing the right man.

[6] *Journal of Primary Council of Diocese of Lexington* in 1895, pp. 10, 13, 17. The final vote was: Burton, clergy 13, laity 13; Talbot, clergy 3, laity 4. No record of individual votes was published.

The new Diocese of Lexington was a unique territory, composed of three distinct sections—the central Bluegrass Region with Lexington as its center and with many old and beautiful churches; the southern part of the Ohio River Valley, extending roughly from Covington to Ashland, with important industries; and the mountainous region with its rugged terrain, the foothills of the Appalachians. The emerging problem was to build a homogeneous atmosphere among these heterogeneous areas and to establish among them an independent household of faith.

The Diocese of Lexington comprised all the territory lying east of the western boundary line of the counties of Anderson, Mercer, Boyle, Casey, Pulaski, and Wayne, an area of 19,983 square miles, just nineteen square miles less than the area of the Diocese in the western half of the state. It contained sixty-three of the 119 counties in Kentucky in 1895. There were seventeen clergymen, including the Bishop, fifteen parishes, and seven organized missions. The church property was valued at $367,550, and the new Diocese started out with an Episcopate Endowment Fund of $20,000.[1]

The fifteen parishes and their rectors were:[2]

Christ Church, Lexington: The Rev. Edward H. Ward
St. John's, Lexington: The Rev. John Sword
Ascension, Frankfort: The Rev. Richard L. McCready
Trinity, Covington: The Rev. Robert Grattan Noland
St. John's, Covington: The Rev. William Worthington
St. Paul's, Newport: The Rev. William G. McCready
St. Peter's, Paris: The Rev. Frank Hallam
Advent, Cynthiana: The Rev. Rolla Dyer
St. John's, Versailles: The Rev. Alexander G. Hensley
Trinity, Danville: The Rev. Frank Earl Cooley
St. Philip's, Harrodsburg: The Rev. Frank Earl Cooley

Nativity, Maysville: The Rev. Densmore D. Chapin
Ascension, Mt. Sterling: Vacant
Holy Trinity, Georgetown: The Rev. Augustine J. Smith
St. John's, Dayton: Vacant

The organized missions and the clergymen in charge were:

Lee County Mission: The Rev. John E. H. Galbraith
St. Mary's, Middlesborough: The Rev. Henry H. Sneed
Calvary, Ashland: The Rev. Andrew Fleming
St. Andrew's, Lexington: The Rev. Charles H. Thompson
Christ, Richmond: The Rev. Lewis M. Wilkins
Emmanuel, Winchester: Vacant

There were in addition a few mission stations which had been entirely dependent upon the Board of Missions of the Diocese of Kentucky. These were now vacant, but there were a few in the charge of clergymen of nearby parishes, who held occasional services. In Lexington there was the flourishing parochial mission of the Good Shepherd, under the auspices of Christ Church.

The part of the Diocese of Kentucky which had elected to become a new diocese had developed rather irregularly since 1870. Churchmen in the older, proud communities of the Bluegrass and southern Ohio Valley regions were, for the most part, and by circumstance rather than design, more parochial than diocesan-minded, and their efforts had gone toward the maintenance of their churches and the establishment of parochial institutions, both charitable and educational, rather than into participation in Church affairs at diocesan level. During the postwar period, under Bishops Smith, Cummins, and Dudley, Louisville had become more and more the center of diocesan activity, and only those Churchmen in and near the state's largest city had much experience of this kind. Modes of travel over Kentucky were not easy, and clergy and laity alike found it difficult to take the necessary time from their parishes or businesses to travel long distances to Louisville. One of Bishop

[1] *Burton and Wallace Family Histories,* Vol. II, Edited from materials in the possession of the Rt. Rev. Lewis William Burton by Donald W. Fein (Lexington, 1939). Courtesy of Mr. Hendree Milward of Lexington, grandson of Bishop Burton.
[2] *Journal of the Primary Council of the Diocese of Lexington,* 1895, p. 7.

Burton's first tasks was to establish an esprit de corps between the widely scattered officers and diocesan workers.

The histories of the seven organized missions which became a part of the Diocese of Lexington and the three post-war parishes, St. John's, Covington, St. John's, Dayton, and St. John's, Lexington, from their founding until 1895, have already been recounted in earlier chapters. However, the histories of the dozen antebellum parishes, which played so vital a role in the Diocese of Kentucky, have been related only up until about 1870. Their later history, however, is pertinent to a proper prospective of the heritage of the Diocese of Lexington.

CHRIST CHURCH, LEXINGTON

Christ Church had weathered the War Between the States remarkably well, largely through the efforts of its dynamic wartime rector, the Reverend Jacob Shaw Shipman (1861–1877). One of the parish's truly great rectors, Shipman also stands out among the important clergymen of the Diocese of Kentucky, who helped guide its course through sixteen of its most tempestuous years. In 1875 he had declined the Bishopric of Fond du Lac, Wisconsin, and remained at Christ Church for two more years, after which he tendered his resignation to accept the rectorship of Christ Church, New York City.

Suceeding Dr. Shipman was the Reverend Thomas Allen Tidball (1878–1884), a native of Winchester, Virginia. A graduate of the Virginia Seminary, he was ordained to the diaconate in 1872 by Bishop Whittle, and the following year to the priesthood by Bishop Johns. His first charge was Trinity Church, Portsmouth, Virginia, whence he came to Christ Church, Lexington. During his six-year rectorate in Lexington, the parish continued to prosper. He was deeply interested in work among the Negroes of the community, and in 1880 the chapel, known as St. Andrew's, was founded for them. Dr. Tidball conducted services there for several years and left the mission in a prosperous condition, under the charge of a Negro deacon. He was a dedicated pastor, a scholar of note, and a good preacher. Nevertheless, during his last year as rector, a number of communicants made plans to withdraw and found a new and more Catholic parish in the community.

The Reverend Edward Henry Ward was rector from 1885 to 1896. A native of Campbell County, Virginia, he too was a graduate of the Virginia Seminary. Ordained to the diaconate in 1873 and the priesthood in 1874 by Bishop Johns, he was in charge of St. Paul's Church, Petersburg, Virginia, and afterwards of several parishes in California, the last of which was St. John's, Stockton. Dr. Ward was primarily a scholar, and his meticulously written sermons show the marks of careful preparation. His public utterances, however, suggested the philosopher rather than the theologian. He was also a gifted musician, and while at Christ Church was generally head of his own choir. During his ministry the actual withdrawal of nearly fifty communicants, first contemplated during his predecessor's rectorate, was accomplished, and St. John's Parish was founded in the eastern part of Lexington. Christ Church, however, continued to make noticeable progress under Ward. During his eleven years there, many church organizations were formed, notably the Woman's Auxiliary, the Brotherhood of St. Andrew, and the Altar Guild. Ward had also a great deal of executive ability and the finances of the parish were adroitly managed during his rectorship. Dr. Ward was one of the seventeen clergymen who were canonically resident in the new Diocese of Lexington upon its creation, but he remained less than a year, removing to the Diocese of Pittsburgh.

On April 9, 1897, Christ Church became the Cathedral of the Diocese of Lexington.

THE CHURCH OF THE ASCENSION, FRANKFORT

The name of John Nicholas Norton will ever be remembered among Churchmen in Frankfort, where he had labored faithfully for nearly a quarter of a century. He had built the Church of the Ascension from a small, struggling parish of barely two dozen communicants into one of the largest and most flourishing churches in the Diocese of Kentucky. When he resigned in 1870, the number of communicants stood at 454.

Bishop Smith took temporary charge of the parish after Norton's resignation. The vestry asked the Bishop to request the Reverend Daniel J. Edwards, deacon, to preach in the church, in recognition of his "faithful services as lay reader for the last sixteen months." The Bishop, however, did not think it advisable and did not comply with the request. Shortly thereafter he resigned the temporary charge of the parish. A committee was appointed to again request the Bishop to reconcile his differences with Mr. Edwards and allow him to officiate,[3] but a short time later the young deacon was dismissed to the Diocese of Ohio.

The Reverend Lucien C. Lance from the Diocese of Easton became rector on Christmas Day, 1870, but remained less than two years. During his rectorate there was a lamentable decrease in baptisms, confirmations, communicants, and activities of all kinds in the Church of the Ascension. The number of communicants inexplicably dropped from 454 to 175.[4]

Succeeding Mr. Lance was the Reverend Henry T. Sharp (1872–1879). During his ministry a parish meeting requested the vestry "to elect ladies as an Advisory Board, as fast as vacancies occur," and the next month three ladies were present at a meeting of that board. The parish also appointed a "committee to solicit subscriptions for the support of the church."[5] This very probably was the first action of this kind in the Diocese and foreshadows the action of Christ Church, Lexington, half a century later in authorizing the election of women to the vestry. The communicant strength further declined, however, and at the time of Mr. Sharp's resignation was 154.

During the rectorate of the Reverend Edwin A. Penick (1880–1893) from the Diocese of Virginia, the parish awoke to new life. Within two years the communicant strength had increased from 140 to 220. The popularity of the new rector grew constantly, and the parish continued in a healthy state, growing in interest and strength. Its financial condition also greatly improved. Penick's thirteen years as rector were eminently successful, and the Frank-

---

[3] Richard Lightburne McCready, *The Church of the Ascension, Frankfort, Kentucky* (1939), pp. 68–69.
[4] *Ibid.*, p. 69.
[5] *Ibid.*, p. 69.

fort parish once more took its place among the great parishes of the Diocese of Kentucky.

Mr. Penick was succeeded by the Reverend Richard Lightburne McCready, a young deacon from Louisville, who had attended the University of Kentucky and then studied theology under Dr. Edward H. Ward at Christ Church, Lexington. Richard McCready soon endeared himself to his parish and the entire Diocese of Kentucky. He was ordained priest in 1895 by Bishop Dudley in the Church of the Ascension, and was at that time officially elected rector of the parish, which he accompanied that same year into the new Diocese of Lexington.

ST. PAUL'S CHURCH, NEWPORT

Throughout the War Between the States, St. Paul's Church continued to serve the people under its care and responsibility, and by 1870 the political prejudices and antipathies had been largely forgotten.

That year the little church, which had served since 1844, was razed, and the cornerstone laid, amid appropriate ceremonies conducted by Bishop Cummins. The Reverend Albert D. Walker, who had come from the Diocese of Virginia, was rector at this time. During his rectorate a mission was established at Dayton, where services were held twice a month and a thriving Sunday school was conducted by lay workers. Because of ill health, however, Walker had to resign, even before completion of the new St. Paul's Church. For six months thereafter the Reverend Frederick Elwell was rector pro tem, holding services in the city hall.

When the Reverend Foster Ely assumed his duties as rector in 1871 he found "a small but intelligent and attentive congregation. . . ." Many parishioners were attending services in Cincinnati and Covington, some frequently in a chapel on Cabot Street where a deposed minister of the Church regularly officiated. He also found a beautiful and commodious stone church building nearly completed on the site of the old church.[6] On Easter Day, 1872, the interior being

[6] Benaiah H. Crewe, an unpublished sketch entitled "A Brief History of St. Paul's Church" (1935), 14 pp.

finished, services were held for the first time, Bishop Cummins preaching. "Too much praise can hardly be bestowed on the indefatigable, energetic Vestry and the pious, self-sacrificing ladies of the parish," stated Mr. Ely in his parochial report that year.[7] Before long a cross surmounted the spire, and the church was completed and entirely furnished before Ely's resignation in 1875.

During the seven-year rectorate of the Reverend William M. Pettis (1876–1883), the parish continued to prosper and two missions were established, one in a lower part of the city of Newport in a chapel built by the Reverend P. H. Jeffries, a former rector of St. Paul's; the other at Bellevue, a small town adjoining Newport. Services were held every Sunday afternoon at the missions. According to Pettis, there were five hundred confirmed persons in Newport, but the majority had never connected themselves with any parish, never attended services, and contributed nothing to the maintenance of the Church.[8] In 1879 there was a large increase in membership of St. Paul's, brought about by the influx of many families connected with the military headquarters in the city.

The Reverend Reverdy Estill, a Virginian, served as rector from 1884 to 1893. He was a faithful, dedicated pastor, an able administrator, and a clergyman highly respected throughout the Diocese. His ministry in Newport was most successful. The debt incurred in the erection of the new building was liquidated, and St. Paul's was consecrated by Bishop Dudley on April 15, 1888, seventeen years after the laying of the cornerstone. The following year the parish lost a large number of communicants because of the removal from the city of several factories. In 1891 the church abolished the pew system. "The change," stated the rector, "has been received with enthusiasm, and is advancing the prosperity of the Parish."[9] Mr. Estill resigned in December, 1893 and became rector of St. Paul's Church, Louisville.

The Reverend William G. McCready began his duties as rector in January, 1894, and when St. Paul's became a part of the new Diocese

[7] *Journal, Diocese of Kentucky,* 1872, pp. 51–52.
[8] *Journal,* 1878, pp. 73–74.
[9] *Journal,* 1892, p. 120.

of Lexington the following year, it had the largest number of communicants of any parish in the Diocese.[10]

TRINITY CHURCH, COVINGTON

Upon the resignation in April, 1868, of the beloved wartime rector, the Reverend C. G. Currie, the Reverend Frederick Elwell was appointed rector pro tem and served efficiently until the following October, when the Reverend David H. Greer of Clarksburg, West Virginia, assumed charge. During his four-year rectorate, Trinity Church flourished. The church building was much enlarged and was greatly improved by the addition of a transept and an organ tower, adding largely to the capacity of the building and its beauty. The next year the church was seriously damaged by fire, but through the efforts of the rector and people was restored within a month. Two mission schools and chapels were begun in the city and suburbs, with the rector or his assistant maintaining weekly services.

The Reverend Isaac Gibson served as rector for a few months after Greer resigned in 1872 and removed to Rhode Island. The following April the Reverend George F. Bugbee began his six-year ministry at Trinity Church. Both parish and missions flourished. The debt on the church was entirely paid and the mortgage removed. He was succeeded by the Reverend Samuel W. Young, who had been assistant at St. Paul's, Louisville. Under him the mission at Ludlow was constituted in 1882 and soon was ready to pay its own resident minister.

In 1886 the Reverend Frank Woods Baker from the Diocese of Rhode Island became rector and his brother, Dr. Walter Baker, assistant. The church building was completely renovated and greatly enlarged; a 103-foot brick tower with a chime of ten bells and a round baptistry tower were erected. A new ornamental front extended the interior twenty-five feet. A beautiful cathedral window and several memorial windows were added and new pews of quartered antique oak and kneeling benches. In 1890 it became

[10] *Journal of the First Annual Council of the Diocese of Lexington*, 1896, p. 98. There were 892 "souls," 514 communicants.

necessary to erect a chapel farther uptown, and St. John's Church was built on the corner of Eighteenth and Scott Streets.

The Reverend Robert Grattan Noland from the Diocese of West Missouri became rector of Trinity Church in October, 1891. He was a faithful pastor and much beloved rector. Under this able administrator, the debt incurred in the erection of St. John's Chapel was systematically liquidated.[11] Noland accompanied Trinity Church into the new Diocese, where it soon took a foremost place.

ST. PETER'S CHURCH, PARIS

The Reverend George A. Weeks succeeded John Austen Merrick as rector of St. Peter's Church on January 1, 1866, and for nearly nineteen years he served it faithfully and well. A native of Salisbury, Vermont, and a graduate of the General Seminary in New York, he was a thirty-five year old bachelor when he came to the Diocese of Kentucky. In Paris he met and married Maggie K. Spears, who died shortly after the birth of a son a few years later. Reserved in manner, devoted to study and teaching, in his quiet, persevering way he brought many into the Church. During his rectorate in Paris the old church building was rebuilt and greatly enlarged—so thoroughly remodeled as to make it virtually a new church. Much of the ten-thousand-dollar building cost was raised by the envelope system. The building, described by Weeks as "neat and churchly in its appearance and in every way adapted to the wants of the parish,"[12] was completed in 1870 and consecrated by Assistant Bishop Cummins on November 18.

The rector had begun a parochial school in 1870, which he conducted with the help of a competent female teacher. It flourished for many years, its students growing in number from twenty-five the first year to nearly one hundred a few years later. Bishop Dudley later said of George Weeks, "Of all the men whom I have ever known in the ministry he was the equal of any as a teacher. His views were clear, and their presentation lucid and pointed."[13]

[11] *Journals, Diocese of Kentucky,* 1868–1895 inclusive.
[12] *Journal, Diocese of Kentucky,* 1871, p. 69.
[13] *Journal,* 1890, p. 61.

Weeks resigned as rector of St. Peter's in May, 1884 to take charge of the Church of the Advent, Cynthiana.

The Reverend William H. Barnwell from the Diocese of South Carolina served as rector from 1885 to 1889; he was succeeded by the Reverend Rolla Dyer from Ohio (1890–1891). The parish had been without a rector for nearly a year when the Reverend Frank Hallam from the Diocese of Maryland took charge in December, 1892. He was still in charge three years later when St. Peter's became a parish in the new Diocese of Lexington.

THE CHURCH OF THE ADVENT, CYNTHIANA

For the greater part of the three decades prior to the creation of the Diocese of Lexington in 1895, the Church of the Advent, Cynthiana, either shared the services of its rectors with other small parishes or missions or else was without regular ministrations by clergymen. For much of this time the little parish was only partially self-supporting and had to depend upon a stipend from the Board of Diocesan Missions in order to support a rector.

After the departure of the devoted Carter Page in 1862, the parish had no clergyman in charge until February, 1868, when the Reverend Charles Stewart was appointed to the post by Assistant Bishop Cummins. He remained about a year. During 1867–1868 the Reverend Silas Totten, rector of Christ Church Seminary, Lexington, held monthly services in Cynthiana, and the Reverend George A. Weeks of Paris officiated occasionally.

In the spring of 1869 the Reverend Walter Tearne began to visit Cynthiana, holding services and preaching on Sunday until August 1, when at the request of Bishop Smith he accepted the rectorship. At that time, according to Tearne, "The church was in a crushed and deplorable condition, nine discouraged and disheartened souls alone composing it."[14] In less than a year the number of communicants had nearly tripled and a thriving Sunday school, numbering sixty-two pupils and seven teachers, was in operation. During his two-year rectorate the young priest proved the importance of a resident minister in Cynthiana.

[14] *Journal,* 1870, pp. 54–55.

There followed twelve years during which there was no resident minister at the Church of the Advent. The Reverend Charles T. Kellogg, principal of a girls' school in Covington, held weekly services during 1875. From 1876 to 1879 the parish shared a rector with the Church of the Ascension, Mt. Sterling, the Reverend James S. Johnston holding services in each place on alternate Sundays. During part of 1880 the Reverend George Weeks gave a Sunday a month. The Reverend Edward S. Cross, from the missionary jurisdiction of Colorado, accepted the vestry's call to Cynthiana but remained only nine months during 1881–1882.

In January, 1883, a young deacon, a native of North Carolina, the Reverend John Franklin Spivey, became resident minister. He was ordained to the priesthood in May by Bishop Dudley and soon gained the confidence and respect of the people in his charge. The outlook for the future seemed hopeful, but in December he became ill and died the following March.

The Reverend George A. Weeks, who had served the parish from time to time in years past, became rector in August, 1884, resigning the rectorship of St. Peter's, Paris, where he had served for nineteen years. For five years he faithfully ministered to the church in Cynthiana, holding not only regular Sunday services but weekly services during Lent and on holy days. The number of communicants increased, the church became self-supporting again, a sizable endowment fund was begun, and money raised for a rectory. Prosperity prevailed at the Church of the Advent. Then in August, 1889, failing health forced the rector's retirement. He died the following March.

The Reverend C. L. Pindar served as rector for about a year during 1890–1891. On April 1, 1892, the Reverend Rolla Dyer, formerly rector of St. Peter's, Paris, became rector of the Advent. He accompanied his parish into the new Diocese with twenty-five families, sixty-seven communicants, and 124 "souls" on the parish register.

THE CHURCH OF THE ASCENSION, MT. STERLING

When the Reverend Walter Tearne became rector of the Church of the Ascension in March, 1871, he found eleven communicants with no church in which to worship. The burned-out building had been restored after the war but had been leased as a schoolhouse and post office. Tearne held services every other Sunday in the court house until the expiration of the lease the next year, when the congregation moved back into the little church building. He remained as part-time rector until 1876, when he became missionary at Beattyville and Proctor.

The number of Episcopalians in the little mountain town had increased considerably during the early seventies with the influx of Englishmen and businessmen from the East connected with the building of the C. & O. Railroad and with coal and timber interests in the mountains of eastern Kentucky. With increasing membership came plans for a larger church building.

The Reverend James S. Johnston succeeded Walter Tearne, and during his rectorate a beautiful Gothic church was erected. Mr. Hugh Forbes, who had named this town for his native Stirling, Scotland, and Mr. Fred Vischer, a native of Germany, took the lead. The old church building and lot were sold, and part of the proceeds were used to enlarge the rectory adjacent to the church. Mr. Frank Fitch, who had come to Mt. Sterling from Connecticut a few years earlier, was chosen to draw the plans and supervise the construction of the new church. The lumber was contributed by William Magowan, Fred Fitch, Frank Fitch, Mrs. John S. Williams, Colonel A. W. Hamilton, and Miss Ida Hamilton. The wainscoting was of chestnut, and the altar, reredos, sanctuary rail, choir rail and pews were all of solid walnut and handcarved by Mr. Vischer. The imported stained glass windows, exquisite in color and design, were carefully brought over the mountains by oxcart. The very fine Erben organ was the first pipe organ in Mt. Sterling and one of the first in Kentucky. The church was completed in 1878, but it was four more years before it was entirely furnished and the many handsome memorials permanently placed. It was consecrated by Bishop Dudley in 1882. The first vestrymen to serve in the new Church of the Ascension were: Judge H. R. French, senior warden; Harry Campbell, junior warden; C. W. Carpenter, secretary; John Stewart and Colonel Hamilton.[15]

[15] Archives, Church of the Ascension, Mt. Sterling.

Between 1880 and 1896 a series of short-term rectors had charge of the parish, usually dividing their time between Mt. Sterling and other points in eastern Kentucky. They were: the Reverend W. Dudley Powers (1880–1881); the Reverend Alexander G. McCabe (1882–1883); the Reverend Henry Harrison Sneed (1885–1890); the Reverend E. V. Evans (1892–1893); and the Reverend William Hugh McGee (1893–1894). During this period there were long intervals when there was no clergyman in charge; at such time the faithful laymen held the congregation together and ran the affairs of the parish. Clergy from neighboring towns conducted services from time to time. When the Diocese of Lexington was created in 1895, the parish had been without a rector for nearly two years. It was not until November, 1896, that the Church of the Ascension was once again under the charge of a rector. He was the Reverend George Chapman Abbitt from the Diocese of Virginia.

THE CHURCH OF THE NATIVITY, MAYSVILLE

During the score of years following the War Between the States, seven clergymen served as rectors of the Church of the Nativity, Maysville. They were: the Reverend R. H. Weller (1866–1869); the Reverend James B. Craighill (1870–1872); the Reverend R. C. Foute (1874); the Reverend Mortimer Murray Benton (1875–1877); the Reverend James Wilkins Tays (1877–1880); the Reverend W. Dudley Powers (1880–1882); and the Reverend Charles Buckner Hudgins (1883–1887).

During this period the communicant strength remained between sixty and eighty, although the "whole number of souls" was often listed as nearly two hundred. The population of the town of Maysville was not increasing by immigration, and there was little expectation of growth in the Episcopal Church, although the prejudices of former years had been largely removed and there was a growing good feeling toward the Church among the Protestant denominations in Mason County. Financially, however, the Church of the Nativity remained in a good, healthy state.

During the rectorate of the Reverend Mr. Weller in the late 1860's, a parish house was built and a rectory purchased. He conducted a flourishing parish school for girls and a little later began a school for boys.

There were good years and lean during these twenty years; some of the rectors were faithful and dedicated men. Others not very effectual. There were some long periods when there was no clergyman in charge, and the parish was often weak from deaths and removals, but the spirit remained good. In the parochial report for 1874, the parish having been without a clergyman for six months, the wardens stated, "We have reason to be thankful, as we have a beautiful little church, with school and vestry room attached, and a nice parsonage, situated in a commanding view, all in good order, and the parish out of debt."[16]

In September, 1887, the Reverend Densmore D. Chapin from the Diocese of Western Michigan became rector of the Church of the Nativity, and during his thirteen-year ministry, the longest in the parish's history, the church awoke to new life. Outwardly the church building was a perfect specimen of the Tudor Gothic, but the interior had deteriorated greatly since its construction forty years earlier. In 1891 the interior was entirely remodeled, the old gallery was removed, a center aisle was arranged, a proper sanctuary and chancel built, and, with the exception of font and organ, all new furniture was procured.

In his first parochial report to the First Annual Council of the Diocese of Lexington in 1896, the Reverend Mr. Chapin reported the number of families, seventy-five; the total communicants, ninety-six; and the "whole number of souls," about 275.[17]

TRINITY CHURCH, DANVILLE

Only intermittent services were held in Trinity Church, Danville, during the years of the War Between the States. After the resignation of the Reverend Matthew Fontaine Maury in 1862, the church was frequently used as a hospital and services virtually ceased. Next came years of struggle to keep the church open and in repair. Many

---

[16] *Journal,* 1874, p. 60.
[17] *Journal of the First Annual Council of the Diocese of Lexington,* 1896, p. 95.

ministers came and went during the next quarter of a century, each one usually remaining two or three years at most. The Danville and Harrodsburg churches usually shared the services of the same clergymen, and there were many years when Trinity was without any regular clerical ministrations. During such periods the faithful lay men and women held the church together. Lay readers held regular Sunday services, and a visiting clergyman occasionally administered the Holy Communion.

From 1866 to 1888 the rectors were: [18]

The Reverend E. W. Gilliam, 1866–1867
The Reverend Isaac Gibson, 1868–1870
The Reverend David S. Goodloe, 1871–1873
The Reverend C. R. Page, 1875–1877
The Reverend Mortimer Murray Benton, 1878–1880
The Reverend George Stanberry, 1882–1883
The Reverend George C. Sutton, 1883–1884
The Reverend Stanley S. Pentz, 1885
The Reverend Robert Grattan Noland, 1886–1887

During the brief periods these men served, some did good work and the church prospered, but no sooner would the parish be running smoothly than the clergyman would leave the Diocese or take charge of a larger parish in another town.

In the spring of 1888 the Reverend William Y. Sheppard gave up the charge of Christ Mission, Richmond and became rector of the parishes at Danville and Harrodsburg. During his able and devoted ministry at Trinity Church the outlook seemed bright indeed. Indefatigable in his labors, he soon endeared himself to all the region round about. The church grew steadily, the finances were sound, the church lot was improved, and a rectory purchased. Then in June, 1892, the beloved young rector died unexpectedly.

He was succeeded by the Reverend Frank Earl Cooley, who had recently resigned the rectorship of St. Andrew's Church, Louisville. The parish at Danville continued its steady growth during his nine-year rectorate, and by 1895 the communicant strength had

---

[18] *Journals, Diocese of Kentucky,* 1866–1888 inclusive.

increased to eighty-five and the "whole number of souls" was 143.[19] Such was its status when it became a parish in the new Diocese.

ST. PHILIP'S CHURCH, HARRODSBURG

Considered by many as the most perfect specimen of rural church architecture in Kentucky, St. Philip's Church, Harrodsburg, with its graceful octagonal spire, had survived precariously since its construction in 1861. In 1872, however, it was consecrated, and the parish, debt-free at last and with a clear deed to the property, had reason to regard the future with hope.

There followed good years and bad. Never robust financially, the parish shared rectors with Trinity Church, Danville or some other parish during most of its existence, with services usually held on Sunday afternoons. The clergy came and went in rather rapid succession, with the usual length of service about two years.

The clergy roster of St. Philip's Church from the war's end to 1896 was:[20]

The Reverend E. W. Gilliam (1867–1869)
The Reverend Isaac Gibson (1869–1870)
The Reverend David S. Goodloe (1872–1873)
The Reverend Henry Sharp (1873)
The Reverend John W. Venable (1875–1880)
The Reverend George Stanberry (1881–1882)
The Reverend George C. Sutton (1883–1884)
The Reverend A. T. DeLearsey (1885–1886)
The Reverend Robert Grattan Noland (1886–1887)
The Reverend William Y. Sheppard (1888–1892)
The Reverend Augustine J. Smith (1893–1895)
The Reverend Frank Earl Cooley (1896–)

Outstanding among the clergymen above named was the Reverend William Y. Sheppard, who served both Harrodsburg and Danville from 1888 to 1892. The congregation of St. Philip's increased

---

[19] *Journal*, 1895, Summary of Parochial Reports for Year Ending April, 1895.
[20] *Journals*, 1867–1895 inclusive.

considerably because of his untiring efforts, and his untimely death brought sorrow to the community.

The Reverend Augustine J. Smith, a Virginian, was rector at the time of the parish's entrance into the new Diocese of Lexington in December, 1895, but three months later he had left the state. The Reverend Frank Earl Cooley, rector of Trinity, Danville, agreed to take charge of St. Philip's, and it was he who was rector of both parishes at the First Annual Council of the Diocese of Lexington in June, 1896.

ST. JOHN'S CHURCH, VERSAILLES

Two clergymen stand out clearly in the history of St. John's Church, Versailles—the Reverend John W. Venable, who served faithfully for twenty-eight years, and the Reverend William G. McCready, whose nine years were among the most fruitful in the parish's history.

Venable [21] had come to St. John's in 1855 from the Church of the Ascension, Frankfort, where he had served as assistant. Throughout the War Between the States he held the Versailles parish together. He became rector of Holy Trinity, Georgetown, upon its organization in 1864, a charge which he held jointly with Versailles for the next twenty years. An indefatigable missionary, he officiated from time to time in a number of stations in central Kentucky, among them St. Philip's, Harrodsburg from 1875 to 1880.

Since his residence was in Versailles, it was to St. John's Parish that he gave his greatest efforts. Times were hard in the little parish during the war and in the two decades following. The rector's parochial reports were often disheartening. Among his chief desires was a new church building for St. John's, or at least extensive improvements to the present one. Neither was realized during his incumbency, although he waged a constant campaign to this end. In 1871 a heavy debt on the rectory was paid off through the efforts of the Ladies Parish Aid Society, and a fund was started for church enlargement. The promise by a wealthy communicant of a sizable sum for building improvement, to be given as a monument to a

[21] *Journals*, 1855–1882 inclusive.

deceased son, was not fulfilled. It seemed that the rector's efforts were frustrated at every turn. Some years there were heavy losses by removals; at other times there were signs of renewed life and energy. The number of communicants ranged from sixty-two in 1868 to thirty-five ten years later. Venable's labors did not cease, nor did his hope desert him; the groundwork had been laid for another rector to fulfil Venable's dreams for St. John's Church. He resigned in 1882 and became rector of Grace Church, Hopkinsville.

The Reverend William G. McCready[22] became rector of St. John's in April, 1883. A native of Louisville, he had been ordained to the diaconate in 1881 and the priesthood the following year by Bishop Dudley. Since then he had been in charge of St. James Church, Peewee Valley; St. Luke's, Anchorage; and St. James Mission, Shelbyville. He entered upon his duties in Versailles with vigor and great enthusiasm and soon gained the love and respect of his congregation. Like his predecessor, he also assumed charge of Holy Trinity, Georgetown.

Before the end of his first year in Versailles the old church had been razed and a new and commodious church building was under construction. The beautiful new St. John's Church was consecrated by Bishop Dudley on May 28, 1885. At the time of his resignation in 1891 to become diocesan missionary with residence in Louisville, the rector's congregation numbered 245 "souls" and the communicant strength stood at one hundred, larger than at any time in its history.

During the next four years the parish was without a rector for much of the time and relied upon the lay-reading services of Mr. John Amsden. For eight months in 1892 the Reverend W. W. Kimball, called from the Diocese of Georgia, served the parish, but sickness forced his resignation; for a like period in 1894 the Reverend Wiley J. Page was rector.

In 1895 the Reverend Alexander Culbertson Hensley of Frankfort, who had been ordained by Bishop Dudley nine years earlier and had since served as a United States Navy chaplain stationed in Virginia and Washington, D. C., became rector of St. John's, just in time to accompany it into the new Diocese of Lexington.

[22] *Journals*, 1883–1891 inclusive.

HOLY TRINITY CHURCH, GEORGETOWN

Because of two outstanding clergymen who were its successive rectors, the history of Holy Trinity, Georgetown, closely parallels that of St. John's, Versailles. The same two men, John W. Venable and William G. McCready, guided the course of both parishes for three decades.

The Reverend Mr. Venable[23] had been rector of St. John's for eight years when he began in 1863 to hold services in Georgetown in the courthouse. Upon the organization of Holy Trinity Parish the following year, he became rector, holding the charge jointly with St. John's for the next twenty years. The cornerstone of the beautiful Gothic stone church was laid in 1867 by Assistant Bishop Cummins, assisted by Venable, and in June, 1870, Bishop Cummins consecrated it to the glory of God. In order to avoid incurring a debt, the tower and basement were left unfinished for more than ten years.

During the years he had charge of Holy Trinity, Venable resided in Versailles and was able to give only one Sunday a month to the Georgetown parish. His parochial reports were discouraging, for he realized that, in order to prosper and grow, Holy Trinity must have the services of a resident minister. The struggling parish could not afford to employ a full-time rector and the Board of Diocesan Missions could not spare the extra stipend which would be required. And so for a score of years Venable struggled doggedly against overwhelming odds. The monthly services were well attended, especially by young people of the town and college students, but the communicant strength remained at about two dozen. For years there was a strong prejudice against the Episcopal Church among certain denominations in Georgetown.

In 1882 John W. Venable resigned the rectorship of Holy Trinity and St. John's Church and assumed charge of Grace Church, Hopkinsville.

The Reverend William G. McCready[24] became rector in 1883

[23] *Journals*, 1863–1882 inclusive.
[24] *Journals*, 1883–1891 inclusive.

and, like Venable, resided in Versailles. He, too, found the field "exceedingly difficult to work" and soon was confronted with the same problems which had been his predecessor's. He began holding an additional monthly service and gave as much time during the week as he could spare from his parish in Versailles. By 1887 the long-standing debt on the church had been liquidated with the aid of friends elsewhere in the Diocese, and money had been raised for repairs on the building. A few years later a rectory was built next door to the church, the rent from which would pay off the debt incurred in its erection.

Upon McCready's resignation in 1891, the Reverend W. W. Kimball served as rector for eight months. The Reverend Augustine J. Smith had charge of the parish from 1893 to 1895, serving simultaneously at St. Philip's, Harrodsburg. He was listed among the clergy of the new Diocese of Lexington but resigned less than two months after its creation. Holy Trinity had no clergyman in charge at the time of the First Annual Council in June, 1896.

BISHOP LEWIS WILLIAM BURTON
FIRST BISHOP OF LEXINGTON

Lewis William Burton was consecrated to the high and holy office of bishop on January 30, 1896, in St. Andrew's Church, Louisville, the parish of which he had been rector for a little over two years.[25]

The new Bishop chose Lexington as his residence and see city and shortly thereafter accepted the offer, tendered him by the wardens, vestry, and congregation of Christ Church, that it be designated the cathedral of the new Diocese. It remained the Bishop's church throughout Burton's administration. A large and handsome episcopal residence was built for the Burtons on West Sixth Street. Not since Benjamin Bosworth Smith's early years in Kentucky had a bishop resided in Lexington, and the Burtons were graciously and joyously received in Christ Church Parish and the community. The

[25] *Journal of the First Annual Council of the Diocese of Lexington,* 1896, pp. 32–33. Bishops participating were: Dudley; Peterkin of West Virginia; Leonard of Ohio; Randolph of Southern Virginia; Vincent of Southern Ohio; White of Indiana; Nelson of Georgia.

Bishop's affable personality and courtly manners and Mrs. Burton's charm and friendliness soon endeared them to the people of Lexington.

While Lexington and its cathedral naturally became the hub of activity in the Diocese, the Bishop by no means confined himself to the seat of his episcopacy. There was not a parish or mission which did not soon receive his personal and strengthening attention. In and out among his people he went, into every corner of his jurisdiction, often traveling on muleback or on foot in the rugged mountainous areas, preaching, baptizing, confirming, celebrating the Holy Communion, ministering to his far-flung flock. And as had Bishop Dudley before him, he knew his people and they loved him. The problems of each parish and mission were his own and it has been said of him that "he knew more intimately the conditions of the parishes than the rectors themselves."[26]

It was indeed fortunate that the first Bishop of Lexington was possessed of remarkable administrative ability, for in a comparatively short time the machinery of a new Diocese was operating smoothly, although it required constant supervision. Soon there was manifest throughout the Diocese a spirit of unity among both clergy and laity.

What was the background of a leader so peculiarly fitted to become the first Bishop of Lexington? What manner of man was he and what were the qualities which so endeared him to his people?

Lewis William Burton was born in Cleveland, Ohio, November 9, 1852, the son of the Reverend Lewis Burton, D. D., and Agnes Jane Wallace Burton. His father was one of the best-known clergymen in the Diocese of Ohio, with which he was connected for nearly fifty years. For twenty-four years he was rector of St. John's Church, Cleveland, and afterwards rector and then rector emeritus of St. Mark's Church there. He was founder and rector of All Saints' Church in the same city. Dr. Burton's brother, the Reverend William Miller Burton, was his immediate predecessor in the rectorship of St. John's Church, Cleveland.

Lewis William Burton attended the public schools of Cleveland

[26] *The Lexington Herald,* February 1, 1921, quoted in *Burton and Wallace Family Histories,* Vol. II.

and Kenyon Grammar School, a preparatory school for Kenyon College, Gambier, Ohio, which he entered in 1869. He graduated from Kenyon in 1873, first honor man and valedictorian of his class. He decided on the ministry of the Church during a period of recuperation from an illness and, in 1874 entered the Philadelphia Divinity School. He rode his horse, "Pet," from Cleveland to Philadelphia, a distance of almost five hundred miles, taking seventeen days for the journey. Commenting upon his decision to enter the ministry, his father wrote in his journal, "The Lord be praised for guiding him to this decision. Make him, O Lord, a workman that needeth not to be ashamed. Prayer answered."[27]

After his graduation in 1877, he was ordained to the diaconate in 1878 by Bishop Bedell of Ohio and became assistant to his father at All Saints' Church, Cleveland. After his ordination to the priesthood the following year, he served as rector of the parish until 1880. After six months travel abroad, he became assistant and then successor to his father at St. Mark's Church.

In 1883, in Decatur, Georgia, he married Miss Georgie Hendree Ball, the daughter of Dr. George Rieley Hendree and Cornelia Jane Paine Hendree. She had been adopted by her father's sister, Mrs. James Martin Ball, and Colonel Ball.

In 1884 Burton accepted a call to St. John's Church, Richmond, Virginia, the church in which Patrick Henry made his immortal speech. His rectorate there was eminently successful, resulting in the erection of a new chapel and the beginning of a mission for Negroes. He left the parish entirely free of debt and with the largest communicant list of any Episcopal Church in the Diocese of Virginia.[28] While in Virginia, he was a member of the Missionary Committee of the Diocese, vice president of the Richmond City Missionary Society, and examining chaplain. In Richmond, three children were born to the Burtons: Lewis James Hendree, who died at the age of two; Sarah Louise; and Cornelia Paine Wallace.

On October 1, 1893, Lewis Burton became rector of St. Andrew's Church, Louisville, which had been founded as a mission nearly forty years previously by an uncle, the Reverend John Singer Wal-

[27] *Burton and Wallace Family Histories,* Vol. II.
[28] *Ibid.*

lace, while he was assistant to the rector of St. Paul's Church in that city.[29] While in Louisville, Burton took a prominent place among the clergy of the Diocese of Kentucky, serving on many important committees and establishing for himself a name as an excellent administrator, a fine preacher, and a faithful pastor.

He was forty-three years old when he became Bishop, determined, forceful, and capable. His whole life had prepared him for the lofty office. Brought up in the ecclesiastical atmosphere of his father's house, he had been influenced toward the ministry at a very early age. He had proved his intellectual and scholarly ability in college and seminary, and his administrative acumen in the parishes which he had served as deacon and priest. He was an able and persuasive preacher, his diction impeccable, his sermons models of reason. Dignified and erect both in his youth and later years, he wore, after the fashion of the day, full beard and mustache, which in his early years turned to snowy white. His gracious and friendly personality won him a host of friends. To match the perseverance of Smith, the eloquence of Cummins, and the magnanimous leadership of Dudley, Burton brought to his office a lifetime commitment to the Church.

Ask any person today who knew Bishop Burton, "What is the quality which best sums up his character?", and invariably comes the reply, "His saintliness," or perhaps, "His holiness." The congregation of Christ Church Cathedral, Lexington, once expressed its feelings toward him in a letter, stating, "Your life has made it easier for us to believe in the Christ, for we have seen His image reflected in you."[30] And in an editorial in *The Lexington Leader* appeared the words, "His life has been like the clear flame of a lamp in the night. His spirit has inspired all who have come under his influence."[31] A layman of another persuasion wrote of Bishop Burton, "I am not a theologian, but I have the impression that only those who have passed through the Church Militant into the

[29] *Journal, Diocese of Kentucky,* 1856, p. 44.

[30] *Burton and Wallace Family Histories,* Vol. II. The Dean, the Associate Dean, the Vestry, the heads of all the departments, and the entire congregation of Christ Church, Lexington, Kentucky, to Bishop Burton, August 6, 1928.

[31] *The Lexington Leader,* August 1, 1928, quoted in *Burton and Wallace Family Histories,* Vol. II.

Church Triumphant are canonized, else I should regard you as a saint who had been sent to us not only for the strengthening of your own communion but for the inspiration and encouragement of all Christians."[32]

During the thirty-three years Lewis William Burton would serve as Bishop of Lexington, the Diocese would grow in strength and numbers. New missions would be founded throughout, some in places where the Church had established a foothold in earlier years, others in places where no Episcopal service had ever before been held. The parishes and organized missions would grow stronger, and nearly all would become self-supporting; church buildings, parish houses, and rectories would be built; educational and charitable institutions would be founded and would flourish. Now, at the beginning of 1896 a new ecclesiastical unit was beginning its life.

Bishop Burton's predecessors in this fertile field had been many. An Anglican clergyman preaching in a green wilderness; a gentle parson who dreamed a dream and made it a reality; a quiet clergyman who organized the first parish; a profound theologian who formed a Diocese; a pioneer Bishop who labored and taught and builded; a beloved peacemaker; an Assistant Bishop, whose evangelical zeal precipitated revolt; a magnanimous missionary Bishop —of these we can be proud. But there were many, many more— giants of both the clergy and the laity, whose voices are now stilled, but whose works will long be remembered. Nor should we, in the timeless brotherhood of faith, forget the lesser people who have gone before, serving our Lord and His Church. As testimonials of their devotion, they have left us beautiful churches of solid yet gracious structure, like that of the faith they represent. Their spires reach ever heavenward. Some are richly dight, some are humbly chaste, but all are noble in their Christian purpose. It is a goodly heritage.

[32] Charles H. Manning to Bishop Burton, quoted in *Burton and Wallace Family Histories,* Vol. II.

Epilogue

Such is the story of the planting of the Episcopal Church in Kentucky, and of its nurture and growth until the time of the setting apart of the Diocese of Lexington—the eastern half of the Commonwealth—as a separate jurisdiction.

The story of the Diocese of Lexington remains to be written, a moving story in its own right, for America has been on the march since the turn of the century, and Central and Eastern Kentucky march with the nation into an era of great and germinal change.

Since its establishment, the Diocese of Lexington has been under the leadership of three bishops, each a very different man from the others, which is right and proper, for each brought to the Diocese his own peculiar talents and his own personality. And the times in which these bishops served have, themselves, been vastly different. It is difficult for people today even to imagine the difficulties which Bishop Burton faced in visiting his mountain churches, or those met by Bishop Abbott in the midst of a savage depression, not only national but world-wide in scope, having its deep and tragic results in Kentucky as well.

Today, the chief problem before the Diocese of Lexington is to find means to buy up its opportunities in a changing and rapidly developing world. Industrialization is sweeping like a great wave from Northern Kentucky, through the Bluegrass, and on toward the Tennessee border. Thousands of people are moving in to run the factories, and they come from the North and the East, changing the ethnic character of the region, churning it up, and producing a new kind of Kentucky. Industrialization is also penetrating the mountain area. Fine highways, better schools, new means of livelihood are coming into being. An exciting time to be alive, and an exciting place to live and to work! And an exciting world of opportunity for a Church which is alert and alive!

Seeing this coming, the Diocese of Lexington revived the ancient

Episcopal Theological Seminary in Kentucky, and this school, now flourishing, is turning out ministers to man the churches throughout the area. The Seminary occupies its own quarter of a million-dollar building, which was constructed without debt of any kind, and has a fine faculty of able teachers. Graduates now serve throughout the United States and in some foreign lands. This has not been accomplished without work, "blood, sweat and tears" but it is paying off in dividends for the Episcopal Church in this area, and for the Gospel of the Lord Jesus, which it constantly and steadfastly holds forth.

Another vital link in "renewal for the future" was the successful establishment of the Cathedral Domain in the Kentucky mountains, and the building in that place of "The Cathedral of St. George the Martyr." This unique foundation serves the purpose of drawing together men, women, and children from all over the diverse regions which make up the Diocese of Lexington, so that they may meet, know one another, become friends, learn to pray together, and so to become in truth the Family of God, the Church. The fame of "The Mountain Cathedral" has gone throughout this region, so that it is advertised by agencies quite unrelated to the Church as "something which a visitor to Kentucky simply must see!"

The growth of the Episcopal Church in the city of Lexington in the past ten years has been dramatic, and almost unbelievable. From two parish churches and a small mission, Lexington now has nine churches, not to mention new churches in neighboring towns. More, of course, must and will be built in this rapidly growing center of population, which includes the expanding University of Kentucky, Transylvania College, a great Medical Center, two very large Federal Government hospitals, and other foundations and institutions too numerous to mention.

The past has given the Episcopal Church a good foundation. It is for us to take hold of the opportunities which are before us, and to claim them for the future. Soon there will be another Bishop of Lexington. He will be a new and different man, with God-given talents all his own. We, of the past—the long past—give on to him our work, and look to him, under God, for what he will contribute toward its perfection.

WILLIAM R. MOODY
Bishop of Lexington
Diocese of Lexington,
Lexington, Kentucky
January, 1969

Index

Curtis, Rev. Judson M.: 301
Cynthiana, Kentucky: 153, 172, 176, 178, 179, 210–216, 226, 228, 230, 273

Daisy, A. E.: 326
Dallam, Col., of Maryland: 38
Danville, Kentucky: 38, 53, 54, 72, 73, 74, 83, 87, 157, 172, 192, 252, 274, 424
Dartmouth College: 45, 77, 87, 143, 181
Davidson, Dr. Robert: 96, 97, 109, 144
Davis, Benjamin O.: 116, 163
Davis, Rev. Edmund: 80n, 93, 117, 210
Davis, James E.: 42
Davis, Robert: 178
Davis and Force, Printers: 239
Dawson, Wade H.: 330
Dayton, Kentucky: 325, 326, 327, 353, 415
Deacon, Rev. Daniel H.: 76, 80n, 89n, 94, 99, 117, 128, 129, 149, 255n, 262
Dehon, Rt. Rev. Theodore: 22, 23n
DeLancey, Rt. Rev. William H.: 182, 183, 281, 296
DeLearsey, Rev. A. T.: 425
Dickinson College: 292
Diocesan Convention (Diocese of Kentucky): 1829 (Primary), 56–58, 189; 1830, 62–63; 1831, 72–73; 1832, 76–77; 1833, 80, 81–82; 1834, 89–91; 1835, 98–99, 211; 1836, 116–121, 124, 170; 1837, 127, 129–132, 170, 212; 1837 (Adjourned), 131–132; 1838, 147–148; 1839, 153–154, 167; 1840, 156; 1840 (Special), 156–157; 1841, 157–158; 1842, 160; 1843, 244; 1844, 160, 197; 1845, 192; 1846, 182; 1847, 184, 214, 217, 230, 231; 1848, 184, 204, 205; 1849, 185, 204; 1855, 258; 1857, 222; 1858, 231, 370; 1859, 206, 235, 254–257; 1860, 206, 232, 236; 1861, 224, 286, 371; 1862, 286; 1864, 225, 227; 1865, 233, 282–283; 1866, 290; 1867, 287, 294; 1868, 236, 285, 294; 1870, 288, 328, 356; 1872, 310; 1873, 310, 311–312, 326, 332; 1874 (Special), 334–336; 1879, 345, 363; 1886, 373; 1891, 380; 1894, 394–399; 1895, 400–403; 1895 (Special), 404
Diocesan Convention (Diocese of Lexington): 1895 (Primary), 404–409
Diocesan Council. See Diocesan convention
Diocesan statistics, 1859: 255–257

Diocese of Alabama: 197, 281, 364
Diocese of Albany: 385
Diocese of California: 391
Diocese of Central Pennsylvania: 391
Diocese of Colorado (Missionary): 420
Diocese of Easton: 414
Diocese of Fond du Lac: 349, 412
Diocese of Georgia: 282 (PECCSA), 357, 385, 406, 427
Diocese of Illinois: 89, 146, 304, 305
Diocese of Indiana: 146, 218
Diocese of Iowa: 363, 365
Diocese of Kentucky, division of: 399–404
Diocese of Louisiana: 269, 274
Diocese of Maryland: 8, 14, 17, 37, 38, 42, 43, 44, 81, 194, 239, 419
Diocese of Massachusetts: 222
Diocese of Milwaukee: 390, 392
Diocese of Minnesota: 271
Diocese of Mississippi: 237
Diocese of Missouri: 146, 327
Diocese of New Jersey: 271
Diocese of New Mexico and Arizona: 358
Diocese of New York: 102, 177, 271
Diocese of North Carolina: 56–58, (PECCSA) 284, 384
Diocese of Ohio: 169, 197, 286, 354, 393, 414, 430
Diocese of Pennsylvania: 126, 131, 178, 231
Diocese of Pittsburg: 346
Diocese of South Carolina: 419
Diocese of Southern Ohio: 327, 393
Diocese of Tennessee: 88, 146, 275, (PECCSA) 284, 381, 397
Diocese of Texas: (PECCSA) 284
Diocese of Vermont: 69
Diocese of Virginia: 8, 68, 196, 214, 280, 286, 294, 414, 415, 422, 431
Diocese of West Missouri: 418
Diocese of Western Michigan: 271, 422
Diocese of Western New York: 182, 217, 281, 393
Diocese of Wisconsin: 208
Disciples of Christ. See Christian Church
Dobb, Rev. A. F.: 182
Doctrinal Controversy, 1866–1874: 302–308, 312–313
Dodge, Rev. W. W.: 199